Peacemonger

PUBLISHING FOR THE WORLD
125 Years

THE JOHNS HOPKINS UNIVERSITY PRESS

Peacemonger

MARRACK GOULDING

The Johns Hopkins University Press
Baltimore, Maryland

© Marrack Goulding 2002, 2003
All rights reserved.
Printed in the United States of America on acid-free paper
2 4 6 8 9 7 5 3 1

First published in the United Kingdom in 2002
by John Murray (Publishers) Ltd., London
Johns Hopkins edition published in 2003.

The Johns Hopkins University Press
2715 North Charles Street
Baltimore, Maryland 21218-4363
www.press.jhu.edu

Library of Congress Cataloguing-in-Publication Data
Goulding, Marrack.
Peacemonger / Marrack Goulding.
p. cm.
Includes bibliographical references and index.
ISBN 0-8018-7858-6 (hardcover : acid-free paper)
1. United Nations—Peacekeeping forces. 2. Goulding, Marrack.
3. United Nations—Officials and employees—Biography. I. Title.
JZ6374.G68 2003
341.5′84—dc21
2003012838

A catalogue record for this book is available from the British Library.

This book is dedicated to Irvine Goulding (1910–2000), polymath, naval officer, lawyer, judge and loving father, who taught me most of the important things I know – and contributed greatly to this work by describing an early draft chapter as 'phenomenally dull', and to Susan Goulding, née D'Albiac, whose courage, love and loyalty gave me strength and solace during the adventures described in these pages.

Contents

ENDINGS

Preface

This book is an account of seven years, 1986 to 1992, which I spent in New York as the United Nations official in charge of the Organization's peacekeeping activities. Peacekeeping is the use of international military and police personnel to help prevent, control and resolve conflict. It can take place only if the hostile parties give their consent; it cannot be imposed on them. The peacekeepers' task is not to use force to end a war or impose the will of the international community. Their task is to help settle disputes peacefully. This they do either by creating the conditions required for the successful negotiation of a peace settlement or by helping the belligerents to implement an agreement which has already been negotiated.

Because this book is based on my personal experiences, it does not offer the reader a continuous narrative of the conflicts described in it. All of them had origins which long preceded my recruitment to the United Nations Secretariat, and in some of them I was only intermittently involved. Readers should therefore think of themselves as being in a cinema where the projector flickers, and sometimes fails altogether, leaving them to piece together the story from the episodes which it permits them to see. The account of each conflict summarizes that conflict's origins and history, and brief explanations are given to illuminate periods of darkness between the episodes in which I was involved and which are therefore more fully described.

My seven years in peacekeeping included the end of the Cold War, with the new opportunities it brought for international action to settle some long-standing conflicts, many of them fuelled by the Cold War itself. As a result those years saw an enormous expansion in peacekeeping. In 1986 there were five United Nations operations in the field with about 10,000 uniformed personnel; by the beginning of 1993 there were thirteen operations and their soldiers and police officers numbered almost 55,000. The annual budget had increased from $240 million to $2.7 billion. The successes and failures of those seven years ought to have defined the form that peacekeeping would take during an even more intensive period of activity which was about to begin. But not all the lessons of the previous period were learnt and disasters were to follow in Somalia, Rwanda and Bosnia.

Two more threads are accordingly woven into the autobiographical fabric of this book. The first consists of detailed accounts of three United Nations peace operations which introduced us to the opportunities and perils created by the end of the Cold War and acted as laboratories in which we could refine techniques for seizing the opportunities and avoiding the perils. These operations took place in Namibia, where the United Nations staged its first attempt to help hostile parties implement a comprehensive political settlement of their dispute; in Central America (Nicaragua and El Salvador; Guatemala was to come later), where the United Nations took the lead in resolving three civil wars which had become proxies of the East–West conflict; and in Yugoslavia, where the United Nations was introduced to the horror and complexity of the wars that so often accompany the break-up of federations or the collapse of states.

The second thread consists of observations on the lessons to be learnt from the United Nations' performance during those seven years and on how its peace operations can be made more effective. Most of the precepts that emerge from the observations are addressed to the governments of the member states rather than to the Secretariat, for it is governments that determine the policy of the United Nations and their action or inaction which largely, but not exclusively, determines the ability of the Secretariat to put that policy into practice.

This examination of peacekeeping operations gave rise to the most difficult question I have encountered in writing the book: how frank should I be about the performance of individual members of the Secretariat? The ethos of diplomatic memoirs is to be guarded and discreet in such matters, especially where colleagues are concerned. My initial inclination was to respect that ethos. But as the writing proceeded it became clear that the drawing of conclusions and the definition of precepts that would enhance the United Nations' efficacy would be impeded if I did not write frankly about the performance of individuals, myself included. If these observations cause hurt to colleagues with whom I worked, I crave their forgiveness and beg them to understand that the writing is motivated only by the desire to create wider understanding of the Organization which we served and to help prevent repetition of the mistakes which we made.

Many have contributed to the writing of this book. Foremost amongst them are Grant McIntyre and his team at John Murray. Their patient guidance of a novice author turned what could have been a nightmare into an enjoyable and enriching experience. Another major contribution has come from the many past and present colleagues and friends who found time to make comments on successive drafts as the book developed, especially those who told me frankly about the shortcomings of those drafts. I am also grateful to the dozens of individuals who responded to e-mailed requests for confirmation of facts imperfectly remembered by me. Finally, I salute the Fellows and students of St Antony's College and my family and friends who have so patiently tolerated the neglect of my obligations to them during the writing of this book.

The discourse of the United Nations, like that of the governments of its member states, is plagued by abbreviations and acronyms. In particular, the Organization's peacekeeping operations are invariably referred to by their initials. I have struggled to reduce the use of these; but many remain. A glossary of them is provided in Appendix I and Appendix II contains a full list of United Nations peacekeeping operations established between 1948 and 1996. Because so many individuals feature in the narrative, biographical notes are offered in Appendix III.

For me, the writing of this book has been a pleasurable revisiting of past experience. For the reader, it is intended to provide both entertainment and insight. For those who worked, and too often died, to prevent, control and resolve wars in countries that were not their own, the book will, I hope, enhance recognition of their courage and dedication and demonstrate that in the often violent and ugly world of international relations peacekeeping is, for all its faults, an ethical enterprise that is fully in keeping with the noble purposes stated in the Charter of the United Nations.

Marrack Goulding
Oxford, England
December 2001

Maps

CYPRUS

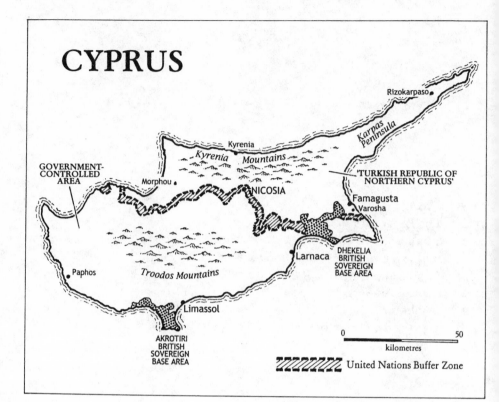

Rizokarpaso

Karpas Peninsula

Kyrenia

Kyrenia Mountains

GOVERNMENT-CONTROLLED AREA

Morphou

NICOSIA

'TURKISH REPUBLIC OF NORTHERN CYPRUS'

Famagusta
Varosha

Larnaca

DHEKELIA BRITISH SOVEREIGN BASE AREA

Paphos

Troodos Mountains

Limassol

AKROTIRI BRITISH SOVEREIGN BASE AREA

0   50
kilometres

United Nations Buffer Zone

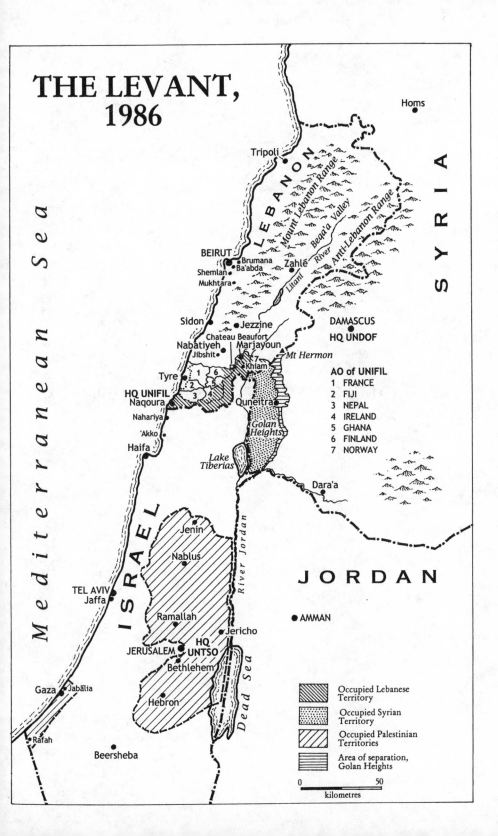

THE LEVANT, 1986

Homs

Tripoli

Mediterranean Sea

L E B A N O N

Mount Lebanon Range

Beqa'a Valley

Anti-Lebanon Range

BEIRUT
Brumana
Ba'abda
Zahlé
Shemlan
Mukhtara
Litani River

S Y R I A

Sidon
Jezzine

DAMASCUS
HQ UNDOF

Chateau Beaufort
Nabatiyeh
Marjayoun
Jibshit
Mt Hermon
Khiam
7

Tyre
1 6
2 5
HQ UNIFIL
Naqoura
3
Quneitra

AO of UNIFIL
1 FRANCE
2 FIJI
3 NEPAL
4 IRELAND
5 GHANA
6 FINLAND
7 NORWAY

Nahariya
'Akko
Haifa

Golan Heights

Lake Tiberias

Dara'a

I S R A E L

Jenin

Nablus

River Jordan

J O R D A N

TEL AVIV
Jaffa

AMMAN

Ramallah
Jericho

JERUSALEM HQ UNTSO

Bethlehem

Dead Sea

Gaza Jabālia

Hebron

Rafah

Beersheba

	Occupied Lebanese Territory
	Occupied Syrian Territory
	Occupied Palestinian Territories
	Area of separation, Golan Heights

0   50
kilometres

SOUTHERN LEBANON, 1986

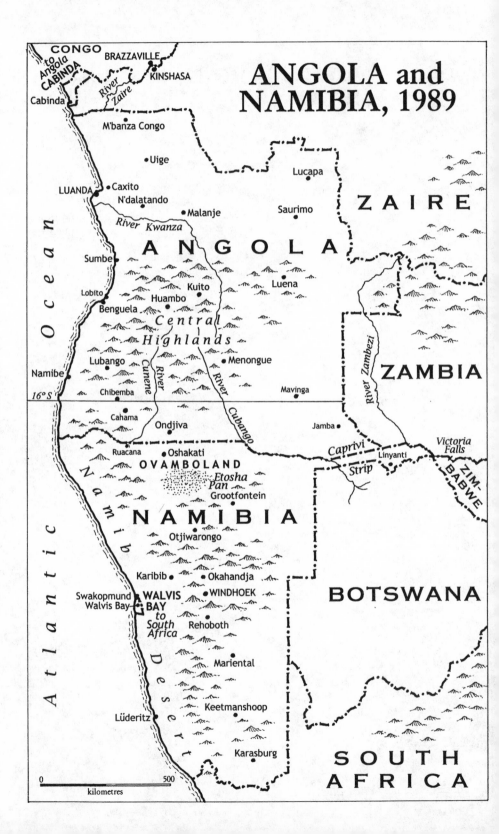

ANGOLA and
NAMIBIA, 1989

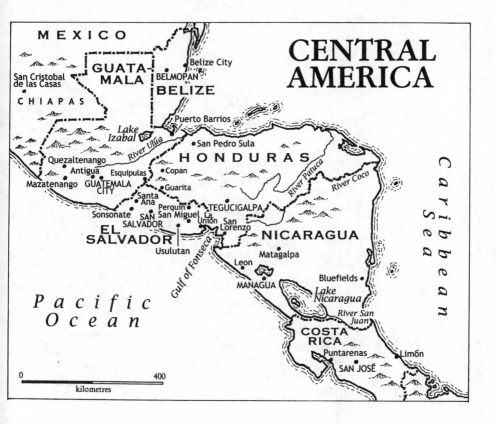

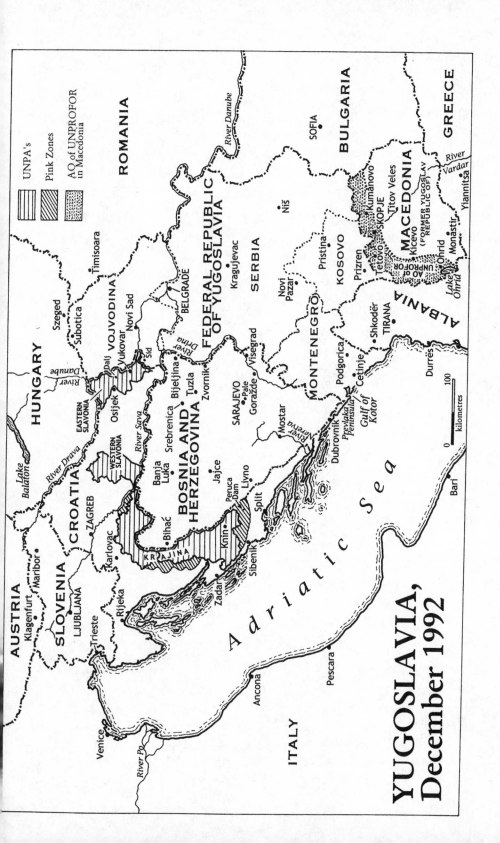

YUGOSLAVIA, December 1992

Introduction

1

Beginnings

'Well, yes,' said Secretary-General Pérez de Cuéllar, with the grimace of mild pain that always accompanied a remark he expected to displease, 'but I don't think I could commit my successor.' I had dropped my first UN brick. And I was not yet appointed.

We were sitting in Pérez de Cuéllar's rented summer house on Long Island on a sunny morning in August 1985. I had run him to ground there, with the support of the Foreign Office, to seek confirmation that he was ready to appoint me to succeed the legendary Brian Urquhart. Urquhart, who was to retire from the United Nations Secretariat at the end of the year, was a 'Mohican', almost the last of the officials who had founded the Secretariat forty years before. Latterly, he had come to personify 'peacekeeping', the stop-gap technique developed by the Secretariat during the years when the Security Council, paralysed by Cold War rivalry, was unable to apply the measures prescribed by the United Nations Charter for dealing with conflict. As peacekeeping was not mentioned in the Charter, the Soviet Union questioned its legitimacy from time to time. The post to which I aspired was accordingly entitled Under-Secretary-General (USG) for Special Political Affairs, a characteristic UN circumlocution designed to avoid causing offence to Moscow.* Urquhart's courage, intelligence and political street-wisdom had made him a model international civil servant, committed to the multilateral ideal, but realistic, and often very funny, about the shortcomings of the institutions and individuals charged with putting it into practice.

As a permanent member of the United Nations Security Council, the United Kingdom can expect at least one USG post in New York and the Foreign Office was determined that a Briton should succeed Urquhart. He had, unusually, risen through the ranks of the Secretariat, whereas most other USGs had been made available to the Secretary-General by their governments after successful careers at home in politics, administration

---

* The Secretariat also included a USG for 'Special Political Questions', a euphemism for decolonization which had been chosen to avoid offending the colonial powers.

or diplomacy. None of the existing senior Britons in the Secretariat was deemed right for the job and the search began for some other candidate. Meanwhile, British ministers repeatedly sought assurances from Kurt Waldheim and then from his successor, Pérez de Cuéllar, that they accepted the principle that Urquhart's post should remain with the United Kingdom. The answers ministers received were equivocal.

My name was first floated as a possible successor in 1982 when I was serving in the United Kingdom delegation in New York as Head of Chancery (i.e. Chief of Staff) to Sir Anthony Parsons, the UK Permanent Representative (as ambassadors to the United Nations are known). Three years before, in 1979, Parsons had rescued me from the British Embassy in Lisbon. I was posted there in 1977 after two years of secondment to the Central Policy Review Staff in the Cabinet Office. While in the 'Think Tank', as it was called, I had headed a team that produced a report on Britain's overseas representation which had been ill-received by the Diplomatic Service – and the British Council and the BBC. Aggrieved but not cruel, the Service devised an exquisite punishment for the sinning radical. I was posted to the Embassy in Lisbon, as Counsellor, squeezed uncomfortably between an Ambassador and a Head of Chancery, both of whom were intelligent, experienced and fluent in Portuguese and held defiantly traditional views about the Service. Lisbon was nevertheless better than Ovid's Tomi as a place of exile and I passed two happy years there. But professionally it was a relief when Tony Parsons telephoned in the spring of 1979 to say that he was insisting on taking me to New York as his Head of Chancery.

My subsequent good fortune in obtaining the succession to Brian Urquhart owed something to the folly of General Galtieri, the President of Argentina who invaded the Falklands in March 1982. As the British Task Force steamed south to recover the islands by force, first the US Secretary of State, Alexander Haig, and then President Belaúnde of Peru tried to mediate a peaceful outcome. Both failed, and in early May Pérez de Cuéllar picked up the baton. It was a brave move. He was the first Latin American to be Secretary-General and had been in office for only three months when a Latin American country went to war with a permanent member of the Security Council. In two weeks of intensive negotiation in New York, he got the British and Argentine delegations to accept, *ad referendum* to their governments, an interim arrangement under which the Islands would pass under United Nations administration while the sovereignty dispute was resolved through negotiation. Parsons succeeded in persuading the War Cabinet in London to accept the deal, but the Argentine delegation failed with Galtieri in Buenos Aires, and combat was joined.

The negotiations in New York were highly confidential and each delegation had only three principal members. For the United Nations, they were the Secretary-General himself; Rafeeuddin Ahmed, a long-serving UN official of Pakistani nationality; and Álvaro de Soto, an able Peruvian diplomat whom Pérez de Cuéllar brought on to his staff for the purpose and who thereafter went on to a distinguished career in the Secretariat. The Argentine trio were led by Enrique Ros, the Under-Secretary for Foreign Affairs in Buenos Aires. The British team consisted of Tony Parsons, David Anderson, the UK Mission's Legal Adviser, and myself. As a result, Pérez de Cuéllar got to know me well. This led Parsons later in the year to propose to London, and then to Pérez de Cuéllar, that I should succeed Urquhart. The Secretary-General was non-committal and a few months later my time in New York came to an end.

I had been rehabilitated by my performance there and was rewarded with a small but highly active post of my own, the British Embassy in Angola, at what in those days was the young age of 46. I had been in Luanda for only two months when Pérez de Cuéllar made a brief stop-over on his way back to New York from a visit to South Africa. I went out to the airport to pay my respects and was told by a member of his staff that 'the Secretary-General wants you to be on standby to succeed Brian'.

The wind had blown hot and cold several times during the succeeding months. But here I was, my two years in Angola completed, on a mission to persuade the Secretary-General to say unequivocally that it was his intention to appoint me to the post. I had told the Foreign Office that my wife and I wanted the move to the United Nations to be a lasting one and not just a three-year secondment. Angola had been tough. The civil war was getting closer to the capital and life was sometimes hard, even for diplomats. But the work was exciting. I had negotiated the release of British mercenaries imprisoned in 1975. Alone among the Ambassadors, I was allowed to visit the diamond mines in the north-east where more than a hundred British workers were exposed to kidnapping or worse at the hands of Jonas Savimbi's UNITA guerrillas. I had been a clandestine channel of communication between Washington and Luanda in the negotiation of a deal under which Cuban troops would be withdrawn from Angola and South Africa would permit implementation of the UN plan for the independence of Namibia. There were almost no representational chores. No future Embassy seemed likely to offer such satisfaction. The prospect of spending the next ten to fifteen years in New York was therefore attractive. The Foreign Office welcomed my decision but gave me the option of returning to the Diplomatic Service during the first three years if things did not work out with the United Nations.

In preparing for the conversation with Pérez de Cuéllar, I had assumed that he would be pleased to hear that I would not be a transient on se-condment, watching who was being promoted at home and calculating what jobs would be available in two or three years' time. Our conversation went well until, oozing sincerity, I made clear my determination to offer a lifetime's commitment. Well yes, he said, but he could not commit his successor; his term of office would expire at the end of the following year; he did not know whether he would stand again or, if he did, whether he would be elected; he could offer me only a short-term contract.

The conversation ended shortly thereafter. I climbed into the British Permanent Representative's Rolls-Royce and proceeded to the nearest diner to reflect over a dry martini. Perhaps, I concluded, the meeting had not gone so badly. The Secretary-General had at least promised a contract. It was natural that he should think of me as someone seeking a secondment rather than a long-term change of career. Certainly borrowing the British Ambassador's Rolls-Royce and chauffeur had not been the most intelligent way of signalling ardent multilateralism. I decided to send a positive report to the Foreign Office.

But Pérez de Cuéllar's reaction highlighted a problem that was not going to go away. A senior UN official nominated by his or her government was, I already knew, assumed to be in the Secretariat to do that government's bidding; this assumption was not always right but it could poison relations within the Secretariat. I wanted to be an impartial international official like Urquhart and had already decided that I would decline invitations to stay at British Embassies when on my travels.

I would take the same decision today. The efficacy of the United Nations depends on the Secretary-General and his senior advisers remaining independent of governments, whether their own or those of other countries. Not everyone in the UN would be convinced by my insistence that I had severed my relations with Whitehall; why in that case, they would wonder, had Whitehall made such an effort to get me appointed? What I did not foresee that August day was that distancing myself from Whitehall could reduce my usefulness to the Secretary-General himself. Boutros-Ghali, in particular, expected his British USG to give him private insights into Her Majesty's Government's thinking and their likely reaction to initiatives which he might take. My insistence on my independence as an international civil servant thus made me something of a misfit on the 38th floor (the floor given over to the offices of the Secretary-General, to which Urquhart had been closely attached). Not only was its sincerity doubted; because it was in fact genuine, it reduced my value to my boss.

Style was also to make me a misfit. I tend to be direct, in speech and in writing. The circumlocutions beloved of the United Nations did not come naturally to me. I would say 'Secretary-General, you must call the Secretary of State now', not 'Mr Secretary-General, you might wish to consider calling the Secretary of State fairly soon'. Evasion and understatement were especially prevalent in the reports about peacekeeping submitted by Secretaries-General to the Security Council: 'armed elements' meant guerrilla fighters; in Cyprus 'the events of July and August 1974' meant the Turkish invasion, which if referred to directly had to be called the Turkish 'intervention'; in reports on Cambodia the Khmer Rouge genocide had to be referred to as 'the policies and practices of the past'. My propensity to call a spade a spade was especially troubling to Viru Dayal, the able Indian who was Pérez de Cuéllar's Chef de Cabinet and had previously worked on peacekeeping with Urquhart. Viru was a generous guide and mentor during my first months in the Secretariat but we tussled often when he toned down the draft reports which I submitted through him to the Secretary-General.

Insistence on good drafting was a trait that Dayal and I shared. In the Diplomatic Service, great importance is attached to the quality of drafting, partly because that is the tradition of the Service but also because both precision of language and constructive ambiguity are important in diplomacy. In my three Head of Chancery posts (Tripoli, Cairo, New York), I had been something of a martinet where drafting was concerned. Now English was not the native tongue of most of my staff. Many of them had a remarkable ability to draft in it. But some did not, and in those cases I had to make a choice: either tolerate less than perfect drafting or spend hours revising the drafts myself. Too often I chose the latter course.

Another field in which adjustment was necessary was document security. In the Foreign Office, one could confide secrets to paper, in the knowledge that the paper would be kept secure and the secrets would not leak. I soon learnt that this was not so in the United Nations, but old habits died hard and my staff often urged me to write less frankly.

The Foreign Office had arranged that if Pérez de Cuéllar confirmed his intention to appoint me at the beginning of 1986, I would spend the intervening months at St Antony's College in Oxford. This would help me make a discreet transition from British ambassador to international civil servant, while educating myself about United Nations peacekeeping, of which I had had little direct experience during my four years in New York. Not knowing that I would one day be Warden of St Antony's, I spent a shamelessly idle term there. The then Warden, Raymond Carr, made no demands of me and the only academic task I was given was to lead one seminar on UN peacekeeping. Otherwise I was left to read, talk and walk, as I pleased, ending the term better informed about the UN and fitter and more relaxed than I had been for some time.

But the weeks in Oxford passed without a whisper from New York. Being accustomed to the methodical way in which the Diplomatic Service managed postings, I was worried by the silence. Finally, on 11

November Brian Urquhart's resignation and my appointment were announced by the Secretary-General in New York. Before leaving I called on ministers and officials in London. The call on Mrs Thatcher took place on 9 December, the day the Westland Helicopter crisis broke. She came into the room an hour late, shook herself like an animal emerging from water, called for a whisky and, without apparent distraction, applied herself for half an hour to the tasks that awaited me in New York.

My wife and I arrived in New York on 2 January 1986. By the end of February we had rented an airy 18th floor apartment on East 61st Street. It was to be my home until I left the Secretariat more than eleven years later, the longest I have lived anywhere. Our pets were summoned from England, two miniature dachshunds and an African grey parrot which the Queen of Libya had given my wife in 1969, three months before Mu'ammar Qadhafi overthrew the monarchy there. All three of the pets had been with us during our previous sojourn in New York. Their arrival at JFK in 1979 had given us early warning of the embarrassments that could arise from an inadequate knowledge of the differences between American English and English English. 'What does he like doing best?' asked a federal official, pointing at the male dachshund as he barked for release from his box. 'Chasing pussies,' replied my wife. A look of amazement crossed the official's face; then he rubbed his forehead and said, 'Gee, Ma'am, I guess I like doing that too.'

But settling into the office was another story. Brian's retirement did not come into effect until the end of January. Handovers are always difficult, but this one was especially so. Brian was a hero of the United Nations with over forty years' seniority. His retirement had been reluctantly accepted by the Secretary-General and was regretted by his colleagues. His successor was almost an upstart, inserted by a major power at a young age into a prestigious post which the bureaucracy would have preferred to see occupied by one of its own. Brian, sensitive as ever, did all he could to ease the passage. But as I camped in the 'Map Room', the holy of holies where Dag Hammarskjöld and Ralph Bunche had planned the first UN peacekeeping force in 1956, I itched for the day when Brian would leave and I could move into the Under-Secretary-General's office and take charge.

Meanwhile I tried to acquaint myself with the Secretariat. It was not an easy task. Despite my four years in the British delegation I knew little about the Secretariat of which I was now a member. International bureaucracies have a poor reputation; charges of inefficiency and corruption abound. In my experience, the charges of inefficiency are better justified than those of corruption. There is minor corruption in the Secretariat, and the temptations in some field missions are great, but I doubt whether it is worse than in the public services of most member states. It is the inefficiency that strikes someone arriving from an environment as efficient as Her Britannic Majesty's Diplomatic Service. But the inefficiency too is not as bad or all-pervasive as is alleged by the Organization's enemies.

In the preparation of documents or the running of meetings, which account for much of the work done in New York, the Secretariat is first rate. Where inefficiency does exist, it is often due less to the inadequacy of individuals than to the convoluted procedures imposed on the Secretariat by the member states. If, for instance, I needed to fly to Washington to talk to the State Department, I could not buy a ticket on the shuttle and claim my expenses on return. Before travelling, I had to obtain signatures from six minor officials. Without them the official travel agent could not issue the ticket, I could not claim incidental expenses and I was not 'on travel status', which meant amongst other things that I was not insured against death or injury in the line of duty. Similarly cumbersome procedures mean that it takes on average fourteen months to recruit a new staff member and ten weeks to procure a piece of equipment for a peacekeeping operation.

Some inefficiency is due to cultural and linguistic diversity but, contrary to a widely held view, it is not necessarily a consequence of the policy of 'equitable geographical distribution'. Article 101(3) of the Charter states that 'The paramount consideration in the employment of the staff ... shall be the necessity of securing the highest standards of efficiency, competence, and integrity. Due regard shall be paid to the importance of recruiting the staff on as wide a geographical basis as possible.' For some, this paragraph is like the Balfour Declaration, an attempt to render incompatible ideas compatible by putting them side by side in a text.* I have to confess to having arrived in the Secretariat with this prejudice in mind. But I soon discovered that it is neither morally justifiable nor empirically true. There is no correlation between efficiency and region of origin and it is offensive to suggest that there is.

What also became quickly clear, however, was that the Secretariat was suffering from decades of poor personnel management. There was no confidential reporting on an officer's (or, in UN parlance, 'staff member's') performance. The reporting officer had to rate the staff member

---

* The Balfour Declaration, which is several times referred to in this book, was contained in a letter dated 2 November 1917 from the then Foreign Secretary, Arthur Balfour, to Lord Rothschild. It stated that: 'His Majesty's Government view with favour the establishment in Palestine of a national home for the Jewish people, and will use their best endeavours to facilitate the achievement of this object, it being clearly understood that nothing shall be done which may prejudice the civil and religious rights of the existing non-Jewish communities in Palestine, or the rights and political status enjoyed by Jews in any other country.'

for thirteen qualities in a range from A ('Excellent') to F ('Unsatisfactory'). It was normal to mark A throughout, save for a sprinkling of two or three Bs ('Very Good') to create the illusion of serious assessment. Departure from this norm was likely to expose the reporting officer to 'rebuttal' by the reportee, a time-consuming and wordy procedure which reporting officers tried to avoid. Thus was the dead wood protected from the pruner's knife. Without a pattern of unsatisfactory reports there was no basis for disciplinary action or 'early separation'. The financial crisis resulting from the United States' failure to pay its contributions in full would soon necessitate a series of recruitment freezes, which had the effect of further consolidating the status quo. When Secretary-General Kofi Annan announced his first package of reforms in 1997, he revealed that the average age of the Secretariat had risen to 49 years and less than 5 per cent of its members were under 35 – hardly the dynamic new management the Americans said they wanted.

In early 1993, Secretary-General Boutros-Ghali moved me from peacekeeping to his new Department of Political Affairs. He had created this a year before in order to strengthen the Secretariat's capacity for political work, especially preventive diplomacy, and to put all political functions in a single department, instead of distributing them amongst half a dozen different units as his predecessor had preferred. I complained to him that the new Department contained some dead wood; it had been thrown together by amalgamating the previous political offices without any attempt to match individuals with the skills that were now required; through no fault of their own, some of the staff were not capable of doing the tasks entrusted to them. 'Get rid of the dead wood,' said Boutros-Ghali; 'give my Chief of Staff a list. I will support you.' As a first step, I produced a geographically balanced list of six names whom I asked to be moved to other departments. Believing in transparency in such matters, I told each of them that I was doing so and why. Uproar ensued. My flouting of procedures was publicly denounced by the Under-Secretary-General for Administration and Management. Some of the six lodged appeals in the administrative tribunal, in one case claiming punitive damages. 'Ethnic cleansing in the UN Department of Political Affairs' screamed the Lagos press, though no Nigerian was involved. I should have known better.

All this was very different from the orderly and friendly world of the Diplomatic Service. Like everyone else I had criticized its Personnel Department. But I now began to see how humane it had been and how clear and relevant its regulations were. The problem with the UN's regulations was that they were rarely revised, contained many gaps and were sometimes superseded by subsequent decisions of the General Assembly. Arguments with my colleagues in the administrative offices revealed that they could draw on an inexhaustible armoury of rules, regulations and resolutions to shoot down an unwanted proposal from a 'programme manager'. In an attempt to level the battlefield, I asked for a day's briefing on the Organization's administrative, financial and personnel procedures. Though repeated frequently, the request was never met. A couple of years later, I complained about this to an Argentine friend, Luís María Gómez, a wise and cynical operator who had become acting head of administration. 'But my dear Goulding,' he said, 'what on earth caused you to think that they would let you into their secrets?'

A pleasing surprise in the Secretariat was the way its members use the English language. The UN has six official languages – Arabic, Chinese, English, French, Russian and Spanish – and two working languages – English and French. The two working languages are supposed to enjoy parity, but English dominates, even in francophone Geneva. It is, however, an English that is often delightfully idiosyncratic in vocabulary and spelling. I do not grieve for the King's English. On the contrary I relish the regional Englishes in every continent which are standing up so well to global standardization. Soon after 'coming on board', as they say in the UN, I received a note from a colleague which included the statement that 'the . . . Government is noted for its *hypocracy*'. There were many other such gems. Some were orthographically adventurous: 'the diggings [of unauthorized fortifications] have prompted the US and the UK to make *day marshes* to the Turkish side'. Others were wrong but logical: 'General X has lost his place in the *higherarchy*'; 'relations between India and Pakistan *registered a very low peak* this month'. Others seemed to change geography: 'my wife and I drove into *the bush* in Westchester County on Saturday'. Others created expressive neologisms which deserve a place in the language: 'the Minister of Energy is blaming the distributors for *hamstering* fuel'; 'we must develop an even stronger *amityship* between our two nations'; 'Iraq's allegation that Kuwait is creeping *inchmeal* into Iraqi territories'; 'we must act in the *beforemath* of events'; 'problems that arose in this situation should be *creased out*'. And sometimes the orator expressed an unintended truth: 'this Organization was founded to forge *words* into ploughshares'.

At the end of January 1986, Brian Urquhart left the United Nations and moved across First Avenue to the Ford Foundation. There was no ceremony or party to mark his going. I assumed that that had all happened the month before. But as I accompanied him, visibly moved, to the elevators that Friday evening, I felt guilt at not having arranged some fanfare to salute his unique achievements in the service of peace. He turned out to be a perfect predecessor. Throughout my time in the Secretariat he was to be generous with advice when it was requested but never proffered it on his own initiative.

2

United Nations Peace Operations

I served in the United Nations Secretariat for eleven and a half years.
This book is about the first seven years and two months of that
period. My prime responsibility during that period was for the
Organization's activities in the field of peacekeeping, though at times this
included a good deal of peacemaking.

In 1945 the Charter of the United Nations established procedures for
international action to deal with conflict between states. It distinguished
between the 'Pacific Settlement of Disputes' (Chapter VI) and 'Action
with respect to Threats to the Peace, Breaches of the Peace, and Acts of
Aggression' (Chapter VII), which could involve coercion including, in
the last resort, the use of armed force. The Cold War, which dominated
the United Nations' first four decades, impaired the Organization's
ability to use the procedures laid down in the Charter. There was no
direct fighting between the two power blocs, but in most conflicts
throughout the world, including many conflicts within states, the East
supported one side and the West the other. As a result, it was rarely possible for the Security Council to agree on the use of non-coercive means,
let alone coercion; each side could veto a proposal that it considered
damaging to its protégés.*

There were, however, occasions when the East–West logjam was
briefly broken and the two superpowers agreed on short-term action,
even though their long-term objectives differed. This was most likely to
happen when the West was divided, usually because the issue related to
decolonization. There were three such occasions in the Arab-Israeli conflict: when the State of Israel was proclaimed in 1948, the Soviet Union
and the United States were the first to recognize the new state; when

---

* The exception was the Council's decision in 1950 to authorize the use of force to stop
North Korea's aggression against South Korea, a decision that was possible only
because the Soviet Union happened to be boycotting the Council at the time in protest
against Nationalist China's retention of the China seat after the Kuomintang had been
defeated by the Communists.

Britain, France and Israel, in secret collusion, attacked Egypt in 1956, the superpowers were united in opposing that action; and when war between Egypt/Syria and Israel in October 1973 threatened to draw their superpower champions into the fray, the latter recognized that they had a common interest in bringing the conflict under control.

It is no coincidence that these were the only occasions when the United Nations was able to take effective action in the Arab-Israeli context. For the momentary accord between the superpowers enabled them to use the United Nations as a third party which could play an impartial and neutral role. Because these opportunities for the UN were short-lived and the Security Council would soon be immobilized again by East–West discord, the emphasis tended to be on rapid interim measures to bring a conflict under control rather than on the longer-term task of helping the parties negotiate a political settlement to their dispute. This was the origin of UN peacekeeping, which involved the deployment, with the consent of the parties, of military personnel under UN command to help stop the fighting and thus create the conditions necessary for political negotiations. The first peacekeeping operation was established in 1948 during the first Arab-Israeli war when the UN Truce Supervision Organization (UNTSO), a group of unarmed military observers, was sent to Palestine after the Security Council had ordained a truce there. The first armed peacekeeping operation was the United Nations Emergency Force (UNEF I) which was deployed in 1956 to 'secure and supervise' the cessation of hostilities following the Anglo-Franco-Israeli invasion of Egypt.*

Dag Hammarskjöld referred to peacekeeping as 'Chapter Six-and-a-Half'. Chapter VI of the Charter did not mention the possible use of military personnel in the peaceful settlement of disputes. Chapter VII provided not for consent-based peacekeeping but for what is now called peace enforcement, reflecting the prevalent view in 1945 that the League of Nations had failed during the inter-war years 'because it lacked teeth'. The deployment of troops by the UN, with the consent of the hostile parties, was thus neither specifically provided for in the Charter nor contrary to any of its provisions. That is what Hammarskjöld meant by 'Chapter Six-and-a-Half'. This concept suited the Russians well, for it enabled them to question the legitimacy of peacekeeping when they wanted to be awkward but to let the Security Council set up peacekeeping operations when this suited their purpose or was desired by their friends in the Third World. However, for most of the Cold War the Soviet Union refused to pay its share of the costs of peacekeeping and in

---

* A list of all the peacekeeping operations established by the UN between 1948 and 1996 is to be found in Appendix II.

1964 this led to a politico-financial crisis which paralysed the General Assembly for almost a year.

When I joined the Secretariat in 1986, the United Nations' role in the maintenance of peace and security was seen almost entirely in terms of peacekeeping. This was because peacekeeping was more visible and extensive than the limited attempts at mediation which the UN had been able to undertake during the Cold War. But the Cold War was about to end and with its end the UN would be able to enlarge its repertoire of techniques for dealing with conflict. In January 1992, the first ever Security Council meeting at the level of heads of state and government asked the newly-elected Boutros-Ghali to prepare recommendations on strengthening the United Nations' capacity 'for preventive diplomacy, for peacemaking and for peacekeeping'. This gave Boutros-Ghali the opportunity to establish, in his report entitled *An Agenda for Peace* (1992), a coherent conceptual framework for the UN's efforts to help maintain peace and security in the post-Cold War era and to define some of the techniques that would be needed.

That framework has since been developed by Boutros-Ghali himself and by many others who have studied the successes and failures of a decade of hectic activity. Consensus does not yet exist on the terminology of UN peace operations but this book uses a simple taxonomy in which all United Nations action in relation to conflict is placed in one of five categories: peacemaking, peacekeeping and peacebuilding, all of which be done only with the consent of the hostile parties; and sanctions and peace enforcement, which are forms of coercion and therefore by definition do not require the consent of the party against which they are used.

Peacekeeping, the primary topic of this book, has evolved a long way since its debut in 1948. Its defining characteristics remain unchanged, however. A peacekeeping operation invariably includes military personnel, and often police as well, who are made available to the United Nations by their governments. The operation is established by the Security Council.* It is placed under the command of the Secretary-General who is required to report regularly to the Council. It is deployed with the consent of the parties to an actual or potential conflict and is required to be neutral and impartial between them. If it is armed, it will be authorized to use its arms only in self-defence. Its tasks, or 'mandate', are agreed in advance with the parties. The costs of the

---

* Or very occasionally by the General Assembly if the Security Council is blocked because a permanent member is opposed to the operation and would therefore veto it, as was the case with the first UN Emergency Force deployed in Egypt at the time of the Suez crisis in 1956.

operation, including some reimbursement of the costs incurred by the troop-contributing governments, are apportioned amongst all the member states of the United Nations.

There are four main types of peacekeeping, based primarily on differences in the tasks the operation is given. The types may, however, overlap or evolve from one to the other.

Traditional peacekeeping operations are deployed after an armed conflict has been temporarily suspended. Their tasks are to ensure that the fighting does not re-start and to work in other ways to create propitious conditions for the negotiation of a lasting settlement of the dispute which has led to conflict. They monitor cease-fires, control buffer zones, verify compliance with provisional agreements and endeavour to build confidence between the parties. Their tasks and personnel are primarily military and they are normally headed by a military officer. They face two main problems, both of which will be encountered in this book. The first occurs if the parties start fighting again. Not only does this remove the political and operational basis for the peacekeepers' presence; it also exposes them to humiliation and danger. The second problem occurs if the peacekeepers do their peacekeeping well but the peacemakers fail to make progress towards a negotiated settlement. This creates several dangers: one of the parties may lose confidence in the peace process and resume fighting; 'donor fatigue' may cause governments to withhold the troops and money needed to keep the operation in the field; it may even be argued that by protecting the parties from the consequences of their intransigence at the negotiating table the peacekeepers themselves have become part of the problem.

During my time in charge of peacekeeping, traditional operations were deployed in Afghanistan, between Iran and Iraq, in Angola, in Central America, between Iraq and Kuwait, in Croatia and in Somalia; another briefly preceded the multifunctional operation (see below) in Cambodia.

The second type is *preventive peacekeeping*. This is the deployment of peacekeepers at the request of only one of the parties to a potential conflict and only on that party's territory. The operation's mandate is thus based not on an agreement between the parties but on a unilateral request by one of them. The only example to date is the force deployed in Macedonia from 1992 to 1999.

Third is *multifunctional peacekeeping*. This denotes a peacekeeping operation established to help the parties implement a negotiated settlement to their conflict; the peacekeepers are deployed after the peacemakers have done their job. This task requires a larger, more complicated and costlier operation than traditional peacekeeping because the functions performed extend far beyond the traditional supervision of cease-fires and buffer zones. They can include the demobilization of combatants and their reintegration into civilian life; the supervision of local administrations and police forces (and sometimes the creation of new ones); the promotion and verification of human rights; the establishment of truth commissions; the supervision, and sometimes the actual conduct, of elections; the return and resettlement of refugees; de-mining; and economic reconstruction and rehabilitation. Multifunctional peacekeeping thus requires major civilian components and the operation is normally headed by a senior civilian with the title of 'Special Representative of the Secretary-General' (SRSG).*

During my peacekeeping years multifunctional operations were deployed in Namibia, Angola, El Salvador, Western Sahara, Cambodia and Mozambique.

Finally, there is the problem type: *complex emergency peacekeeping*. This denotes an operation which finds itself in the middle of an active conflict where there is no cease-fire agreement, let alone a negotiated settlement. This usually happens because of the collapse of the agreement on which a traditional or multifunctional operation's mandate has been based. The logical thing to do in such circumstances is to withdraw the operation; the task it was given is no longer feasible. But the Security Council may not want to appear to wash its hands of the conflict and will therefore look for other tasks which would justify keeping the operation in the field. Those tasks are usually humanitarian ones and they tend to be defined by the Council rather than the parties. The latter's consent may be difficult to obtain, especially if the tasks include the provision of humanitarian relief to civilian communities which a party is trying to displace through terror and deprivation. The danger then is that the peacekeepers will be drawn into the conflict and themselves become a party to it. For they can protect humanitarian activities only if they are prepared, in the last resort, to use force against those who threaten such activities. But if they do that, they forfeit the impartiality which is both a surer protection for peacekeepers than their weapons and a necessary condition for success in any peacekeeping tasks they may have.

---

* Senior civilians appointed to support the Secretary-General's efforts in the peace and security field enjoy a bewildering variety of titles. Special Representative, Personal Representative or Representative *tout court*, in that order of seniority, are the most frequent. Most of these are based in the field as heads of peacekeeping operations or peacemaking missions. Special Envoys and Personal Envoys are more likely to be based in New York or, if they are engaged – as many are – on a 'when actually employed' basis, in their home cities. They are usually involved in peacemaking and peacebuilding. Special Advisers and Senior Advisers are also usually based in New York, with wider and more generic areas of responsibility than their field-based colleagues. There are also a few Special Coordinators and High-Level Coordinators. But there are no standard criteria for who should be called what and exceptions exist to all the above generalizations.

For a long time the United Nations' peacekeeping doctrine was that coercion cannot be combined with consent-based peacekeeping; they are alternatives and a choice has to be made between them. This doctrine was stated uncompromisingly in Boutros-Ghali's *Supplement to An Agenda for Peace* of January 1995. I adhered to it throughout my time in the Secretariat; 'there is no halfway house', I would say, 'between peacekeeping and peace enforcement'. But I now realize that we in the Secretariat adjusted too slowly to the demands of the new types of conflict which proliferated after the end of the Cold War. No longer was the UN dealing with wars between the duly constituted and internationally recognized governments of sovereign states whose consent, once given, could usually be relied upon. Most of the new conflicts were conflicts within the boundaries of a sovereign state. At least one of the protagonists was a guerrilla movement with little understanding of the norms of international relations and with poor mechanisms for command and control. The 'consent' of such parties was an uncertain quantity and rarely absolute.

By the second half of the 1990s it had become clear that there was a need to revise peacekeeping doctrine. It had to provide for situations in which a party's consent had been given in general terms but the peacekeepers could nevertheless expect to encounter armed resistance from some of that party's adherents or, in states without effective government, from armed bandits with no political agenda. This made it necessary to change the peacekeepers' rules of engagement and provide them with sufficient firepower to assure military superiority. The essence of the new doctrine is that force is, if necessary, used against armed persons because of what they do, not because of the side they belong to. It was pioneered by a multinational force, authorized by the Security Council and led by the United States, which was deployed in Somalia in December 1992 to protect international humanitarian operations there. UNITAF, as it was called, had overwhelming military superiority and a patent will to use it against any armed person who threatened humanitarian workers, whatever faction that person belonged to. At the time of writing similar rules of engagement have been given to NATO and UN forces in conflicts such as those in Bosnia (after the Dayton Agreement of 1995), Kosovo, East Timor and Sierra Leone. I regret that this was not done sooner.

In the forty years before I joined the Secretariat in 1986, the UN had fielded thirteen peacekeeping operations. All but one of them had been in the traditional category. The ones in the Congo and southern Lebanon degenerated into complex emergency operations and in the Congo there had also been an element of peace enforcement. The thirteenth operation, in West Irian (also known as West New Guinea), was the only multifunctional one, and it was on a very small scale. During my seven years in charge of peacekeeping, sixteen new operations would be established: eight of them traditional, six multifunctional (of which one degenerated into complex emergency), one preventive and one complex emergency from the outset.* When I left peacekeeping in March 1993, there were fifteen operations in the field with 55,000 uniformed personnel and an annual budget of $2.7 billion. The comparable figures in 1986 had been five operations with 10,000 uniformed personnel and a budget of $240 million. In the year after Kofi Annan succeeded me as Under-Secretary-General for Peacekeeping, the number of uniformed personnel would climb further to over 75,000 and the annual cost would exceed three billion dollars.

This enormous expansion in peacekeeping was due to one cause, which has already been mentioned. The end of the Cold War in the late eighties had at last made it possible for the Security Council to take action to try to end many conflicts in the Third World, especially internal conflicts which were in reality proxy wars between East and West. Initially the United Nations responded to this opportunity with conspicuous success. But the success bred over-confidence in member states and Secretariat alike. As a result, some unwise decisions were taken, disasters occurred in Angola, Bosnia, Rwanda and Somalia, and the United Nations ended a dizzy decade with its peacekeeping reputation tarnished. By the end of the century the number of peacekeepers in the field would drop to less than 19,000.

The two other categories of action which can be undertaken only with the consent of the hostile parties are peacemaking and peacebuilding.

Peacemaking is the use of diplomatic means to persuade hostile parties to settle a dispute which has led, or could lead, to armed conflict between them. In the first instance, the best that can usually be achieved is agreement on a cease-fire and the deployment of peacekeepers to help the parties observe and consolidate it. But the peacemakers' goal is always to proceed to a comprehensive agreement which will not only end

---

* For curious taxonomists the breakdown is as follows:

traditional	UNGOMAP (Afghanistan), UNIIMOG (Iran/Iraq), UNAVEM I (Angola), ONUCA (Central America), UNIKOM (Iraq/Kuwait), UNAMIC (Cambodia), UNPROFOR (Croatia), UNOSOM I (Somalia)
preventive	UNPROFOR (Macedonia)
multifunctional	UNTAG (Namibia), UNAVEM II (Angola) (until October 1992), ONUSAL (El Salvador), MINURSO (Western Sahara), UNTAC (Cambodia), ONUMOZ (Mozambique)
complex emergency	UNPROFOR (Bosnia), UNAVEM II (Angola) (from October 1992)

the existing conflict but also minimize the risk of its breaking out again. A classic example of peacemaking by the United Nations is the negotiation of the peace settlement in El Salvador which is described in more detail in Chapter 13. It was an attempt not only to deal with the military aspects of the civil conflict in that small and crowded country but also to tackle the economic and social issues which had caused the conflict.

Peacebuilding is longer-term action to consolidate peace by tackling the root causes of a potential or past conflict. One of the lessons learnt by the United Nations since the end of the Cold War is that it is not enough to negotiate a peace settlement, help the parties implement it and then withdraw after a couple of years. The peace will last only if parallel, long-term action is taken to eradicate the causes of the dispute that has led to armed conflict. Peacebuilding is especially important, and especially difficult, in internal conflicts within states. What makes it difficult for the United Nations is that in such conflicts the root causes are, by definition, domestic matters. They usually relate to human rights, justice and law and order, ethnic discrimination, economic policy, the distribution of wealth, all of them matters which sovereignty-sensitive governments will be reluctant to open to foreign governments and inter-governmental organizations. The UN's role therefore has to be cautious and discreet, supporting local forces for peace and reconciliation and not taking direct action itself. The international community has much to learn in this field.

The first of the two coercive categories of United Nations action is sanctions, which usually take the form of economic and/or arms embargoes imposed by the Security Council. Although the United States remains a staunch advocate of sanctions, and imposes many unilaterally, there is declining enthusiasm for sanctions amongst the wider membership. They are regarded, rightly in my view, as a blunt instrument which rarely causes a government to change its policies. They usually result in disproportionate suffering to the civilians who have the misfortune to live under that government's misrule; they give the governing class unmatched opportunities to amass illegal wealth; and they can inflict collateral damage on the neighbours of the sanctioned state. Their failure in Iraq since 1990 has, especially, undermined confidence in them.

In 1988 the South African State President, P.W. Botha, gave a luncheon in Pretoria in honour of Pérez de Cuéllar. I was seated next to the Minister of Finance, Barend du Plessis, and asked him whether the easing of South Africa's policy on Namibia had been in any way due to sanctions. In a long reply, he said that military and commercial sanctions had not been a problem: if South Africa had a good product, it could sell it and if it needed an import, it could obtain it, though in both cases it would take some pain on the price. The country's industrial development had probably benefited from the challenge. Sports sanctions had had more of an impact, in causing National Party supporters to question whether existing policies were worth the price of South Africa's exclusion from international competition. But what had finally caused the government to reconsider its position was the denial of access to short-term financial markets. This had led to unmanageable cash-flow problems and 'forced us to close schools and hospitals'.

This anecdote illustrates the need for patient research into the kinds of sanctions which will, in such cases, persuade tyrants to change their policy, rather than the precipitate imposition of general sanctions as a knee-jerk expression of international anger. Boutros-Ghali said this, in more diplomatic language, in his *Supplement to An Agenda for Peace* when he urged the Security Council to set up a 'mechanism' to ensure that sanctions were more accurately targeted and their undesired collateral effects reduced. No action was taken. The need for action remains.

The other coercive category is peace enforcement. Despite the hopes expressed in the Charter, the United Nations Organization does not have the capacity to go to war. It can manage the deployment of peacekeeping troops contributed by member states for non-combat missions, but it cannot provide the planning, the command and control, the communications, the intelligence or the logistic support that would be necessary if it were to send an expeditionary force to make war against a violator of the peace in a distant theatre. Nor would governments be ready to entrust their soldiers, their weapons systems and their military reputations to a command structure in which their own military would have little confidence. The Charter's provisions for enforcement action required member states to enter into binding agreements under which they would make military resources available to the Security Council on demand and the Council would deploy these to stop acts of aggression and breaches of the peace. Efforts to put this concept into practice ran aground on the rocks of the Cold War and no such agreement has ever been concluded. This being so, an alternative arrangement has evolved: when peace enforcement is required, the Council invites member states to assemble a multinational force, under the command of one of them, and authorizes that force to use its arms in order to achieve an objective approved by the Council. The first such case was the Korean War in 1950. The liberation of Kuwait from Iraqi occupation in 1990–1 has become the standard modern example. This is a perfectly satisfactory alternative provided that the participants in the multinational force keep the Security Council informed of what they are doing and do not exceed the authority it has given to them.

There is one further category of action that should be mentioned in this brief survey. Humanitarian action is different from the five categories just described in that its primary purpose is not the maintenance of peace and security but relief of the suffering, especially the suffering of civilians, which invariably occurs when peace and security break down. However, humanitarian agencies often get caught up in the conflict, and the manner in which they do their job can have a direct effect on the ability of peacemakers and peacekeepers to do theirs. Coordination is therefore necessary, but often difficult.

I have described the five categories as categories of United Nations action. But the UN does not claim a monopoly in any of them. On the contrary, all of them can be, and have been, used by one or other of the constituent parts of 'the international community'.* Indeed, it is rare for the UN to perform all functions. Each of the successful peace operations since the end of the Cold War has been a cooperative effort by several elements in the international community. Take the independence of Namibia: as is described in Chapter 10, the outlines of the peace plan were negotiated with the parties by a 'contact group' of five Western governments; the plan was then endorsed by the UN Security Council; when unforeseen difficulties arose, the United States stepped in and mediated an additional agreement which made it possible for the plan to be put into effect; the United Nations supervised its implementation; and many governmental and non-governmental agencies have since contributed to peacebuilding.

There is also imprecision in the phrase 'the United Nations'. Does it mean the United (or not so united) Nations which are members of the 'United Nations Organization' created by the Charter in 1945? Or does it mean that Organization, with its six 'principal organs' – the General Assembly, the Security Council, the Trusteeship Council,† the Economic and Social Council, the International Court of Justice and the Secretariat? Or does it just mean the last of those organs, the Secretary-General and his (or soon, one hopes, her) staff? Or does it mean all of the above, plus the alphabet soup of programmes, funds, offices and agencies which since 1945 have accreted to the original Organization? The answer is that 'the United Nations' can have all or any of these meanings. In the Secretariat one used to feel that if the context was congratulatory ('the UN has eradicated smallpox', 'the UN has brought Namibia to independence') the phrase meant the member states, but that if the context

---

* There is academic debate about what this phrase means. In this book it means the United Nations and its agencies, governments individually or in *ad hoc* coalitions, regional organizations, non-governmental organizations and distinguished individuals who have the wish and the capacity to help deal with a particular conflict.

† Now inactive as there are no longer any UN trust territories.

was critical ('the UN ought to be doing something', 'the UN has missed another opportunity') it was the Secretariat that was meant. In an effort to achieve greater precision, I urged my staff to observe the following usage: 'the United Nations' for the Organization; 'the United Nations system' for the alphabet soup; 'the member states'; and 'the Secretariat'. I did not succeed, but that usage is followed in this book.

As regards the five categories of action, the UN has relied more on the three consent-based techniques than on the two coercive ones. There are various reasons for this: doubts about the efficacy of coercion; worries about its cost, both financial and human; a lingering pacifist ethos – the United Nations was set up to save succeeding generations from the scourge of war and should not be waging war itself; and, above all, sensitivity ab----- sovereignty. Given that most of the wars since the end of the ----- e been civil wars within states, sovereignty has been a major ----- the UN's ability to deal with conflict; the Secretariat has ----- willing but the member states unwilling.

The United Nations has paid a price for this. Its reliance on the consent-based techniques and its respect for sovereignty have often condemned it to impotence. At any one time there are dozens of actual or potential conflicts in the world. But only in a small minority of them are all the parties ready to give their consent to outside mediation. In most cases, at least one of the parties will still believe that it can achieve its objectives by military means; or, as Lakhdar Brahimi, former Foreign Minister of Algeria and an experienced mediator, has said of the multi-party conflict in Afghanistan, 'the trouble is that each of the parties has a first choice which is unattainable, and all of them have the same second choice which is to continue the war'. If the conflict drags on long enough without a decisive military outcome, the protagonists will in the end let third parties in. But the end can take a very long time to come, and meanwhile the question 'Why doesn't the UN do something?' can be answered only by the lame 'Because the parties won't allow us to'.

Professor William Zartman of Johns Hopkins University has developed the concept of the 'ripe moment' when conflicts become ready for third-party mediation. If each party to a conflict believes that it is more powerful than the other and that it can prevail in an armed struggle without incurring excessive costs, they are both likely to choose war rather than negotiation. Conflicts become 'ripe' for negotiation when both sides come to see that they cannot prevail in the armed struggle. This realization usually comes about in one of two ways: when a conflict has reached an intolerable, 'mutually hurting stalemate' which is unlikely to be broken in the foreseeable future; or when a catastrophic escalation of the conflict seems imminent or has been narrowly missed. While the 'ripe moment' is clear conceptually, in reality it is often difficult to see until it has passed.* When, in 1993, I became responsible for the UN's efforts at peacemaking and, especially, preventive diplomacy, I found Zartman's concept a useful tool for identifying which actual or potential conflicts might be worth the UN's attention. The conflict between India and Pakistan, for instance, was – and still is – one of the most threatening in the world, with two enormous armies, each with a nuclear potential, confronting each other across a line that has already seen three major wars. But there was no point in devoting time and energy to attempted mediation because India had been insisting for twenty years that the conflict could be settled only through bilateral negotiations and that third parties had no role, not even in trying to get bilateral negotiations started.

The requirement for consent derives, of course, from the sovereignty of states, which was uncompromisingly reaffirmed in the UN Charter:

> Nothing contained in the present Charter shall authorize the United Nations to intervene in matters which are essentially within the domestic jurisdiction of any state or shall require the Members to submit such matters to settlement under the present Charter; but this principle shall not prejudice the application of enforcement measures under Chapter VII.

Only three years later the Universal Declaration of Human Rights gave states the right to take an interest in how well other states were respecting human rights. Since then, and especially since the end of the Cold War, there have been a growing number of cases in which the UN has involved itself in internal or 'civil' conflicts (which are of course 'within the domestic jurisdiction' of the state concerned). Usually this has been with the consent of the government, as well as the government's armed opponents, but in 'failed states' such as Somalia there has been no government to give consent and consent has had to be sought from the heads of the opposing factions.

Legally, the position remains as described in the Charter: sovereignty is paramount. But since the end of the Cold War a number of precedents have been created and these will in time, perhaps, come to constitute customary international practice and will legitimize some forms of intervention by the United Nations in domestic matters. At the outset of the civil war in Liberia in 1990, the horrors of the fighting in Monrovia led the African Group at the UN in New York to beg Pérez de Cuéllar to do something. The Secretary-General, being a good Latin American jurist, said that he regretted that the Charter permitted him to do nothing; the

---

* I. William Zartman, *Ripe for Resolution: Conflict and Intervention in Africa* (Oxford: Oxford University Press, 1986), pp. 232–3, 236–7 and I. William Zartman and Saadia Touval, *International Mediation in the Post-Cold War Era* (Washington DC: United States Institute of Peace Press, 1996), pp. 450–2.

conflict was an internal one. But a year later, when he learnt of the horrors that were taking place in Mogadishu, again in an internal conflict, he did not hesitate to tell the Security Council that he had decided to take an initiative to restore peace there. Ten years on, the international ethos has changed and no Secretary-General would now feel able to say he could do nothing because the conflict was internal.

In 1991 Pérez de Cuéllar himself stated in a speech at Bordeaux that international law must not stagnate but must keep pace with changes in international life; perhaps a balance was being established between the rights of states, as confirmed by the Charter, and the rights of individuals, as confirmed by the Universal Declaration of Human Rights; did this not call into question the notion that sovereignty was inviolable? Boutros-Ghali, in *An Agenda for Peace* and in his response to individual crises, promoted a more interventionist role for the United Nations. Kofi Annan, speaking in 1998 at the Ditchley Park conference centre near Oxford, said that forceful intervention was a lesser evil than allowing massacre and extreme oppression to continue; but intervention should be a collective decision and only the Security Council had the authority to take it.

Intervention nevertheless remains an ill-defined and controversial aspect of the UN's role in the maintenance of peace and security. It causes particular concern to the countries of the Non-Aligned Movement.* That movement grew from the Bandung Conference of 1955, with the first Non-Aligned Summit being held in Belgrade in 1961. Its moving spirits were Jawaharlal Nehru (India), Gamal Abdul Nasser (Egypt) and Josip Broz Tito (Yugoslavia). Membership was open to all states which wished to remain neutral in the Cold War. In 1986 the movement included almost one hundred states and two liberation movements and had become a force to be reckoned with at the United Nations, where its members attempted to coordinate their policies and to vote as a bloc. On most issues they succeeded, though there were often one or two dissenters. In the Security Council they had what was in effect a sixth veto if they remained united. This was because the non-permanent members of the Security Council usually include seven Non-Aligned countries. As Security Council resolutions cannot be adopted without the positive votes of at least nine of its fifteen members, the Non-Aligned members can prevent a resolution being adopted if none of them votes in favour of it. But the solidarity of the Non-Aligned tends to collapse if the conflict concerned is between Non-Aligned countries, as in the case of Kashmir or Iraq's invasion of Kuwait in 1990.

---

* In this book the phrase 'the Non-Aligned' is used variously to indicate the Non-Aligned Movement (NAM) itself, its members as a whole or its members in a particular institution, usually the Security Council.

As regards intervention, the Non-Aligned may, in specific cases like Liberia, have demanded, or at least acquiesced in, UN involvement in domestic matters for humanitarian reasons. But generically they remain strongly wedded to the principle of sovereignty. Their initial reaction to Boutros-Ghali's *An Agenda for Peace* was not unfavourable. But when they saw the enthusiasm with which the West espoused the ideas of preventive diplomacy and humanitarian intervention and its comparative lack of interest in the UN's role in economic and social development, there was a reaction. For the Non-Aligned development is as important a purpose for the UN as peace and security. As a result, the General Assembly was never able to agree on a substantive response to Boutros-Ghali's report. Since then further disquiet has been aroused by the blurring of distinctions, in Iraq and the former Yugoslavia, between enforcement action specifically authorized by the Security Council (the liberation of Kuwait, for example) and enforcement action undertaken by Western powers on the basis of contested interpretations of Security Council resolutions (such as the no-fly zones in Iraq or the bombing of Kosovo in 1999).

Two linked constraints have thus limited the United Nations' ability to meet expectations that, with the Cold War over, it would at last be able to play the central role in the maintenance of peace and security which had been envisaged for it in the Charter. The first constraint is its reliance on techniques which require the hostile parties to give prior consent to any efforts the UN may make to maintain or restore peace. The second is the uncertainty about how far it can side-step the principle so clearly stated in the Charter that it may not involve itself in domestic matters.

There is a third ever-present constraint: the political will of the member states. There are limits, albeit ill-defined ones, to the political commitment, the money and the troops which states are prepared to devote to peace efforts by the United Nations. This is a factor which the Secretariat must always have in mind. A conflict must not only be ripe, in Zartman's sense, for third-party mediation. It must also be one where a UN effort will attract the necessary political and material support from member states. A politically uncomfortable reality is that in this context a few member states are vastly more important than all the others. In 1990 the member states of the OECD paid (or, in the case of the United States, usually did not pay) 82.9 per cent of the costs of UN peace-keeping operations.* In revised arrangements agreed in 2000, their share has risen to 93.7 per cent. They include three of the five states which have the power of veto in the Security Council. They cannot impose an

---

* The OECD members comprise the Western industrialized democracies, South Korea, Japan, Mexico, the Czech Republic, Hungary, Poland and Turkey.

operation on the United Nations; China and/or Russia could veto. But no operation can be established without their active support.

As a result, the peace efforts undertaken by the United Nations tend to reflect Western priorities and this gives rise to charges of double standards. Why, one is asked, should suppression of a secessionist minority in Serbia lead to war when similar action in Turkey receives so little attention? Why should one Middle Eastern state be so fiercely punished for occupying its neighbour's territory and developing weapons of mass destruction when another Middle Eastern state does the same and gets off scot-free? Pérez de Cuéllar made reference to this in his speech in Bordeaux. International law, he said, must not be applied selectively; 'a principle invoked in a particular situation but disregarded in a similar one is as good as no principle at all'. He was right. To Western readers the questions about double standards may seem misguided and offensive, but they are standard fare for a UN official who travels and speaks in the Third World. One night in 1991 unknown assailants fired rocket-propelled grenades at the headquarters in Tegucigalpa (Honduras) of the UN's military observer group in Central America (ONUCA); it eventually transpired that the attack was a protest against the UN for allowing itself to be used by the United States to persecute the hero Saddam.

It is because the West is seen as setting the agenda for the UN's peace efforts (and devaluing its role in economic and social development) that there has been so much talk in recent years about lack of democracy in the UN and, especially, about the need to reform the Security Council. Little progress has been made in negotiations to change the Council's composition. Even if they eventually succeed, he who pays the piper will still call the tune and the priorities of those who have the money will continue to be a major factor determining which conflicts receive the United Nations' attention.

3

First Foray to the Field

On 3 February 1986 I moved into Brian Urquhart's office on the 38th floor of the Secretariat building. I was to stay there for six years until Boutros Boutros-Ghali became Secretary-General in 1992 and took the whole of that floor for his personal staff. There was a fine view westwards across Manhattan to New Jersey and the sunsets could be spectacular. Peregrine falcons sometimes powered their way past my window, scattering the house finches which used the Glass House as though it was a canyon wall in their native Arizona.

I was one of two Under-Secretaries-General for Special Political Affairs. The other was Diego Cordovez who was later to become Foreign Minister of Ecuador. We had separate staffs but jointly our department was known as the Office for Special Political Affairs (OSPA). One of the funniest men in the Secretariat, Cordovez was charming and good company. But I was warned that he was not an easy colleague. He had been jealous of Urquhart, it was said, and would seize the opportunity to cut the new British USG down to size. I soon learnt, however, that setting colleagues against each other was a house sport in the Secretariat and such warnings were best ignored.

I had a small, talented but somewhat top-heavy staff. It was headed by F.T. Liu, the son of a great Chinese landscape painter. He had been brought up in Paris, joined the Secretariat in 1949 and seamlessly transferred his allegiance from Taipei to Beijing when the People's Republic of China won China's seat at the United Nations in 1971. He was the high priest of peacekeeping and the master of its procedures. These were useful attributes given the weakness of the UN's institutional memory. He had his excitable moments but he imparted much wisdom and gave me loyal support until he retired a year after my arrival.

Liu was an Assistant-Secretary-General (ASG), the second most senior rank in the Secretariat. The next level was Director (D-2). I had three of them: Jean-Claude Aimé, Gus Feissel and Vladislav Misharin.

Aimé, a Haitian who was to become a close friend, began his UN career in the United Nations Development Programme (UNDP).

Urquhart spotted his political talents in Amman in the mid-seventies and appointed him as Political Adviser, first to UNTSO in Jerusalem and then to UNIFIL in Lebanon.* He is a self-effacing man of intelligence and charm, master of a vast telephone network and intensely discreet. Pérez de Cuéllar was to take him into his *cabinet* three years later and he subsequently became Boutros-Ghali's Chief of Staff. But meanwhile he was an invaluable guide as I picked my way through the Secretariat minefield.

Feissel, an American of Alsatian origin, had come recently to peacekeeping after twenty years on the economic side of the Secretariat. He quickly donned the mantle of another American, George Sherry, as the house guru on Cyprus and was to devote most of the rest of his UN career to that intractable problem.

Misharin was the token Soviet. As already mentioned, the Soviet Union often questioned the legitimacy of peacekeeping; it did not feature in the Charter, they said, and it gave the Secretary-General political functions which as 'the chief administrative officer of the Organization' he should not have. But the Soviet Union's support for the establishment of a new UN force in Sinai after the October War in 1973 provided an opportunity to draw it into peacekeeping. The then Soviet USG, Shevchenko, took part in the Secretariat's planning of the operation (UNEF II) and Poland became the first Warsaw Pact country to contribute troops to a UN peacekeeping operation. Urquhart then persuaded Waldheim to accept an oft-repeated Soviet request that a senior Soviet official should be seconded to OSPA. He explained to the secondee, Nicolai Fochine, that he knew Fochine would have to report to the Soviet Mission and that he would sometimes therefore have to withhold information from him. Fochine accepted this without demur. Misharin had succeeded Fochine just before I arrived. He was a modest and decent man and he too accepted these limitations. They troubled my conscience and I was sad that he had already moved on when, a few years later, changes in Soviet policy made it possible to give his successor, Dmitry Titov, a real job as desk officer for Angola.

In addition to Liu and the three D-2s, I had three other civilian professionals and six support staff. The tiny military staff was headed by Major General Timothy Dibuama, an officer of the Ghanaian Army who had joined OSPA in 1974 as a Major with the title of 'Military Liaison

---

* The titles of UN peacekeeping operations tend to be wordy and the operations are usually referred to by their acronyms. UNTSO is the United Nations Truce Supervision Organization and UNIFIL the United Nations Interim Force in Lebanon. A complete list of the peacekeeping operations established in the half-century from 1948 to 1996 can be found in Appendix II.

Officer'. By 1981 his government had promoted him to the rank of Brigadier-General and it was decided that his title should become 'Military Adviser to the Under-Secretaries-General for Special Political Affairs'. In 1987 I was told that Pérez de Cuéllar wanted him to be called 'Military Adviser to the Secretary-General'. I did not demur. Dibuama got the title he wanted but in practice remained a member of my department and under my authority. He was conscientious, loyal and, like Liu, a master of precedent and procedure. He did a good job in helping to keep the flame of peacekeeping alight during the dark decade that preceded the end of the Cold War.

My part of OSPA had three functions. The first was to run the five peacekeeping operations which were in the field at that time. Three of them were connected with the Arab-Israeli conflict: the United Nations Truce Supervision Organization (UNTSO) with its headquarters in Jerusalem and military observers deployed in the Gaza Strip, Egypt, Jordan, Lebanon and Syria; the United Nations Disengagement Observer Force (UNDOF) on the Golan Heights in Syria; and the United Nations Interim Force (UNIFIL) in southern Lebanon. The fourth operation was the United Nations Force in Cyprus (UNFICYP). Finally, there was the United Nations Military Observer Group in India and Pakistan (UNMOGIP), a tiny group of military observers deployed on either side of the 'line of control' between Indian and Pakistani forces in Kashmir. Our second function was to plan any new operations which seemed likely to be needed. The only one under active consideration in 1986 was an operation in Namibia which was not fielded until 1989. The third function was to support the Secretary-General's diplomatic efforts (peacemaking) to resolve conflicts for which a peacekeeping operation had been deployed. In 1986 active negotiations were in progress on the Arab-Israeli conflict, southern Lebanon and Cyprus.

There was to be a major shift in OSPA's structure, functions and staff at the end of 1988. On his appointment as Foreign Minister of Ecuador, Cordovez resigned and was not replaced. Pérez de Cuéllar took the opportunity to reduce OSPA's functions, limiting us to the management and planning of peacekeeping operations and nothing else. Responsibility for peacemaking was transferred to his own office. Aimé and Feissel went with it, together with Lisa Buttenheim, an outstanding political affairs officer of American nationality who had moved from UNTSO to OSPA in late 1986 and subsequently married Aimé. From Cordovez's team I inherited Hisako Shimura, a Japanese D-2, who became my deputy. She was hard-working, methodical and loyal; but in a hierarchical bureaucracy she found it difficult to contest the views of her seniors in other departments and she was reluctant to take substantive decisions in my absence.

This reduced staff was adequate for the limited amount of peacekeeping work that was required at the end of 1988. But we were on the eve of expansion. During 1989 three new operations would be fielded, including a pioneering multifunctional mission to bring Namibia to independence. There would be a pause in 1990 and then five new operations in 1991. This placed on my OSPA colleagues a burden which was beyond their capacity to bear.* By 1991 I had, in addition to Shimura, four staff members at the Principal Officer level (D-1). Joachim Hütter, a very able German, had been Senior Adviser in UNIFIL and then in UNFICYP and understood peacekeeping better than anyone. Michel Pelletier from France was an excellent linguist and gave me good support in the Central American negotiations. Felix Downes-Thomas from Gambia had just joined the office and was my main support on Western Sahara. Dmitry Titov from the Russian Federation had also arrived very recently and was soon to shine as the desk officer for Angola.

My task was made difficult by the fact that I had no direct authority over two administrative divisions on whose performance the efficiency of peacekeeping operations was critically dependent. The Office of Field Operational and External Support Activities (OFOESA), which later became the Field Operations Division (FOD) in the Department of Administration and Management, was responsible for providing peacekeeping operations with personnel and logistic support of every kind. The Peacekeeping Financing Division in the Budget Office was responsible for all the financial issues. Both Divisions were under the authority of the USG for Administration and Management and would take no orders from OSPA. Behrooz Sadry, the Director of FOD, had also established a high degree of autonomy within his department. Bureaucratic and diplomatic skills were thus needed to win the administrators' cooperation, especially when procedural corners had to be cut at the beginning of a new operation.

By early 1991, OSPA was wilting under the strain and so was I. Something had to be done to reduce the overload. I put two complementary proposals to Pérez de Cuéllar. The first was that he should appoint an Assistant-Secretary-General to serve as my deputy; the second was that he should put FOD under my command. Aimé supported both ideas. Pérez de Cuéllar was inclined to favour the first and I asked for Sadry. Pérez de Cuéllar preferred Kofi Annan, who was then Controller (as the senior financial officer in the Secretariat is called). I said that I was happy to accept him. There was stronger opposition to my taking charge of FOD and Pérez de Cuéllar commissioned a study by Swedish consultants. It found against me and Pérez de Cuéllar decided to take no

---

* The diagram in Appendix IV charts the growth in their workload from 1986 to 1992, the seven years in which the author was in charge of peacekeeping.

action on either of my proposals because he was by then close to the end of his term of office and he felt, rightly, that the matter should be left for his successor to resolve. So I continued for another year to struggle in hotel rooms around the world with vast quantities of undigested documentation faxed to me by Shimura with the plea: 'Please advise'.

When Boutros-Ghali assumed office as Secretary-General at the beginning of 1992, he gave himself two months to restructure the Secretariat. The Office of Special Political Affairs was renamed the Department of Peacekeeping Operations (DPKO). I was reappointed as USG and was at last given a deputy at the Assistant-Secretary-General level. Boutros-Ghali too proposed that the post should be given to Kofi Annan. Again I was delighted to accept the proposal. Annan had had a long and successful career in the Secretariat, including several senior posts in the Department of Administration and Management, giving him experience and skills that were sorely needed in my department. At an earlier stage he had served in the first United Nations peacekeeping force, UNEF I, in Sinai and in UNHCR, both of which gave him experience relevant to his work in the new DPKO. He would be my deputy across the board but we agreed to divide the field operations between us. He would be responsible for those in Africa and the Middle East (except for Angola, which I would retain for old times' sake) and I would do the rest of Asia, Europe and Latin America.

Boutros-Ghali also created a new Department of Political Affairs (DPA), which would assume responsibilities previously held by half a dozen different departments, including the peacemakers whom Pérez de Cuéllar had moved into his own office. Boutros-Ghali declared that from now on substantive issues were to be handled in the departments and not in his office. However, he also appointed three Senior Political Advisers, two of them at the USG level, and some doubted whether these senior and experienced officials would be satisfied with a purely advisory role. Aimé, however, who would shortly replace Dayal as the Secretary-General's Chief of Staff, was a fierce defender of the departments' prerogatives and Boutros-Ghali's wishes were on the whole respected, though perhaps less so towards the end of his term.

The new structure raised the question of where the boundary lay between the two new departments in the case of conflicts where a peacekeeping operation had been deployed or was under discussion. Would peacemaking remain departmentally separate from peacekeeping? Or would we return to the pre-1988 arrangement under which the USG for peacekeeping was responsible for peacemaking related to any conflict for which a peacekeeping operation had been deployed? In February 1992 there were thirteen such cases. Boutros-Ghali and Aimé said it was simple: the Department of Political Affairs should do the political work and the Department of Peacekeeping Operations should do the operational work. I had again to argue that peacekeeping *is* a political activity; it serves a political purpose; it can take place only on the basis of a political agreement between hostile parties; and those doing it, even at the administrative level, are in an essentially political relationship with the two sides. So, where do you draw the line, Secretary-General? Since 1988 I had recovered a good deal of lost ground and was now playing a full part in the political work related both to the establishment of new operations, with the sole exception of Rafeeuddin Ahmed's *chasse gardée* in Cambodia, and to the management of existing ones. I did not want to lose this again, especially when I had at last gained an able and senior deputy with whom I could share the work.

The new Department of Political Affairs was headed by two USGs: James Jonah, a long-serving Sierra Leonean member of the Secretariat who had worked with Urquhart and knew a lot about peacemaking and peacekeeping; and Vladimir Petrovsky, a former First Deputy Foreign Minister of the Soviet Union who had played an important part in Mikhail Gorbachev's remodelling of Soviet foreign policy but had no direct experience of the UN. Jonah was determined to play a leading role in the new African operations (Somalia and Mozambique) but did not challenge me over Angola and had the good sense to steer clear of Western Sahara. Petrovsky was keen to get involved in Yugoslavia but was handicapped (as was I when I succeeded him a year later) by the grinding difficulties of forging an effective instrument for preventive diplomacy and peacemaking out of the disparate elements which had come to DPA from the 'political' departments extinguished in Boutros-Ghali's *perestroika*. So ambiguities remained about the boundary between the two departments, and much heat was sometimes generated.

Meanwhile in March 1986, I made an introductory tour of four of the five operations that existed then. To my chagrin it did not include UNMOGIP. This group of military observers was set up in 1949 to 'supervise' the cease-fire established after the previous year's war between India and Pakistan over Kashmir. Initially the Indian Government cooperated with it but New Delhi later took the position that the UN's role in Kashmir had been superseded by agreements signed by the two countries in 1972. These revised the cease-fire line and provided that the parties' differences over Kashmir and other issues should be settled through bilateral negotiations. Pakistan did not accept India's view that the agreements superseded UNMOGIP's mandate. It insisted that the Security Council was still seized of* the Kashmir issue

---

* Another example of UN-speak, meaning that the item was still on the Council's agenda.

and that India was still obliged to implement a decision taken by the Council in 1948 that a plebiscite should be held on Kashmir's future. Meanwhile India stopped sending UNMOGIP its complaints of alleged cease-fire violations by Pakistan and refused to respond when UNMOGIP forwarded Pakistan's complaints to it. As a matter of principle, Pakistan nevertheless continued to submit complaints. Successive Secretaries-General took the position that the operation could be terminated only by decision of the Security Council. Such a decision would, it was assumed, be blocked by the veto of China, Pakistan's friend. So UNMOGIP stayed on as a political symbol without any operational role.

From time to time Secretaries-General tentatively suggested to New Delhi that an agreement to resolve a problem through bilateral negotiations did not necessarily exclude them from using their good offices to get the negotiations started.* But such approaches never prospered. Nor did my own occasional attempts to persuade the Indian delegation in New York that I should at least be permitted to make a brief visit to inspect the operation. The most senior official whom the Indians allowed to visit UNMOGIP during my tenure was James Jonah, who was at the time the ASG in charge of the administrative support of peacekeeping. Like many before and since, he fell foul of the sensitivities of the Indian authorities who took exception to some innocuous remarks he made at a press conference in Pakistan.

UNMOGIP took almost none of my time. All I can remember are various personnel problems and an exciting few days in 1991 when Kashmiri militants kidnapped an Israeli tourist and said that they would release him only to the UN, something which the Indians initially refused to accept but eventually conceded. This episode revealed UNMOGIP's inability to manage even a minor crisis and provided a pretext for another effort to persuade the Indians to let me visit the operation. I did not succeed.

My introductory progress through the peacekeeping parish began in Cyprus. I was happy to be there again. Twenty-six years before, Cyprus had been a weekend destination when I was learning Arabic in Lebanon. Once, in a nightclub in Kyrenia, I danced cheek to cheek with an Israeli air hostess. The thrill was more political than sexual: so nervous were the

---

* 'The Secretary-General's good offices' is one of the more useful examples of UN-speak, since the phrase sounds beneficent and is conveniently vague. Pérez de Cuéllar has described it as 'a very flexible term as it may mean very little or very much'. Its basic meaning denotes action to explore whether opportunities exist for third-party mediation between two hostile parties and, if so, the undertaking of such mediation. Dag Hammarskjöld and Pérez de Cuéllar were particularly active in the exercise of their good offices, usually on their own initiative and in strict confidence, and thereby extended the powers of the Secretary-General.

British authorities about the future of their language school in Lebanon after the 1958 civil war that we students were told not even to utter the word 'Israel' where we might be overheard (we used 'South Wales' instead). As Head of Chancery in the British Embassy in Tripoli in the late sixties I was ex officio chairman of a peripatetic body called the Local Intelligence Committee (Libya). It met in various agreeable places in the eastern Mediterranean, including the British Sovereign Base Area at Episkopi in Cyprus, where the post-prandial high jinks in the Officers' Mess were a riot but the hangovers appalling.

My second career started disastrously in Cyprus. Jet-lagged from New York I slept through the appointed hour for breakfast, was awakened courteously but with undisguisable disapproval by the Deputy Force Commander, Brigadier Robin Duchesne, and arrived an hour late to inspect the guard of honour which had been paraded to greet the new Under-Secretary-General. I rarely felt comfortable inspecting guards of honour. One walked down the front rank, stopped in front of a soldier and tried to say something which was neither banal nor so interesting that it would be difficult to end the conversation a few seconds later in order to move on. There was also the nagging insecurity of 'What do *they* think of *me*?' The Finnish honour guards were the easiest. I was taught to stand in front of them and bellow 'Hyvää päivää suomalaiset sotilaat' ('Good day, Finnish soldiers'); they bellowed back 'Hyvää päivää herra alipääsihteeri' ('Good day to you, Mr Under-Secretary'); protocol was respected and no small talk required.

The other initial disaster in Cyprus was sartorial. Urquhart had told me to dress casually when visiting the field. He was right, but I overdid it. An old and ill-fitting pullover from British Home Stores accentuated my paunch and compared ill with the smart turnout of the soldiers in the field. Brigadier Duchesne saved the day: 'Wear something that looks military but without badges of rank.' Commandant Barney Goulding of the Irish Army not only shared my name but was of similar height. He gave me an Irish Army pullover, a warm and figure-enhancing garment, with the UN roundel on the right arm but no other insignia. It became my standard field attire for the rest of my time in the UN, except in hot weather when I wore a short-sleeved khaki shirt, again with the UN roundel on the right arm.

The commander of the force in Cyprus (UNFICYP) was Major-General Günther Greindl of the Austrian Army. He was good company – jovial, self-confident and realistic. He was also an experienced peace-keeper and had already commanded the UN operation in Syria. The main contingents in his force were from Austria, Canada, Denmark, Sweden and the United Kingdom. At that time, when peacekeeping was in the doldrums, the troop-contributing countries were few in number. Britain and France had troops in Cyprus and Lebanon respectively and Canada was in every operation; but most of the others were small, multilaterally-minded European democracies – Austria, Ireland and the Nordic countries. Only in Syria was there a Warsaw Pact contingent (Poland) and only in Lebanon were there contingents from the Third World (Fiji, Ghana, Nepal).

These peacekeeping stalwarts competed for the few command positions that were available. The Secretariat went along with this. We were happy to reward governments which remained loyal supporters of peacekeeping, often at considerable expense to their taxpayers.* It was also in the UN's interest to appoint commanders with previous peacekeeping experience, for command of a multinational headquarters staffed by officers from varying military and cultural backgrounds is no easy task. Personnel problems at field headquarters were one of the heaviest crosses the USG had to bear. It became especially heavy when the great expansion of peacekeeping that was soon to come brought in many new peacekeeping nations whose right to a share of senior positions had to be respected but which had difficulty in finding senior officers with the requisite experience.

But in this first round of visits in 1986, I was conscious of moving into a milieu where the culture of peacekeeping (its 'law and lore', as Álvaro de Soto used to say) was well established and well understood by officers and soldiers alike. There was evidence of this in the briefings which began every visit, be it to a force's headquarters or a remote observation post. They followed a standard pattern, prepared with such meticulous care that I felt ashamed at causing so many people so much work. Initially much of the information was new and valuable. But on subsequent visits there was a growing sense of 'been here, heard this'. I never succeeded in persuading force commanders that I was already familiar with the conflict, the identity of the protagonists and the force's mandate, deployment and standard operating procedures, and that the briefing could therefore be confined to what had happened since my last visit and what was expected to happen next. There seemed to be a mandatory procedure for briefing VIPs which neither the force commander nor the 'Victor India Papas' themselves had power to vary.

It was often a relief to get out of the briefing room and into a car or helicopter for a tour of the area of operation (AO). The terrain was always interesting, often spectacularly beautiful and sometimes rich in bird- and other wildlife, for buffer zones are *de facto* nature reserves in

---

* Calculations made in 1987 suggested that the troop costs which the UN reimbursed to Norway covered barely a quarter of the costs actually incurred by Norway in contributing an infantry battalion to UNIFIL.

heavily hunted countries like Cyprus or Lebanon. In the field one heard less than at Force HQ about the intractable administrative and budgetary problems and more about the life-and-death operational issues. These were easier to understand there than in the briefing room; one minute's view of an unauthorized fortification in no man's land can explain more than fifteen minutes of briefing. And one could relate better to the soldiers, not by a snatched exchange in the formality of the honour guard but in extended conversations over a sandwich in an observation post. Later on, I sometimes asked to accompany a foot patrol for an hour or two. This was the best way of all to learn about the terrain, the operational problems and the morale of young people from distant places whose lives were at risk in someone else's war.

In between the briefings and the visits to the field there were calls on the leaders of the hostile parties. Sometimes these were courtesy calls only. But usually there was substantive discussion about the party's cooperation, or lack of it, with the peacekeepers. One could also do peacemaking business: had anything happened to make this party more amenable to negotiation of a peace settlement? As will be described in later chapters, the conflicts in Cyprus and the Middle East were frozen at that time and the answer to the question was usually: 'Of course we are ready to negotiate; we always have been. Go and put your question to the others.'

From Cyprus, I flew on to Beirut. Although much calmer than during the Israeli invasion of 1982, the city was still divided by civil war and a dangerous place. On Aimé's advice, I nevertheless made it the starting point for every one of my visits to Lebanon. By coming first to the capital I hoped to signal to Lebanese of all religious and political persuasions that the UN remained committed to the sovereignty, independence and territorial integrity of their country. Starting in Beirut meant flying into the wrecked airport in UNTSO's F-27 Fokker Friendship and then skirting the coast in a UNIFIL helicopter to a secure landing place either in the Muslim West or the Christian East. After visiting the leaders on that side, we would cross to the other side either by going round the coast in the helicopter again or, if the front line ('the Green Line') was quiet, by driving through no man's land.

I had spent fifteen months in Lebanon in 1959–60, just after the brief civil war of 1958, learning Arabic in the Foreign Office's Middle East Centre for Arab Studies (MECAS) at Shemlan in the hills above Beirut. The Centre was run with strict efficiency by a true Scots dominie, Donald Maitland, who was later to be my Ambassador in Libya. Egyptian propaganda had demonized it throughout the Arab world as *madrasat al-jawāsīs* (the spy school). Reality was more prosaic – grinding hours of old-fashioned, but effective, language tuition, and allowances so exiguous that the fleshpots of Beirut were beyond the reach of most of us. Almost none of us were intelligence officers, but the double agent George Blake was a fellow-student at MECAS when his treason was detected.

Beirut twenty-six years later was a horrid revelation. The city had been devastated by eleven years of civil war. The Green Line ran right through its Piccadilly Circus, the Place des Martyrs or *al-burj*, where late at night I had haggled with *taxi-service* drivers to take me back to Shemlan without waiting for other passengers to fill the vehicle. Now it was inaccessible even to visitors protected by the immunity of *al-hai'a* ('the Organization'), as the Lebanese called the UN. Away from the front, however, the streets were crowded with vehicles and pedestrians. On the many visits that were to follow, my little convoy would force its way through traffic some-times so dense that the escorts provided by the local military faction would fire their Kalashnikovs in the air to clear a way. Even at the worst times, when there was nightly shelling and electricity and water were cut, the pedestrians would include perfectly turned out young women teeter-ing through the rubble on high heels. I was to be cheered in other war zones by this determination, especially on the part of women, to main-tain standards, however awful the mayhem around them. Certainly the Beirutis who survived those fourteen years of civil war in their city dis-played a *sumūd* (steadfastness) as impressive as that shown by the Palestinians who were soon to rise up against Israel's occupation of the West Bank and Gaza Strip.

The next stop, reached by helicopter, was the headquarters of the United Nations Interim Force in Lebanon (UNIFIL) at Naqoura, a small village south of Tyre. When UNIFIL was established in 1978, it set up its headquarters in what had been a French border control post between France's Lebanon and Britain's Palestine. In the eight years that followed, a large camp had spread along the shore of the Mediterranean to accom-modate the people and goods needed to command, care for and supply a force nearly six thousand strong. This made it the largest UN peacekeep-ing operation in 1986, accounting for more than half the UN troops in the field. During my first three years I was to spend more time with UNIFIL than with any other operation. The force commander in 1986 was Lieutenant-General William Callaghan of the Irish Army, a peace-keeping veteran who had served in the Congo and was about to leave UNIFIL to take command of the UN Truce Supervision Organization (UNTSO) in Jerusalem.

What struck me on arrival in Naqoura was the contrast between UNFICYP and UNIFIL. In Cyprus there was political and geographical tidiness: two enemies, each in full control of his territory, and in between them UNFICYP in control of a clearly defined and internationally recog-nized buffer zone; hardly a shot had been fired for more than twenty years. In Lebanon nothing was tidy. There was a multitude of enemies: the Israel Defence Forces (IDF); their Lebanese ally, the so-called South Lebanon Army (SLA); Palestinian guerrillas, whom the Israelis had not succeeded in removing entirely from the area; the Lebanese Government, which claimed sovereignty but was itself divided by civil war; the moderate Shi'ite movement supported by Syria, Amal; and a more extreme Shi'ite movement supported by Iran, Hizbullah. There were no internationally recognized front lines between the various enemies; not even the IDF could claim to be in full control of Israel's self-declared 'security zone', though at that time it had come close to achieving that goal. 'Armed elements' fired katyusha rockets at the Israelis; the latter responded with artillery and air strikes. Both sides infiltrated armed groups through UNIFIL's area of operation in which it was supposed to prevent all 'hostile activities'. In short, there was no peace to keep.

As will be described more fully in Chapter 5, UNIFIL had been deployed in 1978, following an Israeli invasion of southern Lebanon, to confirm Israeli withdrawal, restore international peace and security and assist the Lebanese Government to re-establish its authority in the area. This mandate assumed that Israel would withdraw, that the UN force would have the capacity to prevent violations of international peace and security and that the Lebanese Government was in a condition to exercise authority. None of these assumptions was correct. As a result UNIFIL's mandate was unachievable. The gap between the mandate and reality was reflected in UNIFIL's deployment. Its HQ was not in, or even adjacent to, its area of operation but in Israel's security zone and therefore open at any time to pressure from Israel and the SLA, which had gone so far as to shell the headquarters on at least three occasions during the force's early years. One of its seven battalions (Norway) was out to the north-east, alone in Israeli-held territory. The other six (Fiji, Finland, France, Ghana, Ireland, Nepal) were contiguous, but the AOs of three of them overlapped the security zone.

It was to Bill Callaghan's credit that he held this force together so well. But UNIFIL suffered, like so many operations, from strained relations between military and civilians. A particular bone of contention was the force commander's lack of full access to the correspondence exchanged between his (civilian) chief administrative officer (CAO) and the department in New York responsible for the administrative support of peace-keeping operations (OFOESA). The force commander felt that he was excluded from administrative and financial decisions which could affect the operational capacity of his force; the CAO argued that authority in such matters had not been delegated to the field and that he was therefore entitled (indeed, required) to communicate directly with his civilian superiors in New York.

Visits to the field in UNIFIL were made mostly by helicopter. To the north was Château Beaufort, a Crusader castle on top of a cliff where the Litani river turns west towards the sea. It had been a PLO stronghold before 1982 and bombarded by the Israelis, but it had survived. Beyond Beaufort were the foothills rising to Mount Hermon, still deep in snow at the time of my first visit. To the south, the ridges fell away to the Israeli border, Galilee and the watery plain which had once been Lake Hula. To the west was the crescent of coast leading up to Tyre and, beyond it, the Mediterranean. Above the Mediterranean, in the late afternoon, one could occasionally discern the mountain tops of Cyprus. Beneath the helicopter, every hilltop seemed to be crowned, some with ancient fortifications, some with UNIFIL's modest positions, some with the bristling fortresses of the IDF and SLA, but most with extravagant villas built, or more often half-built, by the merchant adventurers of the Lebanese diaspora in the Persian Gulf, West Africa and Latin America. They were not beautiful. Could one be moved by them as an expression of love for a troubled homeland? Or were they just there to impress the neighbours?

Bill Callaghan had telephoned me in New York to say that there would be two hours of free time on my last day with UNIFIL; how would I like to use them? I had replied that I would like to do some bird-watching. A snort: 'Bird-watching? Do USGs go bird-watching these days?' But there it was in the programme, after a visit to the isolated Norwegian battalion on the lower slopes of Mount Hermon: '1100–1230 hrs: Birdwatching.' Off we drove in convoy: armoured personnel carrier (APC) in front, three staff cars, another APC in the rear. On a mountain road we stopped by a ruined house. A platoon was already deployed in defensive positions. I was invited to walk into an olive grove, where an immense telescope had been erected on a tripod. 'Right, sir, bird-watching.' A Norwegian private was brought forward to brief me on the bird-life (always a briefing, you see). He read nervously from notes and then, at the end, ad-libbed: 'As you come from northern Europe, sir, you will be surprised that there are no *teetmouses*.' I advanced to the telescope, alone and under scrutiny. For operational reasons (quick getaway) the APCs had to keep their engines running, so there was plenty of noise and diesel fumes. Not a bird was to be seen or heard. Swivelling the telescope to right and left, as though there were actually birds to observe, I prayed to the Great Birder in the Sky to make something happen. The embarrassment became intense; how was I going to get out of this? And then my prayer was answered. Low over the ridge, bright in the sunlight, there flew in perfect V-formation thirty-five white pelicans – beautiful, large, identifiable birds on their way down to Hula. Mission accomplished, everyone was happy and away we went.

The next stop was Jerusalem to visit the headquarters of the United

Nations Truce Supervision Organization. Having been established in 1948 to supervise a truce ordered by the Security Council in the first Arab-Israeli war, in the following year UNTSO was given the additional responsibility of helping the parties implement four armistice agreements negotiated by Urquhart's predecessor, Ralph Bunche, between Israel and, respectively, Egypt, Jordan, Lebanon and Syria. Four mixed armistice commissions were established, all of them to be chaired by UNTSO.

In 1986 this remained the formal basis for UNTSO's mandate. But the political and military geography had been changed by the wars of 1956, 1967 and 1973. Israel had denounced the armistice agreement with Egypt following the outbreak of war in 1956, and the other three at the time of the 1967 war. The UN, however, had not recognized the validity of these unilateral denunciations. The Egypt–Israel mixed armistice commission was formally dissolved by the peace treaty of 1979 but the others still survived, though only on paper. The Arab states were determined that they should continue to survive until peace was achieved. For its part, Israel tolerated the continuing presence of UNTSO headquarters in Jerusalem and, more reluctantly, a small group of military observers in the occupied Gaza Strip. But UNTSO's main task had become the provision and administration of military observers to work alongside UNDOF in Syria, following the Israel–Syria disengagement agreement of 1974, and UNIFIL in Lebanon, following the establishment of that force in 1978.

This untidy legal basis was typical of these long-standing peacekeeping operations. In the case of UNTSO, the untidiness gave rise to command and control problems, especially as regards the military observers working with UNDOF and UNIFIL who were under the command of the Chief of Staff of UNTSO but under the 'operational control' of the commander of the force with which they were working. In Damascus it was necessary to conform both with the pretence that the Israel–Syria Mixed Armistice Commission still existed and with Syria's insistence that officers from the five permanent members of the Security Council should not serve on the Golan Heights. The result was institutional discord and an organigramme of bewildering complexity.* My immediate reaction was to rationalize by removing the UNDOF and UNIFIL military observers from UNTSO and making them part of the forces for which they worked. But my colleagues all said that this would enrage the Syrians and Lebanese and might give the Israelis a pretext to challenge UNTSO's tenure in Jerusalem; it was impossible to remove the barnacles without breaking the vessel itself.

---

* Connoisseurs can find it on page 410 of *The Blue Helmets*, second edition, United Nations, 1990.

The commander (formally 'Chief of Staff') of UNTSO was Lieutenant-General Alex Erskine of Ghana, another peacekeeping veteran. After a first stint as Chief of Staff, he had been transferred to Lebanon in 1978 to take command of the newly established UNIFIL. In 1981 he had returned to Jerusalem but he too was now about to leave his command. With his expansive West African charm, he gave the novice a generous welcome. I was sorry that this was to be the first and last time I would visit him in Jerusalem.

I took advantage of being in Jerusalem to see Yitzhak Rabin, the Israeli Minister of Defence, about southern Lebanon. This was the first step in a mini-shuttle that in the succeeding days would define what was to be my major preoccupation during the coming two years, namely the withdrawal of Israeli troops from Lebanon. Meanwhile most of the two days in Jerusalem were devoted to briefings about the complexities of UNTSO and to some sightseeing.

I had not been in Jerusalem since 1960 when I had spent two weeks there improving my colloquial Arabic as a paying guest in the home of a postal worker and his family. At that time the city was divided by a tense front line and I was unashamedly committed to the Palestinian cause. Now the city had been united by force of arms and enjoyed a kind of peace. I did not enjoy the Israeli occupation of Arab East Jerusalem, including the Old City, and still felt that the Palestinians were victims of a great wrong that had to be at least partly righted. But now I was responsible for peacemaking and peacekeeping in the Arab-Israeli conflict. Impartiality was a necessary condition of success. I must take care not to say or do things that would call my impartiality into question.

In Syria I had two objectives: to visit the UN Disengagement Observer Force (UNDOF) on the Golan Heights; and to try to enlist the Syrian Government's help in creating conditions which would make it easier for Israel to withdraw its troops from southern Lebanon. The latter turned out to be a forlorn hope. But UNDOF showed me how effective peacekeeping can be if certain basic conditions are fulfilled. It had been set up in 1974 to help Israel and Syria implement a disengagement agreement negotiated by Henry Kissinger after the 1973 war. Both protagonists were prickly partners for the UN. The Syrians, in particular, were forever detecting what they interpreted as bias towards Israel and lack of respect for Syrian sovereignty; their current speciality was to seize and destroy any UNDOF equipment marked with Hebrew characters, for instance fire extinguishers that had been serviced in Israel. But neither side wanted to fight over the Golan and it suited them well to have a UN force interposed between them. Pinpricks were plenty, but there was no serious obstruction of UNDOF or violations of the disengagement agreement.

The area of operation was even more interesting and beautiful than UNIFIL's. In the north it reached the summit of Mount Hermon; in the south it extended to the valley of the Yarmouk river. In between were the Golan Heights, a volcanic plain littered with basalt rocks that had played havoc with the tracks of tanks engaged in battle there in 1973. Battlefield debris abounded; de-mined patrol paths were marked by red-painted stones; one ventured from them at one's peril. The UN soldiers were outraged by the fatalistic nonchalance with which shepherds wandered with their flocks into mined areas, only too often to return as mangled remains on UN stretchers. In the middle of the area of operation was the town of Quneitra, the capital of the Golan, which had been systematically destroyed by the IDF as they withdrew in 1974, giving the Syrians a propaganda stick which they never tired of wielding.

UNDOF was only a quarter the size of UNIFIL, with infantry battalions from Austria and Finland and support units from Canada and Poland. Its commander was Major-General Gustav Hägglund of the Finnish Army. Lean and keen, he was an impressive leader and I had no hesitation in proposing to Pérez de Cuéllar that he take over the heavier responsibility of UNIFIL when Bill Callaghan moved to UNTSO two months later.

Only one peacekeeping unit remained to be visited. This was UNTSO's outstation in Egypt, Observer Group Egypt, based in Cairo. It had no military *raison d'être*. The Egypt–Israel Peace Treaty had envisaged that UNEF II, the UN force that had been in Sinai since 1973, would take on the peacekeeping tasks arising from the Treaty. However, the Soviet Union, joining the other Arab states in their condemnation of Egypt for having made a separate peace with Israel, would have none of this. UNEF II's mandate accordingly lapsed and it was later replaced by a non-UN force, the Multinational Force and Observers (MFO). Egypt remained anxious, for political reasons, that the UN not be totally excluded from the Egypt–Israel sector and managed to get the Security Council to agree that UNTSO should maintain a presence in Sinai, thus adding another level to the complex archaeology of UNTSO's mandate.

While in Egypt, I called on the Foreign Minister, Ismat Abdul Meguid, whom I had known in New York, and his deputy, Boutros Boutros-Ghali. Rereading the record of the latter conversation, I find little evidence of either the intellectual power or the wit that Boutros-Ghali was to bring to the Secretary-Generalship of the UN less than six years later. Perhaps that was my fault; I wanted to concentrate on southern Lebanon and the situation in the Occupied Palestinian Territories (the West Bank and the Gaza Strip) and this provided little scope for the breadth of vision he revealed in *An Agenda for Peace*, his inaugural report to the member states in 1992. But as we left, he said: 'Remember, Egypt has a kind of weakness for the UN, we think it is *the* organization that can help us and we believe in it.'

I did not linger in Cairo, tempting though it was to do so. The southern Lebanon shuttle called: Defence Minister Rabin in Tel Aviv on Friday, Chairman Arafat in Cairo and President Gemayel and Prime Minister Karamé in Beirut on Saturday, Rabin again in Tel Aviv and Prime Minister Shamir in Jerusalem on Sunday. I left the Levant excited by the possibility of negotiating a gradual pullback of the IDF from southern Lebanon.

This proved to be an unattainable dream. I now realize that my error was not only to overestimate the chances of success. I also allowed myself to be distracted by diplomatic fantasy from a perhaps more achievable, if more boring, task. That was to wield a new broom that would sweep away the administrative, budgetary and personnel cobwebs that made peacekeeping less efficient than it could have been and caused unnecessary stress and strain. I might not have succeeded. My new colleagues discouraged the idea; it was not easy for the newcomer to break into the UN's management culture and I had no authority over the administrators and logisticians in New York. But if I had devoted more effort to that task in the comparatively quiet years of 1986 and 1987, the United Nations might have been better placed to exploit the opportunities that the end of the Cold War was soon to bring.

Relics from the Past

4

Cyprus

The conflict in Cyprus had, and still has, many features that were to recur in the former Yugoslavia: ethnic-religious hatred, obsession with history, self-righteousness, unwillingness (perhaps inability) to understand the other side's position, cruelty in combat. I have heard it said that these features, especially the cruelty, are peculiar to the successor states of the Ottoman Empire. That is untrue and unfair; the Ottomans never ruled Belfast.

The UN Force in Cyprus (UNFICYP) took the field in 1964 when, less than four years after independence, hostilities between the Greek and Turkish communities became so intense that the Security Council decided that they were likely to threaten international peace and security and set up a peacekeeping force to help restore law and order. At that time the Greek and Turkish communities were spread throughout the island, creating many potential flashpoints. UNFICYP had to be deployed accordingly, interposing itself between the front lines where they existed and maintaining a capacity to intervene quickly if intercommunal violence should break out in other sensitive areas. This was a difficult task militarily, and the force's capacity to prevent violence was limited. Intercommunal fighting, with intervention from time to time by the Turkish air force, continued throughout the first ten years of UNFICYP's mandate.

The force's difficult mandate gave rise to the question of how far it could use force. The doctrine hitherto had been that UN peacekeepers could use their weapons only in self-defence, which was rather strictly interpreted as meaning when their lives were in danger. In the Congo operation, which immediately preceded the creation of UNFICYP, UN troops had repeatedly found themselves unable to carry out their orders because armed persons from one or other of the factions threatened to shoot them if they did so. As a result the Secretary-General's guidelines for UNFICYP went into some detail about what 'self-defence' means. They stipulated *inter alia* that the use of force could be deemed to be self-defence if armed persons were attempting by force to prevent

UNFICYP personnel from carrying out their responsibilities as ordered by their commanders. This formulation subsequently became a standard ingredient in the 'rules of engagement' given to peacekeeping operations. Ostensibly it was an important extension of peacekeeping doctrine. In practice, it was rarely used, in Cyprus or elsewhere, because UN forces are seldom equipped to go to war with the hostile parties. Commanders have rightly feared that if they use force when their troops are not actually under fire they will forfeit the neutrality and impartiality which are necessary conditions for successful peacekeeping; and they have been concerned, also rightly in most cases, that the use of force might escalate the confrontation to a point where they would be outgunned and suffer military defeat.

In 1974 Cyprus was afflicted by a new tragedy. In mid-July a *coup d'état* against President Makarios, staged by the military junta which then ruled Greece, led Turkey to invade the island (or, as Ankara prefers, to 'intervene' to preserve Cyprus' independence, in accordance with the 1959 Treaty of Guarantee which gave that right to Greece, Turkey and the United Kingdom). Two rounds of fighting in the fierce heat of the Cypriot summer were accompanied by mutual atrocities against civilians. In less than four weeks the Turkish forces succeeded in occupying the northern third of the island. The outcome was partition through exchange of population, some of it as a result of the fighting and some of it subsequently negotiated. A year after the war, few Turkish Cypriots remained in the two-thirds of the island controlled by the government in Nicosia and even fewer Greek Cypriots remained in the Turkish-controlled north. The government in Nicosia has continued to enjoy recognition as the government of Cyprus by all states except Turkey. The Turkish Cypriots, however, with Ankara's support, have insisted that they be treated as the political equals of their Greek enemies and have tried to assert this unilaterally. In 1975 they proclaimed themselves to be a separate Turkish Cypriot state within a new federal republic; in 1983 they declared their independence as the 'Turkish Republic of Northern Cyprus', which is recognized only by Turkey.

Tragic though it was, the 1974 war left the UN force with an easier military task. No longer did it have to try to protect minority communities in enclaves and mixed villages all over the island. No longer did it have to keep the peace between, and with, irregular forces of the two sides who thought they could protect their communities more effectively than UNFICYP. Now UNFICYP's task was the traditional one of controlling a buffer zone between the front lines of two reasonably disciplined armies. In the divided city of Nicosia the zone was in places only three metres wide, which led to occasional incidents, some of them fatal. In the late eighties UNFICYP eased this problem by persuading the two sides to 'unman' their positions and reduce patrolling in a few sensitive spots. Serious incidents occurred elsewhere, however, often sparked by ill-judged Greek Cypriot demonstrations and marches in the buffer zone. But they were not many; UNFICYP's busiest time was usually during the hunting season when the locals could not resist the lure of abundant game in the buffer zone and took their weapons where weapons were not supposed to be.

As a traditional peacekeeping operation, UNFICYP's task was to maintain calm on the island while a political settlement was negotiated. Since the *de facto* partition of 1974, it has performed this task well and at little cost to the international community. The complementary task of negotiating a settlement has been entrusted to successive Special Representatives of the Secretary-General, a post which, until the mid-nineties, went by convention to a Latin American. Pérez de Cuéllar himself held it from 1975 to 1977. With infinite patience and diplomatic skill the Special Representatives had 'used their good offices' in efforts to bridge the unbridgeable.* Almost nothing was achieved during the decade preceding the 1974 war. But negotiations about its aftermath paved the way for a continuing intercommunal dialogue which began to produce results. In 1977 and again in 1979 'high-level agreements' established that the settlement should be based on the concept of an independent, non-aligned, federal and bicommunal republic.† But it had proved difficult to put flesh on these bones and when I took over in 1986 the talks were in exhausted suspense.

This lack of progress in the peacemaking had undermined international support for UNFICYP. I was startled to be told by critics in Washington and elsewhere that the peacekeeping force had 'become part of the problem'. UNFICYP's success, it was argued, was actually an obstacle to peace because it protected the leaders from the consequences of their intransigence at the negotiating table; if it were not there, fear of war would make both sides readier to compromise. I rejected this argument, and still reject it, for two reasons. First, withdrawal of UNFICYP would not lead to compromise; it would lead immediately to a fight for control of the buffer zone which covers 3 per cent of the island's territory and contains rich arable land. Secondly, the implicit reliance on the threat

---

* The verb 'mediate' must never be used in the Cyprus context. It has been anathema to the Turkish Cypriots since an allegedly anti-Turkish report was submitted in 1965 by the 'Mediator', Galo Plaza Lasso of Ecuador. He was obliged to resign as a result, and the principal peacemaker has since been known as the 'Special Representative of the Secretary-General'. This is an example of the terminological pitfalls which await the unwary in Cyprus. For 'good offices', see page 33n.

† Later reformulated as 'an independent, non-aligned and federal republic, bicommunal in constitutional terms and bizonal in its territorial aspects'.

of war to bring about a settlement is contrary to one of the main purposes of the United Nations, which is to settle disputes by peaceful
means.

The argument also raises the question why the same is not said about
the Golan Heights, where for a quarter of a century a small UN force has
been even more successful than UNFICYP in maintaining calm in spite
of non-existent or failed peacemaking. The answer, I think, is that neither
Israel nor Syria agitates internationally about the status quo: Israel is
content with it; Syria is not, but is playing a long game and does not
meanwhile want military confrontation with Israel. By contrast, Greek
Cypriot leaders agitate continuously about the existing situation and,
with the partial exception of George Vassiliou who was President from
1988 to 1993 and his successor, Glafcos Clerides, they do little or
nothing to prepare their people for a settlement which, if it comes, will
fall far short of the expectations aroused by their rhetoric.

On the other hand, the Turkish Cypriot leader, Rauf Denktash, is reasonably satisfied by the *de facto* partition of the island and tends therefore
to block progress towards a settlement. By objective standards, he ought
not to be satisfied. The GDP per head of his unrecognized statelet is
barely a third of that enjoyed by the Greek Cypriots; much of his natural
market in Europe is closed to him by the European Union at the behest
of Greece; and his middle class are emigrating and being replaced by
peasants from Anatolia. But his policy makes sense to him because it is
based on two convictions, which I believe to be genuinely held: Greek
and Turkish Cypriots cannot live peacefully together; and any settlement
acceptable to the Greek Cypriots would be worse for the Turkish
Cypriots than the present state of affairs. He is also confident, probably
rightly, that Ankara will support him through thick and thin and that the
Western powers will not put intolerable pressure on Ankara to do otherwise.

At the core of the peacemakers' difficulties in Cyprus, both substan-
tively and procedurally, is Denktash's insistence that the two communities
are political equals and must be treated as such by anyone who attempts
to make peace between them. As far as he is concerned, the Republic of
Cyprus that attained independence in 1960 died in the intercommunal
strife which began in December 1963. The negotiations are about a new
federal republic which is to be formed by two politically equal communities or, if he is being particularly provocative, 'peoples'. There is, he
argues, no such office as 'President of Cyprus' and it is improper for the
UN to accord such a title to the leader of the Greek Cypriot community.
This position is understandably rejected by the Greek Cypriots who
point out that the Republic of Cyprus is recognized by every country
except Turkey. To Denktash's fury, they use every available international

stage – including the United Nations, the Commonwealth and the Non-Aligned Movement – to win support for their cause and internationalize a problem which he insists can be resolved only through negotiation between two equal communities/peoples.

This basic disagreement between the two sides demands terminological gymnastics from the United Nations. The peacemaking talks, it is agreed, are between 'the two communities' and every effort is made to avoid using the name of either of the two leaders or giving either of them a title. So in this context 'President Clerides' does not exist; he is 'the leader of the Greek Cypriot community'. However, it was the government of Cyprus that asked for the establishment of UNFICYP in 1964 and signed the agreement that defines the force's status on the island. So in the peacekeeping context, Clerides becomes 'President' again.

This terminological complexity affected Cyprus more than any other conflict I dealt with: the one thing the two sides appeared to agree on was not to call a spade a spade. The Turkish invasion (Greek version) or intervention (Turkish version) is referred to as 'the events of July and August 1974'. The declaration of the Turkish mini-state is 'the Turkish Cypriot action of 15 November 1983'. The 'intercommunal talks' led in 1977 and 1979 to two 'high-level agreements' and the drafting of a 'partial interim agreement'. This having failed, it was decided in 1982 to make a 'major effort of synthesis', which facilitated the drafting of a 'scenario' in 1984. Next was a series of 'high-level proximity talks', which enabled the Secretary-General in early 1985 to table 'the documentation for a draft agreement' which was accepted fully by Denktash but by the Greek Cypriot leader, Spyros Kyprianou, only 'as a basis for negotiations in accordance with the integrated-whole approach'. The next step was 'incorporation of the components of the documentation into a single consolidated draft agreement'. This time Kyprianou accepted but Denktash rejected. In 1990, a new effort was launched; the earlier material would be re-presented as a 'set of ideas', including a map for a 'proposed territorial adjustment', which would form 'the basis for an overall framework agreement'. But by the end of 1992 it was evident that it would be impossible to reach agreement on the 'set of ideas', so the UN warmed up some ideas from the mid-1970s as 'confidence-building measures', mainly the reopening of Nicosia International Airport and the resettlement of an abandoned beach resort called Varosha. Agreement remained elusive and, by the time I left the Secretariat, attention was focussed on the discussion of 'a broad range of possible trade-offs for an overall settlement', with the Secretary-General bravely repeating the refrain: 'all the elements for an overall settlement are on the table'.

Perhaps it is unfair to dismiss so lightly two decades of patient and tireless effort by intelligent and committed people. But the circumlocutions concealed the reality of what was a patently unsatisfactory state of affairs: an island and capital city divided like Germany and Berlin; a gross concentration of armed forces (those of Turkey alone are equivalent to a quarter of the British Army); the taunting Turkish symbols outlined in stone on the slopes of Pendedaktyl, the five-peaked mountain to the north of Nicosia; the Turkish north dirt-poor; the Greek south prosperous but resentful; the sense that another war in Cyprus could set the Aegean alight. It was also infuriating to get the circumlocutions wrong and be accused of having changed the Secretary-General's position. For most of my time the principal negotiators were Glafcos Clerides and Rauf Denktash, both of them clever, London-trained barristers and merciless exploiters of looseness in language. Another irritant was the self-centredness of the Greek Cypriots. 'Delphi is no longer the navel of the world,' I used to say, 'now it's Cyprus', whereupon wiser colleagues would point out that it was natural that the parties should consider their conflict to be the only important one in the world, and at the same time remind me that there were probably microphones in the room.

On my first visit to Cyprus in March 1986, the peacemaking was totally frozen following the failure of Pérez de Cuéllar's 'documentation for a draft agreement' initiative. In New York's view, blame for the failure lay more with Kyprianou than with Denktash. I did not warm to Kyprianou, whom I found stiff and sententious. He introduced me to the terminological complexities already referred to and asked several times whether I really meant what I had just said; was I telling him that the Secretary-General had changed his position? The first encounter with Rauf Denktash was not much better. He too exploited my unfamiliarity with the issues and displayed the power of his intellect and his skills as a negotiator. In many subsequent meetings I never came out of an argument feeling that I had made any headway against him. I could not help liking him, in spite of regretting that his intellectual prowess was used to block progress rather than to devise new ways of bridging the gap between the two sides.

I concluded from this visit that the gap was probably unbridgeable. Even Georgios Iacovou, the Foreign Minister, had said gloomily that for the first time he was beginning to think that the least bad option was continuation of the status quo. But there was no way in which this could be formalized, and the military build-up on both sides did constitute a threat to the peace. The peacemaking therefore had to continue. Hopeless it might seem, but there was no alternative, and unexpected breakthroughs can occur. Peacemaking was also necessary in order to reassure the governments which contributed troops to UNFICYP and were bearing an unusually heavy financial burden. The other four operations existing at that time were funded from contributions levied on all member states of the UN. Not all of them paid, but the UN was able to reimburse the nations contributing troops for at least part of the costs they incurred. From the beginning, however, and by decision of the Security Council, UNFICYP had been financed almost entirely by the troop contributors, who were less and less willing to carry this burden.

The year 1987 had been a sterile one in Cyprus, but 1988 opened promisingly. An unexpectedly successful meeting in January between the Prime Ministers of Greece and Turkey was followed in February by the election of a new President in Cyprus, George Vassiliou. The son of Communist parents, he had grown up in Hungary but had prospered in capitalist Cyprus. He was the antithesis of Kyprianou; open, relaxed, informal and innovative, he was going to be a more testing adversary for Denktash than his stolid and predictable predecessor. Coincidentally, Pérez de Cuéllar appointed a heavy-weight Special Representative in the person of Oscar Camilión, an Argentine distinguished by his intellect, political finesse and charm, who had been scholar, diplomat, newspaper editor and briefly Foreign Minister of his country. His first round of conversations with Vassiliou and Denktash confirmed that new possibilities existed but that Denktash was wary of them. Pérez de Cuéllar invited them to a working lunch in Geneva in August, at which they agreed to try to negotiate a settlement by 1 June 1989. This was followed by a series of increasingly difficult talks between the two leaders in Camilión's presence, culminating in a breakdown at a second meeting with Pérez de Cuéllar in New York in June 1989. But by this time I no longer had responsibilities for peacemaking and was concerned only with UNFICYP, which fortunately distracted me hardly at all from the new operations that proliferated during the latter years of Pérez de Cuéllar's term of office.

However, this proliferation had its impact on UNFICYP. With several new operations being created each year at growing cost to member states, it was felt that long-established operations should be reviewed to see if savings could be made. The governments contributing to UNFICYP were particularly keen for that operation to be reviewed because it was the only one whose costs were almost entirely borne by the troop contributors themselves. As a result a review team was appointed, led by Gus Feissel, who had by now been transferred to the Secretary-General's office, and I accompanied it to the island in November 1990, the first visit I had made to UNFICYP in over three years. By then the opportunities which seemed to have been created by Vassiliou's election had proved to be illusory and peacemaking was at a standstill (or so I thought at the time; more may have been going on than the secretive Feissel cared to reveal). Both sides were strengthening their positions along the edge of the buffer zone, in violation of the cease-fire, and some hotheads on the Greek Cypriot side were even advocating a suicidal attack on the Turkish forces in order to draw international attention to 'the Turkish occupation'.

After eight years, Günther Greindl had been replaced as Force Commander by a Canadian officer, Major-General Clive Milner. I liked Milner a lot but was not entirely happy with his performance. I shared his discontent at the separation between peacemaking and peacekeeping but could not condone his shortness of temper and his distrust of civilians, which had complicated his relations with both the Special Representative, Oscar Camilión, and his own political adviser, Joachim Hütter. But he had a clear understanding of UNFICYP's task and had developed some good ideas for streamlining the force.

In New York some had advocated converting it from an armed infantry-based force into an unarmed observer mission like the one deployed after the cease-fire between Iran and Iraq two years before. Our tour of the buffer zone quickly demonstrated that this idea would not work. We would have had to replace the armed soldiers who currently manned the force's 148 observation posts with unarmed officers. Quite apart from the cost, this would mean that the UN was no longer able to deploy armed troops instantly when an actual or threatened violation of the status quo was observed. The team was convinced that removal of the capacity for rapid reaction would compromise UNFICYP's ability to stop small incidents developing into serious confrontations. But if armed infantry were essential, how could we reduce the cost? By doing what had been done in Namibia the year before: we would improve the teeth to tail ratio, by having fewer infantry battalions but asking the governments to make them larger so that UNFICYP would have the same strength on the line as before.

This was a good outcome as far as the teeth were concerned. But I failed on the tail. During my earlier visits to UNFICYP I had heard mutterings that the British Government was overcharging the UN for the logistic support which the British contingent provided to the force, drawing on the resources of the UK's two Sovereign Base Areas in Cyprus. I had not been able to determine whether these complaints were justified. The review now provided an opportunity to do so. With Milner's help I probed hard. But the British contingent and UNFICYP's Chief Administrative Officer, who happened to be British too, erected a wall of obfuscation which proved to be impenetrable. My diary records: 'When I asked on what basis the British calculated the prices they charged UNFICYP and whether those prices had ever been compared with those prevailing in the Cyprus market (which is, after all, now one of the strongest services-based economies in the Near East) there were no clear answers. Milner fumed.'

I enjoyed this return to Cyprus and vowed to visit UNFICYP at least once a year in future. The review team's report was well received by the troop contributors. But they were unwilling to enlarge their contingents unless UNFICYP, like other peacekeeping operations, was funded by the UN membership as a whole and not by them. The prospects were not good; twelve members of the Security Council were in favour but the Soviet Union had instructions to veto and China and France said that they might do so too. The resolution was withdrawn. Support for the proposal declined and two years later Britain was the only permanent member that was not threatening to veto. The troop contributors became more and more angry. A new peacekeeping operation was being created every few months, they said, all of them funded by the whole membership; why should the contributors to UNFICYP be discriminated against in this way? By mid-1992, the Danes had decided to withdraw their whole battalion; the other three main contributors (Austria, Britain, Canada) all intended to reduce their contingents; and Canada said that its contingent would be withdrawn completely by the end of the following year. As a result the force's strength would fall below the level which the November 1990 review had declared to be the minimum needed if the force was to implement all its existing tasks.

In July and August 1992, Boutros-Ghali had brought Vassiliou and Denktash to New York and was trying to get them to agree to the territorial aspects of a settlement. The question, to put it simply (which one should never try to do in Cyprus negotiations), was how much territory currently held by the Turks would be transferred to the Greek zone in the new bizonal republic? In particular, would it include the important town of Morphou and the arable land surrounding it? Boutros-Ghali was good at this sort of negotiation and was manoeuvring Denktash into a corner from which he could not emerge without either giving up Morphou or demonstrating that, as many of us had long believed, he preferred the status quo to a settlement.

Within the Secretariat this caused a certain tension: Boutros and the peacemakers welcomed the imminent collapse of UNFICYP because it demonstrated the urgency of the need for a settlement; the peacekeepers worried about how to maintain the cease-fire and the buffer zone and wanted to discuss with the troop contributors which of its tasks a smaller UNFICYP could still perform. I was told firmly by Boutros not to do this; let the Cypriot parties fear the worst. This illustrated well the dangers of putting peacemaking and peacekeeping into separate departmental boxes; mistakes would be made if the peacekeepers were not *au courant* with what the peacemakers were up to. During my first seven years in the Secretariat I ran with the peacekeeping hares; in the remaining four years I hunted with the peacemaking hounds. And at no time did I

Relics from the Past

succeed in persuading either Pérez de Cuéllar or Boutros-Ghali that in the valleys of peace the hares and the hounds must lie down as one.

Finally in mid-1993 the Security Council agreed that the force should be financed in the normal way. The Canadians nevertheless left and were replaced by an Argentine battalion, with the pleasing result that eleven years after the Falklands War the former enemies were serving shoulder to shoulder in a mission of peace.

5

Lebanon

My first three years in the Secretariat were dominated by the Arab-Israeli conflict. I had three parts to play. The first was to manage the three peacekeeping operations in the Middle East – the group of military observers based in Jerusalem (UNTSO), the force on the Golan Heights (UNDOF) and the force in southern Lebanon (UNIFIL). The second was to try to persuade the Israelis, the Syrians, various Lebanese factions and the Palestine Liberation Organization (PLO) to bring about the withdrawal of Israeli troops from southern Lebanon and the restoration of the Lebanese Government's authority there. This required political negotiation and involved more peacemaking than peacekeeping. The third role was pure peacemaking and will be described in the next chapter. It related first to Pérez de Cuéllar's determination to get the United Nations back into Middle East peacemaking and then to the *intifāda*, the Palestinian uprising in the Israeli-occupied West Bank and Gaza Strip at the end of 1987.

The demands made on me by the first role – managing the peacekeeping operations – depended on the circumstances of each force and the quality of its commander. UNDOF required almost no management. It was a stable operation, had a workable mandate and enjoyed the cooperation of Israel and Syria, at least at the strategic level.

UNTSO was more complicated. It had an ancient and complicated collection of mandates and its main function had become the administration of UN military observers assigned to work with UNDOF in Syria and UNIFIL in Lebanon. I was tempted to transfer this responsibility to the two forces themselves. But I was persuaded not to do so for four reasons. First, any change in the status quo might weaken the United Nations' title to property and rights in Israel and Israeli-occupied territories which it had acquired over nearly forty years and which Israel would have been glad to terminate. Secondly, it would have enraged Syria and Lebanon which wanted to keep in being the structures created by the United Nations in 1949 as evidence that the Arab-Israeli conflict had yet to be resolved. Thirdly, UNTSO provided much logistical support, including an aircraft, to myself and other UN officials who needed to move quickly around the capitals of the Levant. Fourthly, it had in the past been, and would again be, a useful reservoir of UN military observers (UNMOs) which could be drawn on when new operations had to be set up at short notice.

UNTSO did require some management from New York but the issues were usually minor and responsibility for it and UNDOF should have been delegated to one of my subordinates. But I had to make frequent visits to Israel and Syria in connection with southern Lebanon and could not ignore the issues, however trivial, which were on the UN commanders' minds.

The Lebanese question itself was of considerable complexity and needs some preliminary exposition. Think of Lebanon as a cockpit. But it is not a normal cockpit. The fights are not single combats between two cocks; they are fights between teams of cocks, in ever-changing alliances. And the floor of the cockpit is strewn with brightly coloured beads. They are called 'assets' and they come in various colours – blue for political assets, yellow for economic assets, khaki for strategic assets, white for ideological and religious assets, red for criminal assets. Inside the cockpit there are several resident teams of cocks. The four principal ones are the Maronite Christians, the Sunni Muslims, the Shi'ite Muslims and the Druze, a heretical Islamic sect. There are other lesser teams of cocks. Each team includes some fighting cocks, called 'militias'. The teams fight with each other to accumulate and control as many of the assets as possible. Alliances between teams are frequently formed and frequently dissolved. Sometimes teams fight within themselves and split into two or more smaller teams. The fights are violent and cruel; many team leaders are assassinated, sometimes by members of their own team.

Around the cockpit there are several gamblers. The principal ones are Israel, Syria, Iran and the Palestine Liberation Organization (PLO). Lesser ones are Egypt, Iraq and Jordan. Like the resident teams, the gamblers' objective is to accumulate and control assets in the Lebanese cockpit. Three of them (Israel, Syria and the PLO) have, or have had, their own fighting cocks in the cockpit. But all of them also hire the services of one or more of the resident teams, as do Iran and the lesser gamblers.

The distribution of some important political assets amongst the teams was determined in 1943 by an unwritten agreement called the National Compact. It was based on Lebanon's only census, which had been conducted in 1932. At that time, the ratio of Christians to Muslims had been six to five. The Maronite team was accordingly given the posts of President of the Republic and Commander of the Army. The Sunni Muslim team were allotted the post of Prime Minister and the Shi'ite

Muslims that of Speaker of the National Assembly. By 1986 the demography of Lebanon had changed. Muslims now outnumbered the Christians, and the Shi'ite Muslims were believed to be the largest team. But the distribution of assets laid down in the National Compact had not been revised, because the Christians, still enjoying a six-to-five majority in the Assembly, had blocked the holding of a new census.

When I assumed responsibility for UNIFIL in 1986, the line-up in and around the cockpit was as follows. The Maronite team was ostensibly led by Amin Gemayel, the President of the Republic. But the real power lay with Samir Geagea, the leader of its main group of fighting cocks, known as 'the Lebanese Forces'. The Sunni Muslims, the team most affected by the demographic changes and no longer the power-brokers of Lebanon, were led by Rashid Karamé, the Prime Minister. Their militia, known as the *Murābitūn*, was smaller than the others. The Shi'ite Muslim team was ostensibly led by Shaikh Muhammad Mahdi Shamsuddin, but had in fact split into two separate teams. One, Hizbullah, was led (though he denied it) by Shaikh Muhammad Husain Fadlallah and the other, Amal, by Nabih Berri. Each had its own fighting cocks. The Druze team was led by Walid Jumblatt. At that time the Maronite team, in association with lesser Christian teams, was locked in battle, especially in Beirut, with the three Muslim teams, known collectively as 'the National Movement'. Amongst the latter, there was hostility and potential conflict between the two Shi'ite teams, Amal and Hizbullah.

As regards the gamblers, Israel had deployed its own fighting cocks, the Israel Defence Forces (IDF), in the self-declared 'security zone' which it had established in the southern part of Lebanon along the Israel–Lebanon border. It had also armed, funded and directed a group of Lebanese fighting cocks, the South Lebanon Army (SLA).* The SLA consisted mainly of Maronites who helped Israel to control the security zone and the neighbouring Jezzine region where there was a significant Maronite community. Israel also received support from the Maronite team, which shared its hostility to the various Palestinian teams in the cockpit and valued the SLA's protection of Christians in the south. The Syrian fighting cocks were detachments of the Syrian Armed Forces, numbering about 15,000 men and deployed mainly around Beirut and in the Beqa'a, the broad valley which runs north–south in the centre of the country. Syria also enjoyed the services of the Amal faction of the Shi'ite team and sought those of the Druze team. The PLO had its own fighting

---

* In UN-speak the security zone was referred to as 'the enclave' and, later, 'the Israeli-controlled area (ICA)', which more accurately described what it was, and the SLA was 'the *de facto* forces (DFF)'. In this book, however, 'security zone' and 'South Lebanon Army' will be used throughout as they are more widely recognized than the UN variants.

cocks in the form of the Fatah movement led by Yasir Arafat, but several smaller groups of Palestinian fighters were more or less independent of the PLO. It enjoyed much support from the Sunni team. Iran had procured the services of the more radical of the two Shi'ite factions, Hizbullah. Iran also had a certain hold over Syria, as a result of Syria's dependence on Iran for oil, its indebtedness to Iran and the two countries' common hostility to Iraq, with which Iran had been engaged in war since 1980. Iran exploited this relationship to ensure that Hizbullah was permitted to operate in and through zones controlled by Syria. This sometimes caused strains in Syria's relations with its ally Amal, which was contending with Iran's ally Hizbullah for the allegiance of the Shi'ite community.

The UN Force in Lebanon (UNIFIL) had been established in March 1978 in great haste following an IDF invasion of southern Lebanon aimed at the PLO, which had become the dominant military power there and was making cross-border attacks against civilian targets in Israel. The haste was due to the United States' wish to resolve this new crisis quickly before the negotiations which were about to take place at Camp David between Egypt and Israel. In its resolution 425 the Security Council gave UNIFIL the mandate to 'confirm the withdrawal of Israeli forces' from Lebanese territory, 'restore international peace and security' in the border area and 'assist the Government of Lebanon in ensuring the return of its effective authority in the area'. That mandate was based on the assumptions, or perhaps just the hopes, that Israel would entrust its border security to the UN, that the PLO would accept the Security Council decision and stop its attacks on Israel, and that the Lebanese Government had some authority to restore. None of these assumptions was sound.

The IDF did withdraw from Lebanese territory in June 1978. But it turned over all its positions in the vicinity of the border not to UNIFIL but to the South Lebanon Army. UNIFIL was thus prevented from deploying down to the border, for it had neither the mandate nor the capacity to do battle with an SLA which was assured of military support from its Israeli paymasters if it came under attack. Nor could the Lebanese Government assert its authority, for Lebanon was three years into a civil war which was to deny it an effective government and army for another thirteen years.

As for the Palestinians, they had no intention of giving up their fight against Israel. Their right to operate out of southern Lebanon, they insisted, had been recognized in an agreement mediated between Lebanon and the PLO by President Nasser of Egypt in 1969. But the PLO was involved hardly at all in the sketchy negotiations which preceded the adoption of SCR 425. Secretary-General Waldheim had wanted to talk to its representatives about UNIFIL's tasks, its deployment and the cooperation it would need from the Palestinians. He had been blocked, however, by United States' and Israeli objections to his having anything to do with the PLO, on the spurious grounds that the Israeli and Lebanese Governments were the only parties to the conflict. But in reality it was the Palestinian and Lebanese militias fighting Israel who would determine whether there would be a peace for UNIFIL to keep. If they would not accept a truce, Israel would retaliate and the war would continue. That is what happened. UNIFIL's efforts to carry out its tasks were seen by the militias as an obstacle to their *jihād* and they were not above killing its members if they got in the militias' way.

Trouble started as soon as UNIFIL began to deploy. When the PLO denied it access to Tyre, on the grounds that the city had not been occupied by the Israeli forces, shots were fired and several members of UNIFIL, including the commander of the French contingent, were killed. In order to secure the PLO's cooperation, the United Nations had to accept that Tyre was excluded from UNIFIL's area of operations. It also had to accept that the PLO would retain six positions and a number of arms caches in the area of operation. After these initial difficulties, UNIFIL established checkpoints and observation posts throughout its area and disarmed or turned back armed persons who tried to enter it. But small groups could easily bypass the checkpoints and the PLO and other groups had little difficulty in maintaining an armed presence in what the Security Council had intended to be a demilitarized buffer zone between the two sides. Nor could UNIFIL impose similar restrictions on the SLA which, secure in its support from Israel, established new positions in UNIFIL's area and harassed the force at will, kidnapping its personnel and bombarding its headquarters at Naqoura. This robbed UNIFIL of such credibility as it had with the PLO and the latter's Lebanese allies and exposed it to danger and humiliation.

In June 1982 Israel invaded again. Some brave Nepalese denied the invading force the use of a strategic bridge across the Litani for two days until their position was directly targeted by the invaders' artillery. Otherwise, UNIFIL's only action was to place obstacles on the roads, which the Israeli soldiers removed without difficulty as the UN soldiers looked on helplessly. UNIFIL was much blamed, in Lebanon and elsewhere, for not doing more. This was unfair, for the force had neither the mandate nor the capacity to resist an Israeli invasion.

In 1982 the Israelis had a more ambitious objective than in 1978. This time they were to occupy Beirut and, with Western help, bring about the expulsion of the PLO from Lebanon. This outcome, which was preceded by Lebanese atrocities against Palestinian civilians in the refugee camps in Beirut, was as devoutly desired by the Lebanese Christians as it was by Israel. Syria too had long been opposed to Yasir Arafat's Fatah wing of the PLO, and was pleased to see it driven from Lebanon. Its departure also opened opportunities for Amal (the moderate Shi'ite faction) to strengthen its position in the south.* Amal did not disguise its satisfaction at the departure of the PLO fighters. Only thus would it be possible to end the suffering visited on the largely Shi'ite population as a result of Israel's retaliations against PLO attacks. This was a strong card for Amal in southern Lebanon. It was also a card which won tricks in Damascus because of Syria's hostility to Arafat.

Meanwhile, however, the focus was on Beirut where, after the IDF's withdrawal, the Western 'multinational force', with contingents from Britain, France, Italy and the United States, provided easy targets for more radical Shi'ite groups supported by Iran and Syria. These turned out to have an unsuspected military ('terrorist' in their enemies' vocabulary) capacity and in two truck-bomb attacks on the same day in October 1983 killed 243 United States and 58 French troops. The force quickly pulled out of Beirut but the IDF remained to the south of the city. When it too was effectively attacked by the Shi'ite militias, it started to move southwards. Israeli-Lebanese negotiations at UNIFIL headquarters in early 1985 failed to produce agreement on full Israeli withdrawal in accordance with SCR 425 and Israel unilaterally imposed its own plan: the security zone would be established along the border, the IDF would retain positions on Lebanese territory and the SLA would be strengthened. This military occupation would soon be complemented by an Israeli-run civilian administration which controlled the police, issued permits for people to travel outside the security zone and levied taxes.

By 1986, therefore, UNIFIL's original mandate bore little relation to the political and military realities on the ground. But all the factions represented in the Lebanese Government said, honestly, that they valued the force. For them it was a symbol of the international community's commitment to the preservation of their fractured state within its internationally recognized boundaries. Every six months the Security Council would meet to renew the force's mandate. For a few days this gave Beirut the opportunity to parade centre stage as the victim of occupation by Israel, which was still at that time a pariah state at the United Nations. The pretence could be maintained that 'the Lebanese Government', at whose request the mandate was to be renewed, actually functioned as a government; the existence of civil war within Lebanon could be forgotten.

---

* Amal, which means 'hope', is an acronym of the militia's Arabic name, *afwāj al-muqāwama al-lubnāniyya*, 'the Battalions of the Lebanese Resistance'. Its resistance was as much against the PLO guerrillas who had taken over southern Lebanon as against Israel and its Lebanese allies.

Unfortunately the pretence did not end when the Security Council's proceedings were over. Back in Beirut 'the Lebanese Government' made demands on UNIFIL which they knew to be wholly unrealistic. 'Compel the Israelis to withdraw,' various political leaders would say. 'Allow the Lebanese Army to deploy alongside UNIFIL and share with it the task of maintaining security in the south.' But the army was as riven by civil strife as the so-called government, and attempts to deploy it in the past had been forcefully resisted by Israel and the SLA. 'Do not obstruct the resistance; they are entitled to use force against the occupation.' This was true, and acknowledged by the Secretary-General, but the Security Council did not change UNIFIL's mandate; it was still supposed to ensure that its area of operation was not used 'for hostile activities of any kind'. 'Stop the Israelis from stealing water from the River Litani.' This accusation was made annually but no evidence was ever produced that the Israelis were actually committing the alleged offence. None of the Lebanese political leaders, except occasionally the wise, calm and moderate Salim al-Hoss, who became Prime Minister in 1987, would admit to understanding the limitations on UNIFIL's ability to do what they demanded of it.

As for the Israeli Government, it prevented UNIFIL from carrying out its mandate but nevertheless saw some value in its presence in southern Lebanon. Israel did not regard the mandate as realistic because, it said, only the IDF and the SLA could protect northern Israel from cross-border 'terror attacks'; the Lebanese Government was evidently unable or unwilling to do this, and the UN lacked the necessary military and intelligence capacity. Israel admitted that UNIFIL did, to a limited extent, help to maintain calm north of the security zone. But if the UN or the troop contributors were inclined to withdraw the force, Israel was not going to pay any political or military price to keep it in place. Senior officials and officers in Israel thus accorded UNIFIL some respect, but for many Israelis it was an object of undisguised contempt and often referred to as 'UNFULFIL'.

In short, UNIFIL was a textbook case of how not to establish a peace-keeping operation. In 1978 the Security Council took a precipitate decision without giving itself time to make sure that it understood what it was doing. In particular, it failed to ensure that all the parties involved in the conflict (which included the PLO far more than the Lebanese Government) agreed to the deployment of the UN force and to the tasks the Council was going to give it. The Council did not even define what the new force's area of operation would be. When it became clear, three months later, that Israel was pursuing a policy which would make UNIFIL's mandate inoperable, the Council took no action either to dissuade Israel or to change the force's mandate. Four years later the Israeli

invasion of 1982 and its aftermath made the mandate even more irrelevant. But again the Council failed to take the opportunity to correct its
earlier mistake and give the force tasks which could actually be carried
out.

These errors had grievous consequences for the civilian population
living immediately north of the security zone. By 1986 it had become
standard practice for the SLA to shell villages in order to discourage their
inhabitants from harbouring members of the increasingly active
Lebanese resistance; and the SLA were holding scores of suspects,
without trial and in appalling conditions, in a prison at Khiam in the
security zone to which the International Committee of the Red Cross
(ICRC) was denied access. The United Nations itself also suffered from
the Security Council's errors. For the failure of UNIFIL undermined the
credibility which UN peacekeeping had regained as a result of the successful operations in Sinai and the Golan Heights after the Arab-Israeli
war of October 1973. It was exploited by the UN's enemies in
Washington,* including even the State Department's Assistant Secretary
for International Organizations, Alan Keyes, who wanted the Congress
to withhold or reduce funding for peacekeeping.

By early 1986 UNIFIL's plight was understandably causing concern to
the nine countries which were contributing troops to the force. Unless
UNIFIL was enabled to do the task it had been set up to do, so they
informed the Secretary-General, they would have to withdraw their contingents. Moreover, since the United States, the Soviet Union and other
countries were not paying their share of UNIFIL's costs, the troop contributors were not receiving the reimbursements to which they were entitled. Their troops were less unhappy. On my introductory visit to the
force, I was impressed by the strength of their morale. True, there was
some danger, and the winters were cold and wet; but there was adventure
too, their tours lasted only six months and most of their governments had
given them incentives to volunteer for UN service – duty-free imports of
gold for the Nepalese, for instance, and of motor vehicles for the Finns.

As I studied UNIFIL during the transitional term I spent at Oxford, I
had reached a positive conclusion: it was the most troubled of our five
operations but it was also the only one which offered the new USG an
opportunity to achieve something more impressive than merely maintaining the status quo. In reaching this conclusion I was helped by an

---

* When I was invited in October 1986 to address the National Democratic Women's
Club in Washington about UN peacekeeping, all the Jewish and pro-Israeli members
boycotted the meeting in order to demonstrate their disapproval of the UN. In October
1987 I received a telephoned death threat from a known Zionist zealot in New Jersey
and was placed under tight security for several weeks.

Israeli scholar, Clinton Bailey, who came to St Antony's to give a lecture on southern Lebanon. He had been a civilian adviser to the Israeli Ministry of Defence, initially in Sinai and then in southern Lebanon (and was later to resume this role in the Occupied Palestinian Territories at the time of the *intifāda*).

Bailey's argument was that Amal and Israel had essentially the same objectives in southern Lebanon. Both wanted the PLO out and both wanted the area to be peaceful. Amal's problem was that it was dependent on Syria's support; it would lose that support if it failed to heed Syria's desire to exploit southern Lebanon as an arena in which military pressure could be put on Israel without causing problems on the Golan Heights. This was why Amal was simultaneously fighting both the PLO and Israel, demonstrating that 'my enemy's enemy is my friend' is not always a reliable guide in Lebanon. In these circumstances, argued Bailey, the UN had an opportunity to mediate, and help implement, an undeclared deal between Amal and Israel which would make it possible, at last, to put SCR 425 into effect. Syria's desire to keep the pot boiling in southern Lebanon might cause it to obstruct such a deal but it was worth trying.

This analysis seemed to me to provide the UN with a powerful case to put to the government of Israel. We could argue that by continuing to occupy the security zone and condoning the SLA's brutality there Israel was creating enemies it did not need to have and was giving an advantage to the extremists of Hizbullah. It thus risked radicalizing Amal, for that movement would lose its support if it was seen to be less effective than the extremists in fighting the hated Israeli occupation. Would it not be wiser for Israel to recognize that a community of interest existed between it and Amal? On that basis it could give the UN and Amal, working together, an opportunity to show that they could maintain security in southern Lebanon.

These were the ideas I drew on during my introductory visit to the Levant in March 1986. It began with a preliminary canter round the course with the politicians in Beirut. I was to know that course well. In order to underline the United Nations' impartiality, each visit to Beirut had to include calls on the holders of the three main offices of state – President Gemayel (Maronite), Prime Minister Karamé (Sunni Muslim) and the Speaker of the National Assembly (Hussein Husseini, Shi'ite Muslim). But Husseini had little political power and I had also to see Nabih Berri, the leader of the Amal movement. To complete coverage of the four resident teams in the cockpit, I usually added to the list the Druze leader, Walid Jumblatt.

President Gemayel had succeeded his brother Bashir who was elected President in 1982 but was assassinated before he could assume office.

Amin was in his mid-forties, dignified, intelligent and well-informed but embarrassed by awareness of how little power he had either as President of the Republic or within his own Maronite community. Prime Minister Rashid Karamé was a much older man, who personified the decline of the Sunni Muslims as a political force. He was courteous to the point of flattery and effusive in his support for the UN's efforts. But on substance he had little to offer – only requests for the impossible and sententious rhetoric about the wickedness of Israel and the United States. He was to be killed the following year by a booby-trapped briefcase while returning by helicopter to Beirut from his native Tripoli. Speaker Husseini, a Shi'ite version of Karamé, was no match for Berri who had replaced him as the leader of Amal.

Berri also served as Minister of the South in the Lebanese Government. He was then in his late forties, speaking American English as a result of several years' residence in Detroit, though he had been born in Sierra Leone and once held a British passport. He was witty and informal but easily offended. He could also be disarmingly frank about his own people and their shortcomings. He once said to Jean-Claude Aimé: 'I advise you to remember, Mr Aimé, that we Shi'ites are the best liars in the world.' He was right; for the Shi'ites, dissimulation (*taqīya*) is not a sin if the person being deceived is not also a Shi'ite. The other political leaders received me in grand offices dating from the days when Beirut was indeed the Paris of the Middle East. Not so Berri; although a Minister, he worked from a dingy and smoky office in what always seemed to me a particularly hazardous part of West Beirut.

The Druze leader, Walid Jumblatt, had succeeded his father Kamal after the latter's assassination in 1977. He was a salouki to Berri's terrier – lean, elegant and languorous in manner, but sharp of mind and something of a philosopher. At one of our meetings he said: 'the Druze and the Maronites, the People of the Mountain, do massacre each other from time to time, but we are the true Lebanese and, now as always, we suffer together, squeezed between the Wali of Damascus and the Wali of 'Akka (Acre)' – that is, between Syria and Israel.*

My colleagues on these visits were Aimé from New York and Lisa Buttenheim, an American from the civilian staff of UNTSO in Jerusalem. Rolf Knutsson, a Swede and senior political adviser at UNTSO, was also sometimes in the party. Like Aimé, he had come into peacekeeping from the UN Development Programme, was a friendly and reliable colleague and had good political judgement. He was also a pessimist who seemed to enjoy bearing bad news, especially about dissension within the UN,

---

* In the Ottoman Empire a *wali* was a provincial governor. Jumblatt was likening Israel's and Syria's policies in Lebanon to those of the former imperial power.

and I soon learnt not to be excessively dismayed by what he said. At the end of the day's meetings we would drive into the mountains on the Christian side and stay in a huge hotel, echoing and empty, in the summer resort of Brumana. A kilometre down the hill there were two small restaurants in the French style, La Gargote and Le Gargotier, one managed by a Lebanese man and the other by his wife. For a few dollars each, we could eat and drink royally at either of them, serenaded by the French night-club singer Patachou on an ancient tape and occasionally reminded of reality by a loud noise from the city below.

Aimé and Knutsson were sceptical about Bailey's approach and my readiness to follow it. For years they had seen Urquhart deploy all his skills and authority in the search for a solution which would get the IDF out of Lebanon. They knew better than I that in Lebanon almost nothing is what it seems to be, that alliances can change overnight and that the hostilities in the south of the country were part of a wider regional conflict. It would end only when the regional leaders decided it should end and their logic was rather more convoluted than the simple logic of the United Nations' peacemaking mandate. I should remember, my advisers said, that Amal is part of the Syrian apparatus in Lebanon. Do not assume that President Assad wants an early end to the Israeli occupation. Does it not serve his interests by putting Israel at odds with the international community and giving him opportunities to needle the IDF in its security zone, while keeping things calm on the Golan? His priorities are to recover the Golan and ensure that any settlement in Palestine takes account of Syria's interests. He probably thinks that both priorities can be served by keeping the fires burning, but not too fiercely, in southern Lebanon.

It was only gradually that I came to see that Aimé and Knutsson were almost certainly right. Meanwhile I had the Secretary-General, the Security Council and the troop contributors behind me in trying to avoid the withdrawal of UNIFIL, which would, I was convinced, lead to another war. So I pressed doggedly on – and was pleased when some months later President Gemayel said to me at the end of a meeting: 'Mr Goulding, I am glad that someone else, like me, is an extremist in his determination not to be discouraged.'

In March 1986, after the introductory visit to Beirut, I met Yitzhak Rabin, Israel's Defence Minister, in Jerusalem. We were to have about a dozen such meetings until the eruption of the Palestinian uprising in the Gaza Strip and the West Bank in December 1987 changed Rabin's priorities and made him even more reluctant to take risks in southern Lebanon. I enjoyed negotiating with Rabin. He was invariably punctual, courteous and even-tempered, allowing one to say one's piece without interruption. What is more, he seemed to think seriously about what one had said and, without having taken a note (perhaps it was all too predict-able), gave a point-by-point reply. This inspired confidence and made it possible to forgo the circumlocutions which cloud so many diplomatic exchanges and were *de rigueur* in Beirut or Damascus. He consumed avidly during our meetings – tobacco, coffee, biscuits, fruit. At first, the lighting of a cigarette or the sinking of his teeth into a pear appeared to be a sign of boredom; but I learnt otherwise – it was a sign of intensified thought and therefore to be welcomed.

Rabin's gravelly voice and sombre expression suggested world-weari-ness, but a sudden smile would reveal a warmth, unexpected at the first meeting and eagerly awaited at subsequent ones. In 1987, when I was briefly his go-between with persons in Lebanon who were thought to be holding the remains of two Israeli soldiers captured in southern Lebanon, I went to see him alone in his office in the Ministry of Defence in Tel Aviv. We talked about where the remains might be held. 'Do you want to see what's going on in Beirut?' he asked. You bet I did. He led me into a room behind his office. On one wall was an enormous screen with a live aerial shot of a street in what looked like the slums of south Beirut. A tank was moving along the street. Rabin pressed a switch and we zoomed in on the tank. 'Syrian,' he said, 'T-55.' He was excited, like a child with a complicated new toy.

It would be presumptuous to say that Rabin was a friend, but I became fond of him during those months. The last time I saw him was in New York on 20 October 1995 when, as Prime Minister, he called on Boutros-Ghali. He talked of how the hardliners, Hamas on the Palestinian side and Jewish zealots on the other, were helping each other in what was, in effect, a common effort to destroy the Palestine peace process; the suicide bomb attacks were making it difficult for him to maintain popular support for the Oslo Accords. 'But with Jordan', he said, 'we have a beau-tiful peace.' Two weeks later he was assassinated by a Jewish zealot. Incongruously, the awful news reached me, via the duty officer in my department and my mobile phone, in a pool hall in Lower Manhattan where I was having my Saturday afternoon game.

At the first meeting with him in March 1986 I made the case rehearsed above: the security zone is not working; you and Amal have a common interest in keeping Hizbullah out of southern Lebanon; let the UN and Amal show you what we can do. Rabin's reply was: your analysis is wrong; Hizbullah's advances in the south are nothing to do with the security zone; they result from Tehran's efforts, abetted by Damascus, to create an 'Islamic Republic of Lebanon'; cross-border terrorism is due, as it always has been, to the absence of an effective government in Beirut; UNIFIL cannot fill that gap; it is a peacekeeping operation with a 'mission impossible'. I made a proposal: let the IDF withdraw to the border, experimentally, in the western part of the security zone and announce its intention to withdraw from Lebanon completely by a certain date, provided it is not harassed meanwhile. This would give Amal the opportunity and incentive to show what it could do. It would also open the way for the UN to get the political leaders in Beirut to talk seriously about security arrangements and the future of the SLA.

Rabin did not respond directly. He spoke of Israel's desire to talk to Amal face to face, which the Amal leadership had previously refused. This was encouraging; he was implicitly accepting that Amal could have a role to play. Would Israel talk to Amal through the UN, I asked. He replied that 'unfortunately' the Cabinet had decided to maintain existing policy; he did not want to close the door to talks with Amal, though he would prefer them to be direct. He agreed that we should meet again.

In Damascus the following week I obtained nothing that would help with Rabin. Vice-President Abdul Halim Khaddam was affable but arrogant and implacable – and suffering from flu, thanks, he claimed, to receiving so many delegations from Lebanon each of whose members insisted on kissing him three times. Of course the IDF should withdraw from Lebanon, he said, but this would not put an end to operations against Israel, though they would not be on the present scale. Israel would not be secure until there was peace in the region and that would not come while Israel continued to occupy Arab lands. Indeed, if Syria could create trouble in any village or city in Israel, it would not hesitate to do so.

I saw Rabin again, ten days after our first meeting. He had a counter-proposal: let there be six months of 'tranquillity' in a designated sector in the western part of the security zone; if Amal and the UN passed this test, Israel would consider (repeat consider) redeployment of the IDF in that sector (he was careful not to use the word 'withdrawal'). I said this was too difficult a test for Amal; they had to be able to demonstrate that they were achieving results. But at Rabin's insistence I agreed to put the proposal to Berri. I did so the next day in Beirut. He rejected it without ceremony: it had been made twice before. He could not switch the resistance on and off; Hizbullah would step into the gap left by Amal's exit; it was Israel which should pass a test, not Amal; his people would not obey if they received such an order (this was not just an excuse; he really was under pressure from less moderate elements within his movement). His counter-proposal was that Israel should withdraw its troops, on the understanding that if there were then attacks against Israel, the IDF could return.

I went on to see Prime Minister Karamé and President Gemayel. The latter seemed to know that we were putting our eggs in the Amal basket. He said firmly that he could not countenance any talks outside the legitimate Lebanese Government or agreements between Amal and the SLA.

'We know our sovereignty is a fiction but we are trying to restore it.' However, in a subsequent tête-à-tête I told him about Rabin's proposal and he became more flexible; he could accept the kind of arrangements we had in mind, provided that the government was involved in some way from the outset, for example by including one pro-Amal army officer in the negotiations. But he dismissed both Rabin's proposal and Berri's counter-proposal as unrealistic. He had an alternative: Israel should announce its intention to withdraw on a certain date provided that in the meantime (a) there was no harassment of the IDF and (b) there would be Israeli-Lebanese negotiations about how the border would be controlled in future. Gemayel also said that I was wrong to believe that there was consensus in Lebanon on the necessity of IDF withdrawal; the IDF and the SLA were needed to protect the Christian population in the south, especially those in and around Jezzine.

Rabin was not surprised by any of this when I saw him in Tel Aviv the next day. Berri, he said, had a lot of enemies: his own extremists, Hizbullah and Iran, Walid Jumblatt and the Druze, Arafat's wing of the PLO. The interesting question now was whether Syria would continue to back Berri. It ought to if it was aware of how rapidly Iran was extending its influence in Lebanon. He thought it unlikely that Berri would ever agree to the kind of arrangements that Gemayel had proposed. But we should wait for a few weeks and see how the power struggle in Amal between Berri and the extremists worked out. I agreed.

I was to return to the Levant five times during 1986, in a triangular shuttle between Beirut, Damascus and Jerusalem/Tel Aviv. But the reader should not despair; neither those five visits nor the two which followed in 1987 will be chronicled in such detail. For the essentials of the plot remained unchanged. There were, however, external developments which obliged the principal players to change their lines.

The first was that in April France insisted that the Security Council should renew UNIFIL's mandate for only three months instead of the customary six. France's motives were not clear. Some saw a link with the French citizens held hostage in Beirut, one of whom had recently been murdered. Their captors were extremist Shi'ites; the regime in Tehran had stated its rejection of SCR 425 because that resolution recognized the State of Israel; *ergo* the dissolution of UNIFIL at French initiative was part of a deal to free the hostages. Paris, however, declared a more convincing, and more proper, motive: it was unworthy of the Security Council to treat renewal of the mandate as a routine matter when absolutely no progress was being made towards implementation of its earlier resolutions. France got its way.

The second development was that the PLO began to re-establish itself in the south, using its considerable financial resources to build up a military capability in the refugee camps in Beirut, Sidon and Tyre. It was said (but everything was said in Beirut) that it was doing this with the support not only of Hizbullah but also of President Gemayel and the Christian militias. They had previously been the PLO's bitterest opponents. But they were equally opposed to the Syrian hegemony which had been consolidated since the PLO's expulsion and they were now ready to form an alliance with their old enemy Arafat, who was also Syria's enemy. Syria's ally Amal could do nothing in Sidon, which was already controlled by the PLO and its Lebanese Muslim allies. But Berri laid siege to the Palestinian refugee camps in Tyre and in those parts of Beirut which were under Syrian control and subjected them to intermittent shelling for over two years.

This clarified the line-up in the cockpit in a way that was not helpful to our efforts to get the IDF out of Lebanon. On the one side were Syria and Amal and perhaps the Druze; on the other were Iran, Hizbullah, the PLO and some of its Lebanese allies; others were hesitant about joining an alliance in which Iran and Hizbullah were prominent. But also on that side, it seemed, were the Maronites, whose objection to the assertion of Syrian suzerainty over Lebanon was strong enough to put them in the same coalition as their previous enemies, the PLO and Hizbullah. This raised questions about Syria's position. In theory it had the capacity to rein in Hizbullah because it controlled the territory through which Iran sent money, weapons and *agents provocateurs* to Lebanon. Might Damascus think again about whether it was in its interests to aid and abet Tehran's policy in southern Lebanon?

President Assad went to Tehran that summer (this was the third development) and nothing changed. This brought home to me that UNIFIL's problems were a minor sideshow on the regional stage. Assad could not afford to antagonize Khomeini, for reasons already mentioned (oil, debts, Iraq). The fate of Amal was important for Syria but less important than its relations with Iran. Berri was stoical about this: 'Assad asked me last week: "Why do you want to create problems with Hizbullah if Israel is not going to withdraw?" Syria has its own policy. Sometimes we agree with them; sometimes we don't.' Rabin kept on asking me to find out from Syria what its policy would be if the IDF withdrew. All Khaddam would say was that the Lebanese resistance would consider its objectives achieved once the IDF had withdrawn; meanwhile, it did not want to see a return to 'the pre-1982 situation', meaning the re-establishment of a PLO military presence in the south. Syria, said Khaddam, supported the resistance's position on both points. This cut little ice with Rabin; what he wanted was to see Syria controlling Hizbullah's activities where it had the capacity to do so.

The fourth development, which occurred in August and September

1986, was a series of deliberate attacks against UNIFIL personnel. An Irish officer was killed by Amal because, in spite of warnings, he had been too assiduous in defusing roadside bombs planted by Amal on tracks used by the IDF and the SLA. In a separate incident, an altercation at a checkpoint led to the killing by a French soldier of two Amal members, one of them a leader of the more extreme wing of the movement. For the next seven weeks the French contingent was submitted to revenge attacks which cost it three dead and twenty-four wounded. Prime Minister Chirac was strident in his public criticism of the United Nations for putting the lives of French soldiers at risk. The Defence Minister told me that it was an intolerable affront to the dignity of the French Army that its soldiers should be deployed in positions monitored by armed elements whom they were supposed to be monitoring. Aimé and I went out for another gruelling ten days of shuttling between Beirut, Naqoura, Tel Aviv and Damascus.

These four developments invalidated the ideas which had been aired in March. Both Rabin and I had to change our lines. He stuck to his proposal of a six-month trial to see whether Amal and the UN could maintain tranquillity in what came to be called 'the Triangle' at the western end of the security zone. But he added a new condition for even a partial withdrawal. The Lebanese had to accept the SLA as a 'legitimate' militia; otherwise the SLA would feel that they were being betrayed by Israel. This was an absolute non-starter but Rabin affected not to understand why. He also moved the goalposts by saying that the IDF's withdrawal from the Triangle would not include a technical surveillance position overlooking the stretch of coast south of Tyre; nor would it include the port of Naqoura, the only one in the security zone and thus of commercial importance for the SLA. For my part, I recognized that the tranquillity test was going nowhere. Although Berri had rejected it, Amal had in fact exercised restraint in the Triangle for two months. But it had started to shell the Palestinian camps and faced the growing power of Hizbullah; it could not afford doubts about its commitment to the fight against Israeli occupation.

We had to find another way of persuading the troop contributors that there was some movement towards implementation of SCR 425. With Pérez de Cuéllar's agreement, I got all the Lebanese players and Israel to accept a form of words about a new diplomatic initiative by the UN to establish, through separate negotiations with the governments of Israel and Lebanon, a basis for implementation of SCR 425. In his report to the Security Council in mid-June the Secretary-General stated:

I have come to the conclusion, subject to the Council's deciding to renew UNIFIL's mandate, that the United Nations should pursue a process of negotiation with each of the two Governments concerned in order to establish agreement with them on practical measures for UNIFIL to fulfil its mandate . . . I believe that this is a realistic approach which offers the best prospect of achieving full implementation of resolution 425 (1978).

This was a much diluted version of what I had originally proposed, but it did the trick and the Council renewed UNIFIL's mandate until mid-January 1987.

By the end of 1986, the naivety of my earlier hopes was apparent. The going became tougher, though I still enjoyed my regular visits to the Levant.* During 1987 all sides maintained their established positions and there was no further negotiation. But paradoxically there was some progress on the ground. In July UNIFIL learnt that the SLA intended to establish a new position on a feature known as Tell al-Janajil in the force's area of operation. Gustav Hägglund, the force commander, telephoned in the middle of the night to say that he intended to occupy the hill pre-emptively. With my encouragement he did so, to the irritation of the SLA and the Israelis, and was kind enough to name the new position 'OP Marrack'. Three months later, UNIFIL successfully negotiated the with-drawal of the IDF/SLA from a hill called Tallet Huqban, from which they had regularly shelled two neighbouring Shi'ite villages. But when I saw Rabin in December 1987, he complained that Iranian Revolutionary Guards and Hizbullah activists had accompanied the civilians when they returned to their villages. What was Amal doing about that?

The outbreak of the Palestinian uprising in December 1987 made it even more unlikely that Israel would change its policy in Lebanon and my involvement with UNIFIL thereafter was confined to operational issues. The most serious of these concerned Lieutenant-Colonel William 'Rich' Higgins, an American officer who was kidnapped near Tyre in February 1988.† But I continued to visit the force in January and July each year to prepare the report in which the Secretary-General would recommend renewal of the mandate. In July 1988 Gustav Hägglund had been suc-ceeded by a Swedish officer, Lieutenant-General Lars-Eric Wahlgren, who, like Hägglund, brought a charming wife and generous Nordic hos-pitality to the force commander's house. This was an austere prefabri-cated bungalow but it was on the Mediterranean shore and I could watch

---

* An account of one such visit, given in a letter to my daughter Rachel in January 1987, is reproduced in Appendix V.
† This tragedy is described in Chapter 7. Higgins was a member of UNTSO and com-manded the group of military observers from that operation who were attached to UNIFIL. He was kidnapped by members of Hizbullah who were assisted by extremist members of Amal. All our efforts to locate him and negotiate his release failed and he was murdered by his captors in 1989.

the Yelkouan shearwaters glide amongst the Lebanese boatmen fishing with hand grenades inshore and the Israeli patrol craft out at sea. The focus of the visit in July 1988 was on Beirut where the political situation was deteriorating further. There was little hope for a constitutional succession to President Amin Gemayel and, after Parliament failed that August to elect a successor, the outgoing President appointed a Maronite general, Michel Aoun, as head of a military government. This was not accepted by the Muslims, who insisted that the acting head of state be the Prime Minister, Salim al-Hoss. The myth that there was a single, constitutional government of Lebanon could no longer be sustained.

It was about this time that I began to have doubts about whether UNIFIL should be continued. Its mandate could not be implemented; my efforts to facilitate its implementation had failed; the risk of casualties remained great; its ineffectiveness placed a flail in the hands of the UN's enemies in Washington; and it cost a lot of money when demand for peacekeeping was growing. On the other hand, it provided succour to the civilians who tried to keep their lives going on the fault-line between Israel and its enemies, and it did symbolize the UN's commitment to the independence and territorial integrity of Lebanon. I concluded that if it could not be withdrawn completely, it should at least be withdrawn from the security zone where it could do nothing to control IDF/ SLA aggression against the 'liberated areas'. I put this thinking to Pérez de Cuéllar. He was not keen but authorized me to make discreet soundings of some of the troop contributors. The Norwegian Defence Minister, Johan Jörgen Holst, one of our staunchest and most realistic supporters, said that his government could handle the reaction in Norway if UNIFIL withdrew from the Norwegian sector, which was wholly within the security zone. But in Paris the French Foreign Minister told Pérez de Cuéllar that any withdrawal would send the signal that the UN was washing its hands of Lebanon. The idea was dropped.

On my next UNIFIL circuit, in January 1989, I gave the two Lebanese 'governments' a gloomy assessment: collapse of the Lebanese state; consolidation of Israel's security zone; the kidnapping of Higgins; harassment of UNIFIL personnel; lack of funding for UNIFIL. They listened, and Berri even admitted that the Lebanese had to come together if they were ever to rid Lebanon of all the foreigners fighting their wars on its soil. But they were confident that UNIFIL would be kept in place. The meeting with Aoun was disturbing. He received us, alone and in military fatigues, in the President's office. He was brisk, frank, to-the-point and totally unrealistic: his policy was all-out diplomatic war against Syria; he would personally lead attempts in the Arab League and the UN to have its occupation of Lebanon classified as aggression.

There was also some good news. At Arafat's initiative, Amal and the

PLO had signed a pact banning all military activity by the PLO in southern Lebanon, a significant revision of alliances in the cockpit; and Amal was now at war with Hizbullah in the south. These developments, if they held, might make it possible to revive our earlier proposals for a gradual pull-back by the IDF, though not until the situation in the Gaza Strip and the West Bank had stabilized. But in March 1989 three members of UNIFIL's Irish battalion were killed by a roadside bomb, apparently deliberately. I asked Wahlgren to meet me in Amman on my way back from a visit to the new UN observer group on the cease-fire line between Iran and Iraq. The Irish Chief of Staff, Lieutenant-General Tadgh O'Neill, joined us there. Wahlgren reported that the bomb had been a professional job on a road that the Irish had been using several times a day for over two months. He had no doubt that it had been targeted against them, though the motive was not clear. Berri had suggested that it was a warning by Hizbullah to Amal not to be so close to UNIFIL. O'Neill was admirably robust, confirming a long Irish commitment to the United Nations. He would recommend to his government that it continue to contribute to UNIFIL. Martin Vadset, the Chief of Staff of UNTSO, also came to Amman to discuss how we could protect UN military staff in Beirut from the consequences of the intensifying hostilities there. Answer: withdraw as many of them as possible and reduce crossings of the Green Line to a minimum.

So worrying was UNIFIL's plight that Pérez de Cuéllar changed his mind and instructed me to consult the five permanent members of the Security Council about the possibility of at least reducing the size of the force. None of them favoured this, however, especially at a time when Lakhdar Brahimi's Arab League mission to end the civil war was at last making progress. By now I was so engrossed with the new multifunctional operation in Namibia that I had little time for these Lebanese problems and did not make the usual visit to UNIFIL in July 1989 (though I did have to go to Lebanon at short notice when Colonel Higgins' captors announced on 31 July that they had 'executed' him).

My next visit to Lebanon was in January 1990. Much had changed. Brahimi had arranged for the sixty-two surviving members of the Lebanese Parliament elected in 1972 to be transported to Taif in Saudi Arabia, where they agreed on a Charter of National Reconciliation. The immediate effect was to intensify the civil war. Almost all the teams in the cockpit criticized the Taif agreement, and General Aoun, the head of the Christian government in East Beirut, rejected it altogether, threatening to shell the parliament building if the deputies gathered there to elect a new president, who would still be a Maronite. So the deputies did the deed in a Syrian-controlled airbase in the Beqa'a, but the President they elected, René Mouawad, was almost immediately assassinated.

Undeterred they elected another, Elias Hrawi, who set up his government in Muslim West Beirut. The Security Council expressed unequivocal support for the new government, but Aoun rejected its authority and refused to give up either command of the army or the presidential palace at Ba'abda in East Beirut.

The Taif agreement had changed the dispositions in the cockpit. Aoun, entrenched at Ba'abda, was about to go to war not with the Syrians or the Muslims but with the main Christian militia, the Lebanese Forces led by Samir Geagea, who was challenging him for leadership of the Maronites. Aoun was receiving military supplies from Iraq, including FROG missiles, allegedly with the connivance of Egypt and Jordan. All those countries were lesser gamblers but they saw Taif as a victory for Syria and therefore tried to undermine it. In the south the two Shi'ite movements, Amal and Hizbullah, were still at war with each other and the South Lebanon Army, Israel's creation and the arch-enemy of them both, was allowing Hizbullah fighters safe passage through its territory in order to add fuel to the inter-Shi'ite fire. Under pressure from Hizbullah, Amal was seeking help from the PLO, its other arch-enemy which it had been trying for years to remove from the south.

My main concern in this mayhem was that the Lebanese Christians should not target the UN in protest at the Security Council's unqualified endorsement of the Hrawi government (which had meant that I could not make my customary visit to Aoun). There was a protest but it was not life-threatening, just a few bursts from heavy machine guns in the flight path of the UN helicopter which was to take me to Naqoura. Next day UNIFIL's complaint produced an apology: Aoun's forces had been conducting anti-aircraft exercises and had unintentionally fired close to the helicopter. To complete the picture, the flight down the coast to Naqoura gave us a grandstand view of two Israeli jets conducting a mock air raid against a Palestinian refugee camp near Sidon. How was UNIFIL ever going to fulfil its mandate in the midst of a conflict of such complexity?

At Naqoura it was confirmed that Taif had done nothing to change UNIFIL's plight, and morale was low. There were no new ideas about how to end the Israeli occupation; the force continued to be harassed by the Israelis and all the 'armed elements'; some of the contingents were below standard; and some of their commanders were bypassing Wahlgren and taking too many orders from their capitals. A few weeks later the Irish Government was to order the Irish contingent commander to pay compensation to the families of two Amal fighters who had been shot dead in a clash with Irish soldiers. I had urged Dublin not to do this, because Wahlgren had rightly instructed the Irish commander not to pay any compensation until UNIFIL's procedures for such cases had been completed. This led to a series of painful exchanges with the Irish mission in New York.

Government interference in the UN chain of command has always been a problem in peacekeeping. When, on the eve of the 1967 war in the Middle East, President Nasser demanded the withdrawal of UNEF I, the Indian and Yugoslav governments decided that, whatever Secretary-General U Thant's response to Nasser might be, they would withdraw their contingents from the force, thereby removing much of its military capacity. Enhanced telecommunications have made it easy for governments to keep in minute-by-minute touch with their contingents. Force commanders and I were conscious that every significant order we issued in the name of the United Nations would be scrutinized in the capitals of the troop contributors concerned. This was not in itself reprehensible. Governments have every right to watch over the security and welfare of the troops they make available to the UN and to take up with the Secretariat any instances in which they believe that their troops' lives are being put unnecessarily at risk. We were also ready to discuss any misgivings troop contributors might have about the strategy or tactics employed by the UN. What was totally unacceptable, however, was for a capital to order its contingent commander to disobey an order received from his UN commander. It was established doctrine that UN peacekeeping operations were under the operational command of the Secretary-General and that that was the unique chain of command. If it was not respected, peacekeepers' lives would be at risk.

After this dismal visit to UNIFIL I moved on to Damascus where I was able to bask in Syria's delight at the Security Council's endorsement of Taif. But nothing new was said about the south. In Tel Aviv Ze'ev Schiff, the magisterial defence correspondent of *Ha'aretz*, told me to have no illusions: the status quo in Lebanon suited Israel (though Iraq's supply of missiles to Aoun was worrying) and Israel would do nothing to assist the implementation of Taif. Rabin too was uncompromising. His preference for the 'cantonization' of Lebanon was evident; Israel would not 'remain inactive' if force was used against Aoun.

When I returned to Lebanon six months later, in July 1990, the gloom had lifted. True, Amal and Hizbullah were still fighting an ugly war immediately to the north of the UNIFIL area of operations. But there had been a significant decline in harassment of UNIFIL, the crisis over the Irish incident had passed, the south seemed to be enjoying a boom, new bridges, terraces and hideous mansions were sprouting everywhere, roads and public utilities were being restored, UNIFIL had succeeded in establishing a number of new positions along the fault-line with the security zone, and the Norwegian battalion was successfully using 'passive violence' to obstruct Israeli attempts to establish new positions (passive violence being the placing of one's own personnel and vehicles in positions that will oblige the opponent to use violence against them if he is to get his way). But the calm and the prosperity were illusory. My talks with the governments in Beirut, Damascus and Jerusalem produced not a glimmer of hope that progress could be made in ending either the internal conflicts in Lebanon or the Israeli occupation of the south.

Six months later, in January 1991, the Taif agreement was beginning to have some beneficial effects. The Green Line had disappeared; Beirut was a reunited city; the main road to Damascus was open again. The new commander of the armed forces, a naval officer called Emile Lahoud, was making progress in disarming the militias. He had also decided to end the previous practice under which each brigade was dominated by one of the confessions and effectively belonged to that confession's team. In the new army each brigade would contain a mixture of confessions; the Sixth Brigade, for instance, would no longer be the Shi'ite Muslim brigade. President Hrawi and General Lahoud were keen to deploy the army to the south as a step towards re-establishment of the government's authority. Syria supported this and claimed to have told Amal and Hizbullah to facilitate the army's move. The UN also supported the idea, in principle. But we were cautious; in 1978 the SLA had used artillery to block the army's advance as the Israeli invaders withdrew. I explained to Hrawi and his ministers that the critical question was how the army would deal with the militias in the south; if it turned a blind eye to their operations against the IDF and the SLA, it would itself be drawn into the conflict. The new Prime Minister, Omar Karamé (younger brother of the assassinated Rashid), had already raised Israeli suspicions by declaring the army's role to be that of protecting the resistance's communications. But Hrawi understood the point and asked me to sound the Israelis.

Moshe Arens, the Defence Minister, predictably said that Israel would welcome the army if it established law and order and prevented 'incidents' but Israel would not hesitate to strike if it was involved in 'terrorist activities'. Hrawi was downcast at this; it was politically impossible, he said, to order the army to prevent attacks against the IDF and the SLA when Israel remained in occupation of Lebanese territory. This had always been the problem and it had affected UNIFIL too. I wondered why Syria, poor Hrawi's suzerain, had encouraged him to pursue a policy that was bound to fail and thereby undermine his political credibility; the answer seemed to be that Damascus preferred not to have a politically credible leader in Beirut, lest he rally Lebanese resistance to Syrian domination of the country.

But this was unduly pessimistic. During the ensuing six months Lahoud did succeed in deploying his army down to the Litani river, the northern boundary of UNIFIL's area of operations. When I returned in July 1991, the talk was about whether it could next move into the Jezzine area, outside the security zone but controlled by the SLA, on the pretext of protecting the Christians there. Hrawi talked about a possible deal with Antoine Lahad, the commander of the SLA, under which some SLA personnel in Jezzine could be incorporated into the Lebanese Army. But in Jerusalem Arens described Jezzine as being an important part of Israel's security arrangements in Lebanon and it was clear that the decision would not be Lahad's.

Discussions had also begun on the transfer to the army of part of UNIFIL's area of operations; this took place in the following year. By that time, Kofi Annan had become ASG for Peacekeeping and UNIFIL was one of the operations I had delegated to him. My last visit to the force was with him in February 1992. We travelled at short notice. On 16 February Israel assassinated the head of Hizbullah, Abbas Musawi, while he was driving with his wife and son north of the Litani. Heavy exchanges of fire ensued, including rocket attacks against towns in northern Israel. Four days later an Israeli armoured column moved north out of the security zone and assaulted the village of Kafra, pushing aside the obstacles UNIFIL had placed in its path. It withdrew the following day after suffering fatal casualties, as had UNIFIL and the Lebanese militias which engaged it in Kafra. Annan's and my mission was to try to calm a very tense situation. We visited Kafra in a blizzard; as we approached the village we encountered a group of less than friendly militiamen. When my identity was revealed one of them fired a number of shots in the air (a Hizbullah cleric had for some months been denouncing 'the Jew Goulding'). A wire service reported that Goulding had been shot, which caused a mild stir at that day's press briefing in New York.

It was not a bad ending to my relationship with UNIFIL. Lebanon is a violent place; one only has to note how many Lebanese politicians have died by assassination.* Visits there always had a tinge of adventure and I had enjoyed that. But I became more and more disillusioned about Lebanon itself. At the beginning I had believed in the 'commitment to the preservation of Lebanon's sovereignty and territorial integrity'. But did the Lebanese themselves have that commitment? It was true that the gamblers round the cockpit were encouraging inter-Lebanese conflict in the pursuit of their own interests. But if the Lebanese were really patriotic would they go on selling their services to the gamblers? At that point, though, I would think of the civilians in southern Lebanon who had come to depend so much on the protection, albeit limited, that UNIFIL could give them against the depredations of the gamblers and their

---

* Four of the 17 Lebanese politicians listed in Appendix III died by assassination.

hirelings. Perhaps there *was* an ethical justification for the international community's efforts at damage limitation.

That argument held some validity while the UN had only half a dozen operations in the field. But it became less convincing from 1988 onwards, as the demand for peacekeeping grew. At that time, the five permanent members of the Security Council were billed for 57.6 per cent of the costs; the share of the OECD countries was 82.9 per cent. They became increasingly uneasy about the financial burden that peacekeeping imposed on them. In these circumstances, it seemed to me, priorities had to be established. Was it wise to keep UNIFIL in being? It was costing the UN about $150 million a year and had, for a decade or more, been prevented from doing its job by a small power which the United States protected from censure, let alone action, in the Security Council. This state of affairs was made all the more galling by the fact that the United States itself failed to pay its share of UNIFIL's costs, thereby violating the international law which it insisted that other states respect.

6

Palestine

Exciting though I found it, Lebanon was only a sideshow in the wider Arab-Israeli conflict; its problems would not be solved without progress on the central issue, which was Palestine. Such progress seemed an unlikely prospect when I joined the United Nations in 1986. In spite of much coming and going, the diplomatic process was stuck. A plan launched by President Reagan in 1982 had failed. American opinion was disillusioned with the 'Mid East' because of the loss of 243 US Marines in Beirut in 1983, the hostage-taking there and continued acts of terrorism by the PLO in which American citizens were often the target. In 1985 King Hussein of Jordan had signed with Yasir Arafat an agreement for the PLO to participate, as part of a joint Jordanian-PLO delegation, in negotiations for a settlement which would include self-determination for the Palestinians in the context of a confederation with Jordan. While Washington showed a guarded interest in this approach, it found no favour with the others involved, including eventually Arafat himself. In February 1986, Hussein announced that the peace process had broken down and he was ending cooperation with the PLO leadership.

In spite of this setback, the Arab states remained interested in the long-mooted idea of an international conference which would be convened by the Secretary-General and would include the five permanent members of the Security Council and the parties to the conflict. These were assumed to be Israel, its four immediate neighbours (Egypt, Jordan, Lebanon, Syria) and, in some form, the Palestinians. Hussein continued to be active in pressing the idea and initially received support from Israel, ruled at that time by an uneasy coalition between Labour and Likud known as the 'National Unity Government' in which Yitzhak Shamir and Shimon Peres swapped the posts of Prime Minister and Foreign Minister every two years. In an interview in October 1986, just before the changeover, Peres, as Prime Minister, said revealingly that the primary purpose of a conference would be to bring Jordan into the negotiations: 'The formula is: make enough of an international conference so Jordan can enter negotiations, and stop it at the right moment, so that negotiations become direct and bilateral.' Direct negotiations with the Arab states individually were what Israel had always wanted. A month before, Peres had told Pérez de Cuéllar with pride that for the first time three Arab countries favoured them – Egypt, Jordan and Morocco.

Pérez de Cuéllar instructed me to take advantage of my UNIFIL-related travels to pursue 'consultations' about an international conference with the political leaders I met. However frequent the setbacks in a peace process, his policy was to keep 'stirring the pot' by taking every opportunity to remind the parties of the dangers inherent in continuing stalemate. I fully supported his policy, but this was barren land to till in 1986. The consultations that mattered were being done in secret at a higher level than mine. The Secretary-General's role was anyway unwelcome to those who most needed to be persuaded in Israel and the United States, for it derived from resolutions of the General Assembly. In their eyes the Assembly had disqualified itself from any role in the peace process by allowing itself to be manipulated by the PLO, which its resolutions referred to as 'the representative of the Palestinian people'.* In 1975 it had 'determine[d] that zionism is a form of racism and racial discrimination'. It had taken sides, something that mediators should not do.

In 1981, the Assembly decided to convene 'an International Conference on the Question of Palestine'. Two years later it adopted detailed guidelines for the conference. These contained elements which were wholly unacceptable to Israel, the United States and some other Western powers, such as the right of return for the Palestinian refugees, a Palestinian state and the PLO as 'the' representative of the Palestinian people. The 1983 resolution requested the Secretary-General to take urgent measures to convene the conference and this request was repeated annually. Pérez de Cuéllar thus faced a problem. If he consulted the parties about 'the' conference approved by the General Assembly, he would get nowhere because Israel and the United States would have nothing to do with such a conference; but if he consulted them about 'a' conference implicitly different from the Assembly's formula, he risked being accused of exceeding his mandate. He decided to take the risk and, if challenged, to argue that his mandate did not preclude him from exploring the possibility that 'a' conference might be a more effective way of achieving progress. Such semantic minutiae can seem tedious to those not involved in the negotiation. But they are not insignificant; minute distinctions of language can have considerable substantive implications.

In December 1986, the General Assembly's resolution added a new

---

* A designation which nevertheless fell short of the Arab League's then usage of 'sole legitimate representative of the Palestinian people'.

ingredient, namely the establishment by the Security Council of a preparatory committee in which its five permanent members would participate. The Secretary-General was to report back by 15 May 1987. The preparatory committee eventually turned out to be a non-starter but its endorsement by the Assembly gave Pérez de Cuéllar an opportunity to stir the pot again, starting at a summit meeting of the Islamic Conference Organization in Kuwait in January 1987. I was a member of his delegation.

Of the Arab leaders present at the summit, President Assad was of particular interest. This was the only time I was to meet him. Tall, thin, with high forehead and pale complexion, quiet and brief in speech, courteous but aloof, he was a model of inscrutability and lived up to his reputation as the shrewd, calculating and cautious player without whom there could be no settlement of the Arab-Israeli conflict. The Jordanians had claimed that he was becoming more amenable to the kind of conference they had been discussing with Israel and the United States. It would consist of the five permanent members of the Security Council, Israel and its four Arab neighbours; the latter would have individual delegations and not be combined in a joint Arab delegation as Syria had previously wanted; the Palestinians would be represented through a joint Jordanian-Palestinian delegation; the plenary would be multilateral; but direct bilateral negotiations would take place in committees. Assad said nothing to confirm so significant a shift in his position. Pérez de Cuéllar thought he detected some signs of flexibility, but they escaped me.

After our return from Kuwait, Pérez de Cuéllar started a round of consultations in New York with the members of the Security Council and the parties. All the members of the Council accepted, in private consultation at least, the concept of 'a' conference. Only the Soviets and their faithful Bulgarian allies had ideas about how to prepare it. All the rest were ready to go along with whatever preparatory steps the parties could agree among themselves. Although less productive than expected, this outcome did license us to concentrate our efforts on the five state parties, plus the PLO. In April 1987 Hussein and Peres, now Foreign Minister, met secretly in London and agreed on a format for the conference. It fell well short of what the other Arab participants, except Egypt, were looking for but it was nevertheless a step forward. However, Peres failed to get Shamir to endorse it as government policy.

Pérez de Cuéllar was rightly undeterred, and in mid-June 1987 he sent me off to consult the five state parties in their capitals and Yasir Arafat in Tunis. Aimé accompanied me and we were joined in the field by Knutsson from UNTSO headquarters in Jerusalem. We had a checklist of eight issues relating to participation in a conference, its terms of reference, the manner of its convening and its rules of procedure. The aim was to identify what common ground existed and explore how the remaining differences might be resolved. We talked with Prime Minister Shamir and Foreign Minister Peres in Jerusalem; with King Hussein, Crown Prince Hassan and Prime Minister Zaid ar-Rifa'i in Amman; with Foreign Minister al-Shara' in Damascus; with President Gemayel and Prime Minister al-Hoss in Beirut; with Foreign Minister Esmat Abdel Meguid in Cairo; and with Chairman Arafat in Tunis. This rubbing of shoulders with the great and not-so-good in the Middle East was summarized in a letter which I wrote to my children in June 1987:

> Lunch with the King and his brother in Amman; a disagreeable session with the Syrian Foreign Minister who took the line that the UN's only function was to blame Israel for everything; a moment of blind terror in the Bekaa in Lebanon when the escort arrangements broke down and Aimé and I found ourselves being driven at breakneck speed by a Syrian secret police driver to what I assumed was a rendezvous with kidnappers; deep depression in Beirut where things go from worse to worst but there's always something worster to come; a long evening spent with Arafat at his beachside villa near Tunis.

But all our interlocutors took the Secretary-General's initiative seriously and I began to think that perhaps we had been promoted to a level at which substantive negotiation was possible. I reported to Pérez de Cuéllar in Geneva that there was an important measure of agreement between Jordan, Egypt and Peres but many obstacles to a conference remained, the greatest being Shamir. He was adamantly opposed to the whole concept and, indeed, to any negotiations which would put pressure on Israel to give up any part of the West Bank or the Gaza Strip. Peres was confident that he could precipitate early elections and win them on the peace issue, but few shared his confidence. The second biggest obstacle was Syria; Foreign Minister al-Shara' alone had insisted on 'the' conference detailed in the General Assembly resolutions and had said that the procedural issues should not be discussed until Israel had committed itself to attend the conference. There had been no sign of the flexibility which Pérez de Cuéllar thought Assad had hinted at in Kuwait. Arafat had, however, indicated that there could be room for negotiation on how the Palestinians would be represented and on how the concept of Palestinian rights could be worked into the conference's terms of reference. The Lebanese had focussed only on the problem of southern Lebanon; its solution, they insisted, should come first and not be linked to settlement of the wider question of Palestine. There had been uncertainty in all quarters about the intentions of the two superpowers and about how the United States elections in 1988 would impact on the peace process.

From Geneva I accompanied Pérez de Cuéllar to Moscow. But neither

I nor Diego Cordovez, who was mediating an agreement on the withdrawal of Soviet troops from Afghanistan, was invited to be with him when he met Mikhail Gorbachev. I was subsequently told that Pérez de Cuéllar had emphasized the need for Israeli policy to be clarified, preferably as a result of Peres winning early elections in October, and for a more positive response from Syria. Gorbachev had supported his approach but had been evasive about Syria, saying only that the Russians had recently talked to Assad.

Back in Geneva, Peres came to see Pérez de Cuéllar and spoke about the internal problem in Israel: it would be better for all parties in Israel to adopt a common position on the conference; only if this was impossible would the people have to be asked to decide. He quizzed the Secretary-General at length about Moscow, looking for changes in the Soviet position which would help him convince opinion in Israel that the conference was the right way forward.

The next day, I had a tête-à-tête with the Director-General of the Israeli Foreign Ministry, Avraham Tamir. A former general in the IDF, he had been brought by Peres from the Prime Minister's office when he and Shamir had swapped roles in October 1986. He was short, squat, untidy and quite unmilitary in appearance, with a gravelly voice like Rabin's and eccentric pronunciation of English – 'cooperate' came out as 'copulate'. His purpose was to explain Peres' remark to Pérez de Cuéllar about the desirability of a common position in Israel on the conference. What Peres had meant was that it would be better if Labour and Likud could agree on the *launching* of the conference; he had no illusions about their agreeing on its *outcome*; peace could be achieved only after a major split in Israel and in the PLO. I told Tamir about my most recent conversation with Arafat. He smiled ruefully and said: 'The trouble is that he is right in much of what he says.' Israel would have to talk to the PLO one day. Future historians would 'laugh and cry' at the fact that Israel's refusal for so long to talk to the PLO had blocked the possibility of an Israel–Palestine confederation, which was the only sensible solution.

Tamir also wanted me to draw Pérez de Cuéllar's attention to the warmth of Peres' remarks the previous day about the UN. This had been a signal that Peres had been persuaded (by Tamir) that the UN was the most valuable 'instrument' currently available. Having directly experienced the contempt with which most Israelis regarded the UN, I wondered what this remark suggested about the realism of Peres' policy. Were we not being naive in hoping that Peres and Tamir could change Israeli policy over Lebanon and Palestine? For they could deliver only if either their Likud partners agreed or they could beat Likud in an early election. Likud, I was sure, would not agree; and Peres' conversation with Pérez de Cuéllar had shown that, as Tamir himself complained, he was not getting any election-winning cards from the other players in the game, including Moscow and Washington.

Pérez de Cuéllar nevertheless sent me off immediately on another circuit of the capitals. In Amman there had been recent contact with the PLO but Arafat had yet to prove that he accepted the conditions necessary for Jordan to resume cooperation with him (endorsement of SCRs 242 and 338, non-specific language about Palestinian rights in the conference's terms of reference, a joint Jordanian-Palestinian delegation).* In Damascus I had a sour meeting with Vice-President Khaddam. He did not question the legitimacy of the Secretary-General's consultations. But he accused me of making unacceptable assumptions about possible changes in Syria's position, which remained as it was when al-Shara' had explained it the previous month (had he, I wondered, been briefed by the Russians about the conversations in Moscow?); he rejected Egyptian participation in the conference; and he thought that Peres would fail to get an early election in Israel and that if he did he would lose it. In Jerusalem Peres had little new to say but expressed optimism about an improvement in Israel's relations with Moscow. Tamir, on the other hand, was depressed, angry with everyone (especially Khaddam) and uncertain whether Peres would get early elections. He did not. Khaddam had been right – and was proved right again in November 1988 when elections did take place. Both main parties lost seats in a contest dominated by the *intifāda* but Labour lost more than Likud and had to accept that in the new government of national unity Shamir would be Prime Minister without rotation and that another Likud member, Moshe Arens, would be Foreign Minister.

The next development was, for me, a painful one. On a Saturday morning in September 1987, I saw the Secretary-General's limousine parked outside the Regency Hotel, next to the apartment building where we lived. I asked the driver, jocularly, whether Pérez de Cuéllar had come to call on me. 'No,' he said, 'we are here to have lunch with the Foreign Minister of Israel.' I had not been asked to provide briefing nor even been told that the meeting was to take place. This was hurtful when, for four months, I had been shuttling round the Levant on the Secretary-General's behalf. I called Dayal, the Secretary-General's Chef de Cabinet. He said that the meeting was news to him; he assumed it must have been arranged by Giandomenico Picco.

---

* SCR 242 was adopted after the Arab-Israeli war of June 1967. It enshrined the principle of 'land for peace', that is Israeli withdrawal from Arab territories occupied in 1967 in return for acceptance of Israel by its Arab neighbours, on which all subsequent peacemaking efforts have been based. SCR 338, adopted during the Arab-Israeli war of October 1973, called for a cease-fire and, immediately thereafter, the implementation of SCR 242 in all its parts.

Picco, an Italian, was later to earn well-deserved praise for the skill and courage with which he brought about the release of most of the Western hostages in Lebanon. He had joined the Secretariat in 1973 and was sent by Urquhart to be Pérez de Cuéllar's assistant when the latter was the Secretary-General's Special Representative in Cyprus. He won Pérez de Cuéllar's confidence there and when Pérez de Cuéllar became Secretary-General in 1982 he brought Picco into his office as 'Assistant for Special Assignments'. In that role he had mainly been assigned to work with Diego Cordovez, in whom Pérez de Cuéllar had somewhat less confidence, on Afghanistan and the Iran–Iraq war. Picco's interest in the Arab-Israeli conflict and Cyprus had occasionally caused our paths to cross, though never before in so disagreeable a manner.

I asked Dayal to arrange for me to see the Secretary-General as soon as possible. Pérez de Cuéllar does not normally like confrontation but on this occasion he went on the offensive: it was for him, and him alone, he said, to decide whom, if anyone, he took with him to meetings; he did not accept that I had a valid complaint. I said that I did not dispute his right to use his staff as he saw fit, though it obviously boosted our credibility with our interlocutors if we took part in high-level meetings and were seen to enjoy his trust. What really irked me was the subsequent discovery that instructions had been issued in his office that I and my staff were not to be informed of the meeting with Peres. This had denied me the opportunity to offer him advice before the meeting. More seriously, it suggested that he did not trust me. He remained unrepentant and the brief meeting ended without any explanation of why I had been excluded and without any move by either party to start mending the rift that had been created between us.

Picco subsequently gave me a brief account of what Peres had said about an international conference. He had confirmed that he had met Hussein in London and gave optimistic accounts of his recent contacts with the Americans, Russians and Chinese. But when Pérez de Cuéllar asked about the domestic scene in Israel, Peres admitted that the reality was that he and Shamir were as firmly stuck together as Adam and Eve.

In the following months the odds against a conference lengthened. In December 1987 I took advantage of another UNIFIL-related tour around the region to resume consultations, but the results were bleak. Peres had made no political progress in Israel. The Americans were losing what little interest they had ever had in a conference and had floated the alternative idea of a meeting between Shamir and Hussein under superpower auspices, an idea that was predictably rejected by Hussein. At a summit in Amman in November, the Arabs had been distracted from Palestine by their growing fears of an Iranian victory over Iraq in the war that Saddam had started seven years before. The hardliners on both sides reverted to their earlier intransigence, insofar as they had ever departed from it. In December Farouq Qaddumi, the cantankerous 'Foreign Minister' of the PLO, managed to insert into the General Assembly's annual resolution on Palestine a coded reprimand of Pérez de Cuéllar for departing from 'the' conference outlined by the Assembly in 1983.* Shamir was revelling in the Arabs' differences; for him the threat had passed.

However, it was by now evident that the kaleidoscope was being shaken by a new event – the Palestinian uprising or *intifāda* – which would give a new impetus to the search for a settlement of the Palestine question.

The diplomatic stalemate aroused international interest in what was actually happening in the Occupied Palestinian Territories – the West Bank ('Judaea and Samaria' to Israelis) and the Gaza Strip. Already in mid-1986 the Egyptian Foreign Minister had told me that the situation there was 'intolerable', and Peres, then still Prime Minister of Israel, had described the Territories' economy as the over-riding problem. It was true that economic conditions were dreadful, but this was not the problem. What was about to make it impossible for Israel to govern the Territories without violating human rights was its refusal to respect the international norms for the administration of territory occupied in war. Again a life-and-death political issue was clothed in semantics. The United Nations and most countries described the West Bank and the Gaza Strip as 'the Occupied Territories' and took the view that as such they were governed by the Fourth Geneva Convention and its provisions regulating the conduct of occupying powers. Israel, on the other hand, described the territories as the 'Administered Territories', precisely to avoid their being subject to the provisions of the Convention. On this basis, Israel justified a number of practices prohibited by it, such as inhumane treatment, 'physical coercion' to obtain information, deportation, reprisals through collective punishment and the destruction of property, annexation of territory, compulsory acquisition of land to build settlements for citizens of the occupying power and detention without trial. The arrogant and sometimes brutal nature of Israeli rule, combined with the squalor, unemployment and poverty of the refugee camps and the improbability of an early political solution, had produced an explosive situation.

Israelis were aware of how bad things were in the Territories. About

---

* I always felt that Qaddumi's manner did the PLO more harm than good and have since learnt that a prominent British champion of Palestine once said to him: 'I have defended the Palestinian cause for thirty years and do not intend to be discouraged by you from continuing to do so.'

215,000 Jewish settlers lived there, of whom 120,000 were in occupied East Jerusalem; and 60,000 Arab labourers were bussed from Gaza alone into Israel each morning and bussed out again each evening. But most Israelis were less concerned about the plight of the Palestinians than about their birth rate, which in 1984 was 3.1 per cent per annum in the Gaza Strip and 2.4 per cent in the West Bank.* Many concluded that retention of the Territories, whether by annexation (as Likud advocated) or by continued occupation, would confront Israel with two unacceptable alternatives. One would be a democratic binational state in which, as in Israel itself, Jews and Arabs would enjoy the same civic rights. In that case, even with optimistic assumptions about future immigration from the Soviet Union, the Arabs would outnumber the Jews by the end of the first quarter of the twenty-first century; in what sense would Israel then be 'a national home for the Jews'? The second alternative would be a state whose Arab citizens had lesser rights than its Jewish ones; this would produce a Near Eastern replica of apartheid and would expose Israel to the same international opprobrium as the apartheid regime in South Africa. A third and even less acceptable alternative, advocated by extremists like Meir Kahane, was to annex the Territories and expel all their Arab inhabitants. This bleak range of options led many Israelis to conclude reluctantly that the least bad course was to seek a negotiated settlement based on the principle of 'land for peace'.

The breakdown in February 1986 of Hussein's brief agreement with Arafat increased the feeling in the Territories that their plight had been eclipsed by the Arab rulers' fear of an Iranian victory in the Iran–Iraq war. Tension grew when it became evident that Hussein's policy was now to 'Jordanize' the West Bank, and even Gaza, with the undisguised support of Israel and the United States. 'Jordanization' took the form of an ambitious development plan, financial support for pro-Jordanian media in the Territories, the issue of Jordanian passports to stateless people in the Gaza Strip and a declared policy of strengthening links between the two banks of the Jordan. It was accompanied by the closure of all Arafat's offices in Jordan and the expulsion of his leading lieutenant, Abu Jihad. This reopened the wounds of 'Black' September 1970, when the Jordanian Army had forcibly expelled the PLO from Jordan. The pro-Jordanian Mayor of Nablus on the West Bank was assassinated.

The growing hopelessness in the Territories changed the way in which the inhabitants resisted the Israeli occupation. Most of the organized

---

* Rabin once told me that he had commissioned a study on the future of the Gaza Strip. It estimated that the population would rise from 650,000 in 1986 to one million by the year 2000, a forecast so horrifying that he decided to keep the study secret. In the event, a Palestinian census in 1997 found that the population was already 1,022,000.

resistance had been liquidated. What the Israelis now faced was mostly random, uncoordinated stone-throwing and provocation by small groups of youths, the *shabāb*. The IDF often reacted with disproportionate force, 'martyrs' fell, the wounded were displayed to the media as they were rushed to hospital and the population came on to the streets in protest. Control of the resulting disorder required a restraint and professionalism unknown to the Israeli conscripts whose unhappy lot it was to maintain order in the Territories.

Incidents increased during the autumn of 1987. The *intifāda* is considered, however, to have begun on 9 December in Gaza when an Israeli settler killed four Arabs in a traffic accident. Violence quickly spread to the West Bank. Rabin recognized the inadequacy of the conscripts and brought in more seasoned units. But his orders to them were 'to break bones' and their combative violence fuelled yet more dissent, including violent demonstrations by Israel's own Arab citizens. On 22 December Security Council resolution 605 'strongly deplored' policies and practices of Israel which violated the Palestinians' human rights, reaffirmed the applicability of the Geneva Convention and asked the Secretary-General to report on ways and means of protecting the Palestinian civilians under Israeli occupation. Pérez de Cuéllar instructed me to undertake a fact-finding mission to the Territories and draft the report which he had to submit to the Council by 20 January 1988.

I arrived in Israel on 8 January, accompanied by Lisa Buttenheim, who had just joined OSPA from UNTSO. Thirty-four Palestinians had been killed and over 250 wounded during the first month of the *intifāda*, almost all of them at the hands of the Israeli security forces. More than two thousand had been arrested. There had been no fatal casualties on the Israeli side but about sixty soldiers and forty settlers had been injured, mainly by stone-throwing. Seven of the eight refugee camps in the Gaza Strip, and four of the nineteen in the West Bank, were under curfew or had been designated as closed military areas. As a result, tens of thousands of Arabs in the Territories were no longer able to commute to their daily jobs in Israel. The coalition government, and even the Labour Party component in that government, were divided on whether more repressive measures should be taken or restrictions relaxed and efforts made to ease the economic plight of the Palestinians.

As regards my mission, Pérez de Cuéllar had difficulty in getting the Israeli Government to let me come at all. Eventually they agreed, on the understanding that they would receive me as an official who made frequent visits to Israel on behalf of the Secretary-General but that they would not accept any link between my visit and the report requested of him by SCR 605. However, Shamir had already announced that he would not receive me; it would be left to Foreign Minister Peres to repeat to me that the government rejected SCR 605 because Israel was exclusively responsible for security in the Territories and the Security Council had no role to play there.

Normally I stayed in the American Colony Hotel in Arab East Jerusalem. Its fine buildings of the Ottoman era convey a feeling of history which is lacking in the modern hotels in Jewish West Jerusalem. But many Israelis view it as a hotbed of Palestinian nationalism and on this occasion, therefore, it seemed politic to stay at the Hilton in the West. I had to wait for two days before I could see Peres, a necessary preliminary to visiting the Territories. After restating the basis on which the government had agreed to my coming, he acknowledged that the situation in the Territories was a serious one. The IDF had been surprised by the scale of the disturbances and lacked expertise in riot control. The casualties were regretted and steps were being taken to minimize them. But the present disorder could not be tolerated and firm measures would, if necessary, be used to suppress it. Meanwhile I was free to travel where I wished, except for places which were under curfew or had been designated as closed military areas. Peres was evasive when I asked which of the refugee camps had already been so designated.

Pérez de Cuéllar had told me to visit some camps. My mission would lose all credibility if we did not at least attempt to do so. So we decided to try next morning in Gaza. Journalists told us that the IDF were close to losing control of some of the camps; they distrusted the United Nations and would not want a UN visit to add to their problems. We had hoped that we could evade the media; the fewer the cameras, the better the chance of being admitted to a camp. But they were waiting for us outside the hotel and we left for Gaza with a comet's tail of journalists and cameramen in our wake. We crossed the line between Israel and Gaza without trouble, met up with UNRWA's Acting Director for Gaza, Angela Williams, and drove on to Jabālia, the largest camp in the Strip.* At the entrance an IDF lieutenant told us that the camp had just been designated a closed military area; he could not let us in. Williams began to argue, pressing for something in writing. I returned to the car, keeping myself in reserve in case a heavier gun was required. The cameramen filmed me through the car window. I tried to look calm but stern, wondering how these pictures would be received in New York.

The lieutenant remained adamant. Could we visit the nearby Shāti camp? No; that one was under curfew. Admitting defeat, we withdrew.

---

* UNRWA, the UN Relief and Works Agency for Palestine Refugees in the Near East, was established in 1949 to bring relief to the Palestinians displaced by the Arab-Israeli conflict. It provides relief, education, health care and other social services to registered refugees in the Occupied Palestinian Territories, Jordan, Lebanon and Syria.

Williams suggested that we go to a smaller camp, Maghāzi. Her walkie-talkie told her that it was the only camp in the Strip that had not been declared under curfew or a closed military area. This turned out to be true. The IDF were deployed in strength at the entrance but they let us through. Once inside, however, we found our way blocked by burning tyres, a favoured tactic for hampering the IDF. The local *shabāb* advised us not to proceed because the situation in the camp was very tense. We drove back to Tel Aviv, where I had already arranged to see Rabin. On the way, we heard on the radio that the IDF spokesman was saying that my presence at Jabālia had provoked a riot and that this had obliged the IDF to close the area; at another camp, he said, the residents themselves had asked me to go away.

The meeting with Rabin began in the presence of the media. They variously described it as 'tense' and 'icy'. I was glad they were there because this enabled me to deny on screen that I had caused a riot. After they had left, Rabin repeated what Peres had told me the day before. Back in Jerusalem I received confirmation from New York that I should continue to insist on access to the camps. Our tactics clearly had to be refined, so we staged some bogus phone conversations to lead eavesdroppers to conclude that our plan was to go to the West Bank the next day.

Instead, we left Jerusalem before dawn and headed south-westwards on minor roads towards Gaza. When the dawn came, damp and grey, we found to our delight that we had almost no media in attendance. At the Gaza checkpoint Williams advised us to go to Rafah Camp, at the far west end of the Strip, where a Palestinian youth had been killed by the IDF the day before. We drove into the camp without hindrance, parked the cars and walked towards the UNRWA health centre along the open sewer that is Rafah's main street. Hundreds of people emerged from the rows of little houses – happy people, the women ululating. There was not an Israeli in sight. An old man grabbed me by the scruff of the neck and kissed me on both cheeks. We reached the health centre and set up shop in the director's office.

Hundreds wanted to tell us their tales. Our UNRWA colleagues tried to establish some order: form a line; choose individuals to speak for all the young men who have been beaten, for all the families of the missing, for all the merchants whose shops have been sealed; let the people from '*al-hai'a*' (i.e. the UN) tell you their news. But it was to no avail. More and more people gathered outside, shouting louder and louder; the prefab began to shudder and sway under the pressure of the hands – angry hands now, no longer clapping a welcome – of those who wanted to force their way into our tiny meeting room.

Then there was another sound – gunfire. I feared the worst, not yet knowing how to distinguish between the sound of live ammunition, rubber bullets and tear gas rounds. Fortunately it was not live rounds this time. An IDF patrol had approached the health centre; the *shabāb* had thrown stones; the IDF had responded with rubber bullets and tear gas – standard operating procedures on both sides. Soon a few injured people forced their way into the room, not seriously injured but with enough blood flowing to gain them access. The pandemonium intensified. The three UN people in the room – Williams, Buttenheim and I – discussed nervously how we were going to make our exit.

Another UNRWA official came in and said the only way to restore calm was for me to go out and address the crowd. I was uneasy: the place was by now surrounded by the IDF, the crowd was almost hysterical, a speech could cause a riot and lives might be lost. Williams suggested that we should negotiate a deal with the *shabāb*. I would make a speech outside; they would undertake to maintain order and to escort us out of the camp as soon as I had spoken. I agreed. Two *shabāb* were brought in and the deal was quickly struck, so quickly that I wondered whether they were serious about it.

Out we went. The crowd fell silent. A few IDF soldiers watched from the rooftops. I decided to speak through an interpreter. My Arabic was no longer good enough for a speech that would have to strike so delicate a balance; the Palestinians must be comforted and given some grounds for hope, but not in terms that would enable the Israelis to accuse the UN of inciting civil disorder. So I told them that in New York the world was aware of their plight; I had come to get up-to-date information for the Secretary-General; I had urged the Israelis to respect the Fourth Geneva Convention; I praised the Palestinians' *sumūd*, their steadfastness; I urged them not to respond to violence with violence; the only just solution would be a negotiated one. They listened with silent respect; but they were finding no comfort in my words.

True to the deal, the *shabāb* then formed a ring around us and guided us through the cameramen, who had caught up with us, and the now sullen crowd. A little boy pressed a Palestinian flag into Buttenheim's hand. I said, 'Careful; the TV's watching.' She responded with a beatific smile. It was broadcast worldwide. Her mother later said that it had reassured her to know that her daughter had such trust in her colleague on what seemed a dangerous mission. Some of my more ribald friends arrived at a less proper conclusion; but they were wrong.

As we got into our cars, another IDF platoon marched into the camp. 'Here comes the f—ing IDF,' said Buttenheim. I shared the sentiment but hoped it had not been picked up by the ubiquitous boom microphones; even in a situation like this the peacemaker must look and sound neutral. The crowd's discipline broke: some pressed against the car windows to show us new wounds; others banged the roof with fists and stones; one man climbed on top and was only dislodged when the driver, close to panic, accelerated out of the camp. We sped down the road to much-needed calm and refreshment at the UN's 'Gaza Beach Club' – exhilarated, frightened, sad and, later over dinner in Jerusalem, almost hysterical in our recounting of the day's events. Meanwhile the Israelis deported four Palestinian leaders to Lebanon, in defiance of the Geneva Convention, a Security Council resolution and appeals, even from Washington, against such expulsions.

The next day we visited a refugee camp at Dheisheh in the West Bank. Though smaller than Rafah it too had had its riots and casualties, for it lies beside a main road and had provided a grandstand for stoning IDF and settler vehicles, until the IDF built a wire fence higher than even the strongest young arm could throw. This time we avoided the mistake of going into a building from which it might become difficult to make an exit. Instead we walked the streets of the camp and talked to many refugees. The visit was calm and without incident. I returned to Jerusalem to convey to Peres the anger created in New York by Israel's action in deporting the four Palestinians at a time when the Security Council was trying to find ways of easing the tension and an emissary of the Secretary-General was in the Territories. Peres was unrepentant. Like all the Israeli officials we talked to he dismissed as malicious exaggerations what we had been told about the behaviour of the occupying power, even when we had ourselves witnessed violations of the Geneva Convention.

Two days later we made another 'dawn raid', this time accompanied by Rolf Knutsson, the senior civilian in UNTSO, and Bernard Mills, the Director of UNRWA's operations on the West Bank. The target was Balata, a large refugee camp on the outskirts of the city of Nablus. Again we left Jerusalem before dawn, avoided the media and got into the camp without problems. We spent an hour visiting a house that had been blown up by the IDF and another in which several rooms had been sealed off, in both cases because a son of the family was alleged to be a 'terrorist'. Some individuals told us of their suffering at the hands of *al-ihtilāl* (the occupation), others declared their support for the PLO, others demanded more effective action by the UN. But the crowd grew and I began to fear another Rafah. Gunfire was heard a few blocks away; 'rubber bullets', said Mills. Knutsson whispered, nodding nervously towards the accompanying *shabāb*: 'Have you seen what they've got in their hands?' I had: stones. The IDF patrol came round the corner; most of the crowd melted into the alleys; the *shabāb* did not, thank God, throw their stones. The IDF looked at us, perhaps 75 metres away. As we turned to withdraw, they sent us on our way with a few rubber bullets. Some of us ran. Mindful of what I had been taught at a defiantly imperialist prep school in England forty years before, I attempted a dignified exit, with measured pace and shoulders set to convey contempt for those who were taunting us with their rubber bullets. As we got back to the cars, more gunfire was heard. I looked at Mills. 'Live rounds, I fear', was his reply.

This visit lasted eight days and received much attention from the media, for the *intifāda* was still headline news. Friends from all over the world cut from their local newspapers the photograph of the old man's embrace in Rafah and forwarded it to me with mocking or admiring commentary. My father advised me to remind Shamir of Isaiah 26, verses 5–6:

> For [Jehovah] bringeth down them that dwell on high; the lofty city, he layeth it low; he layeth it low, even to the ground; he bringeth it even to the dust. The foot shall tread it down, even the feet of the poor, and the steps of the needy.

My sister wondered, rightly, how a generation reared in the camps with no experience of life outside them could be expected to be amenable to reason. My mother-in-law, who had lived in Jerusalem as an RAF wife in the 1930s, wrote of her concern at seeing me on television 'harassed by a crowd of rather dubious characters'. When I got back to New York on 18 January, I found that I was a local hero in the Secretariat.

Buttenheim and I did the first draft of the Secretary-General's report on the flight back to New York. Pérez de Cuéllar, supported by Dayal and Aimé, thought it was too critical of Israel. I was unhappy about this at the time; after a week's exposure to the realities in the Territories, I was convinced that criticism was justified. Before leaving for New York, I had given a critical interview to the *Jerusalem Post* which, to that paper's credit, was fully and fairly reported. I described the mutual hatred that I had seen in the eyes of the *shabāb* and the young Israeli soldiers; what did this imply for the future of Israel? Could Israel, as a democratic society, tolerate indefinitely the routine use of armed force to suppress unarmed demonstrators? I rejected the government's contention that it was applying *de facto* the humanitarian provisions of the Geneva Convention and I listed the ways in which Israel was daily violating those provisions. How widely was this known by Israelis, I asked. My indignation was justified by what I had seen. But Pérez de Cuéllar was right to insist that his report be less passionate. He also rejected, wisely I now see, a naive proposal for early municipal elections in the Territories.

But Pérez de Cuéllar retained the points that were of most importance to me. As Israeli ministers now admitted, he told the Security Council, the *intifāda* was a spontaneous outburst, supported by Palestinians of all ages and walks of life. It was an expression of protest at twenty years of occupation and despair of its ever ending. The report listed the complaints most generally heard, with specific examples: the harshness, violence, arrogance and inhumanity of the security forces; their classification of any expression of nationalist sentiment as 'terrorist' activity; the seizure of land for the building of Jewish settlements; deportations; the closing of schools and universities; the unfairness of the judicial system; heavy taxation; and economic discrimination against the Territories. The Israeli authorities' rejection of these complaints was also reported. But Pérez de Cuéllar's conclusion was that 'the international community's concern about the situation in the occupied territories is fully justified'.

The report went on to examine the question of how to ensure the safety and protection of the Palestinians. The only way, said Pérez de Cuéllar, of ensuring this was the negotiation of a political settlement which would end the occupation. Meanwhile Israel must respect its obligations under the Geneva Convention; its arguments that that Convention did not apply were without foundation. He recommended that all parties to the Convention which had diplomatic relations with Israel should make a solemn appeal to Israel to apply the Convention in the Territories.

The report then analysed the issue of 'protection' raised by the Council's resolution. There were four possibilities. The first was 'physical protection' provided by armed forces. Some Palestinians had pressed for UN forces to be deployed for this purpose. But the Geneva Convention placed this responsibility on the occupying power; UN forces would anyway not be accepted by Israel. The second possibility was 'legal protection'. This was already being provided by the ICRC, in accordance with its mandate, albeit subject to some restrictions imposed by Israel.

The third form of protection was what Buttenheim and I had decided to call 'general assistance', meaning intervention by an outside agency to help people resist violations of their rights and cope with the day-to-day difficulties of life under occupation. This form of protection, the report said, had traditionally been provided by UNRWA to the 820,000 registered refugees, who accounted for about 55 per cent of the Palestinian population in the Territories. But UNRWA's current ability to provide it was constrained by the paucity of its international staff, whose number had fallen to only fifteen. In the new security situation, international staff were better able than Palestinian staff to provide this form of protection. Pérez de Cuéllar had therefore asked the Commissioner-General of UNRWA to recruit additional international staff for this purpose and, in exceptional circumstances, to provide general assistance to the 680,000 Palestinians who were not registered refugees. The fourth form of protection was protection by publicity. The report welcomed the attention recently paid to the Territories by the international media.

In conclusion, Pérez de Cuéllar stressed his recommendation for a concerted international effort to persuade Israel to apply the Fourth

Geneva Convention and returned to his point about the need for the negotiation of a comprehensive settlement, based on SCRs 242 and 338, at an international conference. He recognized that this would be exceptionally difficult. But 'each side must put aside the often justified resentment it feels at past wrongs and understand better the legitimate interests and legitimate grievances of the other. Such understanding is not assisted by invective and abuse nor by sheltering behind the illusion that the other side does not exist.' Anyone who has been involved in peacemaking will recognize the wisdom of that observation but will also remember how extraordinarily difficult it is to get two hostile parties to act on it, even if they have both committed themselves to negotiate a peaceful settlement of their conflict.

As the Secretariat finalized the report, the PLO delegation in New York pressed us to say that the vast majority of the Palestinians we had met had declared their support for the PLO as the 'sole legitimate representative of the Palestinian people'. We had a very good reason for not doing this. Before leaving for the Territories, I had been aware that Hussein's attempts to 'Jordanize' them had been less than enthusiastically received by the Palestinians. What I had not known was that there was also growing disenchantment with the PLO. Many of our interlocutors had expressed their support for it; but many had also hinted at, and sometimes expressly stated, the feeling that Arafat and his colleagues living in comfort in Tunisia were out of touch with the suffering endured by their compatriots in the Territories; the latter had decided to take action themselves to make the world aware of their refusal to accept the continuing occupation. It would thus have been dishonest for us to say what the PLO delegation wanted us to say – and would have infuriated the Israelis and the Americans.

The Security Council debated the Secretary-General's report at five consecutive meetings. The report received much praise, though many Arab and Islamic delegations had hoped, unrealistically, for strong measures to curb Israeli excesses in the Territories. The protagonists said nothing unexpected. Israel maintained that, faced with an attempt by the Arab rejectionists to create anarchy, it was applying *de facto* the humanitarian provisions of the Fourth Geneva Convention and was cooperating with the ICRC in the Territories but would not accept that it had a *de jure* obligation to apply those provisions. The PLO denounced the Israeli occupation, which must be ended if there was to be a peaceful settlement. In the meantime ways of protecting the civilian population in the Territories were being sought but the mere presence of the UN had a symbolic value. The Council must respond to the tragic situation by acting in accordance with the General Assembly resolutions.

The Non-Aligned members of the Council tabled a draft resolution which endorsed the modest recommendations in the Secretary-General's report in terms that were extraordinarily mild by the standards of their previous pronouncements on Palestine (there was no 'condemn' or 'deplore', not even a 'regret'). It won fourteen votes in favour but the United States vetoed, on the grounds that the resolution could detract from ongoing diplomatic negotiations to resolve the conflict and that by implication it attempted to impose terms upon the parties, which the Council could not do. This was a big disappointment. But my mission had heightened awareness of what was happening in the Territories and it had one practical result which turned out to be of great value. The US veto did not stop UNRWA from responding to the Secretary-General's request that it recruit additional international staff as refugee affairs officers who would provide protection of the 'general assistance' kind. Within two years their number would be quadrupled and it is now recognized that their discreet interventions have done much to protect the refugees from a still harsh occupation regime.

Immediately after the Security Council proceedings Buttenheim and I left for another circuit. It was not productive. It coincided with news that the American Secretary of State George Shultz was about to visit the region with new US ideas for an international conference. This considerably reduced my interlocutors' interest in what the UN had to say. In any case, I had to turn to other matters when Lieutenant-Colonel 'Rich' Higgins, the American commander of UNTSO's Observer Group Lebanon, was kidnapped near Tyre on 17 February. Shultz's ideas were rejected by Syria and the PLO, and Shamir maintained his implacable opposition to a conference. In April 1988 the Non-Aligned members tried again to get the Security Council to adopt a resolution on the Territories. Their draft remained moderate by their standards but this time it did 'condemn' Israel's violation of human rights. It still won fourteen positive votes, but the US vetoed again. In July 1988, Buttenheim and I made what was to be my final circuit on this course, as an extension to my six-monthly visit to UNIFIL. But by then the impending elections in both Israel and the United States made it even less likely that progress could be made. By the time that those elections had taken place, I no longer had responsibility for peacemaking in the Middle East and became only a spectator of the continuing tragedy in Palestine.

7

Hostages

Hostages were a dominant issue in the Middle East during the first four years of my service with the United Nations. After the Iranian Revolution in 1979, the second invasion of Lebanon by Israel in 1982 and the failed Western intervention in that country the following year, Hizbullah and various other Lebanese Shi'ite factions, most of them enjoying some degree of support from Tehran, began taking Western hostages in Beirut.

Their motives for doing so were not, and still are not, entirely clear. If their purpose was to draw attention to the plight of the Shi'ites of Lebanon (the 'deprived', as they called themselves), they certainly attracted attention world-wide. But they had little success in spreading understanding of their cause or of why people and governments in the West should support it. On the contrary, they gave Israel and its friends ample material with which to denigrate 'Arabs' and 'Islamic extremists' in general. It was probably realization of this that caused Iran in the late eighties to withdraw its support for hostage-taking and thus made it possible for Pérez de Cuéllar, assisted by Gianni Picco, to negotiate the release of most of the hostages taken by the Shi'ite groups.

It needs to be remembered, however, that those groups were not the only hostage-takers in Lebanon nor were Westerners the only hostages taken. Indeed, only one of the four United Nations victims of kidnapping was taken by a Shi'ite group; the other three were taken by Palestinians. Iranian diplomats were seized by Lebanese Christian groups in 1982 and have never been accounted for. Israel itself took Lebanese hostages as chips to be used in bargaining for the release of Israeli servicemen captured in Lebanon. At the time of writing, the most prominent of Israel's hostages, Shaikh Abdul Karim Obeid, a Shi'ite cleric seized from his home in Lebanon in 1989, and Mustafa Dirani, the former security chief of Amal who was kidnapped in 1994, are still imprisoned in Israel, notwithstanding the ending in 2000 of that country's twenty-two-year occupation of southern Lebanon.

The first UN person to be kidnapped was a British journalist employed by UNRWA, Alec Collett. He was seized near Beirut in March 1985 by a group calling itself the 'Revolutionary Organization of Socialist Muslims'. This group, a front organization for the Palestinian terrorist Abu Nidal, had claimed responsibility three years before for the failed attempt to assassinate the Israeli ambassador in London, an outrage which provided the pretext for Israel's invasion of Lebanon three days later. The three assassins had been sentenced to long prison terms in Britain and their group proposed that they be exchanged for Collett. This was rejected by the British and in April 1986 the kidnappers announced that they had hanged Collett. They produced a brief videotape to prove that they had done so but this was not accepted by the UN as conclusive and the case remained open. I regularly asked Yasir Arafat to use his influence to get Collett released or his death confirmed. I knew that Arafat had no influence with Abu Nidal, for they were sworn enemies; but I hoped that he might work on Abu Nidal's protector, Mu'ammar Qadhafi, the Libyan head of state. Arafat equally regularly said that he would see what he could do but never produced any result.

I made similar approaches to Arafat when two Scandinavian employees of UNRWA were briefly kidnapped in Sidon in February 1988 just before Lisa Buttenheim and I were to visit the Levant and Tunis for another round of consultations about an international conference on Palestine. It turned out that the kidnapping was due to dissatisfaction with the services UNRWA was providing to the refugees in Sidon. Arafat was able to secure the two hostages' early release.

From time to time, the Israelis sought our help in their efforts to recover the remains of various Israeli military personnel who had been, or might have been, killed in Lebanon. These included three soldiers who had gone missing in action against the Syrians in the Beqa'a valley in 1982 and whose families clung to the hope that they might still be alive. I pressed the Syrians for information about their fate but invariably received the reply that Syria had no information. There were also two soldiers believed to have been captured by Hizbullah in the south of Lebanon in 1986. For several months in 1989 one of the Lebanese faction leaders claimed to have their remains and personal belongings and expressed interest in negotiating a deal, which would include access by the International Red Cross to the South Lebanon Army's prison camp at Khiam. We put him in touch with those who might be ready to facilitate such a transaction and I told Rabin that we had done so. But it was not until 1996 that their remains were recovered. Israel also sought United Nations help in discovering the fate of an Israeli air force officer, Ron Arad, who fell into the hands of Mustafa Dirani, at that time Amal's chief of security, when his aircraft was shot down over Lebanon in 1986. But a series of contacts with Dirani produced no information.

The one case in which I myself was deeply involved was the kidnapping on 17 February 1988 of Lieutenant-Colonel William 'Rich' Higgins, US Marine Corps, a member of UNTSO who was attached to UNIFIL as Chief of Observer Group Lebanon (OGL). This group's mandate dated back to the Armistice Agreement of 1949 and its military observers still manned five observation posts along the international border. For these historical reasons they had greater freedom of movement than UNIFIL itself in Israel's security zone and they liaised with various Lebanese factions on UNIFIL's behalf. They moved in dangerous places; an Australian officer had been killed by a mine blast a few weeks before Higgins was kidnapped. Higgins himself was seized when alone in his jeep on the main road to Naqoura from Tyre. He was driving behind another UN vehicle containing two OGL colleagues but had declined the offer of an escort to ride in his own vehicle. In heavy rain contact was briefly lost between the two vehicles. A UNIFIL truck came on Higgins' vehicle, its engine still running, just as another vehicle, assumed to be that of the kidnappers, drove off at high speed towards Tyre.

The news reached me in Damascus. I left the next day for Beirut and Naqoura. There were few clues. Hizbullah was assumed to be the culprit because it was the faction most hostile to the United States and least enthusiastic about UNIFIL. But there had been no statement. The two UNRWA Scandinavians had been abducted in Sidon twelve days before, one of them a former Swedish military observer in UNTSO. Was there a connection between the two incidents?

In Naqoura I had a meeting with all the members of Observer Group Lebanon. I asked them how they now felt about doing their duties unarmed, as had been UNTSO's practice from the beginning. To my surprise all but one wanted to carry on as before; a side arm, they said, would provide little protection against the weapons that abounded in the area; being unarmed differentiated them from UNIFIL and was probably the best protection they had. Although none volunteered any new information at the meeting, two or three came individually to talk to me afterwards.

Their message was that Higgins had 'asked for it'. He had made no secret of his previous service in the office of the US Secretary of Defense, including working with Colonel Oliver North, or of his wish to establish contact with Hizbullah and visit their strongholds; he had taken risks (such as driving alone in his jeep, which was contrary to OGL's security regulations); he had conveyed the impression that he had his own agenda, or perhaps his government's; and he had ignored advice that it was imprudent to attract attention in this way. I did not enjoy these remarks. They seemed out of place when Higgins was now in such peril; and knowing what little I did about Hizbullah, I was sure there must be some more substantial *raison d'état* behind the kidnapping, the *état* being, of course, Iran. But I had to confess (to myself only) that when Higgins called on me a year before in New York he had conveyed the same impression as his OGL comrades were now describing.

In the days following the kidnapping, the Amal leadership assured Gustav Hägglund, the UNIFIL commander, that they would soon negotiate Higgins' release. Meanwhile, UNIFIL and OGL received a flood of contradictory tips about his whereabouts and the identity of his kidnappers. UNIFIL established additional checkpoints on the roads and, with Amal's help, searched the villages and hills where Higgins had allegedly been seen. The key figure in UNIFIL was Timur Goksel who had been the force's press officer for eleven years and had gained an unmatched understanding of southern Lebanon and its violent politics. He warned us against believing any of the tips; they were likely to be disinformation or naive attempts to curry favour. He was also wary of the assumption that Hizbullah was responsible. It did not fit the facts. Higgins had been taken on a road which was supposedly controlled tightly by Amal; could Hizbullah have done such a neat job there? Hizbullah was Amal's archrival; why then were our Amal contacts so confident about his early release?

UNIFIL came to the conclusion that the kidnapping was probably the work of autonomous cells within Hizbullah who had been involved in the earlier taking of Westerners and were now receiving local help from former Amal personnel. The latter had become disaffected within Amal because they believed that the Israelis should be driven from Lebanon by armed resistance and not by negotiation, which was the option preferred by Berri and Daoud Daoud, the Amal chief in Tyre. As a result, the dissidents were frustrated by mainstream Amal's military inactivity and distrusted Berri's and Daoud's close relations with the United Nations. They were in the process of switching their allegiance from Amal to Hizbullah and were interested in kidnapping a senior UN officer in order to discredit Berri and Daoud. Their initial intention had been to take a French officer but the French were always well escorted and Higgins' high profile and preference for driving alone made him an easier target.

There were thus serious divisions within Amal. It also lacked organizational capacity, as had been demonstrated in the hours following the seizing of Higgins, when thousands of Amal militiamen were placed on the roads round Tyre without being told what they were looking for. It therefore seemed unlikely that the Amal leadership were realistic in their apparent confidence that they could persuade the Hizbullah kidnappers (who variously called themselves 'the Revolutionary Justice Organization' or 'the Oppressed of the World Organization') to deliver Higgins to them. This analysis turned out to be right. No deal could be struck between the Amal leadership and the kidnappers, and on 26 February Berri dismissed Mustafa Dirani, the leader of the militant faction within Amal and its chief of security. This was bad news for Higgins. Dirani was no friend of the United Nations; he had publicly endorsed the kidnapping of Higgins; and it was believed that he already held another prisoner, Ron Arad. Though Dirani never became a member of Hizbullah, his departure from Amal would bring him closer to it. Higgins had in effect become another hostage held by Hizbullah and its allies; his fate would be decided in southern Beirut or Tehran, not in southern Lebanon.

As soon as we got back from the Middle East, Buttenheim and I went to Washington to meet Higgins' wife, Major Robin Higgins, also of the US Marine Corps. The meeting took place in the Pentagon where Major Higgins was on the Public Information staff. She was calm and collected, intensely proud of the Marine Corps and her husband and resentful of the suggestions (of which she had already heard) that he had been taking unjustified risks. Her main concern was to know what the Secretariat was doing to obtain his release. I was embarrassed by my inability to give specific answers to her questions or to produce any convincing assurance that her husband would be released. Even though it was not in our power to extract Higgins from the web of Shi'ite politics in which he had become entangled, I now feel that it would have been kinder to Robin Higgins and better for the United Nations if we had taken more visible measures, if only of a procedural kind, to illustrate the Organization's determination to save one of its own. But that did not happen and when we saw her again two months later there were signs of rising anger, though still a controlled anger, at the UN's inactivity.

During the March visit to Washington, Buttenheim and I also met various US officials. They claimed to have no hard information. We had doubts about whether they were being entirely open with us. In May, at my request, the US Permanent Representative in New York arranged for us to have a more formal inter-agency intelligence briefing, but it was not very informative. In April and May there had been plausible reports of a negotiation between mainstream Amal and Hizbullah about the terms for Higgins' release. But no hard information (or results) emerged.

The Secretary-General sought the help of the leaderships in Iran and Syria but received none, nor even a reply. At my level, I took every opportunity in Beirut, Damascus and Tehran to seek information and to urge my interlocutors that it was in their own interests to save Higgins. Only when speaking to Velayati, the Iranian Foreign Minister, did I feel that I was with someone who understood the point I was making and might have real influence. But he insisted that Iran did not know who had kidnapped Higgins or where he was. One of his deputies, Larijani, claimed in October to have made himself unpopular in Tehran by expressing opposition to hostage-taking and by telling Iran's friends in Lebanon that it was against their interests. His own conclusion was that Higgins was probably dead; if he was alive, why were his captors not using him? Our efforts to find Higgins were helped not at all by this sort of evasive speculation. The trail had gone cold.

In December 1988, when I was in Oslo following the award of the Nobel Peace Prize to the UN's peacekeepers, the trail warmed slightly. Buttenheim telephoned to say that Higgins' kidnappers, who were now using the pseudonym of 'the Oppressed of the World Organization', had announced that they had found him guilty of spying for Israel and the United States and had decided to execute him. This at least implied that he was still alive and gave us an opportunity to reopen the matter with the Iranians. Pérez de Cuéllar did this through Jan Eliasson, the Swedish diplomat whom he had appointed as his Special Representative for Iran and Iraq. Velayati told Eliasson that Hizbullah continued to deny that they held Higgins but that Iran had dug a little deeper and had received indications that Higgins might no longer be alive. Velayati was to repeat this view to Pérez de Cuéllar several times during the coming months. We picked up stories from other Iranian sources that Higgins had been killed in July 1988 by an Iranian Revolutionary Guard in a fit of rage after the USS *Vincennes* shot down an Iranian civil airliner over the Persian Gulf. Some found corroboration of this story in the fact that the photograph of Higgins distributed by his captors with their communiqué in December was the same as the one they had released soon after his capture ten months before.

However, during a visit I made in January 1989 to Lebanon, Syria and Israel, almost everyone said they believed that Higgins was still alive and that Hizbullah held him. I have since learnt that a few weeks later the Israelis told the Americans that Higgins had been killed in December 1988 or January 1989 (presumably in implementation of the Oppressed of the World's 'death sentence'), though the Israelis were vague about the circumstances. Neither the Israelis nor the Americans passed this information to us at the time.

Meanwhile, Goksel had established with a fair degree of certainty where Higgins had been taken after the kidnapping on 17 February. That afternoon, in a well-planned and executed operation involving several changes of car, he had been driven to the Litani river, which marks the northern boundary of UNIFIL's area of operations. The party crossed the river on foot during the night and reached the village of Jibshit near Nabatiyeh. On the night of 20 February Amal failed in an attempt to seize him from his captors, who then moved him to another of their village strongholds, Luwaizeh. Some weeks later he was moved to the southern suburbs of Beirut where Hizbullah's captives were believed to be held.

After the brief flurry over the 'death sentence', the trail went cold again for six months. But on 30 July 1989 the kidnappers in Beirut announced their intention to 'execute' Higgins within twenty-four hours if Israel did not release Shaikh Abdul Karim Obeid, whom Israeli commandos had kidnapped two days before from his village in southern Lebanon. The shaikh was not released and the next day Higgins' kidnappers released a half-minute videotape which purported to show his death by hanging.

I left New York that evening for a diplomatic seminar in Salzburg, which was to be followed by some leave in Britain. As my wife and I walked into the hotel in Salzburg, the receptionist said there was a call from New York. It was Dayal, Pérez de Cuéllar's Chef de Cabinet. The US media, he said, were strongly critical of alleged UN inactivity over Higgins; President Bush had cancelled a trip to the West so that he could be in Washington; I was to proceed immediately to Beirut to establish what had happened to Higgins, to recover his remains if he had indeed been killed and to see what more the UN could do to help end the wider hostage problem. The Revolutionary Justice Organization, which at one time had claimed to be holding Higgins, had announced its intention to kill an American hostage, Joseph Cicippio, on 3 August. Disconsolately my wife and I took the train back to Vienna. Early the next morning I left for Tel Aviv en route to Beirut.

The timing was less than ideal. An Arab League triumvirate, led by Lakhdar Brahimi, former Foreign Minister of Algeria, which was trying to mediate an end to the Lebanese civil war (and was to succeed a few months later), had thrown in the towel the previous day. This was bound to provoke renewed fighting in Beirut, where the Syrian Army had been using 240-mm mortars to shell the Christian areas loyal to General Michel Aoun. Each projectile weighed 110 kilos and could penetrate the concrete shelters which had hitherto afforded the civilian population some protection. Fifteen people had been killed and more than forty wounded two nights before in a shelter close to the UNIFIL and UNTSO offices in East Beirut. Sure enough my planned helicopter flight from UNIFIL headquarters to Beirut had to be cancelled because fighting had broken out on the Green Line close to the UN offices.

The next morning we made it to East Beirut, landing at the razed site of what had been Tell az-Za'atar, the Palestinian refugee camp whose population was massacred by Lebanese Christian forces in 1976, the second year of the civil war. Here be ghosts. But there was no firing that morning and we crossed the Green Line without difficulty, driving straight on to Hizbullah's stronghold in the southern suburbs to see its 'spiritual guide', Shaikh Muhammad Husain Fadlallah. I became increasingly nervous. Hitherto this part of Beirut had been out of bounds for me, a dangerous place where the hostages were believed to be held. I had considered going there to see Fadlallah soon after Higgins was taken but had been strongly discouraged from doing so both by the Amal leadership and by my own advisers. Now Higgins had become a headline issue, emotions were seething in the United States, the Sixth Fleet was deployed over the horizon off Beirut and the risk had to be taken.

Fadlallah was charm itself, an elegant, dignified and courteous man of modest stature and with a ready smile. He did not conceal the fact that he understood English but used Arabic himself, enunciating slowly and with great clarity to assist the MECAS student of thirty years before. I asked him to help me perform the task the Secretary-General had given me, spoke about the disastrous effect hostage-taking was having on Western attitudes towards Islam and the Arabs, described my frequent visits to Tehran in connection with the UN military observer group on the cease-fire line between Iran and Iraq and the credentials I had established there, and urged him to use his influence to ensure that Cicippio was not killed that evening. If Fadlallah's language was clear, the content was slippery. He began by saying that he was a leader of the Shi'ites but not 'the spiritual leader' of Hizbullah; this was a fabrication by the media. He condemned all attacks against UN soldiers and was opposed to hostage-taking, a problem which had been greatly complicated by the involvement of outside powers. He said that he would try to find out what had happened to Higgins. He did not say explicitly that he was dead, while conveying the impression that he thought he was. He declined to act as an intermediary with the kidnappers because he had no links with them (though at a later point he claimed to be doing all he could to dissuade 'those concerned' from killing hostages).

As I rose to leave he called in the television crews, a departure from the normal Beirut practice of filming the beginning of a meeting rather than its end. When they were ready, he said something that made me laugh. I have forgotten what he said but there I was on the front pages the next day, apparently 'sharing a joke' with the spiritual guide of those who claimed to have murdered Higgins. As he showed us out, he winked at Goksel; the message was evident – 'see what a fast one I pulled on the infidel'.

I drove on to see Shaikh Abdul Amir Kabalan, another Shi'ite cleric but allied to the secular leadership of Amal of whose political bureau he was a member. His hunch was that Higgins was alive. He described in some detail a negotiation which he said had begun in October or November 1988 for the release of Higgins in return for a ransom of 3.5 million US dollars (Berri had hinted to Wahlgren at the time that this was happening). During the course of the negotiation a dated photograph had been produced to prove that Higgins was still alive and this was subsequently made available to the American Embassy. The Americans had never mentioned this to us and I therefore doubted Kabalan's story. If true, it would have invalidated the report that Higgins had been killed at the time of the USS *Vincennes* incident in July 1988.

Next I called on the Iranian chargé d'affaires, a sharp and disagreeable young man who spoke with some authority. He too alluded to a complicated negotiation which, he said, had been close to fruition when the Israelis kidnapped Obeid. He thought Higgins was now dead and offered to help recover his remains, provided there was no publicity. But he warned me not to probe too deep, lest I suffer the fate of Terry Waite who had himself been taken hostage in 1987 while trying to negotiate the release of hostages already taken. We then crossed back to East Beirut to spend the night in the inaptly named Comfort Hotel, which also housed UNIFIL's office on that side of the line. Word came from New York about the FBI's analysis of the videotape. Although positive identification of the body was impossible, it was almost certainly that of Higgins. It did not, however, show the characteristics of a person killed by hanging.

There was some small arms fire during the night, followed, soon after dawn, by outgoing tank-fire close to the hotel. I managed to doze through this for a while but was then woken by what seemed to be a tremendous explosion right outside the hotel. I was later told, disappointingly, that it had been caused by a mere anti-aircraft round, fired horizontally at the Christian tanks, which had hit a telegraph pole in front of the hotel. The same thing recurred an hour later when I was in the bathroom and was so frightened that I fell to the floor. So much for glory under fire. I was shamed by my military colleagues' jovial insouciance. But there was good news that morning: Cicippio had been spared.

Goksel and I returned to the southern suburbs to meet a group of six Hizbullah leaders, all of them young and bearded. The only one to give a name was Abdul Hadi Hamadeh who, though I did not know it at the time, was a senior figure in Hizbullah's security apparatus. His two brothers had been imprisoned in Germany for terrorist offences. They were hostile, stiff, doctrinaire and thoroughly unhelpful. My message cut even less ice with them than it had with Fadlallah the day before. They insisted that they knew nothing. I took the helicopter back to Tyre for a meeting with the local Amal leadership. At least they were friendly but they too had nothing useful to impart.

The next meeting, however, cheered me up. It was with Shaikh Muhammad Mahdi Shamsuddin, the head of the Supreme Shi'ite Council and the grand old man of moderate Shi'ism in Lebanon. I had been warned that he did not approve of my having called on Fadlallah and

Kabalan before him and that he thought I should anyway have first seen Husseini and Berri, the two secular Shi'ite leaders. We were left waiting for a while, but in the agreeable company of his brother-in-law, a lesser shaikh of twinkling eyes and ruddy complexion who could have been an Irish farmer but for his beard and turban.

Shamsuddin eventually arrived in sulky mood, refusing to look me in the eye. I took the bull by the horns, explaining that I had wanted to call on him first but could not find him in Beirut and that Berri had been in Damascus and Husseini in Baalbek (to escape the nightly shelling, though I did not say so). His response was to interrogate me about the conversation with Fadlallah. I had to be evasive because any credibility I had with the latter would evaporate if he learnt that I had recounted our conversation to his arch-enemy Shamsuddin.

I switched the conversation to UNIFIL, praising Shamsuddin for his efforts to persuade his people not to attack the UN. This proved to be an easier way of getting him to talk about Higgins. After two and a half hours he had been won round and was complimenting me on my 'wisdom'. He said that there were strong indications that Higgins was dead. However, he and others unnamed had obtained from the kidnappers a promise not to kill any more hostages. Berri, al-Hoss (the Lebanese Prime Minister on the Muslim side) and the Syrian Foreign Minister were all to claim later that they had played a part in this exercise, with the Syrian adding the important caveat that the promise was conditional on American restraint both in language and in deed. Shamsuddin thought that the way was now open for a negotiated solution to the hostage problem, provided that the Americans moderated their hostility to Iran and helped the newly-elected President Rafsanjani to pursue more pragmatic policies.

This proved to be an accurate assessment. Only a week later President Bush asked Pérez de Cuéllar to communicate some 'thoughts' to Rafsanjani. Pérez de Cuéllar sent Picco to Tehran and thus began the tortuous path that would lead to release of the hostages in 1991. I helicoptered back to Naqoura, pleased to have something more tangible to report to New York and bewitched by the evening beauty of southern Lebanon that contrasts so bleakly with the atrocities committed there.

The next morning it was back to Beirut for meetings with the government leaders there, though under the Syrian assault the concept of a 'Lebanese Government' was daily less credible. Only Aoun was available, the Christian general whom Amin Gemayel had appointed in September 1988 to head the 'Government' when his own term expired. We found him in the presidential palace at Ba'abda where I had had so many meetings with Gemayel. The same chief of protocol was there but he was dishevelled and dispirited. All else was changed. The palace had been shelled; not a pane of glass remained and the huge marble entrance hall was under two feet of sand to protect Aoun's bunker below. The general himself again struck me as being slightly mad, with a messianic compulsion to drive the Syrians from Lebanon, whatever the cost. He insisted the Syrians could solve the hostage problem if they wanted to; the Iranian role was exaggerated. How wrong he was.

We crossed the Green Line to the Muslim side and set off by road to Damascus. Our escort decided to save time by driving south along the airport runway and then cutting across country to rejoin the coast road south of the congestion in the southern suburbs. It was a bad decision. My car became stuck in the sand and the convoy was immobilized in full view of the various gunners in the hills above who shelled the airport from time to time. An enterprising TV journalist, who had attached himself to the convoy, filmed me as I tried to be cool and operational while thinking only of all the eyes that must be staring through telescopic sights at this vulnerable target. But we escaped and reached Damascus safely.

The next day I saw Farouq al-Shara', the Syrian Foreign Minister. His first words were: 'Please accept my condolences about Colonel Higgins'; he was sure that Higgins was dead. Syria, he said, wanted to solve the hostage problem once and for all. It could be solved only through negotiation with Syria and Iran (an unprecedented admission that Syria was able to influence the kidnappers) but Washington would have to be more responsive to the new policies evolving in Tehran.

I also saw Nabih Berri in Damascus. It was a stormy meeting. He wanted to know what Kabalan had told me about the alleged negotiations the previous year. I parried by getting him to tell me his version of events. It conformed quite closely to Kabalan's but there were some discrepancies. A particularly interesting one was that, according to Berri, the dated photograph had been provided by the kidnappers in June 1989 (i.e. only two months earlier), not in November or December 1988, and that it had been passed to Higgins' wife, not to the American Embassy. When I pointed out these discrepancies, Berri lost his temper. Why was the UN always blaming him? He had been on the point of securing Higgins' release when the Israelis wrecked everything by kidnapping Obeid. He was scornful about the idea of recovering Higgins' remains, implying that he assumed Higgins was dead. There was no point in trying: Hizbullah would preserve his body in the hope of an eventual trade but their terms would never be acceptable.

At the time Goksel and I concluded that Berri and Kabalan had concocted their story in order to evade blame for Higgins' death and that one or other of them had forgotten his lines. But when I got back to New York a few days later I learnt that Pérez de Cuéllar had been told on 2

August that a private initiative had been launched the previous May to negotiate Higgins' release. The initiative, which was known to senior members of the Administration in Washington, had still been under way when Higgins' murder was announced. The intermediary had been a rich Shiʻite businessman and childhood friend of Berri. Although there were discrepancies, it seemed that the Berri/Kabalan account did have some basis of truth. Pérez de Cuéllar had decided, rightly I think, that the information should not be passed to me in Beirut. I had stumbled on the facts, albeit in distorted version, as a result of following the lead that Kabalan had provided.

The next morning, seven days after the announcement by the Oppressed of the World that they had murdered Higgins, we drove back to Beirut for a second meeting with Fadlallah and to see Salim al-Hoss, the 'Prime Minister' who had not been available the previous week. This time Fadlallah was alone except for a bodyguard. He was even more friendly and flattering, but as firm as ever in his denial of any connection with kidnappers. He regretted, therefore, that he could not help me in my mission, observing that those who had sent me just wanted a media event, even though they knew that the problem could be solved only by political negotiation. Given Bush's impending overture to Rafsanjani through Pérez de Cuéllar, this remark suggests that Fadlallah had already had indications from Tehran of the imminent change in Iran's attitude to hostage-taking. Meanwhile his advice to me was to shun the media but show by my actions that I was as concerned about getting Obeid released as about discovering what had happened to Higgins; Pérez de Cuéllar had made a mistake in not sending me to Israel as soon as Obeid was kidnapped. This was true; I wished that I had spotted it at the time.

The previous night's shelling had been particularly bad and al-Hoss seemed a broken man – old, tired and dispirited, but as kind and gentle as ever. It struck me that he and Shamsuddin were the only Lebanese I had met who were of true presidential calibre, but as Muslims – one Sunni and the other Shiʻite – they were both denied the chance of holding a post that was reserved for Maronite Christians. Hoss declined to express a view on whether Higgins was dead or alive, saying only: '*We* are sentenced to death every night – and it is just as bad for those on the other side.' I felt I was watching the death of Lebanon. His remark also provoked a twinge of guilt. Higgins was one of ours and I would do everything I could to discover his fate. But for the Lebanese, now in the fifteenth year of their civil war and with civilians dying every night, it must be insulting to see so much attention focussed on the death of one foreigner.

We crossed back to the Christian side. The escort was not there. Standard operating procedures required us to wait until it turned up. But as we left the Muslim side Goksel had said that he 'smelt' that the shelling was going to start early that afternoon. After fifteen minutes, we decided that an unescorted drive through East Beirut was a more acceptable risk than standing around in no man's land. Goksel was right, as usual. The shelling did start early and two people were killed on the very spot where we had been waiting.

The next morning Goksel and I were in Tel Aviv to see Rabin. I invited Goksel to tell him about Obeid. Goksel said: 'Mr Minister, you have a lemon in your hands. You will get nothing from him. If he was important, do you think Amal would have let him stay in their territory while they expelled scores of other Hizbullah shaikhs?' As can be imagined, this remark did not win a round of applause from Rabin's officials. After being told what was meant by 'lemon', however, he admitted that Obeid had been a disappointment; the Israelis had learnt very little from him; he was difficult, clever and terrified of deportation to the United States. I criticized Israel's action in kidnapping him. Whether or not it had precipitated Higgins' death, it would complicate the West's efforts to take advantage of Rafsanjani's accession to power in Tehran. Rabin did not argue back very hard: 'Don't let's quarrel over this; let's agree to differ.' Bibi Netanyahu, at that time Deputy Foreign Minister, had asked me to see him in Jerusalem. I later learnt that Rabin had tried to block the meeting, on the grounds that hostage matters belonged exclusively to the Defence Ministry. Netanyahu had nothing interesting to say and one could sense the chagrin that he felt, as a self-proclaimed expert on terrorism, at being excluded from Israeli policy-making on the subject. I pressed him on why the decision to kidnap Obeid had been taken when it was; it seemed that he did not know.

I flew back to New York that night and gave Pérez de Cuéllar six recommendations: he should announce his conclusion that Higgins was almost certainly dead; we should continue to try to recover his remains but not encourage expectations that we would succeed; our diplomatic efforts should be concentrated on Iran and Syria because we had no means of influencing Hizbullah directly; we should generate less publicity; we should decouple Higgins, for whom the United Nations had a special responsibility, from the other hostages; we should encourage governments to take the lead on the wider issue, where the UN's role should be that of a willing auxiliary, if asked. Pérez de Cuéllar accepted all the recommendations. Picco who, unknown to me, was about to be launched on his mission to secure the release of the Western hostages was understandably unhappy about the last one. Fortunately for the hostages and the UN, it was quickly forgotten. Fifteen days later Picco would be in Tehran conveying Bush's 'thoughts' to Rafsanjani; after a further two years of negotiation the hostages would be freed and Higgins' remains recovered.

Meanwhile, Pérez de Cuéllar went down to tell the press that, having received my report, he had come to the conclusion that Higgins was almost certainly dead. To my chagrin he asked me not to accompany him. It had become evident on my return to New York that my trip had been even more of a media event than I had realized and I again had the sense that this caused my chief some discomfort.

A few weeks later I had a chance encounter with Robin Higgins in Pennsylvania. She reproached me for the advice I had given Pérez de Cuéllar; if I had no proof that her husband was dead, we should have assumed that he was alive and continued to try to find him. In late October she sent an eloquent letter to Pérez de Cuéllar. Writing both as Higgins' wife and as a major in the US Marine Corps, she chided him for having failed in his duty to 'make sacrifices' for the welfare of his subordinates. She had hoped, and stated publicly at the time, that the deployment of UN military observers between Iran and Iraq in August 1988 would have been made conditional on the release of UN military observer Higgins. She did not expect this to happen, for reasons of state, but she did expect the Secretary-General to designate a team 'or at least a credible individual' to do nothing but work on Higgins' release. This had not been done. Why not?

Pérez de Cuéllar decided not to reply to Mrs Higgins until Picco had had further discussions with the Iranians, ostensibly as a member of Jan Eliasson's team that was trying to mediate a settlement between Iran and Iraq. Six weeks later he wrote to her that the standard procedure when a UN staff member is illegally detained is for a team of officials to work on the case, coordinated by one of the USGs and reporting regularly to the Secretary-General; that procedure had been followed in her husband's case.

Four days later Mrs Higgins spoke at an event on hostages organized by the UN Staff Association. Pérez de Cuéllar made a brief introductory statement and then left me to face the music. Alec Collett's wife spoke of the 'pain, agony and torture' which she and her son were enduring. Robin Higgins criticized the UN for its failure to appoint a team or individual with the sole mission of finding her husband and for its 'deafening silence' about his plight; the Commandant of the Marine Corps, she said, had not 'made a determination' that her husband was dead because he had not received any convincing evidence that that was the case. She was supported by a Frenchman, Jean-Paul Kaufmann, who had been a hostage in Beirut: 'noise and publicity freed the French hostages; silence prolongs the torture of the American and British ones'. Other speakers criticized the Secretary-General for not having advocated in public the expulsion from the United Nations of those member states which were known to aid and abet hostage-takers. I replied lamely on behalf of the

Secretary-General: all of us in the Secretariat shared the families' agony; but these cases were exceedingly complicated; solving them was not as simple as some of the speakers had suggested; there had to be a joint effort involving the families, the Staff Association, the Secretary-General and the Secretariat, and the governments of member states.

As in previous encounters with Robin Higgins, I was painfully conscious of how unconvincing these platitudes were. But I still do not know what else could have been said. Privately, I had supported the British Government's refusal to ransom Collett and deplored the efforts that had been made to buy Higgins' release. My own view was, and still is, that the only effective way of discouraging hostage-taking is to ensure that those concerned do not gain any benefit from their wickedness; every ransom paid sows the seed of a future kidnapping. Although I did not know it at the time, Anglo-American insistence that the Beirut kidnappers should gain no benefit had helped to persuade Tehran that its tolerance (to put it mildly) of their activities was damaging Iran's interests. But this is too callous a point of view to put to grieving families, and governments and international organizations therefore have no alternative to platitudes. Looking back, however, I believe that if UN operations are deployed in places where hostage-taking is rife their personnel should be given an explicit warning in writing: the risk exists; the UN will do what it can to secure the release of kidnapped personnel; its capacity to do so, however, is likely to be limited; and it will in no circumstances pay ransom.

Just before my six-monthly visit of inspection to UNIFIL in January 1990, Amal announced that they had discovered a 'secret Hizbullah prison' in a village called Kawthariyat as-Sayyad a few kilometres north of UNIFIL's area of operation and that they had documentary evidence that Higgins had been briefly detained there. Jean-Claude Aimé took the view that Amal's purpose was to discredit Hizbullah, with whom Amal were then in open conflict, and that I should not play into their hands by visiting the place myself. His analysis was right but I felt that I had to go and inspect it, given all that had been said to the Americans about our sparing no effort to establish what had happened to Higgins. The 'prison' turned out to consist of five cells and a primitive lavatory, skilfully built under a house on a hillside and concealed by a garage. There was a hook in the ceiling of each cell and a noose hanging from each hook, presumably a bit of theatre by Amal. The place looked new but did not smell new. There was, however, no evidence that it had been recently used. The Amal people said that they had found it ten days before as a result of 'confessions' by an unnamed member of Hizbullah whom they had recently captured. It was he who had said that Higgins had been held there for three days at an unspecified date. There was no documentary evidence to confirm this.

I again saw the rival shaikhs, Shamsuddin and Fadlallah. Neither had anything new to say about Higgins' fate. I pressed Berri, to the point of anger, for clarification of the inconsistencies in Amal's various statements about the prison, but all I could get from him was a promise that Goksel would in due course be told the results of Amal's investigation, following further interrogation of their Hizbullah captive. These results cast little new light. The prison, Goksel was told, had been built in 1986 as a transit facility for prisoners en route to Beirut and only six people at the most had ever been detained there. Higgins had been taken there on the evening of his kidnapping and transferred to Beirut three days later. Goksel pointed out that all this was very different from what Amal had said previously about Higgins being taken to Jibshit. His interlocutors gave no satisfactory explanation of the discrepancy. Either version is plausible; the truth remains hidden behind the veil of Shi'ite *taqīya*.

In July 1990, the Commandant of the US Marine Corps finally made the formal determination that Higgins was to be presumed dead. It was not challenged by Mrs Higgins. This opened the way for ceremonies to be held in Higgins' honour and for the United Nations to pay the compensation to which his widow was entitled. The first ceremony took place on 8 November at the Quantico National Cemetery in Virginia. General Gray, the Commandant of the Marine Corps, was cool and tried to avoid conversation with me. It turned out that he had been told that the UN was refusing to pay the compensation because Higgins had not been working for it but 'under cover for the CIA or some other US agency'. This was totally erroneous, an example of the malicious rumour-mongering which is a besetting sin of the UN Secretariat. The ceremony was moving, on a cold and sunny fall day. Speeches were made, a volley fired, taps played and, in a remarkable drill, seven pall-bearers mimed the carrying in of a coffin and the unfolding and folding of the flag over it.

Two days later, on a bitterly cold morning, I was at Higgins' school, the confusingly named Miami University at Oxford, Ohio, to speak at the unveiling of a memorial to him and all other Miamians who had died for their country. Robin Higgins was as staunch as ever, but still unforgiving. I assured the gathering that the recovery of Higgins' remains was unfinished business for the UN; we would not give up. Ten months were to pass before, thanks to Picco's perseverance, Higgins' body was left near a hospital in the southern suburbs of Beirut. Picco says in his book that it had been refrigerated since Higgins was murdered. But he does not know, or will not say, what it revealed about the manner and date of Higgins' death.

New Opportunities

8

The Thaw Begins

The five peacekeeping operations so far described are relics from the Cold War. When I assumed responsibility for peacekeeping in 1986, they ranged in age from thirty-seven to seven years. At the time of writing (late 2001), all five are still in the field and their ages range from fifty-three to twenty-three years. Only the youngest of them, UNIFIL in southern Lebanon, seems a candidate for early demobilization. To say this is not to question their value. The forces in Syria and in Cyprus have done a particularly good job and received little credit for it. But longevity in peacekeeping operations is not fashionable. They are meant to be interim arrangements whose purpose is either to create conditions in which a peace settlement can be negotiated or to help the parties implement an already negotiated settlement.

In most cases, therefore, it is right to look for 'exit strategies' if an operation has failed to fulfil its mandate within, more or less, the time-frame envisaged when it was established. Given the current demand for peacekeeping, a case can often be made for cutting losses and reinvesting in a new operation which has a better chance of success. But such decisions require careful analysis; if the effect of cutting the losses is to reopen hostilities, the less bad course may be to leave the investment where it is – which is why I always resisted proposals for ending UNFICYP, the force in Cyprus.

By the beginning of 1987 there could be no doubt that the international environment was becoming more propitious for United Nations peacekeeping. It would be dishonest to say that we were predicting the fall of the Berlin Wall less than three years later. But in early 1986 the Soviet Union had begun, for the first time, to pay its peacekeeping dues and had promised action to clear its considerable arrears. Some hoped, naively as it turned out, that this would shame the United States into clearing its own debt to the UN. But at the very least the Soviet move was seen as evidence that Gorbachev's *perestroika* was changing Soviet foreign policy for the better. East–West détente could create new opportunities for the Security Council to tackle some long-standing regional conflicts.

In early 1987 Pérez de Cuéllar persuaded the five permanent members (P-5) to participate in discreet consultations about how to end the war between Iran and Iraq.* This initiative led in July to the Council's unanimous adoption of a resolution which prescribed the ingredients of a peace settlement. Pérez de Cuéllar did well to start with the Iran–Iraq war. Unlike most of the regional conflicts at that time, it was not a spin-off of the Cold War that pitched East against West. On the contrary, the permanent members had a common interest in ensuring the security of the sea lanes in the Persian Gulf and all of them except China had warships deployed in the Gulf for that purpose. Nor did any of them want to see Ayatollah Khomeini win a victory that would enhance the appeal of his fundamentalism in other Islamic countries or countries which had Islamic minorities.

By the beginning of 1988 it had become clear that the new spirit of cooperation between the P-5 extended also to the proxy conflicts of the Cold War: that is, those conflicts between or within Third World countries in which the East supported one side and the West the other. The conflicts may have had indigenous causes resulting from inter-state rivalry over territory, resources or regional influence or, in the case of internal conflicts, from economic and social injustice or from ethnic rivalry and discrimination. But the intensity of these conflicts was due in large part to the fact that one bloc supported one side and the other bloc the other. This gave them a wider international dimension and enabled each protagonist to obtain political, military and financial support from its superpower champion. The classic example was the war between Ethiopia and Somalia. In the sixties Haile Selassie's Ethiopia was supported and armed by the United States, while the leftist regime in Somalia was supported and armed by the Soviet Union. But after the Marxist Colonel Mengistu seized power in Ethiopia in 1977, the two superpowers exchanged roles, with the Russians supporting Ethiopia and the Americans supporting Somalia. The result was the flooding of the Horn of Africa with arms which continue to this day to fuel conflict there.

But in 1988 there was concrete evidence of a new East–West willingness to cooperate in resolving several of these proxy conflicts. In March the UN succeeded, after many years of effort, in mediating an agreement on the withdrawal of Soviet troops from Afghanistan. Soviet diplomats began to cooperate with Chester Crocker, the American mediator who was seeking to negotiate linked agreements on withdrawal of Cuban troops from Angola and implementation of the UN settlement plan for Namibia. Linked agreements on these two issues were signed in

---

* This subject is examined in more detail in Chapter 9 below.

December. In August Pérez de Cuéllar announced that proposals for ending the war in Western Sahara between US-supported Morocco and the Soviet-supported national liberation movement, Frente POLISARIO, had been accepted by both sides. In South-East Asia a slight thaw in Soviet-supported Vietnam's relations with both Beijing and Washington raised hopes for a negotiated settlement of the Cambodian conflict, which was signed two years later.

The Office for Special Political Affairs (OSPA), of which Cordovez and I remained the joint heads, was deeply involved in the implementation of all these agreements, as will be described in the following chapters. With the sole exception of the Geneva Accords on Afghanistan, the task was entrusted to my part of OSPA. The signature of the Afghanistan accords in April 1988 was the culmination of ten years of effort by the United Nations. They facilitated the withdrawal of Soviet troops but they did not end the fighting in Afghanistan; they merely changed the issues at stake and the identities of the protagonists. Nor did they end foreign interference in a country whose strategic location has condemned it, since the days of Alexander the Great or earlier, to be an international cockpit. Like the Lebanese, the Afghans have only rarely been sufficiently united to present a common front against interfering foreigners. When, in the second part of my UN career, I became responsible for peacemaking in Afghanistan, the sermon I preached to all the factions was: 'put your differences aside; unite and you will be able to keep the foreigners out'. The sermon won few converts.

The UN's involvement in peacemaking in Afghanistan resulted from the Soviet invasion of the country in December 1979, ostensibly in response to a request by the pro-Communist head of the government in Kabul. He was, however, killed during the invasion and replaced by a Communist, Babrak Karmal, who arrived with the Soviet troops. In the Security Council a resolution calling for their withdrawal was vetoed by the Soviet Union. This was the occasion of a rare diplomatic error by my then boss, Tony Parsons. Alphabetical order placed the United Kingdom and the Union of Soviet Socialist Republics next to each other at the Security Council's horseshoe table. Parsons had long been a friend of Oleg Troyanovsky, the personable Soviet Ambassador who had been brought up in Washington where his father served during the Second World War. 'Don't look so solemn, Tony,' said Troyanovsky after he had cast the Soviet veto, 'your predecessor once told me: "casting the veto is like adultery; you worry about it the first time but after that it's fun".' Parsons roared with laughter and a malevolent photographer caught this moment of fraternization with the enemy for publication on the front page of the next day's *New York Times*.

The Soviet invasion was then referred to an emergency session of the

General Assembly. There the Soviets had no veto and a strongly anti-Soviet resolution was adopted. Secretary-General Waldheim appointed Pérez de Cuéllar, then an USG in the Secretariat, as his Personal Representative to try to negotiate a settlement. Two years later Pérez de Cuéllar himself became Secretary-General and passed the Afghan baton to Diego Cordovez. For the next six years Cordovez worked with enthusiasm, patience and wit to create conditions in Afghanistan which would permit the Russians to withdraw their troops. Meanwhile the United States and other anti-Communist powers, with the support of neighbouring Pakistan, funded and armed a loose coalition of guerrilla forces, the *mujāhidīn* (or 'Mooj' in Washington parlance), who were united only by their *jihād* against the Communist government and the hundred thousand Soviet troops that backed it. Six million refugees, almost 30 per cent of the population, fled the country, placing heavy burdens on Iran and Pakistan. By late 1987 Moscow was signalling that it was ready to withdraw its troops, even though the Afghan factions were far from agreeing on what form the government would then take.

The Geneva Accords signed in April 1988 requested the Secretary-General to appoint a representative who would make his 'good offices' available. The representative was to be assisted by a 'good offices mission' (UNGOMAP) which would monitor non-interference by Afghanistan and Pakistan in each other's affairs, the withdrawal of Soviet troops and the return of refugees. The first two of these tasks were to be carried out, in the traditional way, by military observers. Precedent dictated therefore that UNGOMAP was a 'peacekeeping operation' and as such would be deployed and directed by my part of OSPA. But Cordovez and Picco insisted that as a 'good offices mission' UNGOMAP was not a peacekeeping operation and would be rejected if presented as such to Moscow. My staff urged me, on solid grounds, not to concede this point. But having offended Pérez de Cuéllar a few months before over his failure to include me in his working lunch with Shimon Peres, I decided not to fight.

I was, therefore, involved only tangentially in the deployment and operations of UNMOGAP, which was in the field for less than two years. I did, however, attend one meeting of its troop contributors, turning the other cheek, to help Cordovez get out of a mess which he had created by telling the governments concerned that they would receive partial reimbursement of their officers' salaries while they were in UN service, whereas established practice was that the UN paid only the UNMOs' living costs in theatre.

Meanwhile a cease-fire had come into effect between Iran and Iraq and significant progress was being made in ending other conflicts in which East and West were no longer protagonists. In September 1988 it was announced that the UN's Peacekeeping Forces had been awarded the Nobel Peace Prize. For the United Nations, 1987 and 1988 had lived up to their promise; there was a new sense of purpose and achievement. The *Diplomatic World Bulletin*, a gossipy fortnightly distributed free to delegates and Secretariat, enthused:

> As 1988 wound down, one of the most successful years for the United Nations in its 43-year history, the world body basked in a warm glow of nearly universal esteem and Secretary-General Pérez de Cuéllar hailed what he termed 'a time of extraordinary hope and promise'. The euphoria infected the New York staff, which, in a stroke of genius, organized the first UN Open House, inviting visitors in off the street to tour the headquarters for free, meet representatives of peace forces and, as USG Marrack Goulding put it, 'share with us the joy and pride at the award of the Nobel Peace Prize'.

Pérez de Cuéllar flew to Oslo to receive the Prize. I accompanied him and went on to Stockholm to represent him at the celebrations there. This involved giving a speech in the Storkyrkan, the 'Great Church' in the centre of the Old Town, and attending a dinner hosted by the King and Queen in honour of all that year's Nobel Prize winners. The church was lit by candles and packed by an audience-congregation including many former UN peacekeepers and one old man who had served in the international force in the Saarland in 1935. As befitted the place, I preached a sermon on the moral worth of peacekeeping and peacekeepers. The latter, I said,

> embody the noble paradox of peacekeeping, which is its combination of moral strength and practical vulnerability. For peacekeeping soldiers carry arms only to avoid using them; they are military forces but their orders are to avoid, at almost any cost, the use of force; they are asked in the last resort to risk their own lives rather than open fire on those between whom they have been sent to keep the peace . . . the notion of sacrifice is central to all the great religions. One can see an element of sacrifice – sacrifice in the tradition of Bernadotte and Hammarskjöld – in the readiness of so many young soldiers to face the rigours and even the dangers of peacekeeping.

After all the controversy that has since beset peacekeeping, it is painful today to revisit this enthusiastic and confident idealism. But it was the spirit of that year and it fired our work.

Amidst all the rejoicing, however, I suffered a personal setback when Pérez de Cuéllar decided to make me responsible only for peacekeeping and to transfer to his office three key members of my staff. When this 'shake-up' was made public, the general assessment was that I was the loser. It was certainly how I felt. A few weeks later, walking home up First Avenue, I unthinkingly asked Carl-August Fleischhauer, the UN Legal Counsel, how the consultations on the international conference on

Palestine were going. His embarrassed reply was that he was not authorized to tell me. I regretted having asked.

At the time I interpreted this move as a decision by Pérez de Cuéllar to
cut me down to size. A number of factors had perhaps caused cumulative
offence: my reaction to his lunch with Shimon Peres the previous year;
the prominence I had enjoyed as a result of my mission to Palestine at the
beginning of the *intifāda*; my unconcealed doubts about the viability of
his plan for Western Sahara.* Cordovez was known to have made him
unhappy by publicly claiming credit for the Geneva Accords on
Afghanistan. Perhaps Pérez de Cuéllar had concluded that peacemaking
was too heady a drink for USGs and gave them illusions of grandeur;
better to confine it to his inner circle. This interpretation seemed to be
confirmed a couple of weeks later when I learnt that the Secretary-
General's office had asked for an interview with me to be excised from
the UN film celebrating the Nobel Peace Prize.[†] Rumours began to circu-
late that I had indeed offended Pérez de Cuéllar, that his initial plan had
been to exile me to the UN Office in Geneva but that Mrs Thatcher had
wielded her handbag to save me from that fate.

I have never found out what really happened. The reticence of colleagues who might know inclines me to think that my interpretation at
the time was correct. But perhaps it was a little paranoid. Twelve years
later one can see that the impending expansion of peacekeeping did
create a case for having a department exclusively devoted to that activity.
Soon there was to be more than enough peacekeeping to keep me busy.

---

* See Chapter 12.
† The film however had already been distributed. It is interesting in this context to note
that Pérez de Cuéllar's memoir, *Pilgrimage for Peace*, contains no reference to the Nobel
Prize. Another indication of his mood at the time is that on a post-Nobel trip to Oslo
and Stockholm in January 1989 he amended all his speeches to substitute 'peacemaking
and peacekeeping' for 'peacekeeping' *tout court*.

9

Iraq vs. Iran

Saddam Hussein invaded Iran in 1980 in the apparent belief that a quick victory was available and that this would deter Khomeini's regime in Iran from continuing to foment trouble in adjacent parts of Iraq which are inhabited by potentially secessionist minorities, namely the Shi'ite Muslims in the south and the Kurds in the north. The two countries' armed forces were initially about the same size but Iran's population and GDP were three times those of Iraq and the country was still fired by revolutionary fervour.

The quick victory Saddam had hoped for could not be won and as Iran mobilized, Saddam realized that he would be less able than Khomeini to sustain a prolonged conflict. From 1982 onwards his aim was a negotiated settlement to the war. Iran's aim was to overthrow his regime or at least to have him held responsible internationally for having started the war and for the losses suffered by Iran. Each side tried to achieve its aim by keeping up the military pressure and impairing the other's capacity to export crude oil. On land, the war was a kind of desert Flanders, with huge artillery bombardments, poison gas and the sacrifice (or 'martyrdom' as both sides called it) of tens of thousands of lives for paltry territorial gains. At sea, the major powers deployed naval forces to protect oil tankers and other shipping in the Persian Gulf. This brought the risk that they themselves would become involved in the conflict; in May 1987 an American warship, the USS *Stark*, was hit by two Exocet missiles fired by an Iraqi aircraft and thirty-seven of her crew were killed.

In July 1987 the Security Council adopted resolution 598, which contained an outline plan for ending the war. This was a triumph for Pérez de Cuéllar and vindicated his belief that the East–West thaw was creating new possibilities for cooperation between the major powers. The resolution reflected ideas which he had first put to the parties in 1983 and had patiently advocated since then. More than most, he realized that an aspiring peacemaker must never give up. The precise moment when a conflict will become ripe for settlement cannot be predicted. Peacemakers must prepare for that moment by keeping their ideas alive in the minds of the parties. As a peacemaker, one should not be inhibited from saying something because one has said it at every previous meeting. Indeed constant repetition can make ideas seem less difficult or threatening than they sound when first uttered. The new factor in 1987 was not that both parties were ready to accept Pérez de Cuéllar's ideas (one was not, initially) but that the permanent members of the Security Council accepted them and even hinted that the Council might take coercive action against a party that failed to respond to them.

SCR 598 called for an immediate cease-fire and the withdrawal of forces to the international boundaries under the supervision of UN military observers. Prisoners of war were to be released. The parties were to cooperate with the Secretary-General in efforts to negotiate a comprehensive settlement. The Secretary-General was to explore the possibility of setting up an impartial inquiry into responsibility for the conflict and to appoint a team of experts to study the question of reconstruction. He was also to discuss with the protagonists and other states in the region how regional stability might be enhanced. The hint of possible coercive action lay in the Council's decision to adopt the resolution under Chapter VII of the Charter, thereby implying that if it was not respected the Council might resort to sanctions or even the enforcement action increasingly advocated by Reagan and Thatcher. This was almost certainly an empty threat, for China had made clear its opposition even to sanctions and would be likely to veto the use of force, but it nevertheless carried some political weight.

Apart from the impartial inquiry, SCR 598 was the resolution Iraq wanted. Baghdad quickly welcomed it. Tehran criticized its 'fundamental defects and incongruities' but took care not to reject it outright, expressing its readiness to negotiate an end to the war but not on the basis of a resolution which failed to name the aggressor. For its part, Iraq refused to accept any modifications to the resolution. Thus was set the scene for the kind of diplomacy at which Pérez de Cuéllar excelled. He had spotted the opportunity created by the major powers' disquiet at the escalation in the Gulf and a possible victory for Khomeini's Iran and had got the Council to adopt a resolution which Iraq could not refuse. There was now a clear objective for a concerted international effort: bring Iran into line. It took a year. Pérez de Cuéllar was tireless in his diplomacy and was helped both by Iraq's unexpected success in recovering the Fao peninsula and by more aggressive action by the US Navy against Iranian targets in the Gulf.*

---

* Iran had captured the peninsula in February 1986, thereby gaining control of both banks of the Shatt al-Arab through which the combined waters of the Tigris and the Euphrates flow into the Persian Gulf. Control of the Shatt had been one of the contentious issues which led to war in 1980.

On 18 July 1988 Iran accepted SCR 598 and thirty-three days later the cease-fire came into effect.

I had played no part in the negotiations; nor had Cordovez who was fully engaged in his efforts to prevent civil war in Afghanistan after the Soviet withdrawal. Pérez de Cuéllar relied primarily on Picco, who worked closely with Iqbal Riza, a member of Cordovez's team. Riza was a Pakistani diplomat of high ability and moral conviction who had been in the Secretariat since 1978 and was later to play an important role in Central America, before becoming Kofi Annan's right-hand man in the peacekeeping department and then on the 38th floor. It was clear from the moment SCR 598 was adopted that the Office for Special Political Affairs (OSPA), which I shared with Diego Cordovez, should be planning the military observer group that would supervise the cease-fire and the withdrawal of forces to the border. But I was led to understand that the negotiations were so secret that it would be difficult to give me a role in the military planning. Would I please release Timothy Dibuama, the Military Adviser in my office, to help Picco plan the new operation? Picco, I was reminded, had been running two small military inspection teams which had been in Baghdad and Tehran since 1984.*

When UNGOMAP was set up, I had allowed Cordovez to break the monopoly of peacekeeping which the 'British' part of OSPA had established during Urquhart's tenure. That was bad enough; what was now proposed was worse. Responsibility for peacekeeping would no longer rest exclusively with OSPA; an official in the Secretary-General's office would have his own peacekeeping operation. This would fuel the ambitions of other USGs who were working on the settlement of other conflicts (Western Sahara, Cambodia, Namibia). Responsibility for peacekeeping could become diffused amongst several departments. My unhappiness at this trend resulted partly from the need to defend my turf. But I had a more respectable motive. Peacekeeping was (and still is, though to a lesser extent) an unwritten art practised by an organization whose collective memory is not strong. It was already difficult to ensure uniform application of the established principles and customary practices of peacekeeping in the five operations that were being run by my office. Cordovez's mishaps with UNGOMAP had shown how easily things could go wrong if responsibility was entrusted to others who lacked the experience accumulated by the officials I had inherited from Urquhart. They pressed me to stop the trend; if I did not do so now, it would become irreversible, for there were several new operations in the

---

* Each consisted of three military observers seconded from UNTSO and a civilian member of the Secretariat. Their task was to investigate allegations of attacks on civilian areas.

pipeline. Four days after Iran declared its acceptance of SCR 598, I made my case to Pérez de Cuéllar. To my relief he accepted it without argument.

There followed two months of intense activity as we set up the first new peacekeeping operation in ten years (apart from UNGOMAP). A technical mission left for the field immediately. It reported that the cease-fire line extended for 1,400 kilometres from the shores of the Persian Gulf in the south through marsh, desert and grassland to the Kurd-inhabited mountains of the north. The initial deployment would take place at the height of summer, when temperatures of 50°C were not uncommon in the south; six months later the UNMOs in the north would probably have to patrol by ski (at first I thought this was a flight of fancy by the Norwegian leader of the technical mission, Martin Vadset, the commander of UNTSO, but his prediction was right). Landmines and other unexploded ordnance were everywhere and accommodation was scarce in the heavily bombarded rear areas.

The Secretary-General recommended that the new mission, called the UN Iran–Iraq Military Observer Group (UNIIMOG), should include 350 military observers, with their own communications network and air-craft, plus the usual civilian component to provide support in the polit-ical, legal, information and administrative fields. Many of the military observers would initially be borrowed from the existing operations, as few governments were able to make officers available at such short notice. In any case, I wanted to take advantage of the operation to widen participation in peacekeeping by bringing in new contributors, especially from Communist and Third World countries, alongside the Western democracies which had been the main contributors during the Cold War. This took time. First, we had to check informally that a country was willing to contribute; next we had to check that it would be acceptable to the two belligerents; and finally we had to obtain the formal approval of the Security Council. But we managed to assemble twenty-six troop-contributing countries, five of them African, five Asian, three Communist, three Latin American and ten Western.

As Chief Military Observer we appointed a Yugoslav, Major-General Slavko Jović. The son of a racing driver and air force pilot who was killed in combat when the Germans invaded Yugoslavia in 1941, Jović joined Tito's Partisans at the age of 15 but found that his bourgeois background made him suspect. He could only put this right, he was told, if he volun-teered for the most dangerous missions. This he did and by the time he was 16 he was commanding the equivalent of a platoon. But one day his platoon captured some Chetniks, members of a rival guerrilla group loyal to the monarchist, Mihajlović. As they were lined up to be shot, one whispered to Jović a password intended to indicate that he was a Partisan agent who had infiltrated the Chetniks. Jović failed to recognize the password and the man died with the rest. So Jović fell from grace again. He also had chilling tales to tell of what his unit had done to Croatians and Hungarians in northern Serbia after their German allies abandoned them at the end of the war. I found the horrors difficult to believe. But when I saw Jović in Belgrade in 1991 after fighting had broken out between Serbs and Croats in Croatia, his tales became wholly credible, for even in him the new war had reignited the hatreds of fifty years before. Meanwhile, his toughness, patience and wit made him a good choice to command UNIIMOG. He stood no nonsense from the Iranians and Iraqis and this won him the respect of the officers under his command.

The biggest obstacle to the timely deployment of the operation related to communications. UNIIMOG's radio network would eventually be run by UN civilians, but neither they nor the equipment they would operate could be plucked from the air. So I turned, as my predecessors had so often done, to Canada and asked for the temporary loan of a military signals unit. Ottawa immediately agreed. Canada has from the beginning been the most stalwart of the troop contributors – totally committed to peacekeeping, generous in its support, constructively critical of the Secretariat's efforts. It was the Canadian Foreign Minister, Lester Pearson who, with Secretary-General Dag Hammarskjöld, conceived the idea of deploying an armed UN force, the first of its kind, during the Suez crisis in 1956. Canada had contributed military personnel, usually from the outset, to every one of the thirteen operations which had been set up during the Cold War, and Canadian military observers were already serving in UNGOMAP, the first post-Cold War operation. Later in the year I was to make myself briefly unpopular in Ottawa for ending Canada's 100 per cent record by failing to invite the country to contribute to the first UN operation in Angola. My reason for doing so was not lack of respect for Canada's record but, again, a desire to bring new contributors into peacekeeping.

The cease-fire came into effect at dawn on 20 August 1988. By that time 307 military observers and most of the Canadian signals unit were deployed on either side of the cease-fire line. Fifty-one patrols were undertaken on that first day, comparing well with a daily average of sixty-four patrols after the operation had been fully established. Patrols normally consisted of two officers. Their tasks were to check that the cease-fire was being observed, to investigate complaints of violations and, if a complaint was confirmed, to persuade the violating party to restore the status quo ante. Most of the complaints in those first days were about alleged moves forward from the 'forward defended locations' held by each side on 20 August. This created problems for the UNMOs because the line of confrontation was over 1,400 kilometres long and they had no independent information about where the two sides' forward positions had actually been on that day. So how could they determine the validity of the complaints?

Initially, UNMOs on one side communicated by radio with their colleagues on the other side. After the operation had become established, however, face-to-face meetings ('flag meetings') were held regularly, though the parties, and especially the Iranians, were uneasy about these, fearing that details of their defences would be relayed to the other side. Complaints were very numerous (over one thousand during the first two months) and sometimes trivial. But there were some serious incidents, including the capture by Iraq of several hundred Iranian troops on the fourth night of the cease-fire. The most persistent violation, however, came three weeks later when Iran decided to strengthen its defences by flooding a large area of no man's land in the southern sector of the front. This was one of the issues that dominated my five visits to UNIIMOG. Another was Iraq's refusal to let the Iranians extinguish three burning oil wells on their territory in no man's land.

My first visit to UNIIMOG was in October 1988, seven weeks after the cease-fire had come into effect. No progress was being made in the talks which Pérez de Cuéllar was holding with the two sides in Geneva and New York. Iran continued to insist that the provisions of SCR 598 should be implemented sequentially: the cease-fire was in effect; the next step, therefore, should be withdrawal to the international boundaries. This meant Iraqi withdrawal from Iranian territory, of which it still occupied over 2,000 square kilometres. But withdrawal was Iraq's only high-value card and it was not going to play it early. Iraq therefore insisted that priority be given to the release of prisoners of war. My task was to ensure that the cease-fire remained in force while the diplomatic deadlock was resolved and that the two sides gave UNIIMOG the support it needed to do its job.

I started in Baghdad. I had last been there in 1976. The most striking change was the personality cult of Saddam Hussein; towering portraits of him, in various outfits and benign poses, dominated every roundabout and intersection. But the less than benign reality of the regime became evident one evening. I was enjoying the fresh air outside the Al Rasheed Hotel when Saddam's elder son, Uday, turned up in a small convoy of security vehicles. His arrival sent a perceptible tremor of fear through the other bystanders; they did not acknowledge his presence with respectful bows, as would happen in other Arab countries, but scattered from his path like a flock of pigeons fleeing a falcon.

Jović and his deputy on the Iraqi side, Brigadier-General Venky Patil of the Indian Army, gave a worrying assessment (sitting in the garden to escape the microphones which we assumed to be ubiquitous indoors).

Iraq felt that it was being outmanoeuvred and was frustrated by the no-war-no-peace situation which Iran had brought about. Frustration could lead to a punitive strike by Iraq, which it could launch at a few hours' notice. UNIIMOG had identified nine potential trouble spots; in six of them Iraq held the military advantage.

My principal military interlocutor in Baghdad was the Chief of Staff, Lieutenant-General Nizar Khazraji, and the senior civilian was Dr Riad al-Qaysi, the legal adviser in the Foreign Ministry. Their bitter denunciations of Iran confirmed Jović's and Patil's assessment of their mood. They wanted the United Nations to put pressure on Iran. To most of my requests, they replied that they would do what I asked only if Iran did such-and-such. I asked, for instance, that UNIIMOG aircraft flying between Baghdad and Tehran should be allowed to take the direct route over the front lines instead of making a long detour via Turkey or the Persian Gulf. 'No direct flights', Khazraji replied, 'until Iran withdraws from all the new positions it has occupied since the cease-fire.' They accepted only two UN proposals: the establishment of a 'mixed military working group', which would meet regularly in no man's land, under UNIIMOG chairmanship; and the opening of additional crossing points on the front line.

The next day we flew to Basra and accompanied UNMOs on a patrol in a place called Shalamcheh, flat gravel desert on which there had been many armoured engagements and, earlier in the war, human wave attacks by Iran in which thousands of Pasdaran (Revolutionary Guards) had been 'martyred', most of them in their teens. (The entrance to the Pasdaran headquarters in Tehran was decorated by a huge coloured photograph of a victim of one of these engagements, a teenage boy still alive and peering at the bloody stump which was all that remained of his leg.) We met up with an UNMO patrol from the Iranian side and with them supervised an exchange of about twenty corpses found in no man's land, pathetic bundles of bones and tattered uniforms. This was about the only activity in which the two sides worked willingly together.

On the way back from this expedition I probably came nearer to violent death than on any other occasion during my service with the United Nations. Our aircraft was to land at the small military airport in Baghdad. The UN pilot, who had only just arrived in UNIIMOG, mistakenly approached the airport on a course that would have taken us low over Saddam's palace on the banks of the Tigris. At the last moment, Patil saw what was happening and screamed at the pilot to change course. His alertness may well have saved our lives: three months before two Egyptian fighters arriving in Baghdad to take part in the National Day celebrations had made the same mistake and had been unceremoniously shot down by Saddam's air defences.

In Tehran, the Iranian officials concentrated on the need for Iraq to withdraw immediately from Iranian territory, pointing out that Iran had withdrawn from the small parcels of Iraqi terrritory it had occupied. This was predictable and there was little I could offer in reply other than promises that we would go on trying in Baghdad. I concentrated on getting them to provide the facilities they had promised UNIIMOG. Visits to the area of operation had confirmed that living accommodation was a serious problem. Most of the UNMOs were billeted in Iranian military premises, some of them run by the fanatical Pasdaran. Restrictions had been placed on their leisure activities, on the grounds that these were offensive to Islamic culture. This was certainly true of the pin-ups initially displayed by the Canadian signallers; but I could not accept that listening to music or going for a walk or a jog after work was unacceptable behaviour. The other side of this coin was that I had to lecture the UNMOs, and their Ambassadors in Tehran, on the necessity of respecting the customs and traditions of the host country, however unreasonable the UNMOs might find them. I also asked the Ambassadors to underline to their governments the strenuous nature of patrolling, sometimes on foot or mule-back, in conditions of extreme heat and cold. Young and fit officers were required, not those in mid-career who were deemed to have earned a foreign posting.

My next visit to UNIIMOG was in March 1989. Jović had wanted me to come earlier but intensive preparations for the deployment of the big new operation in Namibia had made that impossible. Meanwhile he had been reporting a hardening of Iranian attitudes. They had disliked the Secretary-General's report following my previous visit and in February they had, at the last minute, declined to attend the first meeting of the mixed military working group to which they had agreed in October. This time I started in Tehran, arriving at midnight after a twenty-four-hour journey from southern Africa. Tensions between pragmatists and fanatics within the regime became apparent at the airport, when the Foreign Ministry and the Pasdaran openly competed for the task of escorting me into Tehran; the Pasdaran won.

The next day was spent inspecting the Iranian flooding of no man's land. By now it extended for almost 70 kilometres over the Shalamcheh battlefield. It denied the Iraqis the option of launching a punitive strike over terrain where they could make the most of their superiority in armour. It was a blatant breach of the cease-fire and had recently been the scene of four artillery duels. The status quo must be restored without delay, I said to the Corps Commander, Haj Ahmed – no rank, because this part of the line was held by the Pasdaran. My diary describes him as 'a thirtyish, blue-eyed fanatic . . . quite agreeable in debate but slippery as a fish'. He insisted that the flooding was due either to nature or to Iraqi monkey business with the dykes and sluices under their control. The most I could get out of him was a half-promise not to do anything that would make it worse.

Back in Tehran I told Ali Akbar Velayati, the Foreign Minister, that my colleagues in UNIIMOG were complaining that Iran's attitude had become unfriendly, suspicious and even hostile. Constant harassment and humiliation were undermining morale, operational capability and the troop-contributing governments' support. It was impossible, in particular, to justify the absence of a status of forces agreement (SOFA) more than six months after the operation had been deployed. Velayati seemed almost to welcome this complaint, presumably because it gave him ammunition in the internal struggle. He arranged an immediate meeting with the officials concerned. Good progress was made. He signed the letter we needed from him on the SOFA; agreement was reached on passports, visas, procedures at the airport, licensing of vehicles, UN driving licences and so on; and promises were made about progress the following week on the weightier issues of communications and helicopters.

The next day was 29 March, three days before D-Day in Namibia when implementation of the settlement plan there would start. It began badly. Wintry weather washed out a planned visit to the northern part of the line; the lawyers in New York were not satisfied by Velayati's letter on the SOFA; and three Irish soldiers in UNIFIL had been killed by a landmine which seemed to have been specifically targeted against them.

In the afternoon I had a long meeting with the Pasdaran Minister, Ali Shamkhani, followed by dinner. Our previous meeting, in October, had been so difficult that at one point I had had to relieve the tension by feigning a stomach upset and absenting myself from the room for ten minutes. As a fanatical Muslim, Shamkhani found it insulting that non-believers in uniform should be in the Islamic Republic monitoring the operations of his Revolutionary Guards. His undisguised hostility to UNIIMOG was no doubt felt by the Pasdaran to license the day-to-day unpleasantnesses they inflicted on its personnel at all levels. The meeting with him was again confrontational, especially over the Secretary-General's report to the Security Council in which he had blamed Iran for the flooding, but it was better-humoured than before. Over dinner he revealed that he was an expert on Omar Khayyám, though this proved to be another stick with which to beat the West. The poet's imagery, he insisted, was entirely religious and had none of the amorous or alcoholic connotations perceived by non-believers. The next morning I was finally authorized by New York to accept Iran's letter on the SOFA and left for Baghdad optimistic that, with Velayati's help, UNIIMOG's conditions might improve a little.

The visit to Baghdad was less testing; as far as UNIIMOG was concerned the Iraqis were the good guys. Patil reported that there had been a thinning out of troops in the north and central sectors but a build-up in the south, perhaps reflecting the emphasis Saddam was placing on the reconstruction of Basra. But there was still a risk of cease-fire violations in the centre and north where the Iranian opposition movement known as the *Mujāhedin-i Khalq* had been allowed to establish bases behind the Iraqi front line. The last day of March was spent agreeably in the central sector on a sunny but cool spring day. The scenery was a tonic after the flat drabness of the battlegrounds to the south. Looking east in the afternoon the eye rested successively on the grass and flowers of the plain, then the Petra-pink of the foothills, the almost Attic blue of the lower mountains and the snow-capped peaks south of Bakhtaran in Iran. There were operational hot-spots too – hill 402 on the border where Iraq was levelling the ground for a vast and bellicose war memorial; hill 312 where an Iranian and an Iraqi soldier shared a tiny position on a ridge; and the three oil wells burning noisily and wastefully in no man's land. At a forward Iraqi position, where we stopped for yoghurt and Pepsi-cola, I got a new bird for my life list – Hume's Wheatear, tamely feeding its young within metres of the Iraqi soldiers. This was the sort of day I loved. But in Baghdad that evening, there were ominous messages from New York about Namibia on the eve of D-Day.

The morning of 1 April was spent in meetings with the Iraqis who, as expected, gave full vent to their indignation about the flooding. In the afternoon they took me on a visit to the ancient site of Babylon. My diary records: 'the site is ghastly; what little remains above ground is being bulldozed for a bombastic and fascist reconstruction to the greater glory of Saddam Hussein, the modern-day Nebuchadnezzar. This is a very distasteful regime.' Early the next morning I was wakened with cables from New York reporting that armed SWAPO fighters had made at least four incursions into Namibia the previous day. I offered to go back to Luanda if the Secretary-General thought that would be useful. Before I left Baghdad I had meetings with the Foreign Minister, Tariq Aziz, and his deputy, but my mind was on other things. Thus ended my second visit to UNIIMOG.

During the following months Namibia was dominant and I did not return to UNIIMOG until mid-September 1989. Having begun the previous visit in Tehran, I started this time in Baghdad. UNIIMOG reported that Iraq had reduced its front-line strength by more than two-thirds since the cease-fire. Only in the central sector did it still have the capacity for a sudden strike through no man's land. Three brigades of the Presidential Guard were deployed there and three kilometres of the Iraqi line had been cleared of mines and wire. This was where Iraq was likely to retaliate if the Iranians enlarged the flooding, which remained the most serious violation of the cease-fire.

The Iraqis preened themselves as the side who were respecting the cease-fire agreement. The meetings in Baghdad were cordial and the hospitality lavish. All my requests were accepted. At dinner on the final evening, the Chief of Staff, General Khazraji, who had been sullen and hostile on my earlier visits, was charm itself, talking freely about our families, careers and hobbies and, very positively, about the role of the UN.* I was even taken on a bird-watching trip to the lake at Habbaniyah, though I was asked not to point my binoculars in the direction of the military establishments in the vicinity. Such harmony and bonhomie can be dangerous for peacemakers and peacekeepers; one has constantly to remind oneself to remain impartial, notwithstanding the helpfulness of one side and the obstructiveness of the other.

There were two interesting field trips. The first was to the northern sector, where the Kurdish factor complicated what was elsewhere the simple equation of Iranian-Iraqi hostility. Each side had its loyal Kurds and its rebellious Kurds, who fought the government and the local loyalists. Flying by helicopter a few kilometres west of the cease-fire line, we could see the enormity of what Saddam had done to his Kurdish subjects. In order to create a *cordon sanitaire* along the border, every town and village had been completely destroyed, not a house left standing. The inhabitants had been transported to camps in the lowlands where their plight fuelled the continuing Kurdish insurgency in the north. The next day we flew over the Fao peninsula and the Shatt al-Arab. It was still blocked by the merchant ships sunk there at the beginning of the war in 1980. Clearance of these wrecks and restoration of freedom of navigation were now Iraq's main conditions for complete withdrawal of its troops from Iranian territory. The ferocity of the fighting in the Fao peninsula eighteen months before was still evident in thousands of hectares of topless palms and shell-pocked sand.

As feared, Tehran again took a much harsher line than Baghdad. In a day of meetings with the Foreign Minister, one of his deputies and the Defence Minister I obtained only one positive response to a long list of proposals about respecting the cease-fire and improving cooperation between the Iranians and UNIIMOG. The exception was Velayati's acceptance in principle that UNIIMOG should start patrolling offshore at the mouth of the Shatt. Gianni Picco's newly launched negotiation on the hostages was also creating some turbulence. I learnt about his new

---

* He was wounded and captured by rebel soldiers in the uprising against Saddam which followed Iraq's defeat in Desert Storm and five years later defected to an Iraqi opposition movement in exile.

role only when, before I left New York, he asked me not to raise the Higgins case with Velayati. In Tehran I found that, without consulting me or Jović, he was using Raymond Sommereyns, Jović's senior political adviser, as his go-between with the Iranians. This had produced a predictable crisis in relations between Jović and Sommereyns which grew worse when I had to tell Jović that there was nothing I could do about it. The delights of working for the UN were further highlighted when I learnt from the BBC that Jan Eliasson, the Swedish diplomat to whom Pérez de Cuéllar had entrusted responsibility for negotiating implementation of the other provisions of SCR 598, had started a new round of shuttle diplomacy, an initiative about which I had heard not a word before leaving New York a few days before.

The field trip in Iran also took me to the mountainous north. The headquarters of UNIIMOG's northern sector was in the town of Saqqez which had been mortared the night before by Kurdish insurgents. But it was a rushed visit, with little time to admire the mountains or visit the front, for there was still work to do in Tehran. It had become evident that Jović's 'command group', which commuted weekly between Baghdad and Tehran and which had previously worked so well, was now rent by personality clashes. I had meetings individually with all the members of the group, except unfortunately the main culprit who was on leave, in an attempt to get them to work together as a team. But the attempt was fruitless. In the year that remained before Saddam's seizure of Kuwait brought UNIIMOG to an end, Jović's confidence in Sommereyns was never restored and tension was already evident between him and his new deputy in Tehran, a Swedish Brigadier-General called Per Källström. Back in New York, I advised Pérez de Cuéllar not to conceal from the Security Council Iran's less than adequate cooperation with UNIIMOG. He took the advice and the Iranians complained strongly about his report. Given what is now known about Picco's hostage negotiations, it was brave of Pérez de Cuéllar to risk antagonizing the Iranians at that stage.

My next visit to UNIIMOG was in May 1990. Two months previously, I had received a long letter from Jović complaining about Källström's alleged temper, erratic behaviour, insubordination and failure to consult. It was not a letter which could be left until my next visit to the mission, so I asked Källström to meet me at Frankfurt airport when I was on my way to the independence celebrations in Namibia. I outlined Jović's complaints. Källström defended himself, calmly and at length, and stated his own complaints about Jović and other senior members of UNIIMOG. After two hours I concluded that Jović and he were both difficult characters, that Källström was to some extent responsible for the deplorable state of relations at the top of UNIIMOG but I could not gauge, without great difficulty, the extent of his responsibility, and that in these circumstances my only option was to exhort both officers to put things right. This I did, on the spot to Källström and to Jović in New York ten days later.

I mention this episode not to cast aspersions on either of the protagonists but to illustrate the complexities of directing and managing a multinational military operation. The competence of armies is based on discipline and comradeship: do as you are told and look after each other. Discipline and comradeship are achieved by training, working and living together and by absorbing the ethos of the army, with all its past triumphs and traditions. UN peacekeeping has some of the institutional trappings – medals, accoutrements, memorials, anniversaries, established practices – but it will never achieve the discipline and comradeship which hold a national army together. For well-founded political and financial reasons, the member states will never agree to establish a standing United Nations Army and UN peacekeeping operations will continue to be composed of units and officers on short-term attachment from their national armies. The effectiveness of UN peacekeeping will continue, therefore, to depend on the ability of the Under-Secretary-General and the Military Adviser in New York, and the commanders in the field, to weld together into a coherent force soldiers with widely varying traditions, standards, abilities, systems and languages. The difficulty of this task was aggravated for a while by my decision in 1988 to widen participation in peacekeeping. It was the right thing to do, but it meant that less than a third of the countries contributing to the new operations had previous experience of the art. This undoubtedly impaired the effectiveness of those operations, especially in their initial stages.

It also has to be said that governments were often reluctant to give of their best. When we were looking for a commanding officer, we first decided which country to approach. This depended on political factors relating both to the parties to the conflict in question and to the UN's need to ensure that the top posts were equitably shared between the troop-contributing countries. Once the country had been chosen, we asked its government to propose a slate of three officers for us to choose from. The government often declined to do so, arguing the difficulty of assembling a slate of three at such short notice or insisting on the outstanding qualifications of their chosen candidate. As a result, the Secretary-General had little real control over the appointment of commanding officers, and it sometimes became painfully clear that the officer pressed upon us by a government had not been chosen for the quality of his military skills.

Constant vigilance was therefore necessary, as were frequent visits to the field. The latter became more difficult when Boutros-Ghali took over as Secretary-General in 1992. Six months after assuming office, he was outraged by the number of senior United Nations officials attending the UN Conference on the Environment and Development in Rio. On return to New York, he proclaimed a ban on 'promenades by Under-Secretaries-General', who ought to be in New York running their departments. As a result he blocked many trips proposed by myself and others. In vain did I plead that operations of such complexity cannot be managed by fax and telephone alone and that it is necessary to be on the spot to judge how well, or more often how badly, their heterogeneous personnel are working together.

When I reached Tehran in May 1990, it seemed that my exhortations to Jović and Källström had had some effect. But the visit was dominated by a new management issue which generated great heat. New York had decided to reduce the UNMOs' local allowance. We also decided to pay more of it in local currency at the official rate of exchange (which was much less favourable to the officers than changing their dollars on the black market). These decisions were reasonable. It was true that many of the UNMOs lived in primitive conditions and had to endure the social restrictions imposed on them by the Iranians. But the remuneration they had been receiving was far above what could be justified as compensation for these hardships. This message was ill-received in a long and painful meeting I had with the contingent commanders.

As for the Iranians, their views seemed to have changed little and the issues familiar from previous visits were discussed with Government and Pasdaran as repetitively and unproductively as ever. There were only two glimmers of hope. The Iranians hinted that Tehran might be more flexible about the proposed Mixed Military Working Group, which had still not met because of differences over its rules of procedure; and vague ideas were mentioned about the negotiation of two separate but simultaneous agreements on ending the flooding of no man's land and extinguishing the burning oil wells. As usual, consolation was to be found in the field trips, including one to the Iranian edge of the marshes made famous by Wilfred Thesiger. The bird-life was spectacular but the Marsh Arabs had been driven out by the war and were said to be in camps on the Iraqi side of the line.

Before leaving New York, I had heard that Saddam had recently sent Rafsanjani what he described as 'a message of peace' and that the Iranians regarded this as 'a positive signal'. I could discover nothing more in Tehran, but in Baghdad an Iraqi friend said that Saddam's letter, dated 21 April, had proposed a summit meeting in Mecca a week later. After ten days had passed, Rafsanjani agreed in principle to a summit but sought a preparatory meeting first (a typical Iranian reaction). The Iraqis sought clarification, which was still awaited. Tariq Aziz, I was told, had assured the Secretary-General that the proposed meeting would be 'parallel with' his own efforts, an assurance with which, my informant said, Pérez de Cuéllar had been 'very happy'. I subsequently learnt that he had not been happy at all. Nor was I happy at having to obtain this information from an Iraqi source rather than my UN colleagues.

The Iraqis were scornful of the glimmers of hope I brought from Tehran and my discussions in Baghdad were as frustratingly immobile as those in the other capital. But I was released from them by an instruction from Pérez de Cuéllar to return immediately to New York and thence to Nicaragua where the Contras had suspended their demobilization (the second time I had had to cut short a UNIIMOG visit because of a crisis in another operation half a world away). Little did I foresee that the next time I was in Baghdad the Iraqi Army would have occupied Kuwait. But on the way to the Iraqi side of the marshes that morning we had flown over a huge tank park, with hundreds of tanks lined up like guardsmen, and I had thought that if peace was ever achieved with Iran, Iraq's battle-hardened army would present a fearsome threat to its other neighbours.

Contrary to my first fears, the impact of Iraq's invasion of Kuwait on 2 August 1990 was positive for UNIIMOG. After two weeks, Saddam offered to accept the frontier agreed with Iran in 1975, to withdraw completely from Iranian territory and to return all Iranian prisoners of war. At last UNIIMOG was able to carry out its mandate. Notwithstanding (or perhaps because of) the growing tension over Kuwait, the withdrawal of both sides' forces to the internationally recognized borders was almost complete by the end of September. The Security Council extended UNIIMOG's mandate for two months, with three tasks: to verify the remaining stages of the withdrawal; to help the two sides resolve about fifty differences over the exact line of the border; and to help them establish an area of separation into which neither would introduce armed forces.

UNIIMOG's future became a matter of contention in November when that two-month mandate expired. Iraq wanted it to be renewed for six months; Iran was prepared to accept two months at the most. Pérez de Cuéllar agreed that I should make brief visits to both capitals but he wanted the visit to Baghdad to be as inconspicuous as possible, lest it complicate his own efforts to bring about a peaceful resolution of the Kuwait crisis. Sadly I would not be welcomed by Slavko Jović who had just been flown home after a heart attack. This time I started in Baghdad. Saddam International Airport was eerily silent but there were few other indications of the crisis. The hotel restaurants were full of diners who, I was told, were there on the orders, and at the expense, of the government in order to show visiting foreigners that all was confident and calm in Baghdad. But the UNIIMOG personnel doubted that the crisis could be resolved without war. The civilians were understandably anxious about their security and most of them were keen to leave; but for professional reasons, and undisguised financial ones, almost all the UNMOs wanted to stay. The two parties' positions were the same as before. Baghdad wanted UNIIMOG to stay. Tehran challenged me to explain what value UNIIMOG added to the peace process which was progressing well. I did so repeatedly, but without effect. After two days of argument, the most I could get Iran to accept was a two-month extension, with UNIIMOG's existing strength being cut by half.

This was the least enjoyable of my five visits to UNIIMOG. The Kuwait crisis and Jović's departure had deepened the fissures in an already fractious community (my diary complained: 'how I hate and deplore these personality clashes which disfigure almost every one of our operations and consume so much of my time on these visits'); and the decision about UNIIMOG's future was untidy and inconclusive. My own preference was to close the mission there and then, but when Pérez de Cuéllar was trying to mediate a peaceful settlement in Kuwait, Iraq's wishes could not be ignored.

After 29 November 1990, when the Security Council authorized the use of force to liberate Kuwait, the likelihood of war increased and UNIIMOG's situation in Iraq became more and more perilous. On 9 January, after the failure of the talks between Tariq Aziz and the United States Secretary of State, James Baker, in Geneva, panic seized the UNIIMOG civilians in Baghdad and they had to be told very firmly that they could not possibly evacuate when the Secretary-General was due to arrive in Baghdad three days later. After Pérez de Cuéllar's brave but unsuccessful visit, all UNIIMOG personnel in Iraq were moved to the border area and they left Iraqi territory altogether as soon as the war began four days later. At the end of January the mandate was extended for a final period of one month, during which the UNMOs, working from the Iranian side of the line, helped the two sides to resolve the few remaining disputed positions on the border.

Thanks to Saddam's folly in invading Kuwait, the military provisions of SCR 598 had thus been implemented, to the great benefit of Iran, and UNIIMOG had been able to fulfil its mandate, an outcome which it had been difficult to imagine six months before. UNIIMOG's closure was overdue but it caused a brief moment of nostalgia for the hectic and euphoric days in 1988 when we established the first new peacekeeping operation for ten years. Now there was a new operation every three months, the workload was overwhelming and there was an undeniable decline in the quality of our performance.

10

Namibia

With the end of the Cold War certain conflicts became soluble as the superpowers saw that peace served their interests better than continued war. Namibia was the first of these conflicts and the stage on which the United Nations deployed its first 'multifunctional' peacekeeping operation to help hostile parties implement a negotiated peace settlement. Strictly speaking, there had been one previous multifunctional operation. It was deployed in 1962–3 to assist the implementation of an agreement for the transfer of the western part of New Guinea from the Netherlands to Indonesia. For a transitional period of seven months it assumed responsibility for the administration of the territory, as well as monitoring an agreed cease-fire. But it was of modest size and brief duration and made little impact on the doctrine or practice of peacekeeping. The Namibia operation, on the other hand, was to be of great importance in the evolution of the UN's new role, for it was a conspicuous success and set high standards which few subsequent operations could match.

Namibia had been a German colony known as South West Africa. After the First World War it became a League of Nations mandated territory whose administration was entrusted to South Africa 'as an integral portion of the Union of South Africa'. The validity of this mandate became a contentious issue as soon as the United Nations was established. While South Africa tried to incorporate South West Africa, the opponents of apartheid tried to have the League of Nations mandate declared invalid. They succeeded in 1966 when the General Assembly declared the territory to be the direct responsibility of the United Nations. But South Africa remained in possession and pursued its own plans. The South West Africa People's Organization (SWAPO) started a guerrilla war, which was vigorously countered by the South African Defence Forces (SADF).

In the mid-seventies five Western countries (Britain, Canada, France, Germany, the United States) formed a 'contact group' to discuss with South Africa, SWAPO and the 'Front Line States' of southern

Africa* how the conflict in Namibia could be resolved.† Early in 1978 they presented to the Security Council a proposal that Namibia should proceed to independence through elections administered by South Africa but under the supervision and control of the United Nations. South Africa would continue to administer the territory until independence but the UN would ensure that this did not compromise the freedom and fairness of the elections. Secretary-General Waldheim was asked to prepare a plan for the implementation of the proposal.

The main elements of the Contact Group's proposal and Waldheim's plan were as follows. Before implementation began, the Secretary-General would deploy a peacekeeping operation in Namibia, known as the United Nations Transition Assistance Group (UNTAG). It would be headed by a Special Representative of the Secretary-General (SRSG), who would be the senior UN representative in the territory. UNTAG would have a civilian and a military component, both of which would report to the Special Representative. The civilian component would include the Special Representative's office, a large police element, an electoral division, an administration division and a UNHCR office which would be responsible for the return of some 40,000 Namibian refugees, most of them from African countries. The military component would include a number of infantry battalions, logistics units and military observers.

Implementation of the plan would begin on 'D-Day', when a ceasefire would come into effect between South Africa and SWAPO and both sides' combatants would be confined to base. During the ensuing twelve weeks South African forces in Namibia would be reduced to 1,500 troops and the local forces established by South Africa would be disbanded. Nothing specific was said about the demobilization of SWAPO combatants, other than that those outside the territory would return peacefully through designated entry points. These military aspects of the plan would be monitored by the military component of the UN operation (UNTAG).

Administration of the territory would remain the responsibility of the South African Administrator-General but he would be obliged to carry out his functions 'to the satisfaction of' the Special Representative of the UN Secretary-General. The Special Representative's central task would be to ensure that the necessary conditions were established for free and fair elections and an impartial electoral process; the electoral campaign

---

* 'FLS' for short. They were Angola, Botswana, Mozambique, Tanzania and Zambia and would soon be joined by Zimbabwe. Nigeria sometimes participated in their meetings: the enlarged group was then referred to as the FLSN.
† The General Assembly adopted 'Namibia' as the territory's name in 1968.

would not begin until he had pronounced himself satisfied on this score. Before it began, refugees and SWAPO fighters outside the territory would return, all political prisoners would be released and all legislation that could hinder free and fair elections would be repealed. The Administrator-General would also be required to ensure the good conduct of the South West African Police, whose performance of their duties would be closely scrutinized by the police component of UNTAG.

The voting would be for a constituent assembly that would draw up and adopt the constitution of an independent and sovereign Namibia. The electoral campaign and the election itself would be closely monitored by the electoral component of UNTAG. The Special Representative would determine whether the election had been free and fair. Once he had certified that it had been, the remaining South African troops would leave the territory, SWAPO bases would be closed and the constituent assembly would start work. It was hoped that the elections could be held about seven months after D-Day. Thereafter the timing would depend on how long it took for the constituent assembly to agree on the constitution. UNTAG would remain deployed until independence day.

Waldheim's plan provoked much debate, especially about the military and police functions. Only after he had tabled an 'explanatory statement' addressing some of the concerns expressed did the Security Council adopt resolution 435 which approved his plan. Implementation of the plan did not begin until 1989. In the intervening years certain additional agreements and 'informal understandings' were concluded between the Contact Group, the Front Line States, South Africa and SWAPO. They related primarily to the principles to be included in the constitution, the electoral system, the UN's obligation to act impartially and the monitoring of SWAPO bases after D-Day. Another issue which was much discussed was the need for an unqualified amnesty for all Namibian refugees and exiles before repatriation began, but agreement on this was not reached until after D-Day.

The adoption of resolution 435 in September 1978 raised hopes that Namibia would proceed rapidly to independence. The hopes soon proved ill-founded. South Africa raised many obstacles and a 'pre-implementation meeting' in early 1981 failed to restore momentum. A further setback occurred when South Africa, prompted by the United States, made implementation of SCR 435 conditional on the withdrawal of Cuban troops from Angola. These were deployed at the time of Angola's independence in 1975 and had since helped to defend Angola against South African incursions in pursuit of SWAPO guerrillas based there. By 1982 this 'linkage' had become an apparently insuperable obstacle to implementation of SCR 435. The Secretary-General, with varying degrees of support from the other four members of the Contact Group, took the position that the question of Cuban troops was outside the scope of SCR 435 and that the only outstanding issues were the electoral system to be used (this was settled in 1985), the composition of UNTAG and the date when implementation would begin.

Meanwhile, Namibia had been a major part of my work during my two years as Ambassador in Angola. Sam Nujoma, the President of SWAPO, was a neighbour and used to come round for tea and cucumber sandwiches. But these were difficult meetings, peppered with diatribes about the weakness of the Contact Group and London's alleged support for linkage. More valuable were my meetings with the American negotiators, Chester Crocker, the calm, cerebral and somewhat intimidating Assistant Secretary for Africa in the State Department, and Frank Wisner, his more ebullient deputy. I was one of their channels to the Angolan Government, relaying messages to and from the Angolan Minister of the Interior, Manuel Alexandre Rodrigues ('Kito'*), who was at that time their principal interlocutor in Luanda.

Crocker and Wisner were trying to persuade the Angolan Government that Angola need not fear linkage. Once Namibia was independent, they argued, South Africa would no longer have reason to attack Angola or provide military support to UNITA, the Angolan rebel movement led by Jonas Savimbi. Angola could thus afford to dispense with Cuba's military support; and the Angolans would get rid of SWAPO whose presence they disliked, in spite of their public declarations of support for the Namibian people's liberation struggle. This, said Crocker and Wisner, was a good deal for the Angolans; they ought to take it before things got worse. I was always uneasy about the UNITA limb of this argument. The South Africans would still want UNITA to replace the Angolan Government, which they saw as a malevolent Marxist influence in the region. If Savimbi continued to control border areas in the north of the country, they could supply him overland via Zaire. The latter fear proved well-founded, though I did not foresee at that time how illegally mined diamonds would enable Savimbi to maintain his war effort even after the loss of South African support. My other difference with my American friends related to the Cubans. As far as I was concerned, they were a good thing. They had done wonders for Angola's education and health services and were preventing the South African army (SADF) from running wild all over southern Angola.

After I joined the UN Secretariat, I participated in occasional meetings with Chester Crocker or members of his team. The plans for UNTAG were reviewed from time to time by Martti Ahtisaari, who was to be the

---

* Like most senior members of the ruling party, the MPLA, Rodrigues still used, and was known by, his *nom de guerre*.

Special Representative, his Special Assistant, Cedric Thornberry, and the Military Adviser, Timothy Dibuama. Because of the delay in implementing SCR 435, UNTAG was more thoroughly planned than any previous peacekeeping operation – and than any since. The pace quickened in 1988. Thanks to Crocker's diplomatic skills and the thaw in the Cold War, a series of meetings between Angola, Cuba and South Africa, mediated by the Americans with Soviet participation, led to acceptance of linkage. A 'Geneva Protocol', signed in August, provided that Cuban (and South African) troops would be withdrawn from Angola; the settlement plan for Namibia* would be implemented; there would be an immediate 'cessation of hostile acts'† and SWAPO forces would be redeployed north of the 16th parallel (which runs about 150 kilometres north of the Angola–Namibia border). SWAPO was not a party to the agreement but Angola and Cuba undertook to urge SWAPO to comply with its provisions.

The next month Pérez de Cuéllar, who had succeeded Waldheim in 1982, was invited by President Botha to visit South Africa to discuss implementation of SCR 435. On the way back he spent a night in Luanda for the same purpose. Ahtisaari and I were in the party. Pérez de Cuéllar's main task in Pretoria was to convince the South African Government that it could rely on him personally to be impartial in implementing the settlement plan and that an 'impartiality package' agreed in 1982 (one of the informal understandings) would similarly commit the whole UN system to be impartial. The South Africans had confidence in Pérez de Cuéllar and on two previous visits, in 1983 and 1985, he had reassured them on these points. He had no difficulty in doing so again. Meanwhile South Africa had already completed the withdrawal of its troops from Angola. In these circumstances the visit to Pretoria was short and sweet. So it was in Luanda; President José Eduardo dos Santos of Angola confirmed his country's commitment to implementation of the settlement plan and Nujoma confirmed his acceptance of the Geneva Protocol. By early December there was agreement that implementation should start on 1 April 1989. But South Africa would not sign a document to that effect until the Security Council had established a new UN peacekeeping operation (UNAVEM) to verify the Cuban withdrawal. This gave us a week to do what normally takes months. But we succeeded and on 22 December 1988 there was a signature ceremony in New York at which Pérez de Cuéllar formally announced that D-Day would be 1 April 1989.

---

* By 'settlement plan' is meant the plan approved by SCR 435 in 1978 plus the additional agreements and 'informal understandings' that were negotiated in subsequent years.
† Semantics again: this was a full cease-fire but it had to be differentiated from the formal cease-fire on D-Day that would start implementation of the plan.

UNAVEM was deployed in Angola in time to verify, on 10 January 1989, the withdrawal of the first batch of Cuban troops. A total of 50,000 were to depart over a period of thirty months. UNAVEM would consist of seventy military observers contributed by ten countries. Again I widened the net; five of them had never before contributed to UN peace-keeping. The commander was from Brazil, Brigadier-General Péricles Ferreira Gomes. He started badly, giving an interview to the *New York Times* which seemed to endorse South Africa's doubts about whether UNAVEM would be able to check that there were no Cuban troops left in Angola. I sent him a brisk rebuke and received an unrepentant reply. By this time I was in the Middle East. New York agreed that Ferreira Gomes should be summoned to meet me in London and that Knutsson, the senior political officer in UNTSO, the UN observer group based in Jerusalem, should be sent to Luanda for a few weeks to guide him in the UN's ways of peacekeeping. The meeting in London was no fun. But Knutsson did a good job in Luanda and my personal relations with Ferreira Gomes soon recovered.

This episode illustrated the undesirability of entrusting a peacekeeping command to an officer with no previous experience of the art. Peacekeeping is very different from normal soldiering. It is more like police work; the peacekeeper has to persuade individuals and groups to do his bidding without undermining their confidence in him or using the weapons at his disposal, except in the last resort if his own life is in danger. Peacekeeping thus requires soldiers to set aside their training for war and adopt a different ethos while they are on peacekeeping duty. Their governments do not always like this; at the time of the French battalion's crisis in southern Lebanon in 1986, the French Defence Minister denounced me for undermining '*la combativité de l'Armée française*'.

The Ferreira Gomes crisis also exemplifed a common problem. How much were commanders authorized to say to the media? The instinct of Secretaries-General was to demand that they say nothing without prior authorization from New York. But this was obviously impracticable. All the peacekeeping operations at that time were six hours or more to the east of New York. The media could not be asked to wait for a statement from the UN commander to be cleared by New York, especially if it was known that a serious incident had taken place; if the media *were* so asked they would simply concoct their own story from less authoritative sources, including the parties to the conflict. Then there was the problem of who should speak for the UN operation. Obviously again, it should be the head of the operation and his/her spokesman. But this did not take account of the troop-contributing governments' political need for inspiring stories about 'our boys in the field'. The result was that each contingent tended to have its own spokesman. Meanwhile the telecommunications revolution was making it possible for journalists at home to make instant contact with units, however remote their location, as soon as it became known that an incident had occurred.

I tried to establish five rules. First, operations should respond promptly to the media's requests for information, normally through a designated spokesman. Secondly, they should immediately report to New York what they had said, so that the Secretary-General's spokesman could sing the same tune. Thirdly, they should avoid speculating on political issues. Fourthly, they should provide details, especially details relating to responsibility for the incident, only if they were absolutely sure of the facts. Few things discredited the UN more than having to recant when investigation revealed that the facts were not as originally described. And, finally, stories for home consumption should be strictly about the boys' lives in the field and not venture into the politics of the conflict. I thought these rules were simple and obviously right. But it was very difficult to get them followed.

UNAVEM thus had a shaky start but its task proved to be fairly straightforward. The only significant problem arose from attacks on Cuban soldiers by UNITA. Ten Cubans were killed in two attacks and in January 1990 the withdrawal was suspended for a month. But the lost time was soon recovered and withdrawal was completed, ahead of schedule, in May 1991. UNAVEM's success illustrated how much can be achieved if the peacekeepers are given a practicable mandate and the parties cooperate.

Implementation of the Namibia operation was more difficult. The five permanent members of the Security Council pressed for the military component of UNTAG to be halved. The recent détente in southern Africa, they argued, meant that the risks were now less than when UNTAG was designed ten years before. South Africa took the same view. It was vehemently rejected by the massed ranks of the Non-Aligned, the Africans (especially the Front Line States) and SWAPO. The South African Government, they said, had consolidated its power in Namibia; its troops and police were there in greater strength than in 1978; UNTAG's military capacity should therefore be increased, not reduced. However, it would be unwise to tamper with the settlement plan. So they would not press for an increase; they simply wanted the plan to be implemented in its existing form; the P-5 should be similarly prudent.

This was a worrying development. If the plan had to be reworked and approved anew by the Security Council, how could we get the troops and civilians on the ground by 1 April? The Secretariat itself was divided. The Military Adviser, Timothy Dibuama, opposed any reduction in UNTAG's troop strength. So did Dewan Prem Chand, the Indian general who had been Force Commander-designate of UNTAG since 1980. He had begun his career in the Indian Army of the Raj and, to my delight, had never lost the mannerisms he acquired then. He served the UN with distinction in the Congo and later in Cyprus, where he prevented the Turks from seizing Nicosia airport in 1974. I supported Dibuama and Prem Chand, as did Dayal, Pérez de Cuéllar's Chef de Cabinet. But Ahtisaari doubted whether so many troops were needed and was ready to accept the reduction demanded by the P-5. He too had no previous experience of peacekeeping and was much influenced by Cedric Thornberry, an Irish lawyer who was his principal assistant in the Department of Administration. In the early eighties Thornberry had been the Senior Political Adviser in UNFICYP and then in UNTSO, an experience that had left him convinced that the military had assumed too dominant a role in peacekeeping; civilians, including civilian police, should play a fuller part. He was right in this, though I did not see it at the time, and the success of UNTAG owed much to the skill with which he assembled and directed its civilian components.

Pérez de Cuéllar was thus at the centre of a conflict which split the whole United Nations community: on one side were South Africa, the P-5 and Ahtisaari; on the other SWAPO, the Africans and Non-Aligned, Dayal, Prem Chand and myself. His discomfort showed. At a meeting with a South African delegation, my diary recorded, he 'was at his worst, appearing uninterested and distractedly tearing pieces of notepaper into tiny fragments'. His instinct was to support the Non-Aligned and keep the plan as it was. But his vision of the post-Cold War UN accorded a central role to the P-5, whom he had successfully engaged in his efforts to end the Iran–Iraq war. When I returned to New York in mid-January after a visit to UNIFIL in southern Lebanon, the Security Council had just adopted a resolution which called on Pérez de Cuéllar 'to identify wherever possible tangible cost-saving measures without prejudice to his ability fully to carry out the mandate as established in 1978'. This was another Balfour-style attempt to bridge a gap with incompatible words. It placed on the Secretary-General the onus of recommending a reduction which he had told the Non-Aligned he was unwilling to accept.

However, Dibuama recognized the way the wind was blowing and devised an ingenious compromise. Pérez de Cuéllar thought it offered a way out. The original plan was for six infantry battalions to be deployed in Namibia, with a seventh in reserve in its home country. Each battalion would include three line companies.* Dibuama's proposal was for only

---

* An infantry battalion is normally composed of several line companies, one support company and one administration company. The troops in the line companies are available for operational duties in the field. They are the 'teeth'; the other two companies are the 'tail'.

three battalions to be deployed initially but for these to be enlarged battalions, each with five line companies instead of three. The other four battalions would be held in reserve at home. The authorized strength would remain at 7,500 all ranks, as in SCR 435, but the budget would be based on a strength of only 4,650. The reduction in line strength would amount to only three companies (16.7 per cent) but the improved teeth-to-tail ratio would reduce UNTAG's overall budget by about 40 per cent. If during implementation the initial deployment turned out to be insufficient, the Secretary-General would so inform the Council and, with its concurrence, would deploy as many of the reserve battalions as he judged necessary, within the overall ceiling of 7,500 all ranks.

There were some obvious weaknesses in this scheme. It would disappoint the four countries which, after years of planning, would not now be deploying their battalions. Could they be expected to keep them on stand-by for a deployment which might not materialize? Was it realistic to think that the P-5 would ever permit such a deployment, given their financial concerns? Even if they did, could the additional battalions be deployed in time to cope with the crisis that would have revealed the inadequacy of the initial deployment? Prem Chand stubbornly refused any reduction and dismissed Dibuama's plan with scorn. He was an old man now, emotional in his reaction to difficulties and politically careless. His enthusiastic talk, for instance, about what a good chap one of the South African generals was had created the impression that he inclined towards South Africa. But the impression was wrong, as was now demonstrated by the vigour of his support for SWAPO and the Africans. Understandably he found it difficult to stomach the cynical realities of multilateral diplomacy in New York. When he learnt that the Secretary-General was disposed to favour Dibuama's plan, he threatened to resign. Appeals to his loyalty to the UN and the Secretary-General eventually prevailed. But this episode left scars which were to infect his relations with Ahtisaari and, especially, Thornberry throughout the Namibia operation.

The Secretary-General's report recommending the Dibuama plan was published on 24 January 1989. It was denounced by SWAPO and the FLS – and by Ricardo Alarcón, a Deputy Foreign Minister who had come from Havana to reinforce the Africans. Pérez de Cuéllar, they said, had tampered with the settlement plan and sold out to the Permanent Five (both of which charges were substantially true). After a painful meeting with the Africans, I suggested to Pérez de Cuéllar that he might follow Waldheim's example in 1978 and give the Security Council an 'explanatory statement' responding to some of the Africans' concerns. The President of the Council picked up the idea and negotiated a text which the Africans reluctantly accepted. On 16 February the Council approved both the Secretary-General's report and his explanatory statement, and decided to implement SCR 435 'in its original and definitive form'. Balfour would have been proud.

Time was now extremely short. The draft budget was submitted to the General Assembly that afternoon. But the Front Line States again delayed progress by insisting that UNTAG should not be allowed to purchase any goods or services from South African suppliers. As a result, the budget was not authorized until 1 March. The composition of UNTAG was approved by the Council on 23 February, the second day of a conference at which we were already briefing the proposed troop contributors. We were cutting corners. On 26 February Prem Chand and his senior staff officers, accompanied by Dibuama, arrived in Windhoek, the Namibian capital. Ahtisaari and Thornberry, still in New York, were uneasy about the direct communication which then began between Prem Chand and my office. I reassured them that once the mission was established such correspondence would be about technical military matters only; on matters of policy the Force Commander would be obliged to submit his recommendations through Ahtisaari, as Special Representative. All of us were feeling our way. Never before had there been a peacekeeping operation with such a wide range of civilian functions and we had not thought through what this would imply at the New York end. Would Ahtisaari report to various departments in New York, depending on the subject matter of each communication, or would he report to just one department which would then consult others as necessary? The latter is what eventually happened, and worked well, but it took us a little time to establish the modus operandi.

On 14 March, Pérez de Cuéllar sent letters to South Africa and SWAPO formally proposing that the cease-fire come into effect on 1 April and seeking confirmation that they accepted this and had taken the necessary measures to cease all warlike acts and operations. By 21 March both had formally accepted the proposal.

However, at the last moment we had wind that all was not well. The settlement plan had been precise about what should happen both to the South African Defence Forces and to the local forces they had established in Namibia. But all that was said about the SWAPO combatants was that they would be confined to base with effect from D-Day and that those outside the territory would eventually be permitted to return peacefully to take part in the election. The reason for this imprecision was that there was no agreed answer to two questions: where were the SWAPO bases, and who would monitor the SWAPO combatants' confinement to those bases? In 1978 it was not disputed that SWAPO had bases in Angola and Zambia; but SWAPO insisted that it also had bases inside Namibia. This was contested by the South Africans, who maintained that SWAPO had never had fixed bases in Namibia and that its operations there were carried out by guerrillas infiltrated from neighbouring countries. The members of the Contact Group were inclined to support South Africa on this. On the second point, it was agreed that if there *were* SWAPO bases in Namibia, UNTAG would be responsible for verifying that the SWAPO combatants were confined to them. But as regards SWAPO bases outside Namibia, Angola objected, on grounds of principle ostensibly related to its sovereignty, to their being monitored by the United Nations. In 1978 the members of the Contact Group, in their desire to get their proposal to the Security Council, left these questions (like some others) to be resolved at a later stage.

The Contact Group revisited the two questions in 1982. The result was an 'informal understanding'. They told the Secretary-General that in further discussions it had been agreed *inter alia* that 'UNTAG, with the co-operation of host governments . . . would monitor SWAPO bases in Angola and Zambia'. This resolved the second question, though there was no precision about the respective roles of the host governments and the United Nations. But on the first question, SWAPO had continued to insist that it did have bases inside Namibia and that they should be monitored by UNTAG. This had not been accepted by the Contact Group and there was still no provision in the settlement plan for any monitoring of SWAPO troops *inside* Namibia. Now that implementation was about to begin, we in the Secretariat had to establish that SWAPO accepted that it was bound by the 1982 informal understanding. We also had to define the division of labour between the Angolan Government and UNTAG in monitoring the SWAPO fighters restricted to base in that country (it was agreed by all that there were no longer any SWAPO fighters in Zambia).

Following the Security Council's decision to establish UNTAG, I drafted a memorandum on both questions and sent it to the Angolans and SWAPO for their comments. An ominous silence ensued. The South Africans, with American support, pressed for assurances that the arrangements would be in place by 1 April; for them it was of cardinal importance, both politically and operationally, that the international monitoring of their forces should be matched by international monitoring of SWAPO. I was not in a position to give them the assurances they wanted and therefore decided to go to Luanda to sort the matter out on the spot – and to take a look at UNAVEM. On 16 March, a few hours before I was due to leave New York, the Angolan Mission asked me to postpone my visit until after 25 March. This was too close to D-Day, so I decided to bash on regardless, as Prem Chand would put it.

When I reached Luanda, the picture became clearer but more worrying. The Angolan Foreign Minister, Pedro de Castro Van Dúnem ('Loy'), told me that our memorandum had raised issues which could be resolved only by Presidents dos Santos and Nujoma. They, and he, would be in Harare all week for a summit of the Front Line States, after which there would be public holidays in Angola until the 28th. I explained the urgency and persuaded Loy that I should go to Harare to see dos Santos and Nujoma there.

The next three days were devoted to an inspection of UNAVEM. The military observers were already working well together; relations with the Angolan and Cuban authorities seemed to be excellent; and the Angolans had displayed their remarkable ability to improvise. In all but one of the six places I visited they had provided UNAVEM with adequate facilities, a considerable achievement in a country where everything had been degraded by twenty-eight years of uninterrupted war.

But while UNAVEM was no longer a worry, the problem of the SWAPO bases was turning out to be worse than I had feared. In Lubango, the main city in southern Angola, the Chief of Staff, General António dos Santos França ('Ndalu'), agreed that UNTAG military observers could come to Angola to verify that the Angolans were duly monitoring the SWAPO troops and that the observers could be based in Lubango. But he could not yet tell me how the Angolans would do their part; this awaited a decision by dos Santos and Nujoma. Part of the problem, he said, was that there were very few SWAPO bases as such and even these were not fenced, which would make monitoring difficult; most of the fighters were scattered in the bush in units as small as platoons; he supposed that they could be concentrated in 'bases' but only if SWAPO agreed. The Angolans, he said, accepted the commitment they had entered into in 1982 but were worried that they would be blamed if a few armed SWAPO fighters turned up in Namibia. He indicated, as Loy had done, that the Angolans wanted to be rid of them all; they failed to respect Angolan sovereignty and they attracted attacks from their enemy in the south (exactly the same reasons that the Lebanese had for wanting to see the back of the PLO); they would not want cantonment to have the effect of encouraging the SWAPO fighters to stay put in Angola.

President dos Santos lent us his executive jet for the flight to Harare – at 41,000 feet to escape Savimbi's Stingers. The film *Niagara* was screened on the video and Marilyn Monroe was a potent distraction as I tried to explain the political complexities to Michael Moriarty, an Irish colonel who was to command UNTAG's detachment in Angola. I saw dos Santos that evening. He was initially evasive about the SWAPO bases, preferring to speculate about possible South African violations of the settlement plan. But when pressed he confirmed that Angola would honour the commitments it had entered into in 1982; an UNTAG military delegation should return to Angola early the following week to discuss the details.

The meeting with Sam Nujoma the next morning (23 March, nine days before D-Day) was much more difficult. In his view Waldheim's explanatory statement of August 1978 meant that SWAPO troops would be monitored by UNTAG in bases in Namibia. SWAPO had never accepted the 1982 agreement on monitoring in Angola and Zambia; it had been imposed without any account being taken of the amendments SWAPO had proposed. If the SWAPO bases in Angola were not monitored, I replied, there would be no implementation of the settlement plan. Nujoma counter-attacked: what then would happen to the SWAPO fighters inside Namibia? Who would provide them with food and medical care? Why was it that I and the rest of the UN wanted only to humiliate SWAPO and appease the South Africans? It appeared to him that UNTAG's role would simply be to chase SWAPO fighters from Namibia into Angola.

Where were the SWAPO bases in Namibia, I asked. 'We will tell you where they are,' Nujoma replied. I then said, as firmly as I could, that the plan approved by the Security Council did not allow for bases for SWAPO fighters inside Namibia. I began to describe the previous night's conversation with dos Santos but Nujoma interrupted – 'I don't want to hear what Angolans think; they are Angolans and we are Namibians'. Eventually he agreed to give instructions for liaison officers to be appointed to work with the UNTAG delegation in Luanda the next week. But the 1982 agreement remained unacceptable to SWAPO. I insisted that it was an integral part of the UN plan, but assured him that the UN was not going to humiliate or appease anyone.

In his memoir, *Pilgrimage for Peace*, Pérez de Cuéllar says, rightly, that this conversation should have alerted us to the possibility that Nujoma might be going to infiltrate fighters into Namibia, in order to substantiate his claim that SWAPO had always had bases there, but that I did not see it as sufficiently significant to alert New York. I was, in fact, very conscious of the need to pass this information quickly to Ahtisaari in New York. But I had no secure communications in Harare and assumed that the South Africans could intercept a report by telephone or telex. At that stage I trusted them about as much as Nujoma did and feared that they would put a spoke in the wheel if they learnt that Nujoma was questioning what for them was a critical element in the plan. So that afternoon I sent Moriarty to Windhoek with a letter to Prem Chand, asking him to forward it and its enclosures immediately by cryptofax to Ahtisaari in New York. The enclosures were written records of the meetings with dos Santos and Nujoma and a plan for the establishment of UNTAG's detachment in Angola. I told Prem Chand that I had stressed to Moriarty that he must resist any attempt by Nujoma to strike deals directly with UNTAG; it was the Angolans who had the primary responsibility for monitoring the SWAPO fighters in Angola.

Prem Chand faxed the letter and its enclosures to New York on 25 March. But this was Easter Saturday, which probably explains why it did not reach Pérez de Cuéllar until 28 March, the day before Ahtisaari set off to take up his post in Windhoek. Should I have sounded a louder alarm? With hindsight, the answer must be yes. But, as Pérez de Cuéllar recognizes in his book, it was too late to postpone D-Day, even though the deployment of UNTAG had been so much delayed that there were as yet no troops available for northern Namibia. As it was, I had said in my letter to Prem Chand:

> I think Sam recognizes that he has got to accept Angolan monitoring of SWAPO in Angola. It would obviously help if we could give him something on his armed people inside Namibia, however few they may be, but this is likely to cause us problems with the other side.

I had been on the receiving end of many Nujoma tantrums during my time in Luanda, with the result that I took this latest diatribe less seriously than I should have done. Moreover, the Americans had told me before I left New York that they and the South Africans had detected little infiltration since the informal cease-fire had come into effect the previous August. The war did seem to be over. As for the Angolans, I had long admired their skills at improvisation and found it credible that they would be able to set up adequate monitoring arrangements in the week that remained before D-Day.

So the next day, Good Friday, was spent on a visit to Great Zimbabwe, the magnificent, but perhaps over-restored, remains of a city which had dominated this part of Africa from the twelfth to the sixteenth centuries. My companion was Commandant Dermot Earley of the Irish Army, one of Dibuama's assistants in New York. We were to do a lot of travelling together and became good friends. He was from the Gaeltacht, the Irish-speaking west of Ireland, and had, in his day, been a great Gaelic footballer. He possessed, in abundance, the military qualities of loyalty, courage, initiative, accuracy, energy and a readiness to speak frankly to his superiors, the last of which was rather uncommon in the Secretariat.

I was in Baghdad on a mission to the Iran–Iraq military observer group (UNIIMOG) when hints of disaster began to arrive from Windhoek. Dibuama telephoned from New York on the evening of 31 March to say that Prem Chand had proposed that the SADF should not be monitored with effect from the following day because monitoring arrangements were not yet in place in Angola. I rejected this proposal out of hand; two wrongs do not make a right. That night several hundred heavily armed SWAPO fighters crossed from Angola into northern Namibia and the incursions continued throughout 1 April. The intruders were engaged by the South West Africa Police (SWAPOL), and incidents proliferated throughout Ovamboland, the home district in northern Namibia of most of the SWAPO fighters and Nujoma himself. In the afternoon the South African Administrator-General, Louis Pienaar, told Ahtisaari that SWAPOL were unable to deal with the intruders and as UNTAG did not have the troops to do so, the only option was to deploy the South African forces which had been confined to base earlier in the day.

Prime Minister Thatcher happened to be on a flying visit to Windhoek that day and describes in *The Downing Street Years* how she took charge. She told Pik Botha, the South African Foreign Minister, that following SWAPO's violation of the settlement plan South Africa must react with scrupulous correctness; it must not unilaterally move its troops out of their bases but get the UN's authority to do so. She rang Ahtisaari to tell him what was happening. The UN did authorize South Africa to use its forces. As her book puts it, with characteristic understatement, 'I had been the right person in the right place at the right time.'*

Thatcher's role was helpful. She gave Pik Botha the right message, with the vigour and authority that only she could supply. But the reality of the day was a little more complicated than she allows. Botha had already received the same warning against unilateral measures in a telephone conversation with Pérez de Cuéllar. Until corrected by Ahtisaari, he chose to interpret the conversation as indicating that the Secretary-General understood the necessity of deploying the South African army (SADF). When Pérez de Cuéllar learnt this, he instructed Ahtisaari to be tough with the South Africans and stand firm against any sortie by the SADF. The South Africans then laid on the pressure. Interrogation of a captured SWAPO fighter had, they said, revealed that between 4,000 and 6,000 of his comrades would try to infiltrate that night. This led Ahtisaari and Prem Chand to recommend to Pérez de Cuéllar that they be authorized to permit a limited and temporary suspension of the confinement of the SADF to base.

This recommendation caused anguish in the Secretariat; the Secretary-General was being asked to authorize action which could (and did) lead to the deaths of hundreds of SWAPO fighters at the hands of the South Africans. This could cause a crisis with the Non-Aligned and destroy the UN's credibility as the impartial midwife of Namibian independence. On the other hand, SWAPO had blatantly violated the settlement plan and,

---

* Margaret Thatcher, *The Downing Street Years* (HarperCollins, New York, 1993), p. 529.

through no fault of Pérez de Cuéllar's, the UN had neither military observers in Angola to tell him what was happening there nor enough troops on the ground in Namibia to control the situation on that side of the border. Insistence that the SADF should remain confined to base would undermine the confidence that South Africa, the United States and the other members of the Contact Group had in his impartiality; and the South Africans would probably defy the UN's authority anyway. Pérez de Cuéllar would be damned if he did and damned if he didn't, a discomfort that Secretaries-General often have to endure. But if the process was to be saved, he had no choice but to authorize suspension of the SADF's confinement. To his great credit he took that choice. It required considerable political courage.

The next day, 2 April, Ahtisaari sent Thornberry to northern Namibia. He was allowed to interview two SWAPO captives. These said that they had been instructed to enter Namibia, with all their weapons, in order to establish bases where they could be monitored by the UN. If this was true, and Thornberry was inclined to think that it was, it suggested that the purpose of the infiltration was not aggressive, as had been assumed by the South Africans, but reflected a misunderstanding – perhaps a deliberate misunderstanding – of the settlement plan. Ahtisaari accordingly urged the South Africans to be as restrained as possible in their handling of the infiltrators. SWAPO predictably denied that it had violated the cease-fire and said that its fighters in Namibia had simply been looking for UNTAG personnel to whom they could hand over their weapons. The South Africans, equally predictably, said the incursions were continuing.

On the morning of 2 April I had cabled Dibuama from Baghdad offering, if the Secretary-General wished, to return to Luanda to try again to persuade dos Santos and Nujoma to implement the 'informal understanding' of 1982. I left Baghdad that afternoon for Amman, where I was to discuss a new crisis in UNIFIL with Lars-Eric Wahlgren and the Irish Chief of Staff, Tadgh O'Neill. Confirmation came overnight that I should proceed to Luanda as quickly as possible. The day in Amman was mostly devoted to the problems of Lebanon, but I took many calls from the media and one from Álvaro de Soto, Pérez de Cuéllar's Personal Envoy for Central America, to say that the peacekeeping operation in Central America (ONUCA) was going ahead.*

In the evening Earley and I left Amman on a twenty-four-hour journey to Luanda via Cairo and Addis Ababa. In the VIP lounge at Addis I bumped into Robert Frasure, who had been the London member of Crocker's team in the mid-eighties and was now in the US Embassy in

---

* This operation is described in Chapter 13.

Ethiopia.* According to Frasure, Pérez de Cuéllar had the previous day given the Security Council a much-diluted version of Ahtisaari's report, playing down the extent of the SWAPO incursions; this no doubt reflected the Secretariat's reluctance to anger the Non-Aligned and its unhappiness at the decision the Secretary-General had had to take.

Waiting for me in Luanda was a small team from UNTAG, including the Deputy Force Commander, Daniel Opande of the Kenyan Army, and Hisham Omayad, a Ghanaian from the Secretariat in New York who was Director of UNTAG's electoral division. The situation in Ovamboland, they reported, was very serious. Three SADF battalions had joined SWAPOL in hunting down the infiltrators. They were shooting to kill and giving their prey no chance to surrender.

There followed ten days of diplomacy in Luanda, where I had easy access to SWAPO and the Angolan Government, as well as senior Cuban and Soviet officials whose help would be essential if we were to get Nujoma to pull his fighters back from Namibia. The Soviet representative was Anatoliy Adamishin, a Deputy Foreign Minister, who had come out from Moscow at the beginning of the crisis. Besides keeping Pérez de Cuéllar and Ahtisaari informed of what was happening in Luanda, I had to get the Angolans to take seriously their responsibility for monitoring the SWAPO fighters in Angola and to allow UNTAG to verify that they were doing so. This was a sine qua non if the settlement plan was to be put back on track.

Initially, the Angolans denied that there had been any cross-border movements by SWAPO and said that they would not monitor SWAPO fighters until the South African forces ceased fire in Namibia. But I soon learnt from Adamishin that they were already concentrating SWAPO fighters at two sites north of the 16th parallel and that they had come a long way towards accepting our proposals for monitoring, though they still wanted to minimize UNTAG's involvement.

Early on 5 April word came from New York that Pérez de Cuéllar was preparing proposals for: restoration of the cease-fire on a date to be agreed; the establishment of temporary assembly points under UNTAG supervision for SWAPO fighters in Namibia; and the return of the SADF to base forty-eight hours after the restoration of the cease-fire. The SWAPO fighters in the assembly points would have the choice of being escorted back to Angola with their weapons or handing them over to UNTAG and returning to their homes as civilians. I recommended that two elements be added: an immediate end to cross-border movements by SWAPO; and concentration of their fighters in specified

---

* Six years later he died in an accident near Sarajevo when working with Richard Holbrooke on what became the Dayton Agreement.

locations in Angola. Though I did not say so, the omission of these obvious points seemed to indicate a continuing reluctance in New York to accept that SWAPO had committed an egregious violation of the cease-fire. That evening I received authority to put Pérez de Cuéllar's proposals to the Angolans and SWAPO, which I did immediately.

The next day, 6 April, the Front Line States held a summit meeting in the presidential palace outside Luanda. In the morning, I handed Pérez de Cuéllar's proposals to their chairman, President Kenneth Kaunda of Zambia. He received them surprisingly well, unlike Adamishin who had said grudgingly that they contained certain 'holes' but that if SWAPO accepted them Moscow would too. Kaunda asked me to stand by in case the other heads of state needed clarification. The summons came late in the afternoon. Omayad accompanied me. It was, he said, the first time UN officials had appeared before an FLS summit.

The presidents were seated on leather sofas and armchairs arranged in an oblong. At the far end of the oblong sat Kaunda; at the near end were chairs for Omayad and me. The first sofa on my left contained Nujoma and Tambo (ANC), the second Mwinyi (Tanzania) and Masire (Botswana). On my right Mugabe (Zimbabwe) sat in solitary state; beyond him were the two Portuguese speakers, Chissano (Mozambique) and dos Santos (Angola). The Foreign Ministers sat on a row of chairs behind the sofas to the right; the sofas on the left were backed by an enormous plate-glass window giving on to a sunlit swimming pool. The air-conditioning was fierce. After Omayad and I had taken our seats, Kaunda began to welcome us but Nujoma, apparently in sour mood, interrupted to say that the meeting should not begin because Hidipo Hamutenya (SWAPO's Information Secretary) was absent from the row of Foreign Ministers. Proceedings were suspended while he was sought. Chissano and dos Santos whispered together but no one else spoke. Nujoma avoided my eye. I felt as though I was in church.

Finally we started. Only Kaunda spoke. In order to end the unnecessary loss of life, he said, the Summit had, with SWAPO's full support, decided to accept the Secretary-General's proposals. SWAPO had further agreed that all its fighters would be disarmed at the assembly points in Namibia, but the Summit wanted them to remain at those locations under the protection of UNTAG until the SWAPO leadership returned to Namibia and it would be safe for the ex-combatants to join them. This last amendment probably reflected both Angola's desire to remove SWAPO from its territory and Nujoma's desire to have his fighters, albeit disarmed, monitored in Namibia. I confined myself to an expression of gratitude for the Summit's decision, while noting that it did involve amendment of Pérez de Cuéllar's proposals. In my report to him I acknowledged that it would cause trouble with the South Africans but repeated my view that if we were going to get back on course South Africa would have to accept some honourable arrangement in Namibia for such SWAPO infiltrators as were still alive there.

The next day there was good progress on Angola's monitoring of the SWAPO fighters on Angolan territory. Ndalu and the Deputy Foreign Minister, Venâncio da Moura, agreed to all our proposals, except the establishment of a resident UNTAG presence at each SWAPO location in Angola (a point which dos Santos conceded the next day). All SWAPO fighters would be confined to its three existing bases in Lubango and two or three camps which would be set up just north of the 16th parallel.

I was summoned to see President dos Santos early the following morning (8 April). In a staged speech in front of the media, he stated that SWAPO had to make it possible for the peace process to be resumed. After the cameras had left, he said that he was sure South Africa would never accept the Front Line States' wish that the infiltrators remain in Namibia. He had been working hard to get Nujoma to accept this reality and bring all his fighters back to Angola. He thought there was a good chance that Nujoma would agree. This sounded like a major breakthrough. It was confirmed late in the evening when Hamutenya came to the hotel with a statement by Nujoma on the lines dos Santos had predicted. Though it contained much rhetoric about SWAPO's right to have its fighters confined to base in Namibia and about South Africa's 'genocidal onslaught' and 'barbaric carnage', its core was the announcement of the leadership's decision to instruct SWAPO fighters in Namibia to cease fire and report to Angola within seventy-two hours. The decision had been taken against the fighters' wishes 'because we are convinced that this is in the long term interest of our nation'.

This climbdown by Nujoma came just in time for an emergency meeting of the Angola–Cuba–South Africa joint commission, with observers from the Soviet Union and the United States. This commission had been set up in December 1988 to resolve any problems that might arise over the interpretation and implementation of the settlement plan. Its meeting took place at Mount Etjo, a game reserve near Windhoek, on 8 and 9 April, in the presence of Crocker, Adamishin, Ahtisaari and Pienaar. The Mount Etjo Declaration recommitted the three countries to the peace process and set out modalities for the restoration of the status quo ante 1 April. These followed Pérez de Cuéllar's proposals, with the important difference that all the SWAPO infiltrators were to return to Angola. Dos Santos deserves credit for this success. It would not have happened without his determination to be firmer with Nujoma than either his FLS colleagues or the UN Secretariat initially wanted. So the worst of the crisis passed. But it was to take another six weeks to get the settlement plan back on track. And the crisis had planted a thorn in UNTAG's side which would remain there for nearly seven months. This was the reincorporation of Koevoet,* a notoriously brutal counter-insurgency unit of the South West Africa Police which had been disbanded the previous December as a confidence-building measure prior to implementation of the settlement plan.

Who was to blame for the crisis? The immediate blame was Nujoma's. Pérez de Cuéllar's cease-fire letter the previous month had specifically mentioned cross-border movements as one of the categories of 'warlike acts and operations' which were banned. It did not require much imagination to see that so blatant a violation would put the settlement plan at grave risk. I still find Nujoma's motives difficult to fathom. He had always insisted that there were SWAPO fighters inside Namibia and had usually lost his temper when doubt was expressed on this point. Was this an obsession which overwhelmed his judgement and drove him to try to prove his point, whatever the risks involved? Perhaps Robert Mugabe encouraged him to take the risk, with reminders that the presence of his ZANU-PF fighters in camps inside Rhodesia had had an influence on the elections that chose him to lead Zimbabwe to independence. Perhaps he genuinely believed that after his fighters had crossed the border they would find friendly UN soldiers to whom they could hand over their weapons.

But not all the blame should be placed on Nujoma. A share, perhaps a greater share, belongs to the five permanent members of the Security Council. At the last moment they reopened a plan which the Contact Group had exhaustively negotiated with the parties a decade earlier. Three of them were members of that group. As in all such negotiations, the outcome had completely satisfied none of the parties. It was based on a balance of gains and losses which, taken together, made the settlement plan more desirable for everyone than continuation of the war. For SWAPO and the Front Line States the greatest gain was the presence in Namibia of an armed United Nations force of significant size. Reduction of that force by nearly a half changed the equation. The Non-Aligned states' predictable and justified resistance cost several months' delay, as a result of which not even the reduced force was present in the Territory when implementation began.

Should Pérez de Cuéllar have recommended postponement of D-Day until the troops were in place? With hindsight one is tempted to think that he should have. But I failed to advise him thus at the time and would have been opposed by Ahtisaari and Thornberry if I had done so. The recommendation would also have been opposed by the Western members of the P-5 who were to show later in Bosnia how unmoved

---

* The word means 'crowbar' in Afrikaans.

they are by a Secretary-General's pleas that he be given the military resources needed to carry out a task entrusted to him by the Council. There are other questions. If the UNTAG battalions had been deployed in northern Namibia by 1 April, be they the originally planned four light battalions or Dibuama's two enlarged ones, would they have been able to control the situation, or would SWAPOL have engaged the infiltrators before the UN could gather them in and disarm them under its protection? And if UNTAG had succeeded in doing this, would South Africa have accepted the *de facto* establishment of a SWAPO presence in Namibia, albeit a disarmed one? We will never know. But our inability to answer these hypothetical questions does not relieve Britain, France and the United States of blame for their part in the catastrophe that occurred on D-Day.

I had not spoken to Nujoma since the meeting in Harare on 22 March and often wondered what his mood must be after the loss of several hundred fighters in Namibia and the humiliation of having to withdraw the survivors. On the evening of 10 April, I was taken by Hamutenya to Nujoma's residence. He was sitting in a frowsty little room full of video equipment and decorated with a tapestry of Engels, Marx and Lenin – 'a pre-*perestroika* gift', as Hamutenya put it. He was now in truculent mood, complaining that the Angolans had told him nothing about what had been agreed at Mount Etjo (though I had begged them to brief SWAPO as soon as they got back from Windhoek) and insisting that it was the UN's responsibility to clarify the obscurities in the declaration that had been issued there the previous day. I had myself asked Ahtisaari to clarify the same points but had not yet received his reply. For the moment, I could only urge Nujoma to address himself to the Angolans. His reluctance to do so no doubt reflected resentment at the way he had been treated by dos Santos.

Two days later, I sent Pérez de Cuéllar a worried cable: the Angolans had still not briefed SWAPO about Mount Etjo; the Cubans had muddied the water by telling SWAPO that the text published was not the one that had been negotiated in the joint commission; and we could get nothing from the Angolan military about the arrangements for receiving the returning SWAPO personnel. Another problem was that Prem Chand was insisting that UNTAG should have direct responsibility for the cantonment of SWAPO fighters in Angola. I had to tell him firmly that this would not be accepted by the Angolans.

Prem Chand was not happy at being overruled and threats of resignation began to come my way again. He complained that it was 'not cricket' to hold him responsible for operational plans in which he had little confidence. Perhaps the time had come for him to be replaced by someone who would take a new and objective approach. He understood the political constraints within which I had to work; he trusted me to be equally understanding of the operational constraints which he had to take into account.

I had some sympathy with these sentiments. Peacekeeping can require military commanders to accept operational arrangements which make little sense from the military point of view. Sometimes the operational nonsense is so great that generals are justified in questioning the orders they receive from their civilian masters. Generals Janvier and Smith were to do this, with great courage, at the Peace Implementation Conference on Bosnia in London in July 1995. But often the commanders of peace-keeping forces are asked to undertake operations which make little military sense and would be unjustifiable if the force was at war. As the force is not at war, however, the operations can be justified because of the political results they produce. The monitoring of SWAPO in Angola was such a case. Prem Chand was right in saying that the arrangements which I had negotiated did not enable UNTAG to ensure that all SWAPO fighters remained in their 'bases' in Angola. But the Angolan Government was not prepared to accept on its territory the substantial UN military presence that would be necessary to achieve that objective. At that time it was more important for the UN to keep the Angolans committed to Cuban troop withdrawal and implementation of the settle-ment plan for Namibia than to ensure faultless monitoring of the SWAPO fighters in Angola. Military efficiency had to yield to political expediency.

The focus now shifted from Luanda to Lubango. The South Africans had to be persuaded that what had been agreed at Mount Etjo was being put into effect. Most of the next week was accordingly spent in the south. I was trapped within two uncomfortable triangles. The first comprised myself, Ndalu (the Angolan Chief of Staff) and Nujoma. I had to press them to get the SWAPO fighters out of Namibia and credibly confined to base north of the 16th parallel. This irritated Ndalu, who was suffering from malaria, lacked administrative and logistic support and had to clear every detail with dos Santos in Luanda; he asked at one moment why I didn't get out of his way, go back to Luanda and let the soldiers do their job. My pressure also irritated Nujoma who responded with diatribes about Ahtisaari's alleged inadequacies and UNTAG's responsibility for so many SWAPO deaths. I was irritated by the constant waiting and by Ndalu's and Nujoma's repeated failures to carry out promised action. Additional tension was created between the two of them by Nujoma's arrogance and the Angolans' ill-disguised desire to get rid of SWAPO. The first time Nujoma turned up in Lubango I was struck by the number, armament and attitude of his bodyguards. It reminded me of how the PLO leaders had behaved in Jordan and Lebanon before they were driven into exile in Tunis. Nujoma seemed to regard Lubango as his city in the way that Arafat had regarded Sidon as his.

The second triangle in which I was caught up involved myself, UNTAG in Namibia and Headquarters in New York. The cables from New York increasingly revealed Pérez de Cuéllar's disquiet at Ahtisaari's inability to control the South Africans and my inability to establish an effective UNTAG presence at the SWAPO bases in Angola. I shared the disquiet, of course, especially as it became clear that South African troops or police were deployed in the vicinity of every assembly point in Namibia. As a result the SWAPO fighters were trickling back across the border, uncounted and unverified. This could enable the South Africans to claim that many remained in Namibia and the SADF could not therefore return to base. As for the Goulding–UNTAG relationship, there was no problem with Ahtisaari; we remained good friends. But the difficulties with Prem Chand continued; and I was also angered, perhaps unfairly, by UNTAG's failure to deploy quickly to Angola the twenty-eight military observers whom I had with such difficulty persuaded dos Santos to accept. Until they were in place we had almost no capacity to verify that the Angolans were indeed monitoring the confinement of SWAPO fighters to base.

On 18 April, three days before the deadline for the departure of all SWAPO fighters from Namibia, I went with Omayad and Earley to Cahama, the main staging point for returning SWAPO fighters on their way to cantonment in a 'base' called Chibemba. Opande was there with the first eight military observers who were to be stationed at the SWAPO bases. They had with them three SWAPO fighters, one of them lightly wounded, who had been entrusted to UNTAG by a church in Namibia. I handed them over to Nujoma. He did not seem pleased to see them nor they him; it was an emotionless moment. The next day a convoy of about 500 SWAPO fighters passed through Cahama on their way north. They were in open trucks, heavily armed and very glum. The UN team walked along the line of trucks asking if anyone spoke English. Not one admitted to doing so; they just stared at us in sullen hostility. Then two 'officers' appeared. They wanted to speak to the Angolans (Ndalu was there) and the media. They both seemed to be drunk or drugged and told the same familiar tale: they had been fighting in Namibia for ten years and had expected UNTAG to concentrate them in bases where they would be monitored.

We went on by helicopter to Ruacana on the Angola–Namibia border and walked into Namibia to visit a nearby assembly point and look for the remaining twenty military observers and their ten vehicles whom we were supposed to be welcoming to their new duty station. The assembly point was on a small hill and manned by Malaysian military observers,

British signallers and Australian engineers. No SWAPO fighters had reported in. The reason was clear enough. One hundred metres away was a joint SADF/police position, with armoured cars. There was no news of the missing convoy, so we drove on to a South African military settlement.

There we found more Malaysian military observers, demoralized and full of complaints – no cooperation from the South Africans, no support from UNTAG, no communications, no UN flags, no reply to repeated requests for a helicopter to fly in some SWAPO fighters who had reported to assembly points further west. Everything I saw and heard of UNTAG that day disheartened me, including Prem Chand's decision to deploy his military observers in national groups. The standard United Nations practice was to deploy them in mixed groups, making national pride an incentive to perform well. The only sign of the missing observers was the arrival of two UNTAG trucks; their Polish drivers thought that the main convoy was two or three hours away. So we crossed back into Angola and reached Lubango at sunset.

The next day was an epic day of waiting: for the outcome of an emergency meeting of the Angolan-Cuban-South African joint commission, which had been convened to discuss how the SWAPO fighters still hiding in Namibia could be encouraged to return to Angola; for a meeting with Ndalu; for permission for Moriarty to make a reconnaissance visit to Chibemba; for technicians from Luanda who were to install a satellite terminal; and for the arrival of the missing military observers. Only the last happened, at 9 p.m. after a fifteen-hour drive from Ruacana. Their arrival, without any stores at all except for seven generators without cables (another triumph for UNTAG), caused logistic havoc. The chaos was aggravated by the histrionics of a 120-kilo Panamanian major who seemed to expect accommodation in a Lubango Sheraton. By now I was into my sixth week away from New York and found it increasingly difficult to control my temper.

The following day there was a small breakthrough. Moriarty got to Chibemba and had a cordial meeting with Comrade 'Ho Chi Minh', the SWAPO Chief of Staff (who dubbed him Comrade Morality), and Commander Danger, one of the officers we had met at Cahama two days before. But, as feared, the 'base' turned out to be 400 square kilometres of unfenced bush where the concept of monitored confinement was a fantasy. The next morning Ndalu came to the compound to deliver two pieces of good news: the joint commission had decided that all South African security forces would return to base for sixty hours to facilitate the return of the remaining SWAPO fighters to Angola; and Moriarty's observers could now be deployed both at Chibemba and at Cahama.

My job in Angola was done. We drove down the Serra da Leba, the great escarpment to the west of Lubango, and then across a plain which turned from rain forest to savannah to desert as we approached the coast at Namibe. At the airport there was an absurdly comfortable executive jet which Ahtisaari had sent from Windhoek, complete with stewardess, champagne and sumptuous eats. But the end-of-term hilarity was quickly subdued as the two Canadian colonels who had come to fetch us recited a litany of complaints about how UNTAG was being run. Dinner with Ahtisaari and Prem Chand confirmed my growing fears about the latter's state of mind, especially the intensity of his hostility to SWAPO – such a contrast with his support of their position on the budgetary issue only three months before. The next day I learnt that the Australian, British and Canadian contingent commanders were planning a joint approach to their governments to complain about Prem Chand's leadership. Ahtisaari and I agreed that we should scotch any ideas about Prem Chand being replaced. There would be no support for this in New York, for Prem was deservedly popular in UN circles and had served the Organization loyally and well in the past. We had to play with the cards we had been dealt.

I spent four days in Namibia. The first two were devoted to briefings and diplomatic contacts in Windhoek and the third and fourth to field visits in the north of the territory. The briefings were quite encouraging. Yes, there were shortages of almost everything, partly because of the New York-imposed ban on procurement from South Africa, and mobility was limited by the lack of mine-resistant vehicles. But most of the shortages would have been resolved by mid-May and UNTAG was adapting itself to Namibian realities with admirable speed. South African cooperation was patchy. Some officers did not disguise their distaste for what was happening, but they were disciplined and would do what they were told to do. The army units seemed to have received the right orders and were pulling out. It was less clear what instructions the police were receiving. Unlike the soldiers they would remain in force during the transitional period and would retain primary responsibility for law and order. Their concept of policing would have to change if they were to satisfy the Special Representative of the 'good conduct' required by the settlement plan. These first impressions were confirmed during the two days in the north. Message after message arrived about alleged atrocities by SWAPOL in Ovamboland; the so-called 'police' were the ones who would give UNTAG trouble.

The first day in the north was spent in the Caprivi Strip which stretches eastwards like a finger out of the north of Namibia, ending at the confluence of the Chobe and Zambezi rivers where the frontiers of Namibia, Botswana, Zimbabwe and Zambia come together close to the mission which David Livingstone established at Linyanti in the 1850s. The Strip also borders the almost uninhabited south-east of Angola, the *terra ao fim do mundo* (land at the end of the world) as the Portuguese called it, where, with South African and American help, Savimbi had built up UNITA after his defeat at the hands of the MPLA and the Cubans in 1975–6.

We visited a Bushman battalion, one of the 'citizen forces, commando units and ethnic forces' which were to be demobilized. A pre-Bantu people from the Kalahari Desert, the Bushmen were recruited by the South African army (SADF) for their tracking skills. This battalion and its families had been settled in a place called Omega, a company town where the SADF was the company and provided health care, education, municipal services, shop, chaplain – everything, in fact, except the nomadic way of life into which the Bushmen had been born. I was impressed by the SADF colonel's concern about how his people would cope with demobilization from their settled life. But Ahtisaari chided my admiration for this 'colonialist paternalism' which would disappear with independence. I was also impressed by the energy with which the Finnish battalion was establishing itself in the Strip. Finnish missionaries had been active in Namibia since the 1870s and it was pleasing that Finnish soldiers under a Finnish Special Representative should be helping the territory to achieve independence at last.

We spent the night in a German fort – Beau Geste *à l'allemande* – which had been converted into a hotel for tourists visiting the Etosha Pan wildlife reserve. The only other residents were a group of heavy-drinking, middle-aged German settlers. They immediately recognized Ahtisaari and started mocking him. The ordeal began with banter, hugs and kisses but became more threatening when they put funny hats on his head, photographed him thus and taunted him with questions about why he thought *he* could solve Namibia's problems. A serious incident seemed to be in the making and I asked the hotel manager whether he could do anything. A shrug of the shoulders was his only reply. Ahtisaari, however, kept calm and did not allow himself to be provoked. His tormentors eventually became bored and returned to their tables. The next evening, back in Windhoek, I dined with the Chief Justice of Namibia, Hans Berker, and his wife. They too were German Namibians; their liberal principles, patriotism and commitment to the peace process were a welcome corrective to the impressions created by the louts of the previous evening.

Pérez de Cuéllar had reluctantly agreed that I should proceed with Ahtisaari to Cape Town to attend a meeting of the Angola–Cuba–South Africa joint commission. The main issue to be decided was whether the SADF should now be allowed to leave their bases again for a further two weeks in order to verify the SWAPO withdrawal and locate and lift SWAPO arms caches. Our instructions from New York were to oppose this. However, when the meeting opened, South Africa announced that in a restricted meeting the previous day the heads of the five delegations (that is, the three member states plus Soviet and United States observers) had agreed to the South African proposal. By the end of the meeting euphoria reigned: the settlement plan was almost back on course and the disastrous SWAPO incursion was behind us.

The South African Foreign Minister, Pik Botha, gave a celebratory *braai* (barbecue dinner) for 400 people in a marquee on the lawn of his official residence. Wine had been specially bottled for the event. The label bore the South African flag and the words '*Pereunt et Imputantur*', taken from a sundial on the lawn. Pik insisted that this meant 'the hours that are past have not been in vain'. I challenged his translation and was imperiously told to prove my point.* Music was provided by a group from Ciskei called Slo Foot, whose repertoire consisted mainly of familiar Anglican hymn tunes. After introducing each number, the master of ceremonies would say 'Over to you, Slo Foot'. Pik spoke twice, toasting first the leaders of the countries represented in the joint commission and then 'the wives of Angola, Cuba, South Africa, the Soviet Union and the United States'. Ndalu toasted the Secretary-General, and Carlos Aldana, the head of the Cuban delegation, drank to peace in southern Africa. Their speeches all had the same theme: diplomatic history was being made; enemies were talking to each other; this was the way it should be. The *braai* closed with the South African national anthem, followed, astonishingly, by '*Nkosi Sikelel' iAfrika*', the ANC anthem which, we were carefully told, had never before been sung at an official function in South Africa.

Back in the hotel I received a cold and sobering shower. Pérez de Cuéllar's Chef de Cabinet, Viru Dayal, called from New York to complain about the joint commission's decision to let the South African army out of base again: Ahtisaari and I should not have allowed ourselves to be presented with a fait accompli; the Secretary-General had made it clear that he wanted his views to be fully heard before any decisions were taken. Fortified by *Pereunt et Imputantur*, I described the euphoric event that had just ended and argued that the Secretariat could not refuse to accept something which had been decided by the parties and their superpower backers. It was a weak argument. Of course the Secretary-General must insist on his right to comment on, and if necessary oppose, decisions by individual member states which in his judgement are incompatible with a mandate he has received from the United Nations collectively.

---

* I did so subsequently. The quotation is from one of Martial's epigrams (V.20) and means '[days that] pass and are charged to our account' – not quite as optimistic as Pik's version.

Dayal was, understandably, as angered by the weakness of my argument as I was by his call. Pérez de Cuéllar's unhappiness with the outcome was frankly stated in the report he made to the Security Council a few days later, provoking a letter from Pik Botha which he describes in his memoirs as 'the rudest letter I ever received as Secretary-General'.

Back in New York the mood was uglier than I had realized. Dayal, deeply disturbed by D-Day and passionate in his distrust of Ahtisaari and of UNTAG generally, was convinced that the South Africans had known that SWAPO intended a major incursion on 1 April and had let it happen in order to give SWAPO a bloody nose and humiliate the United Nations. During Pérez de Cuéllar's absence (in Geneva in another vain attempt to get Iran and Iraq to implement SCR 598), a Namibia Task Force had been established under Dayal's chairmanship. The majority was strongly pro-SWAPO and anti-Ahtisaari. At the first meeting after my return, I argued that if the operation was to succeed, patience and understanding, and frequent visits, would be needed to maintain good relations between New York and Windhoek. This time my argument was a good one but it was not well-received and provoked from Dayal another outburst about the iniquities of UNTAG. However, at the same meeting Pérez de Cuéllar decided, on Dayal's advice, that the Task Force would meet every afternoon under his own chairmanship.

Its principal members were Dayal, Fleischhauer (Legal Counsel), Farah (USG for Africa), Dibuama (Military Adviser), Giuliani (Spokesman) and myself. It coordinated the work of the relevant departments in New York and ensured that coherent instructions were sent to UNTAG headquarters in Windhoek. Ahtisaari would report by cable each evening. If there were any points that needed clarification, I would telephone him the next morning (New York time). That afternoon I would put recommendations to the Task Force about how the Secretary-General should respond to Ahtisaari's cables. Before going home in the evening I would convey the SG's decisions to Ahtisaari in cables which would be on his desk the next morning (Windhoek time).

At the beginning there was so much animus against Ahtisaari in New York (because of his alleged, but imaginary, subservience to the South Africans) that relations with Windhoek tended to plummet if I was not there to intone my usual plea for less criticism of UNTAG and greater understanding of the difficulties it faced. In early May, for instance, I had to leave New York for two days to meet the Nordic defence ministers in Denmark. When I got back, Ahtisaari was talking of resigning because, without any consultation with him, Pérez de Cuéllar had told the Africans in New York that he had decided to appoint an African as deputy to Ahtisaari. This was a demand the Africans had made after the D-Day disaster. Pérez de Cuéllar was right to accept it and the person he appointed, Joe Legwaila, the permanent representative of Botswana, was an excellent choice. But to reveal his intentions without at least informing Ahtisaari created new tensions with Windhoek which none of us needed.

For the next few weeks every major issue caused dissent in the Task Force. The main concerns were the terms of the unqualified amnesty to which the South Africans had finally agreed, the repeal of discriminatory legislation, the return of refugees, the registration of voters, continuing brutality by the South West Africa Police, and Legwaila's appointment. The latter caused Prem Chand too to talk of resignation yet again; he had, he said, accepted his own appointment on the explicit understanding that he would be the number two in UNTAG; but now Legwaila would be in charge when Ahtisaari was away. Dayal argued daily that Ahtisaari could not be relied on to stand up to the South Africans; the Task Force had to ensure that the Secretary-General was not exposed to embarrassment with the Africans and the Non-Aligned; whenever possible, therefore, negotiations with the South Africans should take place in New York rather than Windhoek. I was often alone in arguing that the United Nations had to assert its authority by doing what it thought right under the settlement plan. Criticism was inevitable and fear of it should not cause the Task Force to second-guess every decision Ahtisaari made. On the contrary, we should stand up to the Africans and the Non-Aligned and not allow ourselves to be blown hither and thither by their tantrums.

The rhythm of communications with Windhoek described above made for late nights but, to adapt the SAS motto, 'Who Drafts Wins'. Because my department (OSPA) was in effect the Task Force's secretariat and the main conduit for its communications with Windhoek, both written and oral, I was able to re-establish its role as the department with the primary responsibility for 'back-stopping' peacekeeping operations. Task Forces were established for some subsequent missions but they were soon so numerous that the Secretary-General had no time to give them the amount of personal attention he had devoted to Namibia. The resulting decline in the quality of support from New York contributed to many of the mistakes that were made in subsequent years. With the level of staffing available, the Secretariat was hard pressed to manage more than one major operation at a time. Yet four years later we would be trying to manage six simultaneously – El Salvador, the former Yugoslavia, Cambodia, Angola, Mozambique and Somalia.

Pérez de Cuéllar gave the Security Council a written progress report at the end of June 1989. The South Africans complained that it was one-sided and partial: it mentioned all South Africa's alleged violations of the settlement plan but almost none of SWAPO's confirmed ones; the

SWAPO 'bases' in Angola were not being monitored; its fighters continued to infiltrate Namibia; South Africa could not therefore remove Koevoet from the northern areas; Koevoet was anyway needed to protect returning SWAPO supporters from right-wing extremists.

In July, Dibuama and I went to Namibia to prepare the way for a visit Pérez de Cuéllar had decided to make to Namibia and South Africa. Our field visit took us to the north. It was not encouraging. The different elements of UNTAG were still not properly coordinated. More seriously, the command structures of South Africa's local forces had not been dismantled. The senior officers and NCOs of each battalion remained at battalion headquarters masquerading as 'paymasters' to whom the soldiers reported fortnightly for their pay. The soldiers' weapons and packs were neatly arrayed in the drill halls ready for instant pick-up if the battalion had to be remobilized. These violations of the settlement plan had been reported by UNTAG but in such mild terms that we in New York had not realized their seriousness. This was a result of Windhoek's lack of confidence in New York and it had the effect, of course, of reinforcing New York's distrust of Windhoek. We were in a vicious circle.

Pérez de Cuéllar's visit broke the circle. Ahtisaari spoke firmly about the need to stand up to the Front Line States, the Non-Aligned and non-governmental organizations (NGOs) whose criticism of UNTAG was often ill-informed and ill-intentioned. Pienaar, the South African Administrator-General, was on his best behaviour, belying the image of him which the demonizers in the Task Force had implanted in Pérez de Cuéllar's mind. Pérez de Cuéllar gently turned down Prem Chand's request, which Ahtisaari declined to support, for two extra battalions, and persuaded him not to resign. A visit to Ovamboland enabled the Secretary-General to see with his own eyes the positive developments that were taking place. Some 23,000 refugees had already been repatriated – 56 per cent of those registered – and three-quarters of them had left the reception centres and returned to their homes. There were very few confirmed cases of intimidation or harassment. Almost 265,000 voters had been registered in the first two weeks, 38 per cent of the estimated total.

Pérez de Cuéllar also observed at first hand the intensity of the Ovambos' hatred for Koevoet. Its personnel remained in force in the north, patrolling night and day in their notorious armoured vehicles known as Casspirs. This was the main issue on which Pérez de Cuéllar pressed the South Africans, both in Windhoek and later in Pretoria. In public, he maintained his impartiality by being equally critical of SWAPO's folly on D-Day and the savagery of the South African response to it; and he preached to all the necessity for Namibians everywhere to approach the elections in a spirit of peace, democracy and reconciliation.

Pienaar was pleased by these public statements. In private, Pérez de Cuéllar took a firmer line with SWAPO's supporters. He told them that the April incursions had been a terrible mistake; they must now help him by doing absolutely nothing which the South Africans could use to justify the continued deployment of Koevoet; there must be no intimidation by anyone. The SWAPO leadership did not like this; they sulked and stayed away from the social events. But a meeting with the representatives of the Front Line States went well; their criticisms were mild by comparison with what we were getting daily in New York.

We flew on to Pretoria for a meeting with Pik Botha, who was accompanied by the Ministers of Defence and Law and Order; this was followed by the usual sumptuous dinner. At the meeting, Pik drank whisky while the rest of us took coffee or tea. He seemed stressed and emotional, interrupting the usual argument about Koevoet with a lachrymose digression about the dangers that would be faced by the Kaokoland elephant (a spectacularly large and powerful subspecies) if SWAPO fighters were to take control of the less populated parts of the north. He parried Pérez de Cuéllar's complaints about Koevoet by criticizing Angola's failure to monitor the so-called SWAPO bases: 'help me with reliable information about the numbers and whereabouts of SWAPO and I will help you over Koevoet'. Pérez de Cuéllar undertook to do what he could with dos Santos and Nujoma the next day in Lusaka.

The visit seemed to be a milestone. The Task Force sceptics had seen the Namibian reality; it was by no means perfect, but it was very much better than the picture painted of it by UNTAG's critics in New York. In Lusaka Pérez de Cuéllar made some progress on the issue of SWAPO fighters in Angola, receiving assurances that almost all of them had returned in civilian clothes to Namibia as refugees. The UNTAG detachment in Angola reported the same. But stories kept surfacing about imminent SWAPO incursions and the South Africans dragged their feet. In late August the Security Council adopted a resolution demanding the disbandment of Koevoet and the dismantling of its command structures. Finally, on 28 September Pik Botha announced that 1,200 Koevoet personnel were being disbanded and another 400 followed a month later. But South Africa paid them until independence and they caused a number of unpleasant incidents in the border areas until the end.

Meanwhile I was distracted from Namibia by the visit I had to make to the Levant after the reported murder of Colonel Higgins.* This was followed by some leave in England. By the time I got back to New York at the end of August, backsliding was evident; relations with Windhoek had become as bad as ever. The issue was now the draft electoral legislation

---

* See Chapter 7.

prepared by the Administrator-General. UNTAG had been instructed to insist on major changes to his draft but had apparently led him to think that the UN had no serious objections to it. As usual Ahtisaari and his team felt that the UN should pay no heed to ill-informed criticism from the Africans, the Non-Aligned and the NGOs, whereas the Secretary-General did not feel able to ignore international expressions of concern about an international operation entrusted to him. Fuel was added to the flames when it was learnt in New York that South African ministers in Pretoria were saying that the settlement plan could easily be implemented if the task was entrusted to Pienaar and Ahtisaari without interference from Pérez de Cuéllar whose entourage, it was said, were determined to engineer a victory for SWAPO. Initially I found myself on New York's side. I liked and respected Ahtisaari and thought the criticism of him unjustified and exaggerated. But it had become so strong that I wondered whether Pérez de Cuéllar might not have to seek his resignation, unfair though that would be, in order to prevent the whole process being disowned by the Non-Aligned. The risk of this would be especially great if SWAPO did less well than expected in the election. But when the pressure on UNTAG increased after the Secretary-General's attendance at a Non-Aligned summit in Belgrade, I felt obliged to resume my earlier role of trying to ease the tensions. Ahtisaari did his part by getting all the Namibian parties to subscribe to a 'Code of Conduct' which had been conceived at Pérez de Cuéllar's meeting with them in July.

In mid-September I spent a week with UNIIMOG in Iran and Iraq. When I got back there was, as usual, a new crisis. Thornberry had received a number of death threats, apparently from hard-line whites in Namibia who had assassinated Anton Lubowski, a white member of SWAPO, a few days earlier in Windhoek. Ahtisaari proposed security works on Thornberry's house and twenty-four-hour protection. The decision in New York, however, was that the UN staff rules required his immediate evacuation. This was vigorously resisted by Ahtisaari and Thornberry himself, to the point of defying an instruction specifically endorsed by the Secretary-General. The row became public knowledge at both ends. The Secretary-General's authority was in question. A blunt message had to be conveyed to Ahtisaari. Neither Pérez de Cuéllar nor Dayal wished to convey it and I was told to do so. It was a painful conversation. Thornberry came to New York two days later, ostensibly 'for consultations'.

The problem dragged on for a month. Ahtisaari was impatient and often angry, threatening to mobilize member states against Pérez de Cuéllar and even, occasionally, to resign. I wanted Thornberry back in Windhoek as soon as possible, lest UNTAG fragment even further without him. But the call belonged to the administrators – Luis Gomez,

Acting Under-Secretary-General for Administration and Management, and Kofi Annan, Director of Personnel. They insisted that Thornberry remain in New York. But Dayal and I eventually succeeded in persuading Pérez de Cuéllar to override them and send him back 'for operational reasons'.

Meanwhile, the Secretary-General had given the Security Council an extensive report on the first six months of the Namibia operation. UNTAG's draft would have set the Africans alight and it took me a week to revise it. I was proud of the result. It was frank about the failure of the South Africans, and, to a lesser extent, SWAPO and Angola, to comply with their commitments under the settlement plan. But it also made clear how much had been achieved since D-Day and looked ahead to what promised to be a successful election a month later. The response from the Non-Aligned and the Africans was angry. Orchestrated by Ricardo Alarcón, they dissected the report to find evidence of UNTAG's alleged connivance with South African violations, especially the absorption of former Koevoet personnel into SWAPOL and the continued presence of SADF personnel in Namibia to perform 'civilian functions' such as air traffic control. They pressed the Security Council to send a mission to observe the elections, because, they said, UNTAG could not be relied upon to do so impartially. The permanent members' rejection of this proposal added fuel to the Africans' anger and the mood turned sour. As the known champion of UNTAG in the Task Force, I became the main target in New York and was openly accused of racism by the Zimbabwe Permanent Representative, Stan Mudenge. Even Pérez de Cuéllar's decision to send Thornberry back, against the advice of an African (Annan), was added to the charge sheet against me. All this was painful, because I shared some of the Africans' indignation, especially about the SADF 'civilian' presence on which I had been fruitlessly pressing Ahtisaari and Prem Chand for months. But I could not say this.

The situation was gradually brought under control, thanks to some skilful diplomacy by the President of the Security Council, Yves Fortier of Canada, and a decision by South Africa, at last, to remove from SWAPOL all former members of Koevoet. The Council adopted a resolution by consensus on 31 October and a flying visit was made to Windhoek by Dayal and other members of the Task Force. To my chagrin I had to miss this. I had known for over a year that I had a heart condition which would eventually make it necessary for a pacemaker to be fitted. That moment arrived in late October and the operation took place at the New York Hospital on 6 November. From my hospital bed I learnt that the first of five days of voting in Namibia had gone well; over 30 per cent of the registered electorate had voted without serious incident (the final total was to exceed 97 per cent). Other momentous events were taking place: the East German Government resigned and the Berlin Wall began to come down; the Security Council voted unanimously to establish a new peacekeeping operation in Central America, an event that was followed by a major rebel assault on San Salvador; a new president was elected in Lebanon, only to be assassinated two weeks later. I resumed work as soon as I left the hospital.

The results of the election in Namibia became known on 14 November: SWAPO led with 57.43 per cent of the votes, followed by the pro-South African Democratic Turnhalle Alliance with 28.58 per cent. This was a dream result. SWAPO had a clear majority and would govern after independence. But they did not have the two-thirds required for adoption of the constitution under which Namibia would become independent. They would therefore have to strike compromises with other parties. The Security Council nevertheless remained divided, with Zambia and Zimbabwe trying to block any endorsement of Ahtisaari's characterization of the elections as 'free and fair'. But now the action that mattered was in Windhoek. The Constituent Assembly convened on 21 November. All the indications were that it would complete its work quickly and Nujoma was talking of independence in February. His confidence was justified; within a month the Assembly had agreed guidelines for the lawyers who would draft the constitution. In New York, there was little to do. The South Africans had accepted the result of the election without question. Their attention to method and detail now became an asset as we monitored Namibia's transition to independence under SWAPO rule. My attention was released for other tasks, especially the establishment of the new peacekeeping operation in Central America.

By the end of January 1990 it had been decided in Windhoek that power would be transferred at midnight on 20 March. But then new problems erupted and I had to go to Windhoek at short notice to resolve them. Ahtisaari and Prem Chand were not talking to each other regarding plans for UNTAG's withdrawal; there were new concerns about law and order; and Pérez de Cuéllar was frustrated by UNTAG's inability to provide information on the part he was to play in the independence celebrations. My task was to establish agreement on UNTAG's role up to Independence Day and to convey New York's determination that the operation should be phased out as soon as possible thereafter. A long morning was spent preparing a withdrawal plan which I cabled to New York for approval. Ahtisaari pooh-poohed New York's concerns about an imminent breakdown of law and order. SWAPO remained vague about their plans for the independence celebrations.

I was glad to be in Namibia again and took the opportunity to visit Swakopmund and Lüderitz on the coast. The former is a very German town and in the municipal park there are, side by side, monuments to both Germany's and South Africa's dead in the two World Wars. But the main point of interest there was the port of Walvis Bay and the offshore islands. The latter's guano deposits caused the British to annex them in the nineteenth century as part of Cape Colony and they would therefore remain South African after Namibia's independence. The absurdity of this was evident at Lüderitz where there were three islands close inshore; the Germans had linked one of them to the mainland by a causeway and it would therefore remain part of Namibia, while the other two would become South African territory. Back in 1978, SWAPO had reluctantly accepted that Walvis Bay and the islands were not covered by the settlement plan, but after independence South Africa agreed to return them to Namibia in 1994.

The next two days were spent in Ovamboland and the Caprivi Strip. The problem there did not seem to be an imminent breakdown of law and order. The statistics showed no increase in crime, with the exception of cattle-rustling. But there was an evident failure to tidy away various semi-clandestine institutions which the South Africans had established to prevent SWAPO incursions from Angola and to support UNITA in its war against the government in Luanda. Most of the border is open and uncontrolled, with kraals of the Ovambo people on either side. The locals complained about cross-border banditry, perhaps by Angolans who had been demobilized from Koevoet or one of the 'citizen forces, commando units and ethnic forces' created by South Africa during the war. The Bushmen seen the previous April were still there and we visited a mysterious place called Delta Village occupied by about 5,000 Angolans, led by a former taxi driver from Huambo, who seemed to be connected in some way to those same South African forces.

Back in New York the calm was troubled by a cable from Ahtisaari predicting that the Front Line States and the Non-Aligned Movement would make a last-minute proposal for UNTAG's mandate to be extended. Sure enough a letter was received on 12 March from President Kaunda asking, on behalf of the Front Line States, that UNTAG should remain in Namibia for at least three further months. This was rich after all the opprobrium that the FLS had heaped on Ahtisaari and UNTAG during the preceding twelve months. Meanwhile the incoming government had, with UN backing, been negotiating with various of the UNTAG contributors bilateral agreements for their troops and/or police to remain in Namibia for a while after UNTAG's dissolution. The Security Council decided to take no action on the FLS proposal.

Thus the way was cleared for the Secretary-General to go to Windhoek for the independence ceremonies on 20–22 March, and for the rapid withdrawal of UNTAG. Enthusiasm and satisfaction at a difficult goal achieved ensured that the ceremonies went well in spite of stormy weather and the incoming government's lack of experience in organizing formal events on this scale. The Secretary-General paid tribute to UNTAG at a parade in the morning. In the afternoon, he had a long meeting with President de Klerk of South Africa who urged that the United Nations involve itself more in southern Africa. His government was 'in a hurry' to bring about internal reform in South Africa by using existing structures to negotiate a 'new constitutional dispensation' which would ensure the full participation of all South Africans in the governance of their country. He would concede no role to the UN in South Africa's internal affairs, but the Secretary-General and his colleagues were welcome in the Republic: 'we have nothing to hide and want people of influence to come and see what's happening'.

The independence ceremony took place in the evening in the sports stadium. The crush was potentially dangerous, especially when Nelson and Winnie Mandela arrived and the crowd went mad. But the UN police officers' proficiency at crowd control compensated for SWAPOL's inexperience and no disaster occurred. Pérez de Cuéllar spoke first, eloquently but at excessive length. He was followed by de Klerk who was listened to in respectful silence. At midnight the South African flag was lowered by a small SADF detachment, to cries of 'down, down, down' from the crowd, but without disorder. The new Namibian flag was raised, Pérez de Cuéllar swore in Sam Nujoma as President of the Republic of Namibia and the new President made an admirably conciliatory speech, followed by a parade by two companies of Namibian soldiers, half of them from SWAPO and half of them from the local forces created by South Africa in Namibia. 'Thus', as Pérez de Cuéllar reported to the Security Council a week later, 'was achieved, in dignity and with great rejoicing, the goal of independence for Namibia for which the United Nations and its Member States have striven for so long.'

The Namibia operation was a success. The settlement plan, albeit in somewhat modified form, was implemented ahead of schedule and under budget. Namibia achieved independence through a democratic process and the political order thus established remains intact more than a decade later. This is an achievement by Africa's current standards. Yet the operation began disastrously and was plagued throughout by conflict within the United Nations Secretariat and within the wider international community. These two phenomena – a successful operation and a divided United Nations – may seem contradictory, but they are not. All multinational bureaucracies are rent by jealousy, intrigue and the clash of personalities. This is not surprising: the officials concerned come from varied backgrounds; most of them are loyal to the institution they serve but they also have loyalties to their own countries; and they often have differing perceptions of the people and situations with which they deal.

This last factor was accentuated in the case of Namibia by apartheid. Everyone detested the system which existed in South Africa. Some in the Secretariat and in the delegations of member states were nevertheless ready to allow for the possibility that South African policies might be changing for the better and were ready to give the South Africans the benefit of the doubt. Others were reluctant to place any trust in them and always assumed the worst. This was the primary cause of dissension within the Task Force.

There were several reasons why the Namibia operation succeeded in spite of that dissension. First, the objective of bringing Namibia to independence through an internationally monitored democratic process was opposed by no one except a few right-wing extremists in South Africa and Namibia. Secondly, there was almost universal international support not only for the objective but also for the settlement plan. Thirdly, that plan had been in existence for ten years; the operational concepts embodied in it were familiar to, and accepted by, almost everyone concerned. This was why Nujoma's attempt to change the rules at the outset was bound to fail. Fourthly, the United Nations was fortunate to have a Secretary-General whose decisions were untainted by emotion or partiality and who had the courage to make difficult choices, as did the Special Representative whom he appointed.

11

Angola

Angola was one of five Portuguese colonies in Africa. The first Portuguese settlements were established there in the early sixteenth century but three and a half centuries were to pass before Portugal extended its authority into the interior and created what is now the third largest country in Africa south of the Sahara. In the early 1960s a nationalist uprising led to fifteen years of colonial war in which three liberation movements fought for independence. The Portuguese Army's distaste for this war and a similar one in Mozambique was one of the causes of the 'Carnation Revolution' which in 1974 liberated Portugal from the post-fascist autocracy of Marcello Caetano.

Both countries won their independence a year later in confused circumstances and ill-prepared for nationhood. In Angola a Marxist party, the MPLA, formed the government, with support from the Soviet Union and Cuba, but was challenged by another of the liberation movements, UNITA, which was supported by the United States and South Africa. South Africa's involvement was primarily due to the fact that, as described in the previous chapter, the Namibian liberation movement, SWAPO, had its main bases in Angola. But the United States was motivated by Cold War considerations; it felt obliged to resist the establishment of Soviet and Cuban power in what had been the territory of one of its NATO allies. Jonas Savimbi, the President of UNITA, took advantage of this by selling himself in Washington as a champion of democracy, which was also a good card to play in Pretoria.

The successful cooperation between the United States, the Soviet Union, South Africa, Angola and Cuba in bringing Namibia to independence inspired hopes that the same recipe could be applied to the conflict in Angola itself. At the independence celebrations in Windhoek in March 1990, the US Secretary of State, James Baker, told Pérez de Cuéllar that he wanted to work with the Russians to bring the Angola conflict under control. He had proposed a cease-fire to the two sides, as the first step towards a negotiated settlement; the UN, he said, should be ready to enlarge its existing operation in Angola (UNAVEM), so that it could monitor the cease-fire. The Americans' initial idea was that Zaire should be the mediator in the peace talks, but by mid-1990 this role had been assumed by Portugal, with the USA and the Soviet Union as observers.

In December 1990 the Americans told us that, after five rounds of talks, agreement had been reached on a 'statement of principles' for a negotiated settlement. In February 1991, there was a setback; the government told the mediators that it would sign nothing until the date of the cease-fire had been agreed. Neither we nor the Americans were surprised by this; it was precisely the position that the government of El Salvador was taking in the concurrent negotiations on peace in that country. In civil wars governments almost always demand a cease-fire before political negotiations can begin. By mid-March optimism had been revived. The two sides were to meet with Portugal and the two observers in Lisbon in early April and give themselves four weeks to reach agreement on all outstanding points: the modalities of the cease-fire; the establishment of the new national army; the elections; and the role of the UN. The UN was invited to send an observer. I chose Dermot Earley for this; a military officer was indicated because monitoring of the cease-fire would be the main task for the UN.

As in the El Salvador negotiations, there were two working groups in Lisbon, a political group chaired by the Portuguese Secretary of State for Foreign Affairs, José Durão Barroso, and a military group chaired by his right-hand man, António Monteiro. The main issues in the political group were the dates of the cease-fire and the elections. There was a possibility that the cease-fire could come as early as May 1991. This was a daunting prospect for my overstretched department and for Field Operations Division (FOD), the division in the Secretariat responsible for the administration and logistics of peacekeeping operations. In the military group, each of the parties began by demanding fifty assembly areas for its troops during the interval between the cease-fire and their integration into the new national army. Earley persuaded them to settle for a total of fifty between them. By the end of April agreement was reached: the cease-fire would come into effect on 31 May 1991 and the elections would take place in September 1992. The Angola Peace Accords, later known as the 'Bicesse Accords', would be signed in Lisbon on 31 May.

The Accords consisted of four documents. The cease-fire agreement provided for a joint political-military commission, whose members would be the government and UNITA, with Portugal, the Soviet Union and the United States as observers; a United Nations representative *could* be invited to its meetings. It would be responsible for overall political supervision of the cease-fire process. Subordinate to it would be a joint verification and monitoring commission with the same membership as the political-military commission, except that a UN representative *would* be invited to its meetings. It was authorized to set up joint monitoring groups consisting of unarmed representatives of the two sides, in equal numbers. A *de facto* suspension of hostilities would come into effect on 15 May and the formal cease-fire on 31 May. The forces of both sides would start moving to their assembly areas on 1 July and assembly would be completed by 1 August. By the date of the elections, all troops in the assembly areas would have been either demobilized or transferred to training centres for the new national army, which would be known as the Angolan Armed Forces (FAA).

The unusual feature in this arrangement was that the parties themselves assumed responsibility for jointly verifying their compliance with the agreement they had signed; on paper, the UN's role was merely to verify that they were doing that. We were told that this reflected the government's unease about infringement of its sovereignty by the UN. Two years before we had been given the same explanation for the government's reluctance to allow UNTAG to verify the cantonment of SWAPO fighters in southern Angola. It may not have been the whole truth. Some years before, I had asked Olusegun Obasanjo, the once and future President of Nigeria, why he thought the government of Mozambique was so unresponsive to offers by the UN to help resolve the civil war in that country. He said the answer was simple. For leftward-inclined Africans of the generation that currently led the ruling party in Mozambique, the United Nations was the organization responsible for the murder of Prime Minister Patrice Lumumba in the Congo in 1961; they simply did not trust us.

The second document in the Accords listed 'fundamental principles' for the establishment of peace: UNITA's recognition of the MPLA as the government until the elections; its participation in political activities as soon as the cease-fire was in effect; consultations about amendments to the constitution; free and fair elections under international supervision; respect for human rights and basic freedoms; creation of the FAA by the time of the elections; declaration and entry into force of the cease-fire. The third document was an expansion of the second, with more detail about how the 'principles' would be applied. The UN was mentioned only in the context of cease-fire monitoring. The fourth document registered agreements reached by the parties on many, but not all, the points listed in the second and third documents, especially elections, the functioning of the political-military commission, internal security, UNITA's political activities, the restoration of government administration in the UNITA-controlled areas and the new army. It contained one new element of importance to the UN: the Organization would be asked to provide police experts to help the parties verify the neutrality of the police. It also mentioned the possibility that the UN might be asked to provide technical advice on some aspects of the elections.

By good fortune, Earley and I were stuck in Baghdad for two days in early May, awaiting the Iraqi Government's response to Pérez de Cuéllar's ideas for a UN police force in the Kurdish areas following the liberation of Kuwait.* This gave us time to draft a report in which the Secretary-General would recommend to the Security Council that UNAVEM be enlarged to undertake the tasks assigned to the United Nations in the Bicesse Accords. We proposed that the enlarged force should include 350 military observers, 90 police observers and the usual support, including a large air unit.

When I was back in New York, Pérez de Cuéllar asked me to give the P-5 ambassadors an advance briefing about his recommendations. It provoked an extraordinary attack from David Hannay, the British Permanent Representative. It was insulting, he said, for the Secretariat to 'consult' the P-5 about a report that was already with the printers; printing of the report must be suspended forthwith. I said that I was there to brief, not to consult; the Secretary-General had the right to present to the Council his own recommendations, which the Council could then accept, reject or modify; it would be improper for the Secretary-General to 'pre-cook' his recommendations with the Five, to the exclusion of other interested groups. This further enraged Hannay, to the undisguised amusement of the other ambassadors who enjoyed seeing two Brits fighting it out. The Soviet Permanent Representative, Yuliy Vorontsov, who was that month's coordinator of the Five, ended the fight by asking me to tell the Secretary-General that they would be grateful if he would delay circulation of his report. Pérez de Cuéllar declined to do so and wrote a firm letter to Vorontsov explaining why. Two days later Vorontsov called on the Secretary-General to express regret at the misunderstanding that had occurred and to assure him that the Five agreed that it was his prerogative to present his own recommendations to the Council.

The arguments that I had used, however, were not entirely sound, for the Charter does give the P-5 special responsibilities in matters of peace and security. Article 106 provides that the Permanent Five 'shall . . . consult with one another and as occasion requires with other Members of the United Nations with a view to such joint action on behalf of the Organization as may be necessary for the purpose of maintaining international peace and security'. This is one of the 'transitional security arrangements' which were to bridge the gap until member states had

---

* See Chapter 16.

concluded 'special agreements' to provide the Security Council with the military resources required for enforcement action. To this day no such agreement has been signed, so the transitional arrangements remain in force. It can also be argued that as the Five pay 46.2 per cent of the costs of peacekeeping (57.6 per cent at the time of the fracas with Hannay), they can reasonably expect to be consulted before a firm recommendation goes to the Security Council.

But there are powerful countervailing arguments. Most members of the UN would prefer not to have any permanent members in the Security Council and there is particular distaste for their power of veto. It is not therefore politic for the Secretary-General to seem more responsive to their concerns than to those of other member states. The preceding chapter has described the difficulties that Pérez de Cuéllar encountered with the Non-Aligned when he gave in to the P-5 over the size of UNTAG. The Five usually get their way in the end, but I used to argue that it is better for the Secretary-General to be publicly voted down by them in the Council than to yield to their demands in private consultations from which the other members are excluded. Boutros-Ghali shared Pérez de Cuéllar's view about the Secretary-General's right to decide what he will recommend to the member states. But, like Pérez de Cuéllar, he respected power and usually preferred to give in privately to the Five rather than be shot down in flames by them in the Security Council. His surrender to them in 1993 over the number of troops needed to implement the safe areas concept in Bosnia was particularly unfortunate, as many of us felt at the time.

Meanwhile, vicious fighting continued in Angola, especially around Luena, the main city in the east of the country. The government complained that UNITA continued to receive massive support from South Africa and threatened to raise this in the Security Council. An intensification of fighting before a cease-fire comes into effect is a frequent phenomenon. At that point in a peace process, neither side has full confidence that a political settlement will be achieved. Even though they may not admit it, both regard the cease-fire as 'reversible' and therefore want to ensure that they will be in the best possible positions, strategically and tactically, if fighting is resumed. It also helps the morale of their troops if they can score a victory or two before going into confined inactivity in an assembly area.

I flew from Caracas, where I was engaged in the unending negotiations for peace in El Salvador, to Lisbon to join Pérez de Cuéllar for the signing of the Bicesse Accords on 31 May 1991. Six days earlier the last Cuban troops had left Angola and UNAVEM I had completed its task. The previous evening the Security Council had approved the enlargement of UNAVEM, on the basis recommended in the report which

Earley and I had drafted in Baghdad, and named it UNAVEM II. Before the ceremony, the Secretary-General met separately with the Angolan President, José Eduardo dos Santos, and the UNITA leader, Jonas Savimbi. Dos Santos was his usual quiet and dignified self but did not welcome our proposal that the new commander of UNAVEM should be a Nigerian. Like other Front Line States, Angola did not always appreciate the overbearing and sometimes arrogant way in which Nigerians conducted relations with their brother Africans. Neither Pérez de Cuéllar nor I had met Savimbi before, though when I was ambassador in Angola he had publicly accused me of being biassed against UNITA (bias was not needed; UNITA's atrocities provided sufficient cause to oppose Savimbi's ambitions). On this occasion, he was charm itself, but after he had left, Pérez de Cuéllar perceptively characterized him as *malin*.

At the signature ceremony dos Santos looked glum throughout and made a stiff and ungracious speech without specific reference to either UNITA or its leader. Savimbi, by contrast, was relaxed and eloquent and greeted dos Santos as the President of the People's Republic of Angola and his compatriot. I felt no joy at this event: my friends in the MPLA had been defeated in the war because of South African and American support for Savimbi and I had been inwardly outraged when James Baker told Pérez de Cuéllar that morning that the United States would continue to support Savimbi financially so that he could campaign effectively.

As 31 July approached (the day on which both parties' troops were to start moving into the assembly areas), I was increasingly worried whether UNAVEM II would be ready to play its role. The mission was desperately short of vehicles and other logistical equipment, mainly because of the UN's habitually slow procedures for budget approval and procurement. These were fine, if time-consuming, for a static secretariat which might, from time to time, have to order a new supply of paper-clips. But they were totally unsuitable for an operational organization which was required, at short notice and under intense political pressure, to deploy multinational expeditionary forces to distant and war-torn lands. The solutions to the problem were clear: a peacekeeping fund to enable the Secretary-General to finance start-up costs (such as the charter of aircraft and ships to get troops and equipment to the field on time) without having to wait for the operation's budget to be approved by the General Assembly (which in the case of UNAVEM II did not happen until two and a half months after the Security Council took the political decision to set up the operation); a reserve stock of standard peacekeeping equipment which would be instantly available to a new operation and would be replenished from that operation's budget once it had been approved; and streamlined procurement procedures for the setting up of new operations. For years the Secretariat had been pressing the member states to accept these reforms, but without success. Nor, a decade later, can it be said that much has changed.

By late September 1991 it was clear that the process was in trouble. The two Angolan parties had both failed repeatedly to meet deadlines and the military programme was severely behind schedule. Much of the delay was due to all-pervasive shortages and transport difficulties in that ravaged land. Another problem was the ineffectiveness of the two joint commissions, which were supposed to be supervising the whole process; for a while UNITA withdrew from them altogether. The Americans and Portuguese complained to me about UNAVEM's apparent inactivity; I complained to them about their failure to get the commissions to function properly. Another destabilizing factor was that both sides had over-stated their troop numbers. At the end of September barely half the declared numbers were in the assembly areas. The initial exaggeration of numbers made it seem that more soldiers were outside the assembly areas than was in fact the case. Nor were we helped by a delay in the arrival of UNAVEM's new Nigerian commander, Major-General Edward Unimna, the first candidate having been withdrawn by Lagos after his appointment had been approved by the Security Council. In these circumstances, I decided that I had better visit the operation and see for myself. The problem was to escape from the El Salvador negotiations, but I got away in mid-October.

I had three main objectives. The first was to determine whether the two sides' delay in assembling their troops constituted a real threat to the peace process or was mainly due to logistic difficulties. The second was to see what could be done to improve living conditions for the UN military observers who were in five-man teams at over forty assembly areas, some of them in very remote places and almost none of them with adequate accommodation. The third was to identify what electoral help, if any, the Angolans were expecting from the UN.

After two days of briefing and meetings in Luanda, I took to the field. The first trip was to the province of Lunda Norte in the north-eastern corner of Angola. I had often visited it as ambassador because at that time about 150 British subjects were working for the diamond mining company there. It was a shock to find officers from the forces of the government (known as FAPLA) and UNITA (known as FALA) standing side by side to greet me at the airport, FAPLA in their usual worn combat fatigues but FALA in fresh green uniforms and Mao caps. We first visited a UNITA assembly area. The UNAVEM observers were living in a tented camp on the edge of a destroyed settlement. The FAPLA and FALA members of the joint monitoring group were camped in the ruined buildings. Water had to be fetched from a river but the UN team had a generator, a cooker, a fridge and a freezer. The assembly area was eleven kilometres away, dispersed over several square kilometres and with tracks neatly cut through the bush to connect small groups of impeccably aligned and stoutly built grass huts, all to a standard design. UNITA had been well trained by the South Africans. The area was supposed to accommodate four battalions, with a separate camp for the soldiers' families (described, with a lecherous grin, as *o acampamento do moral*, 'the morale camp'). But only 425 soldiers had assembled there, about one company per battalion. The area commander, lean and wiry like all the UNITA officers I was to meet, was evasive when I asked where the others were. I asked to see the guardroom where the soldiers' weapons were being held; it turned out to be just another grass hut, with no security at all.

We helicoptered on to Lucapa, one of the mining towns, to visit a FAPLA assembly area. The UN observers were comfortably housed in one of the mining company's villas. The assembly area was about fifteen kilometres away on a bleak and waterless plateau. The FAPLA troops were lined up to present me with a message of welcome. They were visibly miserable, being urban troops who were badly led (their officers were living in the town), ill-disciplined, short of food and water and not adept at living in the bush. As I walked away after receiving their message, they started murmuring, then whistling and catcalling. I thought of the sailors at the end of Britten's *Billy Budd*. The area commander would not say whether they were protesting at me or him or their general lot.

There followed a long meeting with the commander, attended by the FAPLA and FALA members of the local monitoring group. The commander spoke at length about his logistic problems and UNITA's refusal to permit the re-establishment of government authority in some areas which it had recently captured and where, he said, it was now illegally mining diamonds. The FALA representative denied this charge but went on to say that diamonds were the wealth of the people, not the MPLA. Both sides spoke with such vehemence that I doubted whether the joint monitoring group could survive many more sessions like this. The commander of the UNAVEM monitors, an impressive officer from Guinea-Bissau, said that what motivated people in the mining areas was not politics but illegal mining, not warfare but crime. Illegal digging was being done by everybody – FAPLA, FALA, deserters from both armies, civilians who supported the MPLA and civilians who supported UNITA, all of whom were united by their hostility to the mining police. None of those present challenged this assessment of Angola's Wild North-East.

The next day was spent in the centre and south of the country. We started at Huambo, the capital of the Planalto, Angola's *massif central*, visited two FAPLA and two FALA assembly areas and ended at

Lubango, the capital of Huila province, where I had done so much waiting during the first weeks of the Namibia operation. The assembly areas confirmed what we had seen in the north the previous day: UNITA were well led, well motivated, well organized; the government troops were poorly led, demoralized and disorganized.

After a day of comparative rest in Luanda, in which the main event was a meeting with Savimbi, we returned to the field and visited the extreme south-east of the country where Savimbi had long had his headquarters at a place called Jamba. We flew into the town of Mavinga, the scene of heavy fighting and famous victories for FALA as they repulsed successive offensives by FAPLA to take Jamba. There was a huge parade at the FALA assembly area, with a programme of song and dance glorifying UNITA and denigrating the MPLA and its Cuban allies. I was invited to address the parade and told them that they should no longer be singing about victory and defeat; the Bicesse Accords had been a victory for every Angolan; they should be singing about the joys that peace would bring. They looked totally unconvinced but applauded nonetheless.

We flew on to Jamba where UNITA protocol took charge of our programme in a totalitarian style that was not to be matched until I accompanied Boutros-Ghali to the capital of North Korea two years later. The UNAVEM liaison officer, an Irish colonel called Dunne, could say nothing but good of UNITA and bridled when I mentioned some of their violations of Bicesse. But it was soon clear that he and his team were in fact prisoners, invariably accompanied by UNITA escorts and going only where the latter permitted. Our host at lunch was Miguel Nzau Puna, a senior member of UNITA whom Dunne introduced as 'the Minister of the Interior', as though UNITA was the government. In the same spirit, we were asked to complete immigration forms for the 'Free Lands of Angola', as though the UNITA-controlled areas of Angola were an independent state. I instructed my team not to do so and Puna apologized. During lunch, Titov, the desk officer for Angola in my department, was told by the FAPLA member of the local monitoring group that what we were being shown was a sham; the real UNITA headquarters and the real Jamba were seventy kilometres away. This was hotly contested by Dunne, who swore that we were less than a kilometre from UNITA's headquarters. 'OK,' I said, 'let's drive by it on the way back to the airfield.' When we turned off the appointed route, the UNITA minders in the other cars stopped them from following us (I had declined to have a minder in mine). So we rattled alone along the dirt track and, sure enough, soon came to what looked like a headquarters complex, guarded by military police. Presumably the FAPLA officer's remark to Titov was intended to sow dissension between UNITA and the United Nations. When we rejoined the main party, the UNITA protocol officer was beside himself with rage. Our punishment was further pressure to complete the immigration forms but this was successfully resisted.

The next day, a Sunday, was mainly spent in discussion with Unimna and his senior staff about how to accelerate 'cantonment', by which was meant the gathering of combatants and their arms in the assembly areas. Some of the delays, we agreed, were due to gaps and errors in the Accords. It was absurd, for instance, to require FAPLA's town-based HQ staffs, logistic units, training staffs and so on to move to remote assembly areas (the Accords required that 'in so far as possible' the areas be situated away from major population centres). Perhaps we could get the two sides to agree that such personnel should stay where they were. We should also persuade the parties to produce more realistic troop numbers. More seriously, almost no heavy weapons were being brought into the assembly areas and the ones that did appear were mostly old and often unserviceable. Perhaps the parties could accept the idea of regional armouries, where they could place their heavy weapons and ammunition, as an alternative to taking them to remote assembly areas.

The next day I presented these ideas to a meeting attended by the two sides and the three observers (Portugal, the Soviet Union and the United States). No decisions were taken but nor were any of our ideas rejected. Afterwards Ndalu, the FAPLA chief of staff, said that only the United Nations, as a neutral third party, could usefully come forward with such ideas; if either side had done so, the ideas would have been instantly rejected by the other. He was right; this is why it is so important for the UN to be, and to be seen to be, neutral and impartial if it is performing a peacemaking or peacekeeping role.

That evening I left for Paris to attend the signing of the peace agreement for Cambodia, the birth of our next peacekeeping venture. How far had I achieved the objectives identified at the beginning of the week?

As regards cantonment, UNITA was clearly keeping its best troops and weapons in the bush; it was also, unlike FAPLA, sustaining the morale of the troops that it did bring into the assembly areas. The government too had assembled far fewer troops than it had declared. Both sides must therefore be assumed to have the capacity to resume war at short notice. Nor were any recruits being selected and trained for the new army, which was a sine qua non for successful implementation of Bicesse. The three countries which had agreed to support this process (France, Portugal, the United Kingdom) were well advanced in their planning but they needed a response from the government and UNITA.

The second objective related to the military observers. Their quality varied, as did the awfulness of their living conditions. The need to deploy them at short notice to nearly fifty remote locations, almost all of them without ready accommodation, would have tested any logistics system; for the UN's under-funded and over-regulated system it was an impossible task. But I won no applause from the UNMOs when I said that in the circumstances my administrative colleagues in New York had done remarkably well. Some of the UNMOs were outstanding, both in their military skills and in their ability to cope with adversity. I remember particularly an Indian officer, Lieutenant-Colonel Sinha, who in a few weeks had learnt enough Portuguese to communicate with the locals and had persuaded his team to undertake a number of self-help projects to make themselves more comfortable. Others irritated me by talking more about their living conditions than about their professional tasks.

As regards the UN's role, if any, in the elections, the prospects were uncertain. Savimbi wanted the UN to provide technical assistance and possibly to monitor the process. Dos Santos, on the other hand, concerned as always about infringement of his country's sovereignty, was reluctant to allow the UN a monitoring role and non-committal about technical assistance. He was inquisitive, though, about our electoral operation in Nicaragua (in which the Sandinistas were unexpectedly defeated). Was he, I wondered, looking for evidence that UN impartiality could not be relied upon if a Marxist party was a leading contender? Peréz de Cuéllar wanted the UN to play a leading role in the elections. In a report to the Security Council at the end of October, he therefore said that there were strong indications of a growing consensus in Angola that the UN should be involved in the elections. A formal request for both technical assistance and observation of the elections was received from the government in December 1991.

The elections would add a major civilian task to UNAVEM's mandate and Boutros-Ghali, who had become Secretary-General on 1 January 1992, took advantage of this to appoint a civilian Special Representative to head the mission. For this difficult post he chose a Briton, Margaret Joan Anstee, a long-serving UN official of high intelligence and boundless energy who was at that time Director of the UN Office in Vienna. I welcomed this appointment but worried about how the Chief Military Observer, Edward Unimna, would react. He had not made a good impression when I visited Angola the previous year and I had received a number of complaints, then and since, about his short temper and autocratic management. All Joan's diplomatic skills would be needed if she was to get Unimna to work loyally as her subordinate.

She visited Angola in February 1992 and the next month Boutros-Ghali presented to the Council his operational plan for observing the elections. This would require electoral teams in each of Angola's eighteen provinces and a major air operation. Meanwhile implementation of the

Bicesse Accords, he reported, was still badly behind schedule. Ninety-three per cent of UNITA's declared troops were now assembled but the FAPLA figure had fallen to 54 per cent; many of their troops had slipped away from the assembly areas because of the government's failure to pay and feed them. Demobilization had not yet begun and UNITA was blocking the restoration of government administration in many places controlled by it. On the positive side, there had been no serious violations of the cease-fire and joint police monitoring had at last begun.

A boost to the process was provided in early April when demobilization began and it was agreed that the elections for the President and the National Assembly should take place simultaneously on 29 and 30 September. In late June Boutros-Ghali was able to report 'qualified optimism', but neither he nor Anstee disguised the fact that many things that the Bicesse Accords required to be done before the elections would not be done in time. The first weeks of voter registration had highlighted the enormous logistical problems of organizing elections for the first time in such a vast and devastated country. More and prompter help was needed from the international community. At the government's request UNAVEM had agreed to coordinate the air operation; what was needed now was the machines. The Security Council's response was to express its 'serious concern' at the delays in the process and to demand, in unusually firm language, that the parties honour their commitments under the Bicesse Accords.

Three weeks before the elections the Secretary-General issued another report. This time he expressed 'cautious optimism'. Rereading the report nine years later, I am surprised that we advised him to do so; presumably we calculated that a pessimistic report would increase the risk of disaster. Only 41 per cent of the two armies had been demobilized; the political and security situation had deteriorated significantly; UNAVEM's impartiality was being called in question; there was a proliferation of weapons amongst the people; the government was being accused of having transferred tens of thousands of FAPLA soldiers into a new 'anti-riot police' (as the Krajina Serbs were doing in Croatia); the province of Cabinda (which at that time was the principal source of Angola's crude oil) was effectively excluded from the peace process because of a rebellion by two armed secessionist movements and only about 20 per cent of eligible voters in that province had been registered; the formation of the new FAA was 'woefully behind schedule', the only step forward being the swearing in of the officers who would head the command structure; further action would be delayed until tents could be obtained to accommodate the recruits. There were only two pieces of good news. Except in Cabinda, voter registration had been a conspicuous success; in the country as a whole, 92 per cent of the estimated voting population had

been registered; and there had been ample evidence of popular enthusiasm for the elections. Secondly, member states had responded well to
Boutros-Ghali's requests for support for the air operation.

In these circumstances, should Anstee and Boutros-Ghali have recommended postponement of the elections? Their grounds for doing so
would have been political, not logistical. The logistical difficulties were
great but they were being overcome. The danger lay in the certainty that
the political conditions stipulated by the Bicesse Accords for the holding
of elections would not be fulfilled by election day. In particular, three
armies would be in existence: significant elements of both FAPLA and
FALA had not been demobilized and FAA had now been created, at least
in embryo. And Savimbi had begun telling the media that if he did not
win, that would mean that the elections had not been free and fair. I
cannot remember whether we thought of proposing postponement. But
if we had, the proposal would not have succeeded. Dos Santos would
have denounced it as UN interference and Savimbi had always wanted
early elections; the Americans and Russians would have opposed it on
financial grounds and Portugal would probably have followed their lead.

So the Security Council expressed its conviction that the process was
irreversible and forlornly called on the parties, eleven days before the elections, 'to take urgent and determined steps to complete certain essential
measures' which they had failed to complete during the previous twelve
months, such as demobilization, the collection and storage of weapons, the
formation of the new army and getting the police to operate as a neutral,
national force. I often used to feel that more heed would be given to the
Security Council's resolutions and statements if they were fewer, shorter
and less distant from reality; and I applauded the Belgian commander of
the UN force in Bosnia when he said in 1993 that he had stopped reading
the Council's resolutions because they were so totally unrealistic about
member states' political will and the resources they were ready to provide.

In the event the elections were a huge success. During the two days
of voting UNAVEM's observers visited about two-thirds of the almost
6,000 polling stations. On the following day Anstee announced that in
spite of logistical difficulties the great majority of the 4.83 million registered voters had cast their votes in peaceful and orderly conditions. The
votes were counted at each of the polling stations. This limited the
number of counts which UNAVEM could observe, but the mission did a
quick count of the kind that had already been tested by the UN in 1990 in
Nicaragua and Haiti.* The results again provided an accurate prediction

---

* The methodology of the 'quick count' is described in Chapter 15 in the context of the
election in Haiti. It has proved to be a reliable means of predicting the outcome of an
election at an early stage in the counting of votes.

of the eventual outcome (the error being only 0.3 per cent in dos Santos' vote and 2 per cent in Savimbi's). But UNITA soon began to allege that there had been fraud on a massive scale. Eight days had been allowed for the investigation of complaints and the final compilation of votes but so numerous were UNITA's complaints that the results could not be announced until 17 October. During this interval it was known that dos Santos' share of the presidential vote was hovering round the 50 per cent which would assure his election without a second round. As a result Savimbi, sulking in his villa in Luanda and refusing to see anyone, cried foul and began threatening to reject the results even before they were officially announced. Boutros-Ghali had to spend much time on the telephone persuading him not to do so. But on 5 October the eleven ex-UNITA generals in the high command of the new army withdrew from their posts in protest at the allegedly fraudulent elections. Two days later it became known that Savimbi had been smuggled out of Luanda and was now installed in Huambo.

So concerned was the Security Council at these developments, and an accompanying hate campaign by the UNITA radio against Anstee and UNAVEM, that it sent a commission to Angola to urge the parties to respect the Bicesse Accords. The commission's visit coincided with one by the South African Foreign Minister, Pik Botha. There is a splendid account of its meeting with him in Anstee's book, *Orphan of the Cold War*. As our telephone conversations were not subject to the attention of libel lawyers, she gave me orally an even more graphic account of the Minister's behaviour and the fatuity of his efforts to resolve the crisis single-handed. Savimbi was in an emotional mood and far from consistent in what he said to his many interlocutors on the key questions: would he meet dos Santos? What were his conditions for acceptance of the election results? Would he participate in a second round? Would he agree to the formation of a government of national unity, pending a second round? Dos Santos was, by contrast, calm, consistent and statesmanlike, expressing a readiness to meet Savimbi (but not outside Angola) and work for national reconciliation.

On 17 October the official results were announced. Turnout had been over 91 per cent but there had been a high number of blank or spoiled votes. In the legislative elections the government party (the MPLA) had won 53.7 per cent of the votes and UNITA 34.1 per cent. In the presidential contest dos Santos had won 49.57 per cent and Savimbi 40.07; because dos Santos had not quite reached the 50 per cent needed for victory in the first round, there would have to be a run-off between him and Savimbi. Anstee was required to pronounce on the freedom and fairness of the elections. Stating that although there had been some irregularities there was no conclusive evidence of major, systematic or widespread fraud, she certified that 'the elections . . . can be considered to have been generally free and fair'. This finding was undoubtedly correct but it provoked further vicious attacks against her by the UNITA media. There had been serious violence in Luanda and elsewhere during the previous week and disaster now loomed. UNAVEM reported UNITA troop movements and the forceful occupation of municipalities in various parts of the country. Boutros-Ghali urged the two leaders to meet but each set conditions which the other would not accept.

On 30 October UNITA tried to seize Luanda airport. Heavy fighting broke out in the capital and spread the next day to a number of other cities. In Luanda, Anstee was trapped for two days in the British Embassy. The Vice-President of UNITA, Jeremiah Chitunda, and the head of its delegation to the joint political and military commission, Elias Salupeto Pena (a nephew of Savimbi), were killed in the fighting, as were many UNITA supporters. Three dozen senior members of UNITA who had surrendered or been captured were detained at the Ministry of Defence 'under government protection'. A cease-fire of a kind came into effect on 2 November. The government had retained control of the main cities but much of the countryside was now in UNITA's hands; by 23 November UNAVEM had confirmed that UNITA controlled 57 of Angola's 164 municipalities and believed that its control extended to a further 40.

When the crisis broke on 30 October I was on my way, with Álvaro de Soto, the architect of the El Salvador peace settlement, to San Salvador where the peace process had been put at risk by President Cristiani's unwillingness to purge the armed forces. I was due to go on to Beijing for consultations with the Co-Chairmen of the Paris Conference and Prince Sihanouk on saving the Cambodian peace process, which had been put at risk by the Khmer Rouge's refusal to demobilize its troops. These two crises, plus the unending one in Bosnia, left me little time for Angola and the many telephone calls I received each day from Joan Anstee. I was sometimes unforgivably short with her, wishing that she would report events by cable once or twice a day and not by telephone whenever something new occurred. But on 2 November Boutros-Ghali telephoned me in San Salvador and told me to return to New York and proceed as soon as possible for a few days to Luanda to give Anstee support. She had displayed great courage during the fighting in Luanda but, not surprisingly, was now very tired. I had earlier told Boutros that I was worried that she lacked a kindred spirit in UNAVEM, a confidant or confidante with whom she could relax and talk off the record. The military commander, Edward Unimna, was, to put it mildly, a difficult colleague and did not fill this bill, nor did her civilian deputy, Ebrima Jobarteh. The nearest she had to a trusted friend seemed to be the chief administrative officer, Tom White, a Canadian for whom I too had the highest regard. I was glad to be sent on this mission, inconvenient though it was.

Accompanied by Dmitry Titov, my desk officer for Angola, I reached Luanda late on 6 November, just in time to get to the UNAVEM base before the 6 p.m. curfew. I stayed with Joan in her bungalow, where the other inhabitants were Sissy, a housekeeper whom she had brought with her from Vienna and who conjured the most wonderful meals from the limited ingredients available in war-torn Luanda, and Missy, a cat which Joan had adopted in Luanda. The next morning Sissy laid an elegant breakfast on the patio, notwithstanding the presence on neighbouring open ground (red laterite) of three vast UNAVEM helicopters, which for safety's sake had been brought there from the airport. No sooner had we sat down than two of them started their engines. This drove all three females into a frenzy: Joan rushed out into the swirling dust in her peignoir shouting 'Excuse me, excuse me, we are having breakfast'; Sissy, bent double (she had been a teenage skating champion), dashed in and out of the house shutting windows and rescuing the breakfast; Missy desperately sought refuge from noise, vibration, wind and dust. It is never fun to be coated in red dust, but it was particularly trying when water ran for only one hour a day and the next hour would not come until the following morning.

The first call of the day was on President dos Santos. He was less confident than at any of our many meetings during the preceding nine years. He repeated what he had been saying to all since Savimbi challenged the election results: the cease-fire must be respected; the Bicesse Accords remain valid; UNITA must accept the results of the legislative elections so that the Assembly can amend the electoral law and postpone until May the second round for the presidency; and the UN should take a leading role in creating the necessary conditions for that round to be held. The last point was a reversal of the position dos Santos had taken during the negotiation of the Accords and when I had seen him a year before. I said that the Secretary-General would welcome greater UN involvement provided that we could define a mandate that was clear, practicable and agreed by the two sides; but I could not speak for the major powers who were increasingly uneasy about the cost of peacekeeping.

Angola was again the Land of Waiting. We were supposed to see Savimbi the next morning but the meeting was cancelled at short notice and without explanation. After two days of waiting, Savimbi called: yes, it was important that we should meet but the government must first stop accusing UNITA of a premeditated *coup d'état* and allow three of the senior UNITA personalities detained at the Ministry of Defence in Luanda to travel to Huambo with us. I assumed this to be non-negotiable and decided the next morning to put pressure on Savimbi by flying to Huambo even though there was still no agreed hour for the meeting. This we did. The UNITA flag was flying over the airport. The government controlled the centre of the city and UNITA the outskirts; the UNAVEM camp was uncomfortably located in no man's land. We settled into the camp and waited. As dusk fell, Unimna caused a moment of near panic: were we not being lured into a trap in which we would be taken hostage, or worse? Would it not be better to return to Luanda and come back the next morning? After fifteen minutes' discussion, I insisted that we all stay: I did not want to make it easy for Savimbi to avoid a meeting with us and I could not believe that, even in his allegedly disturbed mood, he would do anything so foolish as to harm us.

Sure enough, a UNITA general came at 7.45 p.m. to escort us to the meeting place. We drove through empty streets to a small villa with boarded-up windows. Inside we found a press of people in a small and smelly sitting room, with blue walls, dilapidated furniture and, everywhere you looked, plastic dolls and doll's-house furniture wrapped in cellophane. The human beings included Savimbi, a one-and-a-half armed general called Bock, UNITA's information secretary, Jorge Valentim, and its Deputy Secretary-General, Eugenio Manuvakola. On our side there were Anstee, Unimna, Colonel Roger Mortlock of the New Zealand Army, who was UNAVEM's regional commander in Huambo, and myself.

The meeting lasted for three and a half hours, without refreshment of any kind. Savimbi rambled on, repetitively and at enormous length. He had no trust in the government's word; the government had stolen the election from him; it had made him a hunted man in his native land, obliged to meet us in this malodorous safe house and to change his abode several times a night. He was thinking of withdrawing from politics and giving way to a younger man (his departure would have made it even more difficult to negotiate an end to the crisis and I found myself in the unexpected position of begging him to stay on). His colleagues also spoke, often in more aggressive terms than he. I tried to persuade him to focus on practical steps for putting the peace process back on track, in particular the possibility of a larger role for the UN. He said that he was strongly in favour of this. (Fortunately, I did not have to raise his media's attacks on Joan because he had given her a handsome apology for these in a telephone conversation a few days before.) I talked him through various possible mandates, emphasizing at every point that each of them would have to be based on a sound agreement between the two sides, which meant that he and dos Santos would have to resume the political dialogue. Afterwards, I had to agree with Anstee that nothing had been said to indicate that that was likely to happen.

Back in Luanda everyone wanted to be briefed about the meeting. The representatives of the three observer countries and the British Ambassador disagreed with my conciliatory approach to Savimbi. He should be isolated, they said, and any country which supported him should have sanctions imposed on it; his 'representative offices' in foreign capitals should be closed; visas should not be issued to him or his supporters. He should be given an early deadline for accepting the election results; if he did not meet it, let the heavens fall on him. I was irritated by this criticism of what I was trying to do. I did not believe that Savimbi could be isolated; 40 per cent of the electorate had voted for him; he had shown before that he could recover from defeat; even without South African and American support, he would probably be able to keep the war going. I was also irritated at appearing to defend Savimbi when in reality I loathed him as a monster whose lust for power had brought appalling misery to his people. But I was there as a peacemaker and my job was to try to find ways of restarting the peace process.

The next day I briefed dos Santos and various of his ministers. They too were sceptical about the prospects of getting Savimbi back into negotiations; he was playing for time and intended to pursue power by military means. Dos Santos did not exclude some gesture of goodwill, like the return of Chitunda's and Salupeto Pena's remains, but he would not discuss a future UN role with Savimbi until the latter had unequivocally accepted both the continuing validity of the Bicesse Accords and the results of the legislative elections. I said that he had done the first at the meeting in Huambo; I would see if I could secure his agreement to the second. I spoke to Savimbi that afternoon. Though coming close to saying that he accepted the election results, he was not unequivocal. I suggested that I send him a letter stating what I *thought* he had said; he could tell me if I had got it right. I sent the letter before leaving Luanda that evening to go back to New York.

The days spent waiting for the meeting with Savimbi provided opportunities to congregate in the camp bar with election observers and other UNAVEM officials who had come to Luanda for rest and recreation after service in the interior. They had horror stories to tell: UNITA's violent reassertion of control over the rural areas and small towns; the government's distribution of weapons to civilians; appalling atrocities against Mbundu (Savimbi's tribe) in the northern areas where the Kimbundu (dos Santos' tribe) were the majority; and unpaid FAPLA soldiers who had become bandits, killing, looting and fighting amongst themselves. None of the people in the bar thought that there was any possibility of holding a second round to complete the presidential election or that, if there was, UNITA would accept a second defeat.

The days of waiting also gave Titov and me time to look into the malaise at UNAVEM. What we heard did not please. Both blacks and whites told us that the basic problem was racial prejudice which was splitting the mission into opposing camps. At receptions senior black members of UNAVEM had, it was said, been heard to say that both Anstee and the representatives of the three observer countries were racist. On the other side of the coin, I thought I detected a touch of racism in what was being said by some white members of the mission about some of the senior Africans. It was alleged, for instance, that two of the latter had gone on a weekend trip to Namibia in the UNAVEM Beechcraft accompanied by two young Angolan women, listed in the passenger manifest as 'government officials' who would participate in the UNAVEM officials' supposed consultations with the Namibian author-ities. When I asked why no disciplinary action had been taken, I was told, with a shrug of the shoulders: 'That would have just made things worse.' As I had sensed in New York, Anstee was lonely and somewhat isolated at the head of the mission. She was also doing a desperately difficult job to which she was devoting all her energy. What she needed was a discreet and perceptive manager who would resolve these management issues for her or advise her how to do so herself.

In a brief and busy visit it is difficult to be sure that the information one receives on such sensitive matters is accurate and well-intended. I therefore decided not to take any action on the racism issue. But I came to the conclusion that there were other factors which made it necessary to replace Unimna. He disliked Anstee and did not disguise his reluc-tance to accept her authority. He was also a martinet, short-tempered, autocratic and even violent; he had been observed more than once to strike his driver. This was not the style of command which is needed in a multinational operation. Nor were his professional skills as good as I had initially thought. Just before my visit, I had had to send him a reprimand for failing to keep New York informed about what was happening during the weekend of fighting when Anstee was stuck in the British Embassy and the media were reporting (untruthfully) that UNAVEM had taken casualties. So I spent two and a half hours with him, explaining at length why I thought that the time had come for him to return to his country's service. In the end we agreed that he should leave at the end of the month and we parted harmoniously. Four days later, after I had given a press conference in Portuguese and English he came up to me and said, 'That was a brilliant performance; if you don't offend Africa, you will be the next Secretary-General.' Was that a racist remark? I did not think so, but one of the white officials who overheard it raised his eyebrows and gave me a knowing look.

On 17 November, Savimbi replied to my letter. The Permanent Committee of UNITA's Political Commission had met in Huambo and had concluded that UNITA accepted the results of the 'recognizedly fraudulent and irregular' legislative elections in order to permit implementation of the peace process. This was a step forward, though we had to state publicly that we could not accept UNITA's description of the elections. What was now needed was a positive reaction by the government. It proved difficult to obtain. Dos Santos was still planning a government of national unity and reconciliation. But he was upset by UNITA's continued insistence that there had been fraud and his position seemed to harden. Ndalu, who had, throughout the crisis, been the government's link with UNITA and an advocate of reconciliation, left for Europe, ostensibly for medical treatment, even though Savimbi had said he wanted a meeting with him. Only Lopo do Nascimento, the Minister for the Administration of the Territory and a moderate, tried to get the government to make some concession or at least a gesture of goodwill.

Lopo saw Boutros-Ghali in New York on 23 November. The two sides, he realized, had to show the political will to resolve their conflict or Angola would risk being abandoned by the UN. But the government needed the UN's help in providing security for Savimbi and other UNITA leaders when they returned to Luanda. Could this be done? In return Lopo received a lecture that was to become a standard feature in Boutros-Ghali's repertoire. The government, Boutros said, had won the election and had prevailed in Luanda, but it would face defeat if it did not make a concession soon. As the winner it was responsible for making the first move; the longer it delayed, the more difficult that first move would become. Since the cease-fire on 1 November, three weeks had been wasted. Did dos Santos not realize the urgency? Was he not aware of the level of fatigue in the international community? The government should learn the lesson of Beirut, a prosperous and respected city on which the international community turned its back when the rival factions there rejected dialogue. The same fate awaited Angola. The international community was waiting impatiently for a conciliatory gesture by the government. It would not wait much longer. There was a pressing demand for UN peacekeeping all over the world. The member states were becoming selective; they would not spend their taxpayers' money unless the hostile parties proved that they had the political will to work together. 'Forget about the past; begin anew.'

With Lopo, Boutros-Ghali was preaching to the converted. I hoped that he would convey the message to his President with the same vigour that Boutros had used. Perhaps he did, for three days later the two sides met, though not at a very senior level, at Namibe, a port in the southwest of Angola. They agreed a three-point declaration, affirming the continuing validity of the Bicesse Accords and the continuation of the cease-fire, and requesting that UNAVEM's mandate be renewed and that it be given a larger role. Three days later UNITA launched a major offensive in the northern province of Uige, capturing its capital and an important airbase. Savimbi's intentions were clear; those of us who had advocated conciliatory gestures by the government were left looking foolish and feeling angry. But peacemakers must never give up. Boutros-Ghali invited the two leaders to meet him in Geneva in the last week of December. Savimbi accepted; dos Santos said he was ready to meet Savimbi but only in Luanda.

Early in the New Year the fighting intensified as the government launched an offensive to drive UNITA out of the provincial capitals and other cities where it had established a presence during the previous year. There were reports of massacres of UNITA's civilian supporters, as had happened in Luanda the previous October. The Secretary-General told the Security Council that Angola had returned to civil war and that the conflict was now engulfing centres of population in a way that it had never done before. Anstee worked tirelessly to arrange a meeting between senior military officers from the two sides and/or a second Namibe meeting. Both said that they accepted such meetings but whenever a meeting seemed imminent one or other would back away. Both sides blamed UNAVEM for the resumption of fighting, adding to the perils its personnel already faced. A UN helicopter was destroyed in Huambo and many UNAVEM personnel were assaulted. By mid-January the fighting had become so extensive that UNAVEM had had to evacuate two-thirds of its field stations and abandon UN equipment worth millions of dollars.

UNAVEM's mandate was due to expire at the end of January 1993. The mission's tasks had evolved considerably under the pressure of events. Its original role had been to monitor the two parties' joint verification of the process set out in the Bicesse Accords. This minimalist function reflected dos Santos' unease about what a larger UN role would imply for Angola's sovereignty. But the joint mechanisms for verification did not work well. This was mainly for logistical reasons at first, but as it became clear that neither party was assembling all its troops and heavy weapons, suspicions grew and the effectiveness of the joint mechanisms was further reduced. As a result, UNAVEM gradually became the verification mechanism of first instance, reporting the parties' misdemeanours to the Security Council and using its good offices to persuade them to respect their commitments and to resolve disputes between them. The three observer countries were not always happy about this process but they did not try to block it.

The extended crisis that followed the elections had a complicated impact on the two sides' attitudes to the UN. Both were tempted to blame it for the disasters that occurred and did so from time to time. But both also found it convenient to hand to the UN responsibility for restarting a dialogue between them and both maintained that they wanted the UN to play a larger role in the future. I was never wholly convinced that what they said was genuine. But as it was almost the only thing on which they seemed to agree at the time of my visit in November 1992, Anstee and I tried to use it as a lever to move them towards a resumption of dialogue. In his report to the Council about renewal of the mandate, Boutros-Ghali rightly said that in future the UN should be more closely involved in the negotiation of peace settlements like the Bicesse Accords, so that it could make sure that the role envisaged for it was feasible. But he was too tactful to point out that this had not been possible in the case of Bicesse because the Portuguese did not want the UN to muscle in on their negotiation and the Angolan Government did not want the UN to have more than a minimal role. One middle-ranking military adviser (Dermot Earley) had been all the UN presence they would accept at the negotiations in Lisbon.

The Council adopted its wordiest resolution yet on Angola (the length of resolutions is a reliable indicator of UN impotence) and decided to extend UNAVEM for a further three months, leaving the Secretary-General to decide what levels of personnel and equipment were required and where they should be stationed. Soon afterwards I left the peace-keeping department and had little further to do with the UN's protracted efforts to mediate agreements and get the Angolan parties to put them into effect. Nine years later the conflict grinds on and will continue to do so until Savimbi is removed from the scene. It is important that he should be remembered, for he personifies a lesson that powerful governments need to learn: do not arm and pay and flatter local proxies to fight for your interests in their countries, for those proxies may well become malevolent genies whom you will not be able to put back into the bottle when you no longer need them. Have UNITA in Angola or the Mujahidin/Taleban in Afghanistan been of net benefit to the United States? Has Israel benefited from encouraging the creation of Hamas as a foil to the PLO in Palestine?

One good thing did come out of the UN's failed endeavour to help the Angolan parties implement the Bicesse Accords. It taught us important lessons which we were able to apply almost immediately to a similar situation in what had been Portugal's other large colony in Africa, Mozambique. The peace settlement there, which was signed just before I left the peacekeeping department, was between the Mozambican Government and a rebel movement called RENAMO. Like UNITA, RENAMO had been used by white supremacists in southern Africa as a means of destabilizing a Marxist government. A UN political and military team was admitted to the closing stages of the negotiations and, drawing on what had happened in Angola, was able to persuade the two sides, and the mediators, that the structures for implementation must be such as to give the UN the authority to carry out the tasks entrusted to it.

As a result, the peace agreement in Mozambique accorded the United Nations responsibility for overall supervision of the peace process. It would chair the supervisory and monitoring commission and the subordinate cease-fire and reintegration commissions. It would supervise the cease-fire, ensure the security of key transport routes, monitor demobilization and disarmament, organize the return of refugees, coordinate humanitarian operations and provide technical assistance for, and verification of, elections. This would mean an operation at least as large as the one in Namibia four years before, with a significant infantry element. This was an ambitious mandate and there were bumpy moments. But the mandate was fulfilled and Mozambique was a success for the United Nations. So some good did come out of UNAVEM II's failure in Angola.

12

Western Sahara

Western Sahara is a large, sparsely populated, desert territory which lies between Mauritania and Morocco on the north-west coast of Africa. In 1884 it became a colony of Spain. In the last Spanish census, taken in 1974, its population numbered about 75,000. Early in 1976 Spain withdrew, after setting up a temporary administration based on a local assembly (the *Jema'a*) whose members had been appointed by Spain ten years before. The day after the Spanish withdrawal, Morocco conveyed to the then Secretary-General a message from the *Jema'a* that it had approved the 'reintegration' of the territory with Mauritania and Morocco. The same day a movement known as the Frente POLISARIO, which had been engaged in low-intensity conflict with the Spanish colonial authorities, declared Western Sahara to be an independent state, the Saharan Arab Democratic Republic (SADR). But POLISARIO was not strong enough to take control of the territory and Mauritania and Morocco divided it between themselves.

POLISARIO, supported by Morocco's enemy Algeria, joined battle with the Moroccan forces. The fighting intensified three years later when Mauritania renounced its claim and Morocco occupied the Mauritanian sector. POLISARIO was soon forced back into a narrow strip of land along the territory's eastern and southern borders. Morocco built an immense sand wall or 'berm' to prevent POLISARIO from infiltrating that part of the territory (80 per cent of the whole) which was held by the Moroccan Army. The length of the berm in Western Sahara is about 1,600 kilometres, with a 400-kilometre extension to the north along Morocco's border with Algeria. POLISARIO was defeated on the battlefield but, with Algeria's help, was more successful in its diplomacy. It succeeded in winning recognition of the SADR from more than half the African countries and in 1984 the SADR became a member of the Organization of African Unity (OAU), from which Morocco thereupon withdrew.

The majority view in the General Assembly was that because Western Sahara had been a colonial territory, its people had the right to self-determination. In 1979 it was proposed that this right be exercised through an internationally supervised referendum. In 1981 King Hassan II of Morocco accepted the idea but refused direct negotiations with POLISARIO. However, the central issue was not direct negotiations; it was who would be entitled to vote in the referendum. During the Spanish period most of the population had been nomadic. But more recent exploitation of the territory's phosphate deposits had led to the creation of a number of towns which attracted 'settlers' from Morocco; and the war had driven some 50,000 Sahrawis into refugee camps at Tindouf, just inside Algeria. When the idea of a referendum was put forward, there was no agreed definition of who had been a Sahrawi at the time of the Spanish withdrawal in 1976. The 1974 census was assumed to have omitted many nomads and persons already displaced by the hostilities between POLISARIO and the Spanish forces. This assumption appears to be confirmed by the fact that the 1974 census listed only 74,000 persons but by the early eighties the refugee population in Algeria already amounted to about 50,000.

In 1985 Pérez de Cuéllar launched a joint UN–OAU effort to resolve the conflict. In practice the work was done by the UN, in the person of Issa Diallo, a Guinean member of Pérez de Cuéllar's office. Diallo was in some ways similar to Picco – he enjoyed Pérez de Cuéllar's confidence and was discreet, secretive, possessive of his negotiation and not a team player. But he lacked Picco's patience, realism and attention to detail; he wanted quick results and all doubts were brushed aside. Pérez de Cuéllar quickly persuaded King Hassan that the UN should organize the referendum but failed to dent his refusal to negotiate the details directly with POLISA-RIO. The latter's leader, Mohammed Abdelaziz, was even less flexible: either there must be direct negotiations or the UN must take over the administration of the territory. However, both sides agreed that a UN technical mission could visit the territory and Tindouf in November 1987.

After its return, Diallo prepared his 'Proposals for a Settlement of the Question of Western Sahara'. They provided for the Secretary-General to appoint a Special Representative who would have full and exclusive authority in all matters relating to the referendum, including voters' security, for which purpose he would be assisted by a UN police unit. Those with the right to vote would be persons listed in the 1974 census, plus persons in the refugee camps who would be identified as Sahrawis in a census to be conducted by UNHCR and would be permitted to return to the territory. Voters would be invited to choose between independence and integration with Morocco. The Secretary-General would determine the date of a cease-fire, after Morocco had 'appropriately and substantially' reduced its troops. The troops that remained, and POLISARIO troops in the territory (who were few), would be confined to their bases and monitored by UN military observers.

After much discussion with the parties during the summer of 1988, Pérez de Cuéllar decided in August to present them separately with the settlement proposals. Though purporting to accept them, each side's acceptance was heavily qualified. POLISARIO's was accompanied by a dozen demands and observations that were incompatible with the proposals which they claimed to be accepting. For instance, they demanded bilateral negotiation of the cease-fire and abrogation of all Moroccan laws during the period between the cease-fire and the referendum, neither of which featured in the proposals or was acceptable to Morocco. The latter expressed a number of reservations, including rejection of any role for the Special Representative in matters of public order, which was a central feature of his proposals, and amplified its reservations in a long letter to Pérez de Cuéllar.

Pérez de Cuéllar nevertheless decided to press on. In September he informed the Security Council that the two parties had, 'while making remarks and comments', agreed to the settlement proposals. He did not, however, make the proposals available to the Council, which was not to see them until nearly two years later. The Council duly took note of the 'agreement in principle' and authorized the appointment of the Special Representative. Pérez de Cuéllar chose Hector Gros Espiell, a future Foreign Minister of Uruguay, who had little opportunity to shine in this role and irritated Pérez de Cuéllar by his public statements on what remained a very delicate issue. Fighting in the territory intensified after the parties' 'acceptance' of the proposals. Demands by POLISARIO and Algeria for the withdrawal of *all* Moroccan troops and 'settlers', the reinstatement of Spanish law and other action not provided for in the proposals raised doubts about what had actually been achieved by the UN. Hopes were briefly raised early in 1989 when King Hassan finally met the POLISARIO leadership in Marrakesh. But POLISARIO characteristically overreached itself, claiming that the meeting constituted Moroccan recognition of it as the representative of the Sahrawi people. Hassan refused a further meeting.

Pérez de Cuéllar acknowledges in his memoir, *Pilgrimage for Peace*, that, given the parties' reservations, it was risky to go to the Security Council in the way he did, but '[t]here seemed no other hope . . . of moving forward toward the referendum that both POLISARIO and Morocco said they favored'.* I disagreed with this view at the time and I still disagree with it, for three reasons. First, Pérez de Cuéllar chose to give the Security Council less than the full truth about the parties' 'remarks and comments'. Although he was not pressed for details about them, his reticence could have undermined the Council's confidence in him, a risk

---

* Javier Pérez de Cuéllar, *Pilgrimage for Peace* (St Martin's Press, New York, 1997), p. 343.

that no Secretary-General should take lightly. Secondly, he had at his disposal almost no sticks or carrots that might induce the parties to drop the substantive reservations they had expressed. Thirdly, this normally patient and thorough diplomat seemed to forget some basic principles of peacemaking: make sure that the parties fully understand and accept the implications of the proposed agreement; give them time to 'sell' it to their constituencies; even if they will not meet face to face, let them at least see each other's signatures on a document (there were no signatures on the settlement proposals and there were times during the subsequent negotiations when I even wondered whether the two sides had been shown the same document); do not assume that 'it will be all right on the night'.

The planning of the operation was as unsatisfactory as the negotiations had been. A committee was set up in the Secretariat to work out an 'implementation plan' in consultation with the two sides. None of the Secretariat participants, including myself, had been privy to the negotiations and Gros Espiell was even less informed. As a first step, Timothy Dibuama and I prepared a timetable for implementation. The two sides' negative reaction to it confirmed that there were many substantive issues on which agreement had yet to be reached. But Pérez de Cuéllar wanted the implementation plan as soon as possible and I drafted it over the 1990 New Year holiday.

But Diallo then questioned whether we really had to obtain the parties' consent to our implementation plan; could we not just present it to the Security Council and rely on 'international pressure' to bring the parties into line? Not for the first or last time, much effort had to be expended on persuading reluctant colleagues that there were no short cuts; peacekeeping had its rules; over a period of forty years a corpus of principles, practices and procedures had been established; they could not be ignored. I had to give the same message to Boutros-Ghali when he became Secretary-General in 1992. The frequency of the admonition 'You can't do it that way, Secretary-General' was, perhaps, one of the factors which led him to remove me from peacekeeping a year later.

Early in 1990, Gros Espiell was succeeded as the Secretary-General's Special Representative by Johannes Manz, Director of Administration and Personnel in the Swiss Diplomatic Service. Manz brought a much-needed professionalism to the job and made a good first impression. But he had more difficulty than most in adjusting to the vagaries of the Secretariat, for which the hyper-efficiency of the Swiss public service was not an ideal training. The Western Sahara cast included some particularly trying characters and it is not altogether Manz's fault that he failed to establish good working relations with them.

In March 1990 Pérez de Cuéllar visited Morocco and Algeria to talk to the parties about implementation. On his return, I was told that the main stumbling blocks had been the number of Moroccan troops to be with-drawn and the procedures for identifying which Sahrawis were entitled to vote; substantive agreement had been reached on neither issue; both sides had, however, agreed to an informal cessation of hostilities. The Secretary-General intended to submit his implementation plan to the Security Council by mid-June, in advance of an OAU Summit in July.* The report containing the plan was duly prepared in mid-June but the draft leaked, Algeria and POLISARIO expressed strong objections to it and Pérez de Cuéllar, on Diallo's advice and against mine, put it on hold.

Whatever action a Secretary-General takes will encounter objections from some member state, often from several. I consistently advised that the right course was for the Secretary-General to consult all interested member states, to decide what he was going to say to the Security Council and then to stick to his guns, however noisy the counter-battery fire might be. Boutros-Ghali usually followed this advice; Pérez de Cuéllar did so less often. On this occasion, though, he wavered only briefly and the report, little changed, was published a week later. The Council approved it without delay and 'called upon' the two parties to cooperate with the Secretary-General and the Chairman of the OAU, a rather feeble manifestation of the 'international pressure' on which Diallo rested his hopes. The Council also asked the Secretary-General to provide 'as soon as possible' a further detailed report on his implemen-tation plan, with an estimate of what it would cost.

It was almost ten months before that detailed report was born, after the most painful travail I experienced in eleven years in the Secretariat. The causes of the travail were various: a deeply flawed settlement pro-posal that failed to address the fundamental disagreement between the parties on who would be eligible to vote in the referendum; a top-heavy Task Force, usually attended by five Under-Secretaries-General; a web of personality clashes; and general overload, with four or five new peace-keeping operations being planned simultaneously. As if this were not enough, we were under relentless pressure from the five permanent members to cut costs; how, they asked, could we justify spending almost $250 million on a referendum in which barely 70,000 people would vote?

Unbeknown to the Task Force and the Security Council, King Hassan sent Pérez de Cuéllar in late July 1990 a twelve-page letter reiterating the reservations he had expressed in 1988 and setting out in detail Morocco's

---

* The Secretary-General's efforts were, formally speaking, done 'in cooperation with the Chairman of the OAU'. President Mubarak of Egypt, who was Chairman at the time, made a number of helpful interventions. But the OAU was the junior partner and its role was sometimes neglected by the Secretariat in New York, a failing that was to cause diffi-culties after the UN operation started work.

objections to the implementation plan that had been approved by the Security Council. When, three months later, the Moroccans discovered that the more detailed implementation plan was being finalized by a committee which was unaware of their King's objections to it, they released his letter to the media. There was an ugly showdown in the Task Force. Diallo had repeatedly told us that the parties accepted the implementation plan. Our doubts that this was so were now confirmed. Ahtisaari, back from Namibia and in his previous post as Under-Secretary-General for Administration and Management, was especially critical. Diallo replied, unconvincingly, that the Moroccans had assured him that their document was for internal political consumption only and could be ignored. A month later POLISARIO followed suit by publishing a statement of its own objections to the plan. This had been sent to the Secretary-General in early August but it too had been concealed from the Task Force and the Security Council.

Pérez de Cuéllar was undeterred. When the P-5 asked whether the plan was fully agreed by the parties, they were blandly told that 'the Secretary-General is satisfied that he has the agreement of the parties on all the main aspects'. He met the Task Force to bring us into line: we were not to consult the parties about the detailed implementation plan, lest they reject it. The Legal Counsel, Carl-August Fleischhauer, and I said that it was essential that the parties accept the new plan. They had made public their rejection of the plan approved by the Security Council in June; if we did not obtain their consent to the new detailed plan, either of them could, at any time, withdraw its cooperation. 'Diallo is dealing with that' was the Secretary-General's response. The Task Force was now meeting daily and the mood became increasingly disagreeable. Member states got wind of what was happening and began telling us that the parties must be on board before the Council was asked to set up the new peacekeeping operation. Pérez de Cuéllar was reluctantly persuaded to accept this.

In December 1990 the Task Force met with POLISARIO. In order to save money, we had decided to propose a change in the plan. The deployment of the operation's military component would be for a shorter period than previously envisaged. This could be achieved by starting the identification of qualified voters without waiting for the formal cease-fire and the partial withdrawal of Moroccan troops. Identification, we argued, would not require a UN military presence; the soldiers need not be deployed until the military parts of the plan were put into effect. The POLISARIO envoy, Béchir Mustafa Sayed, vigorously rejected this proposal. The Moroccan troops in the territory, he said, were more than twice as numerous as the civilian population; if they were not reduced and monitored by the UN, the identification process would be manipulated by the Moroccans and would lose all credibility. At this time Pérez de Cuéllar had obtained an undertaking from King Hassan that the Moroccan troops would be reduced to 65,000 (from an estimated 160,000) and had accepted this as being consistent with the settlement proposals. But we were not yet authorized to reveal this to POLISARIO. A senior Algerian official soon arrived in New York to support POLISARIO's position in the brutally direct style that is characteristic of Algerian diplomacy.

At a meeting of the Task Force in late January 1991, Pérez de Cuéllar instructed us to complete preparation of the detailed implementation plan within four weeks. We should stick firmly to the outline plan that had been approved by the Council in June. I was to assume the chairmanship of the Task Force and ensure better coordination. I welcomed this challenge but soon realized that I had been passed a poisoned chalice.

The Task Force struggled to find ways of shortening the peacekeeping operation's deployment in the field. What would need most time would be the sequential process of determining from documents which individuals were eligible to vote in the referendum and then identifying those individuals and registering them as voters. This work would be entrusted to an Identification Commission. Its base document would be the Spanish census of 1974, which would be updated by deleting all persons known to have died. The revised list of names would then be published in the territory and in other places where Sahrawis were known to be living. Persons who considered themselves to be Sahrawis but had for some reason been omitted from the census could then apply to be added to the list. After these applications had been adjudicated by the Commission, with the help of tribal elders, a consolidated list of eligible voters would be published. This work was to be completed by D-Day, when the cease-fire would come into effect. The Task Force estimated that it would require sixteen weeks. A further eleven weeks would then be needed for the Commission to identify persons on the consolidated list and register them as voters. During this period it would also deal with appeals against non-inclusion in the list.

This was clearly going to be a complicated process and the time allowed for it seemed very tight indeed. It was also clear that it would be easy for the parties, if they so wished, to delay the process indefinitely. In particular, we feared that Morocco might swamp the Commission with tens of thousands of applications from persons living in the Tarfaya region north of the territory. This had been ceded to Morocco by Spain in 1958. Morocco might claim that the inhabitants of Tarfaya were just as Sahrawi as those living in the part of Spanish Sahara which had not been ceded to Morocco.

Another question of concern was where POLISARIO troops should be confined during the period between the cease-fire and the announcement of the referendum results. POLISARIO maintained that their troops should be in camps inside Western Sahara. The Moroccans argued that POLISARIO had never had fixed installations in the territory; their troops should stay in their bases inside Algeria (exactly the same position as the South Africans had taken over SWAPO fighters in Namibia). The settlement proposals provided no answer to the question. Nor did Diallo who increasingly took the line that everything had been clear until the Task Force and Manz started meddling with the proposals. By mid-February I had got the Task Force to agree a draft of the Secretary-General's report that would present the detailed implementation plan to the Security Council. Pérez de Cuéllar summoned Manz, Ahtisaari, Diallo and me to discuss it. Diallo, who had stated no objection to the draft at Task Force meetings, disowned its recommendations, claiming that he had told the Task Force they would be unacceptable to the parties. Pérez de Cuéllar's main concern was the P-5's reaction to the still high cost of the operation, but he instructed Manz, Diallo and me to give the two parties an oral summary of the draft.

Two days later we briefed the Moroccan Ambassador, Ali Skalli. His King, he said, would assess carefully how well the new proposals responded to the concerns expressed in his letter of the previous July. After the Ambassador had left, I asked Diallo if I could have a copy of that letter, which I had still seen only in the version published by the Moroccan Press Agency. He disregarded my request, replying angrily that he was not a member of the Task Force and there was nothing he could do to help. That afternoon we gave the same presentation to the POLISARIO representative. Diallo was again present – and silent. Béchir grumbled but did not lead me to expect major problems from that quarter. I felt obliged to send Pérez de Cuéllar a written report on Diallo's behaviour and ask *him* for a copy of the King's letter. I did not get one.

The consultations dragged on. POLISARIO were reasonably content; Skalli maintained that he had no instructions from Rabat but seized every opportunity to denigrate the Secretary-General's revised proposals. The Secretary-General himself decided that he was not prepared to put such an expensive proposal to the Council and instructed us to reduce the cost by at least 20 per cent. Manz returned to Switzerland. Two weeks later he told me by phone that when he took leave of Pérez de Cuéllar the Secretary-General had echoed Diallo (who was present) in saying that everything had been going smoothly until the Task Force became involved. Would Manz please return the next month and help him and Diallo write a new report, without revealing to the Task Force that this was being done? Manz had been struck dumb and had since written to

Pérez de Cuéllar that on grounds of principle he would not draft a new report behind the backs of his colleagues, that he anyway doubted the wisdom of embarking on a new report when we had just briefed the parties on the existing one and that he had lost all confidence in Diallo, whose behaviour was no longer acceptable. When I told Ahtisaari of this, as Manz had authorized me to, he gave the only possible advice: press on regardless. So I set about trying to persuade the soldiers and the administrators to reduce the budget from $245 million to less than $200 million. The target was achieved.

In mid-March 1991, we finally received an official reaction from Rabat. The Foreign Minister, Abdellatif Filali, came to see Pérez de Cuéllar. The Moroccan objections were fewer than I had expected. They related mainly to the length of the pre-cease-fire phase, the confinement of POLISARIO fighters inside the territory and the size of the peace-keeping operation. We set about revising the draft report yet again. Once more Skalli complained about the Task Force's failure to take sufficient account of the points in King Hassan's letter. I could contain myself no longer; he must bear in mind, I said, that the Task Force was a technical body charged with refining the implementation plan and that it was not privy to the diplomatic exchanges which had taken place the previous year. It was a relief to get this off my chest at last. The next day I learnt, also with some relief, that Pérez de Cuéllar had instructed Diallo to assume responsibility for producing the final draft of his report. I decided to withdraw myself from the whole miserable affair. This was easy to do as I was away from New York for most of the next four weeks, first on a visit to Nepal in search of a new force commander for UNIFIL and then to Mexico to participate in extended negotiations on El Salvador.

When I got back to New York the scene was as confused as ever. Kofi Annan, who was then the UN's chief financial officer, had been asked to reduce the budget of the operation but not told which activities were to be cancelled or curtailed. Diallo had made extensive changes to the draft report and had sent it for printing without adequate consultation with the Task Force. An internal storm was brewing; Manz was talking of resigning; Jonah (the new Under-Secretary-General for Africa) had declared that he was no longer prepared to work with Diallo. The Security Council began its consideration of the report on 24 April. The Secretary-General was guarded in what he said about the attitudes of the parties ('I have taken into account, as far as possible, the viewpoints expressed by the parties') but the members of the Council chose to interpret this as meaning that the parties had given their consent. To Manz's surprise, many compliments were paid to the Secretary-General; Manz did not yet understand that the member states do not bother much about squabbles in the Secretariat unless one of their nationals is involved. The Secretary-General's report and the setting up of the new operation were unanimously approved on 29 April. The operation was called 'the United Nations Mission for the Referendum in Western Sahara'; its acronym MINURSO was derived from the French version (*Mission des Nations Unies pour l'organisation d'un référendum au Sahara Occidental*).

I have related this tale at length because it illustrates well, admittedly in extreme form, some prevailing weaknesses of the Secretariat. One of them is the absence of clearly defined divisions of labour between the Under-Secretaries-General and the Secretary-General's personal staff and between the Under-Secretaries-General themselves. This weakness was aggravated in Pérez de Cuéllar's case by his policy of ensuring that no Under-Secretary-General acquired too much power and influence; ambiguity about areas of responsibility helped him to achieve this objective. A second weakness is the failure to enforce discipline. As Pérez de Cuéllar disliked confrontation, this job had to be done by his Chef de Cabinet, Viru Dayal. But Dayal was showing the effects of long and dedicated service in a very demanding post and he had been further distressed the previous year by the West's denial to him of the post of UN High Commissioner for Refugees for which Pérez de Cuéllar had wanted to nominate him. Jean-Claude Aimé, who was being groomed to succeed Dayal and was something of a disciplinarian, agreed that Diallo's behaviour was unacceptable but was as yet powerless to do anything about it. A third obstacle to effective planning is the P-5's perennial pressure on the Secretary-General to cut costs. In this particular case, a further weakness was my own inadequacy as chairman of the Task Force. Someone tougher than I, perhaps Ahtisaari, would have been better qualified to control the *prime donne*, persuade Pérez de Cuéllar to be more open and get him to confront the Diallo problem.

Three weeks after the Security Council vote, the General Assembly approved the budget, whereupon Pérez de Cuéllar proposed, in accordance with the plan, that the cease-fire should come into effect on 6 September. Any optimism created by these events was soon dissipated. It became evident that, as most of us knew, the parties had not actually given their consent to the plan and major differences remained unresolved. Skalli complained that POLISARIO was building camps between the Moroccan sand-wall and the international border and reiterated Morocco's refusal to accept any confinement of POLISARIO troops inside the territory. This became the central issue for the next few months.

In late June, Manz and I went to Geneva for two days of shuttle negotiations with the two sides. We were accompanied by Zia Rizvi, a suave and clever Pakistani who had been working with Sadruddin Aga Khan on the UN's humanitarian relief programme for Afghanistan. Pérez de Cuéllar had appointed him as Manz's deputy against the latter's wishes, thereby fuelling Manz's paranoia about Pérez de Cuéllar and his personal staff; Manz told me at one point that he had come to the conclusion that the Secretary-General and Diallo wanted the operation to fail so that they could blame it on him.

We had an agenda of thirty-eight items which had to be dealt with before D-Day and we were already four weeks behind schedule. But the confinement of POLISARIO fighters was the dominant issue. We made almost no progress on it. On the first day both sides restated their irre-concilable positions. The next morning Manz put a compromise pro-posal to the Moroccans: POLISARIO troops would be gathered at three temporary assembly areas within the territory, where they would be iden-tified and processed before being escorted by MINURSO to Tindouf in Algeria. This was rejected outright by Skalli. But he had no answer to my question of how we were then to deal with the POLISARIO fighters who would undoubtedly be inside the territory when the cease-fire came into effect; and his military minder seemed quite interested in our proposal. I concluded that it might eventually be accepted by the Moroccans. In the afternoon Béchir's reaction was as negative as Skalli's, though less offen-sively conveyed; and he did say, with calm but evident passion, that if the Special Representative determined that there should be no confinement of its troops inside the territory, POLISARIO would loyally comply, while protesting at the liquidation of its armed forces before the referen-dum result was known.

On 8 July, less than two months before D-Day, I convened a planning meeting in New York. The MINURSO participants included Manz, Rizvi, the Force Commander (Canada) and his deputy (Peru), and the Police Commissioner (Uruguay). A painful absence was that of the Chief Administrative Officer-designate who had at the last moment been recalled by his parent organization. All the news was bad, especially Morocco's presentation of a list of 76,000 'Sahrawis' who had allegedly been omitted from the Spanish census. Another list with an additional 45,000 names was to follow a few days later – just what we had feared six months before. My diary reveals my despair: 'Nothing in the last $5\frac{1}{2}$ years has depressed me more than my involvement in this doomed enter-prise.' The brutal facts were: we did not have the consent of the Moroccans to the plan we were trying to implement; we had been com-pelled by the P-5 to accept a timetable so tight that even with Moroccan consent it would have been unworkable; by mischance those who were to hold senior posts in MINURSO included some difficult and excitable personalities; and an imminent review of UN peacekeeping, resulting from an attempt by me to transfer to my office administrative functions performed elsewhere in the Secretariat,* had aggravated turf warfare within the New York team.

I escaped to the Middle East for two weeks. When I got back, there was a new Task Force chaired by Pérez de Cuéllar himself. But the problems had not changed – or been solved. We were so far behind schedule that the Secretary-General, I felt, should tell the Council that we could not adhere to the approved timetable; none of the others however supported my view. Two weeks later King Hassan wrote again to say that his acceptance of the Secretary-General's plan had been conditional on the points in his letter of July 1990 being taken into account. He could not understand why that had not happened. There could not have been a clearer statement that Morocco was not going to cooperate. But still we pressed on regardless. On 9 August Pérez de Cuéllar decided to confirm 6 September as D-Day. Only I pointed out the risks involved: the Moroccans could easily prevent us having enough people and equipment in the territory to monitor the cease-fire; there was still no agreement on the confinement of POLISARIO troops or the criteria for eligibility to vote; the Identification Commission was at least three months behind schedule; there were rumours of an impending Moroccan land operation in POLISARIO's 'liberated territory' between the sand-wall and the international border; the Moroccan Air Force was already bombing POLISARIO's new constructions there. Remember, Pérez de Cuéllar replied, that we are playing a game of poker with the Moroccans.

Four days later in Geneva Morocco raised the stakes. Pérez de Cuéllar was told by the Moroccan Foreign Minister that MINURSO would not be permitted to deploy until the Moroccans were satisfied with the criteria for eligibility to vote and a Status of Forces Agreement had been signed. The first ship delivering MINURSO cargo to the territory was turned away from Laayoune and Rizvi was not allowed to visit. But the Secretary-General continued to reject advice that he inform the Security Council that D-Day would have to be postponed. I left for three weeks' holiday, resisting all hints from colleagues and my own conscience that I ought not to be abandoning my post at this time of potential crisis.

I got back to New York on the morrow of D-Day. It turned out that D-Day had not happened. With Moroccan consent, Pérez de Cuéllar had implemented the cease-fire in isolation from the rest of the plan. One hundred military observers had been deployed to monitor it but neither side's troops were confined. A new date for D-Day would be fixed when agreement had been reached on the criteria for eligibility to vote and other outstanding issues. POLISARIO was unhappy about this development but had not obstructed it. Manz was still in New York, the

---

* See above, page 30.

Moroccans having said that they did not want him to move to Laayoune until the criteria had been agreed. Rizvi was in charge in Laayoune, where he and the Force Commander, Major-General Armand Roy, were fighting cat-and-dog. Rizvi was now perceived as being wholly in the Moroccans' pocket. This was a fate which befell almost all international officials who became involved in this miserable enterprise. I was delighted to learn from David Hannay, the British Ambassador to the UN, that I was not one of them; Hassan II had recently sent his strong man, General Bennani, to London to ask HM Government to tell me to be less 'rigid' about Western Sahara.

By mid-September I was receiving angry messages from General Roy to the effect that the Moroccans were blocking delivery of MINURSO's equipment and supplies, with the result that the operation was logistically dependent on, and therefore controlled by, the Moroccan authorities. Worse was to come. On 17 September Skalli told Pérez de Cuéllar that the King had decided to move 170,000 'Sahrawis' from the 'northern provinces', i.e. Morocco itself, to 'meet the Identification Commission and remain there to vote'. To my amazement, Pérez de Cuéllar struck from my draft cable to Manz a sentence describing this as 'a major departure from the plan'. Even more amazing was the understatement of this development in his next report to the Security Council: 'As is well known, a number of persons who are claimed to belong to Western Sahara have been moved into the Territory.' No wonder that Pérez de Cuéllar and Diallo were perceived by many as being partial to the Moroccans.

Manz went to Morocco and was quickly converted to Rizvi's point of view: the Moroccans were cooperating wonderfully, he said; we must stop suggesting otherwise. Pérez de Cuéllar was persuaded, with some difficulty, to tell him that he must adhere strictly to the plan approved by the Council. In early October King Hassan and his Foreign Minister came to New York but Pérez de Cuéllar saw them both alone and did not brief us about the meetings until Manz returned to New York. There were indications, he then said, that the King might have been spoken to sternly in Washington. He had agreed with Pérez de Cuéllar that the criteria should not be based on tribal affiliation alone but on a combination of *jus sanguinis* and *jus soli* – that is, the criteria would have to include some evidence of residence in the territory. Another promising sign was that Skalli, who had always been uncompromising, had been relieved of his post. And Béchir responded positively to the *jus sanguinis/jus soli* formula. But Hassan's 170,000 'Sahrawis' still discouraged optimism; adjudication of so many individual applications would take months, if not years.

Pérez de Cuéllar was by now playing a more active part, chairing the Task Force regularly and asserting his views more vehemently than was his wont. I came increasingly to feel that he had an undeclared agenda with the Moroccans, to which Diallo and Rizvi, and perhaps even Manz, were privy. Perhaps he was hoping that, before the end of his mandate, he could mediate a political deal based on enhanced autonomy for Western Sahara within the Kingdom of Morocco; approval of this would be the proposition on which the Sahrawis would vote in an eventual referendum. It would have been a sensible goal to pursue given the proven inadequacies of Diallo's settlement proposals and there are some indications in his *Pilgrimage for Peace* that this was what he had in mind. Meanwhile, I was caught in crossfire between Roy, who wanted immediate deployment of a logistic battalion from Poland to support his 200 military observers, and those sympathizing with the Moroccan position who, in alliance with the administrators in New York, wanted no further military deployment.

At the beginning of November Pérez de Cuéllar decided to try to force progress on identification by promulgating his regulations for the organization of the referendum and his instructions to the Identification Commission, which included the *jus sanguinis/jus soli* criteria. Manz was sent to the region to sell these documents to the parties, each of which was expected to approve of one document and disapprove of the other. This tactic might have worked if the two sides had been equally keen to implement the plan. But of course they were not. POLISARIO was desperate for the referendum to be held; Morocco was determined that it should not be held unless there was absolute certainty that Morocco would win. Algeria and POLISARIO, upset by the criteria, foolishly refused to receive Manz.

On Thanksgiving Day 1991 Aimé came to tea to discuss what could be done to save Pérez de Cuéllar's reputation in the five weeks that remained before his departure. It was not a topic I found very interesting but out of friendship for Aimé I went along with it. We agreed that Pérez de Cuéllar needed to replace Manz and launch a renegotiation of the settlement proposals on the basis of a timetable approved by the Security Council.

I was then whisked away from New York by Cyrus Vance to help him negotiate a cease-fire in Croatia and lost sight of Western Sahara. Before returning from Yugoslavia I visited Cairo to see Boutros Boutros-Ghali who had just been elected to succeed Pérez de Cuéllar as Secretary-General. When I raised Western Sahara, Boutros-Ghali sighed and said he had been dealing with the subject for twelve years. I told him about MINURSO's problems in the field, expressing concern that we were not observing our usual impartiality in dealing with cease-fire violations and non-cooperation by the parties. Pérez de Cuéllar, he said, had not told him about this. We agreed that Morocco would not accept a vote in favour of independence, but he showed no interest in the idea of a deal between Hassan II and the President of Algeria which could be put to the voters in the referendum. He did, however, like the idea of asking the Security Council to endorse renegotiation of Diallo's settlement proposals. This too had not been mentioned in his conversations with Pérez de Cuéllar.

On 19 December 1991 Pérez de Cuéllar signed off on the Western Sahara with a bland report to the Council. It announced Manz's resignation, ascribing it to 'the delay that has already occurred', and recommended that while consultations continued about the confinement of troops and the return of refugees 'and other Saharans living outside the Territory' (i.e. Hassan II's additional list of 170,000), MINURSO should function as a military observer group with the sole mandate of verifying the cease-fire. Any personnel not required for this function should be reassigned, though some additional logistic support for the UN military observers would be required. The instructions to the Identification Commission were annexed. POLISARIO expressed vehement opposition to the criteria and was supported by the Non-Aligned, with the result that the Security Council was unable to adopt a resolution approving Pérez de Cuéllar's recommendations. But for me it was a relief that these issues were at last out in the open and I hoped that there would be more *glasnost* in Boutros-Ghali's regime. But at a meeting with him on 3 January 1992 it became clear that he wanted to leave things as they were for the time being.

Three weeks later, on the way back from Mexico City after the signature of the El Salvador peace agreement, I took up the subject again with Boutros-Ghali. He decided that I should visit the territory the following week on the way to Yugoslavia. I had just had surgery on my right hand and therefore took no notes and wrote no diary. I can remember almost nothing of the visit and the few memories I do have are all unpleasant – further evidence, perhaps, of my distaste for the whole project. In Rabat, the Moroccan minister responsible for the Western Sahara, Driss Basri, tricked me into shaking hands, in front of the television cameras, with two senior POLISARIO officials who had just defected from the organization. In Laayoune, Moroccan control was all-pervasive and MINURSO did not enjoy freedom of movement. POLISARIO were angry with me over the handshakes in Rabat and with Rizvi (who was Acting Special Representative, following Manz's resignation) because of his perceived closeness to the Moroccans. I was told that I could not visit their headquarters in Tindouf unless I left Rizvi behind, a condition which I could not accept. Only the desert was beautiful.

At the end of February Kofi Annan joined my department, which had been reborn as the Department of Peacekeeping Operations (DPKO) in Boutros-Ghali's restructuring of the Secretariat. He was a long-desired reinforcement. Western Sahara was part of his portfolio and I was thrilled to be rid of a responsibility which had caused me pain and which I did not carry well.

As it happened, the last task I performed in the Secretariat, apart from writing a valedictory report for Annan when he became Secretary-General, was connected with Western Sahara. In February 1997, the peace process was more or less as it had been when I bowed out five years before. The new Secretary-General asked me to go to Houston, Texas, to persuade James Baker III to accept an appointment as Special Representative and try to negotiate a deal based on enhanced autonomy for Western Sahara within the Kingdom of Morocco. As I flew to Houston, I recalled some prescient observations which King Hassan had made to Pérez de Cuéllar in May 1988. Operational problems relating to the referendum, he said, should not be addressed until it had been determined who would have the right to vote; otherwise the UN could run into financial difficulties if the peacekeeping operation were begun but then had to wait for that fundamental question to be resolved; Morocco would not want the UN to stay in Western Sahara 'eternally' under cover of organizing the referendum. Hassan was right. More than a decade has passed since MINURSO was established. It is still in the field, and there is still no agreement on who may vote in the referendum. Morocco remains in possession of most of the territory and the refugees linger in the camps of Tindouf.

13

Central America

In February 1989, I was asked to attend a whole-day meeting between Pérez de Cuéllar and the Foreign Ministers of five Central American countries: Costa Rica, El Salvador, Guatemala, Honduras and Nicaragua. The purpose was to discuss with the five Ministers whether UN peace-keepers could help them re-establish peace in their region.

Three of the five countries were in a state of civil war. The wars had some indigenous causes but their intensity was due to the Cold War. In Nicaragua a Marxist government faced an insurrection by the Contras, a right-wing guerrilla movement supported by the United States. In El Salvador and Guatemala, right-wing governments confronted leftist guerrilla movements. Moscow and Havana supported the government in Nicaragua and the guerrillas in El Salvador and Guatemala; Washington supported the guerrillas in Nicaragua and the governments in the other two countries. The two superpowers were engaged in a struggle for the political allegiance of Central America and neither cared unduly about the company it kept. During the Reagan Administration, 'my enemy's enemy is my friend' was the doctrine that dominated Washington's policy in Central America. But it is not a sound doctrine, for it can lead to alliances which, when all is later revealed, bring shame to the democracy that has been unwise enough to enter into them.

In August 1987 a comprehensive peace plan for the region was adopted by the Presidents of the five countries at a summit in Esquipulas, Guatemala. It was known as 'Esquipulas II'. One of its provisions committed the five states to discontinue any aid they were providing to guerrilla movements and to prevent their territory being used to attack other states. The Secretaries-General of the United Nations and the Organization of American States (OAS) were asked to participate in an international commission which would verify implementation of the agreement.

By 1989 Pérez de Cuéllar and Álvaro de Soto had spotted that Central America was another region where the thaw between the superpowers created new possibilities for peacemaking. So the Secretary-General invited the five Foreign Ministers to the meeting in New York, in advance of a Central American summit in El Salvador. The meeting turned into an introductory seminar on peacekeeping in which Pérez de Cuéllar, Carl Fleischhauer (the Legal Counsel), de Soto and I reassured our students that any United Nations peacekeeping operation would require their consent and would not therefore infringe their sovereignty. At the end of the day they asked the Secretary-General to prepare a proposal for a UN verification mechanism in their countries.

A month later, the five countries returned to New York to discuss a plan we had prepared for a military observer group that would verify implementation of the security provisions in Esquipulas II and would be known as ONUCA (*Observadores de las Naciones Unidas en Centroamerica*). The paper was well received but differences emerged between the five. Honduras, in particular, wanted the operation to have 'coercive' or 'deterrent' powers so that it could control the Contras based in Honduras and deter cross-border raids against them by the Nicaraguan Army. This would, however, require an armed force, which none of the others wanted. On 3 April 1989, when I was in Amman en route from Baghdad to Luanda, de Soto telephoned to say that the five Foreign Ministers had formally asked the Secretary-General to recommend to the Security Council that ONUCA be established as an unarmed military observer group.

Hopes that the UN could help resolve the conflicts in Central America received a further boost when Pérez de Cuéllar was asked by the government of Nicaragua to send a civilian mission to monitor elections there in February 1990. This mission, known as ONUVEN, was headed by the American statesman and lawyer Elliott Richardson and was directed on the ground by Iqbal Riza, the former Pakistani diplomat who had previously worked with Cordovez on the Iran–Iraq war and was to fill many senior positions in the United Nations during the coming decade. ONUVEN was the first UN electoral mission in a sovereign state, all previous such missions having been part of a decolonization process. Like UNTAG's electoral division in Namibia, it was to be outstandingly successful and set standards for the many electoral missions that the United Nations was to deploy in the 1990s. Because it was a purely civilian operation and not, therefore, classified as peacekeeping, I played no part in its planning and deployment.

In July 1989, the Security Council endorsed the Secretary-General's use of his 'good offices' to help the parties implement Esquipulas II. The next month, at a summit in Honduras, the five Presidents unveiled a joint plan for the demobilization of the Contras and all other irregular forces in the region. They also asked the Secretaries-General of the UN and the OAS to establish jointly an 'International Support and Verification

Commission' (CIAV) to help them implement all aspects of Esquipulas II. Three weeks later, on 15 September 1989, the government of El Salvador and the FMLN, as the rebel movement in that country was called, agreed 'to initiate a dialogue aimed at ending the armed conflict in El Salvador by political means' and to invite the UN to 'witness' the dialogue.

These were positive developments. But the decision that CIAV should be established jointly by the two Secretaries-General caused us concern. It raised an issue which was already causing problems in Namibia, would shortly do so in Nicaragua and was to complicate many subsequent peacekeeping operations. What should be the relationship between the United Nations and a regional organization when both of them have been asked to support the same peace process? The question can be particularly difficult if, as happened in Central America, the division of labour is not clearly defined by those who have done the asking.

During the 1990s there has been much debate about the role and capacity of regional organizations in peacemaking and peacekeeping. Many argue that they are better suited for this task than the UN because they understand their own regions better and will be more familiar with the dispute, its causes and its protagonists. These arguments have led some Western powers, especially the United States, to propose the 'regionalization' of peace operations: each region, it is argued, should be responsible for its own peacemaking and peacekeeping, with some financial and technical support from the West but few, if any, military or police contingents from outside the region. This argument has attracted some support from leaders in the Third World who feel threatened by the West's advocacy of preventive action and humanitarian intervention and therefore like the idea that the West will provide them with some help but will not involve itself directly in the resolution of their problems.

In my view, however, the arguments for regionalization are specious and the arguments against it strong. The real aims of the Western countries that argue for it are to ease the financial burdens placed on them by the post-Cold War proliferation of peace operations and to avoid risking their soldiers' lives in other peoples' wars. These aims are understandable, especially the financial one: the OECD countries currently pay over 93 per cent of the peacekeeping costs incurred by the United Nations, to which must be added the costs they themselves incur when they provide contingents for UN operations.

There are two main arguments against regionalization. First, no regional organization except NATO has the administrative, logistical and command structures needed to deploy and manage multinational military operations. The peace operations deployed by other regional organizations have been ineffective and/or have been used to advance the interests of the regional superpower. Examples of the latter have been the Nigerian-led force known as ECOMOG, which was established by the Economic Community of West African States to perform peacekeeping functions in Liberia and Sierra Leone in the 1990s, and the Russian-led force of the Commonwealth of Independent States in the Abkhaz region of Georgia. Nor does any regional organization have the depth and breadth of experience that the UN has in peacemaking and peacekeeping.

The second argument against regionalization is an ethical one. The United Nations was intended to be a universal organization. Its services are available to all its members on a basis of equality and at the expense of the membership as a whole in accordance with each state's ability to pay. It would be contrary to this vision to insist that member states in a particular region should receive only the level of peacekeeping that their regional organization can provide.

Meanwhile, we worked flat out to field ONUCA before the mood in Central America changed. The commander of UNAVEM, Péricles Ferreira Gomes, led a fact-finding mission to the five countries. It encountered doubts about whether the proposed mandate was realistic (doubts which existed in Washington too) and it received less than perfect cooperation from the military, especially in Guatemala and Honduras. But in New York we relied on the clear commitment of the five Presidents, while acknowledging privately that ONUCA's ability to detect, let alone deter, violations of the security commitments in Esquipulas II was almost nil. Our real objective was to establish a UN military presence in these five countries for two purposes: to raise the political price that would be paid by any of them that reneged on Esquipulas II; and to win for the UN a role in mediating settlements of the conflicts in Nicaragua, El Salvador and Guatemala.

In early November 1989, the Security Council voted to establish ONUCA in the form recommended by the Secretary-General. About 260 unarmed military observers would man nine 'verification centres' (VCs) close to the international borders. They would patrol by helicopter, road vehicle, patrol boat or light river-craft to verify that the five governments were respecting their commitments. A Spanish officer, Major-General Agustín Quesada Gómez, was appointed Chief Military Observer.

ONUCA was born in discouraging circumstances. The Contras had just agreed to peace talks with the Nicaraguan Government but two weeks later these broke down. In El Salvador the left-wing FMLN launched a major offensive against the capital, seizing a hotel in which the Secretary-General of the OAS and US military advisers had taken refuge; in retaliation, six Jesuit priests were killed in cold blood by the army; the

Salvadorian Government suspended relations with Nicaragua because of the latter's support for the FMLN; a few weeks later US troops invaded Panama to depose the President in an old-fashioned assertion of US hegemony in Central America.

The fragile harmony that had been created disappeared and with it went superpower cooperation. The Americans and the Russians squabbled about what, if anything, the Security Council should say about the crisis in El Salvador. Quesada reported from the field that the Salvadorian Government wanted the earliest possible deployment of ONUCA, whereas Nicaragua was now saying that the mission should not deploy until after the Contras had been demobilized. The troop contributors became reluctant to deploy their officers in such a violent theatre. It looked as though Pérez de Cuéllar had moved too soon.

But we pressed on. By early December Quesada had established his headquarters in Tegucigalpa, the capital of Honduras, and was setting up liaison offices in three of the other four capitals, the exception being San Salvador where fighting continued. By mid-January more than half the verification centres were operational. But Washington was pressing us hard to concentrate our efforts on detecting and stopping, or at least reporting, the support which the Sandinistas in Nicaragua were giving the FMLN. It was not easy to persuade people in Washington or in Central America that ONUCA was an impartial operation and as such was obliged to devote equal attention to the support which it was known the Americans were providing to the Contras through Honduras.

In February 1990, I visited ONUCA, just as the anti-Communist Nicaraguan opposition leader, Violeta Chamorro, unexpectedly defeated the incumbent President Daniel Ortega, who had held power since the Sandinistas' victory in 1979. If the transfer of power took place peacefully, ONUCA's tasks would change. The civil war in Nicaragua would end and so would aid from that country to the Salvadorian rebels; the two main causes of cross-border military activity would thus disappear. Meanwhile, my task was to get ONUCA to deploy more quickly and make itself more visible, especially in the border areas where violations of Esquipulas II might be taking place. The delays turned out to be due to two familiar causes: the UN's chronic slowness in providing the logistical and other support needed by the military observers; and the anxieties of Quesada and his senior staff about the military observers' security.

These logistical delays, as in other operations at this time,* were primarily due to the complex financial and procurement regulations that we had to observe. The Secretariat's ability to regulate them was limited. As

---

* See Chapter 11.

regards concerns about security, the extent to which they delay deployment varies with the character of the commanding officer. Some feel that those under their command have been projected into someone else's conflict and that their lives should not be put at risk. Such concerns are reinforced if, as often happens, the commander receives direct (and therefore improper) representations from the troop-contributing governments. Other commanders take a more robust view. While they recognize the special nature of peacekeeping and, like all good commanders, try to avoid unnecessary risks, they accept that in peacekeeping, as in other military undertakings, it is sometimes necessary to put soldiers' lives at risk if the military objective is to be achieved. Callous though it may sound in such a context, I always favoured the latter approach and went out of my way to correct any misconception that peacekeeping is a risk-free activity.

I was in Central America for ten days and visited each of the five countries at least once. There was much scenery to admire and many new birds to identify. But the developments in Nicaragua made this more than an introductory visit to a new peacekeeping operation. President-elect Chamorro wanted the Contras demobilized quickly, if possible before the transfer of power on 25 April. The Americans wanted to proceed carefully and methodically. They were concerned about the security of the ex-Contras if, as seemed likely, the Sandinistas retained command of the armed forces and the police for the time being. They were also desperate to recover about 150 surface-to-air Redeye missiles which they had supplied to the Contras, lest these fall into the hands of the FMLN or other irregular forces in the region. Their concern was heightened by the fear that the Contras might also have captured some Soviet missiles from the Sandinista army; and the latter might have captured some of the Contras' Redeyes.

Early on the third morning of the visit, I was woken in Tegucigalpa by a call from New York: Pérez de Cuéllar required me to proceed immediately to Nicaragua to discuss with the government and the President-elect what ONUCA could do to help resolve the Contra problem. Managua, much of it still in ruins from the earthquake of 1972, was packed with representatives of international organizations and with individuals who had come to Nicaragua to observe the election: the Secretary-General of the OAS; the ONUVEN team who were now playing a critical role in easing the transition from the old government to the new; the UN and OAS directors of CIAV (the joint UN–OAS organization whose creation had caused us some concern in New York); Jimmy Carter; and scores of disconsolate Sandinista supporters from North America and Western Europe, mockingly dubbed 'sandalistas'.

Elliott Richardson, the head of ONUVEN, urged me to work out a plan for the Contras, including a package of 'assurances and guarantees' to persuade them to accept demobilization. That evening I put together the outlines of such a plan. A cease-fire would be declared. The Contras in Honduras (and in Costa Rica, if there were any there) would be demobilized *in situ* and immediately thereafter returned to Nicaragua, where CIAV would arrange their resettlement. For those in Nicaragua, ONUCA would establish, and provide security at, assembly points where they would hand over their weapons, ammunition, other military equipment and uniforms, before being resettled by CIAV. It would be for the governments of the countries concerned to decide how the weapons should be disposed of. The aim would be to complete demobilization by 25 April. ONUCA would have to be temporarily reinforced with armed troops to take delivery of the Contras' weapons and guard them until they were destroyed or otherwise disposed of. The next morning my various UN colleagues accepted this plan. So did the Chief of Staff of the Sandinista army and the leader of Violeta Chamorro's transition team. The Honduran President, however, had reservations; he wanted to get the Contras and their weapons out of his country as soon as possible. The Costa Ricans, on the other hand, welcomed the plan and had no objection to our establishing temporary assembly points on Costa Rican territory if Contras preferred to be demobilized there.

Having reported the plan to Pérez de Cuéllar, I resumed my inspection of ONUCA. In San Salvador the fighting turned out to have been less severe than UN reports at the time had suggested. But my meeting with President Alfredo Cristiani and his Foreign Minister became difficult when they pressed me to share with them any operational information obtained by ONUCA which might be useful to the Salvadorian Armed Forces in their continuing war with the FMLN. I had to refuse: ONUCA's mandate was to verify that the five governments were honouring their commitments to each other under Esquipulas II; it would be *ultra vires* for the UN to take action that would support the Salvadorian Government's campaign against its internal enemies. In saying this, I had it in mind that the Secretary-General hoped soon to play a role in mediating a peace settlement in El Salvador and would not want to be seen to take sides.

But the point was one of wider significance and often came up in other civil war contexts. Internationally recognized governments found it incomprehensible that representatives of the United Nations, an intergovernmental organization, should decline to take their side against opponents who were trying to overthrow them by force. To this we usually had to reply that the Secretary-General's mandate from the Security Council or the General Assembly was to 'use his good offices' to promote a peaceful settlement of the conflict; he could not fulfil that mandate if he and his staff did not remain scrupulously impartial and neutral between the two sides. Sometimes one was asked what the difference was between 'impartial' and 'neutral'. The answer I usually gave was that 'impartiality' was about judgement and 'neutrality' about action. Impartiality means applying common standards in judging the behaviour of two hostile parties and not condoning acts by one that are condemned if committed by the other. Neutrality means not taking action that would serve one side's interests and damage the other's.

As was so often the case, this first visit left me worried about how ONUCA was going to carry out its role. Quesada was a conscientious and hard-working commander, but he had no previous peacekeeping experience, talked too much to the media and had not yet managed to mould his staff into an effective team. Instead of working through the operations branch at his HQ, he was directing his command through a network of middle-ranking officers, all of them Spanish, in the five capitals. This was creating some tension between the Spaniards and Latin Americans, all of whom were new to peacekeeping, and the others (Canadians, French, Indians, Irish, Swedes) who had known other UN operations, had expected to find a similar multinational ethos in ONUCA and resented the fact that the operation seemed to be run as a Spanish enterprise.

As soon as I was back in New York, Pérez de Cuéllar recommended the demobilization plan to the Security Council and Venezuela offered to provide the required infantry battalion. The Americans were, as usual, hesitant. President Bush and Secretary Baker seemed to favour early demobilization but others in Washington remained committed to the Contras as noble freedom fighters and wanted ONUCA to establish a massive presence in Nicaragua before demobilization began and the heroes returned home. But the demobilization plan was eventually approved.

The first Venezuelan troops arrived in Honduras on 10 April 1990 and six days later a small group of Contras were demobilized there. Contrary to expectations (but in accordance with Honduran wishes), almost all the other Contras in Honduras then returned with their weapons to Nicaragua. This would make it more difficult to ensure their security during and after demobilization; it also raised doubts about whether their commanders really intended to demobilize. During the first half of April intensive negotiations took place in Managua about the way forward. In New York we received doom-laden reports from Rolf Knutsson, who was now Quesada's senior political adviser: Quesada and Riza were at odds; so were the UN and the OAS; CIAV was incapable of doing the tasks entrusted to it; some American officials in Managua were supporting the Contra *comandantes'* desire to retain a permanent armed presence in Nicaragua as a means of controlling the new government.

On the night of 18/19 April, however, agreement was reached: a cease-fire would come into immediate effect; the Contras would assemble in a number of 'security zones' from which the army (which was still called the *Ejército Popular Sandinista – EPS*) would withdraw; ONUCA would monitor and verify these arrangements; ONUCA and CIAV would implement demobilization as previously agreed; the whole process would be completed by 10 June. This required the Security Council to approve another enlargement of ONUCA's mandate and to do so very quickly, as the cease-fire was to begin immediately.

Notwithstanding the complaints of Cuba (in the person of Ricardo Alarcón who had been such a thorn in our flesh during the Namibia operation and was now Cuba's ambassador to the United Nations) about 'legitimization' of an armed Contra presence in Nicaragua, the Security Council immediately took the needed decision. But the Contras then declined to begin demobilization, causing Alarcón to raise difficulties about the renewal of ONUCA's mandate. There followed more negotiations in Nicaragua; more debate in the Security Council; another last-minute 'agreement'; more procrastination by the Contras; another outburst of Cuban indignation. This was to be the pattern for the next two months. In mid-May Pérez de Cuéllar decided to tell the Security Council that the Contras were not honouring the agreements they had signed; this being so, they must not be allowed to assume that the UN would go on feeding and protecting them indefinitely. To underline his concern, he summoned Quesada to New York and recalled me from a visit to UNIIMOG in Iraq.

Pérez de Cuéllar's report was ill-received by the Americans because, they said, it put all the blame on the Contras and ignored violations of the cease-fire and the security zones by the Sandinista army. Quesada assured the Secretary-General that there had been no such violations and Pérez de Cuéllar so informed the Council. To my rage, I then learnt that more than a fortnight earlier Quesada's Spanish colonel in Managua had received from the Contra commanders a long list of alleged violations of the cease-fire by the army but had neither investigated them nor even told Quesada about them. As a result Pérez de Cuéllar had misled the Council. But I allowed Quesada to leave the Spanish colonel in place, not wanting to create yet another problem at a difficult time.

I returned to Nicaragua in mid-June with Pérez de Cuéllar's proposals for bringing the demobilization to closure. I saw the Contras' most powerful leader, Israel Galeano ('Comandante Franklyn'), in a village in a security zone to the east of Lake Nicaragua. Just outside the village, ONUCA's Venezuelans had pitched their camp. In a stifling warehouse nearby, the Venezuelan soldiers were destroying the Contras' weapons and CIAV was processing the demobilized, but so slowly, I was told, that the Contras had to wait for up to two weeks for the documents which would entitle them to civilian clothing and food. The meeting with Franklyn went well; he agreed to all our proposals for winding up the demobilization, except for the final date 'because I want to be the last to demobilize, in a ceremony with Doña Violeta'. The new President's advisers also accepted our proposals and so did the Sandinista General Umberto Ortega, who was still Minister of Defence. (At the same time he admitted that the Sandinistas had been the source of a Redeye missile in an arms shipment to the FMLN intercepted in El Salvador a few months before. The purpose, he said, was 'to send a message to the North Americans about what can happen if they bring these sophisticated weapons into the region'.)

But the timing slipped again and closure did not come until 9 July. Over 23,000 Contras had been demobilized and more than 15,000 small arms handed over for destruction, with a reasonably convincing number of heavier weapons. The Contras also handed in just enough missiles to satisfy the Americans. But the latter were less happy about the harvest of small arms: they alone had supplied over 20,000 of these to the Contras and many of the weapons handed in had been unserviceable; it was clear that some had been withheld. So the UN's success was not unqualified. But it felt good at the time.

The end of the civil war in Nicaragua removed much of ONUCA's *raison d'être*. Of the three civil conflicts in Central America, the one that attracted the most external support had been brought to an end. There was no longer a need to monitor Nicaragua's borders with either Costa Rica or Honduras. One down, two to go. Attention turned to El Salvador. If peace could be brought to that country, where 80,000 citizens (one person in every sixty) were believed to have been killed in a decade of armed conflict, only Guatemala would remain.

Good progress had been made on El Salvador. In his inaugural speech in June 1989, President Cristiani had proposed a dialogue between the government and the FMLN. Two meetings took place in neighbouring countries under the auspices of the Church before the process was halted by the FMLN offensive in November 1989. But within a few weeks, thanks to skilful diplomacy by Álvaro de Soto, the five Central American Presidents asked Pérez de Cuéllar to 'ensure resumption of the dialogue' and the FMLN asked him to 'initiate a serious negotiation with the mediation or good offices of the Secretary-General'. In January 1990 Cristiani came to New York to discuss what form Pérez de Cuéllar's role would take. Cristiani impressed me by his mastery of the facts, his fluency and his clarity of thought. But he would not agree that Pérez de Cuéllar should play the role of 'mediator' and he was uncompromising in his insistence on 'dialogue' rather than 'negotiations' with the FMLN. 'We', he said, 'are the products of a democratic process; they are armed rebels, without legitimacy.'

When the UN attempts to mediate an end to a civil war, the relative status that it accords to the protagonists is almost always a problem. The insurgents insist on political equality; in the negotiations the mediator must, they say, treat them and the government as politically equal parties and must not be influenced by the fact that one party enjoys international recognition and the other does not. The government usually rejects this at first and insists that the mediator take into account its legitimacy as the elected and internationally recognized government. Much effort is required to convince the government that if it really wants a settlement it will have to accept that, for the purpose of the negotiations, the parties will be treated as political equals.

Immediately after Cristiani's visit, de Soto set out to persuade the parties to agree on the ground rules for a dialogue/negotiation. This took two months of non-stop shuttling and only at the end of this period did the FMLN agree to a face-to-face meeting with the other side. The resulting agreement was signed by the two sides, in Pérez de Cuéllar's presence, in Geneva on 4 April 1990. Although largely procedural, it committed the government and the FMLN to end the armed conflict as quickly as possible, to democratize the country, to respect human rights and to reunify Salvadorian society.

De Soto pressed on. The next month, in Caracas, he got the two sides to agree on an agenda and timetable. The negotiation of this agreement brought to the surface, but did not fully expose, an issue which was to plague the rest of the negotiation. The government's primary objective was an end to the war and demobilization of the FMLN, an objective which was ardently shared by Washington. But agreement to end the conflict was the only card in the FMLN's hand; they would not play it until the government had committed itself to a programme of political, economic and social reform that would correct the injustices which had caused the armed insurgency.

Two months later in San José, Costa Rica, the parties signed an agreement in which they undertook to respect human rights, notwithstanding the continuing war between them, and asked for a UN mission to verify the observance of human rights throughout the country. It would be called ONUSAL and was to be deployed as soon as the conflict came to an end. But when it proved impossible to adhere to the timetable for negotiations agreed in Caracas, the parties asked the Secretary-General to field the mission as soon as possible, without waiting for a cease-fire.

I had not played any part in the negotiation of the Geneva, Caracas and San José agreements. They were peacemaking and not therefore within the purview of my department. But de Soto decided in July 1990 that the time had come for me to give the FMLN an introductory briefing on peacekeeping and I went to Mexico City for the purpose. The FMLN team was led by Comandante Schafik Handal, President of the Communist Party of El Salvador, one of the five components of the FMLN.* A large man in his sixties, he was a fully-fledged Communist but, like Fidel Castro, had a pragmatic streak which sometimes enabled him to put the dogma to one side. He was nevertheless more sceptical than the others about the peace process and insisted on keeping the war option open right up to the signature of the peace agreement in January 1992 and even beyond. He was a clear thinker and a fine speaker and the younger *comandantes* accepted him as their *de facto* leader and coordinator.

Handal and his colleagues were suspicious of UN peacekeeping (they had also been suspicious of me personally, believing that I was a general from the British Army, and were relieved to discover that I was not). They did not like ONUCA. Its task of verifying that the Central American governments were not permitting cross-border activities by 'irregular forces and insurrectionist movements' amounted to indirect obstruction of the latter's operations and was not impartial. I acknowledged that this was so, but assured them that verification of a negotiated settlement between them and the government would be quite different. The UN would have to be strictly impartial and the task would be done by a new operation which would verify implementation of all aspects of the agreement, military or civilian. I described the recently concluded operation in Namibia, presenting it as the model for this new type of multifunctional peacekeeping operation. They were reassured by this. But discussion of the arrangements for a cease-fire revealed little common ground; unless it came into effect when everything else had been agreed, they said, it would not be irreversible and they would not therefore be able to accept any arrangements which would impair their military capacity.

A few weeks later I went to San Salvador for a matching meeting with the High Command of the Salvadorian Armed Forces (FAES). They were headed by the Minister of Defence, General Emilio Ponce, who had the reputation of being a hardliner but was suave and flexible on this occasion. They clearly disliked the idea of being monitored by the UN and talked a lot about the need to respect *constitucionalidad* and *institucional-*

---

* His parents were Palestinians from Bethlehem. The other four components of the FMLN were, in order of size: the People's Liberation Forces (FPL), led by Comandante Salvador Sánchez Cerén (alias Leonel Gonzales); the People's Revolutionary Army (ERP), led by Comandante Joaquín Villalobos; the National Resistance (RN), led by Comandante Eduardo Sancho (alias Ferman Cienfuegos); and the Revolutionary Party of Central American Workers (PRTC), led by Comandante Francisco Jovel.

idad, two words which were to feature often in the long negotiation that was about to begin. The former related to the sacred duties assigned to the army by the constitution and the need for it to be in a position to discharge those duties at all times; were we really saying that the FAES would have to be confined to base at the time of the cease-fire? *Institucionalidad* related to the honour of the army and its place in the country's institutional structure; if it were discredited in any way, its morale and its ability to defend the republic would be at risk. These concerns were expected. What was more worrying was the difficulty the generals foresaw in establishing security zones for the FMLN fighters; we could not replicate what was done for the Contras in Nicaragua, they said, because El Salvador was so small and so densely populated and because so many of the FMLN combatants were deployed clandestinely in urban areas.

In mid-December 1990 I was back in Mexico City for a further round with the FMLN team, led this time by Francisco Jovel, *comandante* of the smallest of the FMLN factions. One month before, the FMLN had launched another offensive. This time the targets were more specifically military than in November 1989 and its successes were less dramatic than its earlier seizure of large parts of the capital. But they were enough to make the FMLN team more assertive in discussion of the cease-fire arrangements. They now proposed *territorialidad*: the FMLN would retain exclusive control of all territory they 'controlled' when the cease-fire agreement was signed. I carefully dissected the concept of 'control', explaining why it had little validity in a guerrilla war and why their proposal would anyway be rejected by the government.

In January 1991 I went back to San Salvador to put to the FAES High Command the idea that during the cease-fire both sides should withdraw their military personnel from urban areas so that they could be more easily monitored in 'concentration areas' in the countryside. This aroused the demons *constitucionalidad* and *institucionalidad* in all their fury. More agreeable was the subsequent detour to Honduras to meet the new acting commander of ONUCA, Brigadier-General Lewis Mackenzie of Canada. He was later to do the UN great harm after his service with UNPRO-FOR in Bosnia when he told the press that he had never been able to reach anyone at UN headquarters after 5 p.m. New York time. This was grossly unfair to my staff who at that time, like me, rarely left the office before 10 p.m., but it has passed into the canon of abuse levelled at the UN in the United States and will probably never be eradicated; Bill Clinton himself repeated it in one of his speeches to the General Assembly. In this first encounter, though, I rather liked Mackenzie. We did an inspection by helicopter and Zodiac dinghy of the Argentine patrol-boat detachment in the Gulf of Fonseca, the UN's first naval operation since West Irian thirty years before; we flew by helicopter to

Guarita, an isolated village on the Honduran-Salvadorian border where two hundred Salvadorian soldiers had taken refuge with ONUCA during the recent FMLN offensive; and we made a brief visit to the Maya ruins at Copán on the way back to Tegucigalpa.

In February 1991 I saw the FMLN again in Mexico City. This time they agreed that neither side exercised military control in the *zonas conflictivas.* Their main concern now was the preservation of their political and administrative 'control' in the areas in the northern part of the country where they were militarily predominant. Iqbal Riza had been appointed head of ONUSAL, the new operation set up to monitor human rights in El Salvador, and had just visited some of these areas. He reported that the FMLN's claim to 'control' them was not exaggerated. There was no government presence; the only money they received came from non-governmental organizations and foreign governments; the population subsisted mostly on locally grown produce; the only social organizations were committees of FMLN sympathizers and cooperatives formed by them. Law and order was ensured by the 'community', which in practice meant the FMLN.

The next round with the government military was in New York later the same month. They insisted that all FMLN combatants should be concentrated in three security zones, with the FAES remaining in their 'permanent installations' and permitted to patrol for 20 kilometres in any direction. I said this was not negotiable. Three weeks later I was summoned to San Salvador to see Cristiani. According to de Soto, this was standard procedure; Cristiani claimed to have delegated full authority to his negotiating team, but when the going became difficult he would take charge himself. Unlike his generals, he now wanted a replication of the arrangements for the Contras in Nicaragua; the FMLN combatants would concentrate at designated locations where their security would be assured and they would be quickly demobilized. I said that this would never be accepted by the FMLN; the cases were totally different; when the Contras were demobilized their political battle had been won through Violeta Chamorro's electoral defeat of the Sandinistas; Schafik Handal had not been elected President of El Salvador.

This series of meetings confirmed a fundamental flaw in the timetable agreed in Caracas in May 1990. It envisaged a cease-fire which would begin after broad political agreements had been reached on the main issues and would remain in effect until all the details had been worked out, especially those relating to the reintegration of FMLN combatants into civilian life. Only then would the 'cessation of the armed conflict' be declared. This concept had turned out to be unworkable. The FMLN insisted, not unreasonably, that if it proved impossible to agree on the detail, fighting might resume; they must therefore continue to recruit, train and exercise their combatants and receive *matériel* until the conflict was formally ended. The government refused to contemplate this. As a result, the talks I had been having monthly with the two sides lacked reality. Their only *raison d'être* was to deflect Washington's pressure on the UN to give priority to the negotiation of a cease-fire. All of us in the UN team knew by now that there was not going to be a cease-fire until the FMLN had achieved their objectives on the major political issues. My task was to maintain the pretence of a real cease-fire negotiation while de Soto strove to bring the parties to agreement on the issues which had caused the conflict – the role and size of the armed forces, the quality of policing and justice, the electoral system, access to land.

The changes sought by the FMLN in these fields would necessitate amendment of the constitution. This created an urgency which de Soto skilfully exploited. The constitution of El Salvador required that amendments to it must be ratified by two consecutive Legislative Assemblies. The mandate of the existing Assembly would expire at midnight on 30 April 1991. If it had not, by then, ratified either an amendment to the above procedure or the actual constitutional changes required by the emerging agreement, the changes would not become law until ratified by the next Assembly but one, which would not come into being until May 1994. This was evidently unacceptable; the FMLN would not be prepared to wait so long for confirmation that they had won the reforms for which they had been fighting; the war would continue.

To avoid this delay, de Soto persuaded the two sides to participate in three weeks of negotiations in Mexico City, beginning on 4 April; if the negotiations produced results, the Assembly could ratify them before its term ended on 30 April. I missed the first few days, as I was busy in New York with the new peacekeeping operation that was to be deployed astride the Iraq–Kuwait border following the liberation of Kuwait.

De Soto had hoped to get the two sides to accept the option of reforming the procedures for amending the constitution; three weeks would not be long enough to reach agreement on substantive constitutional reforms. While he laboured on this question at his 'political table', my cease-fire table kept itself occupied by exploring the political aspects of the cease-fire. The government clung to the position that the cease-fire must be irreversible; the war would have ended and the FMLN should demobilize as quickly as possible. The FMLN initially maintained their position that *irreversibilidad* could come only when all the substantive issues had been resolved. But then, with a subtlety which the other side found hard to match, they suggested a trade-off: if the government would let them undertake political activities during the cease-fire, they would reduce the military activities needed to keep their combatants battle-ready in case the cease-fire broke down. This concept, labelled *gradualidad*, led to minute discussion of what exactly was meant by 'political activity'.

But we all knew that it was at the other table that the big game was being played. I sat in on some of de Soto's meetings and was struck by how much the quality of the two delegations differed. The FMLN fielded three powerful intellects – those of Handal, Joaquín Villalobos, the leader of the People's Revolutionary Army, and Salvador Samayoa of the People's Liberation Forces. The government team was led by the Minister of the Presidency, a lawyer called Oscar Santamaria, and the Minister of the Interior, Juan Martinez Varela. There was no dialogue between the two sides; they just stated and restated their known positions. Nevertheless the long cohabitation in the hotel where the talks were taking place did seem to be breaking down the hostility between the two sides. I was thrilled one evening when two figures talking discreetly behind some potted palms turned out to be Villalobos and Colonel Mauricio Vargas, the military member of the government team. And when news came that Handal's mother was dying in Managua, the government team agreed that he could travel with them in the ONUCA plane which was returning them to San Salvador and would then take him on to Managua.

In San Salvador, opposition to changes in the procedure for amending the constitution remained very strong. De Soto decided that he and I should fly there in a final effort to persuade Cristiani to accept the procedural option. We did not succeed. He showed some flexibility on the cease-fire issues but would not defy his right-wingers on constitutional amendment, even if this led to the collapse of the talks. When we informed the FMLN of this, they suspended their participation in the work of my cease-fire table. With the prospects looking bleak, de Soto proposed that an attempt should at least be made to agree on a mini-package of constitutional reforms which could be ratified by the outgoing Assembly. On 22 April I returned to New York convinced that the Mexico City round would fail.

To my astonishment de Soto telephoned five days later to say that, at the very last moment, he had got the two sides to accept a package of substantive reforms to the constitution. They covered, *inter alia*, redefinition of the role of the military, the creation of a new civilian police force independent of the armed forces, extensive reforms of the judicial system including the appointment of an ombudsman for human rights, and reform of the electoral system. They also provided for the establishment of a 'Commission on the Truth', appointed by the UN Secretary-General, to 'investigat[e] serious acts of violence that have occurred since 1980 and whose impact on society urgently requires that the public should know the truth'. Given Latin Americans' sensitivity about outside intervention in their domestic affairs, not to mention the United States'

Monroe Doctrine,* the Mexico Agreements were a remarkable achievement. The amendments were, with minor changes, approved by the Legislative Assembly a few hours before its mandate expired on 30 April and the new Assembly promptly ratified most of them, the main exception being those related to the armed forces.

The next round of negotiations took place in late May at Caraballeda, a seaside resort in Venezuela. The negotiating format changed somewhat: de Soto's table would discuss reform of the armed forces and political activity by the FMLN during the cease-fire, and mine would discuss the military and administrative aspects of the cease-fire. My table was weakened by the absence of Villalobos, who was replaced by Salvador Sánchez Cerén, *alias* Leonel Gonzales, leader of the People's Liberation Forces. He was a schoolteacher and closer in age to Handal than the other *comandantes*. He appeared docile but took a hard line and seemed not to have been briefed on the progress we had made in Mexico City the previous month.

I invited the parties to discuss two issues: law and order in 'the areas in which, because of the war, the government has been prevented from exercising its administrative functions' (a euphemism to bypass the FMLN's previous insistence on 'areas of FMLN control' or 'military predominance'); and the criteria for deciding which areas would fall within this category. I made no progress on either issue. Given the repression to which the poor of El Salvador had been subjected for decades, law and order was a deeply sensitive issue for the FMLN. They wanted the new civilian police to take immediate control. The government rightly said that this was impractical; the new police force did not yet exist and it would take two years to recruit and train it. As for definition of the areas, someone proposed that they should be all the municipalities which were in a state of *irregularidad*. This was another of the dreaded *-idad* words which confused more than they clarified. The fact remained that the FMLN would not give up what political control they had in the countryside until they were sure that the eventual peace agreement was going to satisfy their demands.

This issue of territory is critical in all civil wars. We had already encountered it in Nicaragua. It would recur in Angola, in Yugoslavia, in Cambodia, in Mozambique, indeed everywhere. If the peaceful resolution of a civil conflict is in prospect, the government understandably wants to reassert its authority as quickly as possible; *constitucionalidad*

---

* An American warning to European powers in 1823 not to undertake further colonization in the Americas. It was later developed by Washington into a doctrine against 'non-hemispheric' involvement in security issues in the Americas which it regarded as the preserve of the United States.

demands no less. But governments in their impatience fail to see what a huge concession they are demanding from their insurgent opponents. For the insurgents, the control of territory is the last thing to surrender; territory is the fruit of their victories against the forces of oppression, the base from which they will resume battle if the negotiations fail, their source of manpower and food, a safe haven for their supporters, a justification for the suffering they have endured. It always amazed me how blind governments were to these realities and how unrealistic therefore were their ambitions for early restoration of their authority in insurgent-controlled areas.

After five days in Caraballeda I had to leave for Lisbon and the signature of the Angola peace accords. By then both tables were deadlocked and the El Salvador process was in crisis again. It had become even clearer that the FMLN would not play their one ace, acceptance of an irreversible cease-fire, until they were sure that they would get what they needed in the final settlement. The broad political agreements envisaged at Caracas had been reached at Mexico City but they had failed to flush the FMLN ace; the FMLN wanted to see the small print too. Had this been the FMLN's intention all along? The sequential process agreed in Caracas was the conclusion of broad agreements on the main political issues, then a cease-fire, then negotiation of the detailed issues arising from the broad agreements. Had the FMLN's acceptance of this process just been a subterfuge to draw the government into political negotiations? I do not know. Perhaps it was not until the Caraballeda round that they realized that the Caracas process would oblige them to tell their people to cease fire before their political objectives had been finally won.

At Mexico City de Soto had accepted a proposal by Villalobos that some of the FMLN field commanders (*jefes militares*) be brought to Mexico to see what was actually happening at the negotiating table; if all went well they would, on returning to the field, reassure their men and women that their interests were not being betrayed by the leadership. This was a good idea. The FMLN team was small and its composition changed little. It is easy for negotiators to become caught up in the dynamics of a negotiation and lose contact with their constituents at home. One of the things I learnt at the UN, not least from de Soto, is that a mediator must be patient and give the representatives of the two sides the time needed to explain their negotiating objectives to their people and to persuade their people that those objectives, if achieved, will be better than continuation of war. If the domestic constituency is neglected, it may in the end reject the outcome of the negotiation.

The government agreed to Villalobos' proposal – another sign of growing goodwill – and ONUSAL was given the tricky task of getting the *jefes militares* on to the UN plane and returning them to their field headquarters when they came back from Mexico City. They had been a lively addition to the sessions there and their presence had seemed beneficial. But it is possible that concern on their part about what the mid-process cease-fire would imply for the combatants in the field led to a hardening of the FMLN position between Mexico City and Caraballeda.

The next round was in late June at Querétaro in Mexico. The UN team approached it with gloom. Neither side had shown signs of moving from the irreconcilable positions they had adopted at Caraballeda, there had been a resumption of fighting, the government had made difficulties over the extraction of the *jefes militares* to attend the next round of negotiations. We had, however, detected signs that the FMLN were tempted by the idea of abandoning the two-stage formula and going for a concentrated negotiation of all outstanding points which, if it succeeded, would bring the definitive cease-fire into effect. After three days of largely sterile discussion, de Soto and I were invited to meet the five *comandantes* of the FMLN. They confirmed that they would like to change the format and listed a number of points, mainly relating to the armed forces, political activity by the FMLN and land, on which they needed to be satisfied before they would accept a cease-fire. They did not want to put their proposal to the government delegation at that meeting but, said Handal, had already discussed it with Cristiani with whom they intended to maintain direct contact. All this was good news, though the FMLN shopping list contained some difficult items, and we worried about how the Americans would react to postponement of the cease-fire until the whole negotiation was completed.

The FMLN's proposal turned out to be a false dawn. They had second thoughts a few weeks later and Cristiani's position remained ambiguous. The picture was further complicated in July when Carlos Andrés Pérez, the President of Venezuela, without consulting de Soto, summoned both sides' key negotiators to Caracas and put to them proposals for breaking the deadlock. Venezuela was one of the four 'Friends of the Secretary-General' in the El Salvador mediation, the others being Colombia, Mexico and Spain. President Pérez's initiative was a serious violation of the rules which Pérez de Cuéllar and de Soto had set for the Friends and which all of them had accepted.

This concept of 'Friends of the Secretary-General' was pioneered in the El Salvador mediation. Its purpose was to enable the Secretary-General to tap the help of a few countries that had particularly close relations with the parties. The Friends would become, severally and individually, diplomatic assets which he could use when persuasion or pressure had to be applied to a party. It was implicit, and explicitly agreed in the case of El Salvador, that a country's acceptance of the

Secretary-General's invitation to become a 'Friend' precluded independent initiatives by that country; it was to take action only when asked to do so by the mediator. This was essential if what de Soto called 'the unity and integrity of the mediation' was to be sustained. As he has written:

> The worst enemy of mediation is confusion as to who is mediating. Mediators can easily be played off one against the other. Negotiations of a multidisciplinary character – a common feature in complex internal conflict – stand the best chance of success if they are unequivocally controlled by a single, clearly identified mediator. Second-guessing a mediator is a dangerous game for it can undermine the mediation itself.*

There is an important difference between Friends of the Secretary-General and 'Contact Groups' like those for Namibia or, later, Bosnia. Contact Groups are consortia of like-minded states engaged in their own diplomacy, whereas Friends have forsworn diplomacy of their own in order to be able to support that of the Secretary-General.

Fortunately, President Pérez's initiative was blocked by the FMLN which declined to negotiate with the other side unless the UN was present. In August 1991 the Secretary-General received a joint letter from the US Secretary of State and the Soviet (as he still was) Foreign Minister asking him to take personal leadership of the process and offering to join with the Friends in providing support to his efforts. This was helpful. Pérez de Cuéllar, assured of superpower support, invited Cristiani and the five leaders of the FMLN to New York where ten days of negotiation resolved the deadlock. What took place there was essentially what the FMLN had floated at Querétaro – a compressed and accelerated negotiation to obtain agreement on all outstanding points before the cease-fire came into effect. This put the cease-fire on the back-burner for the time being and I played almost no part in this round. For de Soto it was another great success, with agreements on 'purification'† of the armed forces, redefinition of their doctrine, immediate action to establish the new civilian police force and land reform. It was also agreed to create a National Commission for the Consolidation of Peace (COPAZ), which would include two representatives of the FMLN and would enable Salvadorian civil society, in parallel with the international operation ONUSAL, to monitor implementation of the settlement.

---

* Álvaro de Soto, 'Ending Violent Conflict in El Salvador', in Chester A. Crocker, Fen Osler Hampson and Pamela Aall (eds.), *Herding Cats: Multiparty Mediation in a Complex World* (United States Institute of Peace Press, 1999), pp. 380–1.
† '*Depuración*' in Spanish; the English 'purge' was carefully avoided in order not to arouse the army's feelings.

This agreement provoked another outburst of right-wing rage in El Salvador. There were demonstrations in the street and threats against UN personnel. By now Cristiani accepted that the detailed design of the cease-fire would have to come at the very end. But he insisted that I put in an appearance in El Salvador in early November to help him defend himself against the right's accusations that he had allowed the cease-fire to be pushed aside in favour of the negotiation of political agreements, all of which involved concessions by the government. In four hours with Cristiani and his generals I suggested that the government should try to complete negotiation of the remaining political agreements as quickly as possible and then tell the FMLN that if they wanted them implemented they must accept a short process for the demobilization of their fighters. In the end Cristiani seemed to accept this. Of the generals only Vargas spoke; the others sat glum and silent through a conversation which they clearly found distasteful. A few days later the FMLN declared a unilateral truce. This was probably intended to help Cristiani handle the pressure from his right wing. But it revived earlier pressure from Washington on Pérez de Cuéllar to tell de Soto and me to give priority to the cease-fire. This approach had now been overtaken by the FMLN's success in persuading Cristiani that the cease-fire would have to come at the very end and Pérez de Cuéllar resisted the American pressure. Instead of telling me to drop everything and join de Soto in Mexico City to finalize the cease-fire, as the Americans wished, he told me to drop everything and go with Cyrus Vance to Yugoslavia to negotiate a cease-fire in Croatia and insert a UN peacekeeping force there.

Yugoslavia distracted me from El Salvador for almost a month. By mid-December 1991 the process seemed to be stuck again. Within two weeks Pérez de Cuéllar would cease to be Secretary-General, so he invited the government and FMLN negotiators to New York for a last push. Much progress was made, but by Christmas Eve the two sides were in deadlock on the criteria for the admission of former FMLN fighters to the new civilian police force. That afternoon, at a meeting with the two delegations amongst the packing cases in his official residence, Pérez de Cuéllar told me to convene the cease-fire table on Christmas Day; the time had at last come for detailed decisions on the cease-fire. I was puzzled by this instruction: why the urgency? The answer, it turned out, was that Pérez de Cuéllar had decided, as a last throw, to ask Cristiani himself to join the talks immediately after Christmas. Cristiani could be expected to turn down the request unless the cease-fire table was actively at work. In the event, Cristiani came on 28 December and brought with him Armando Calderón Sol, the head of the right-wing ARENA party, which commanded the majority in the Legislative Assembly.

I walked to UN headquarters early on Christmas morning in light snow; the only other pedestrians were dog-walkers and the homeless. Separate meetings with the two delegations showed that our earlier discussions, barren though they had seemed, had identified much common ground. In the afternoon my team drafted an agenda for discussion during the six days that remained. We entitled it *'Carnita para los Huesos'* ('Some Flesh on the Bones'). It was accepted by the two delegations and we moved methodically through it, starting at 9 a.m. each day and going on into the small hours (4 a.m. on the morning of 31 December). It was comparatively easy to reach agreement on the structure and timing of the cease-fire. An informal cease-fire would be observed as soon as the peace accords were signed. On D-Day the formal cease-fire would come into effect. During the five days following D-Day the two sides' forces would remain where they were. That was the first stage. The second stage would begin on D + 6. Between that day and D + 30 the government forces would withdraw to their 'peacetime positions' and the FMLN combatants would assemble at a number of 'designated locations', where they would remain until the military structures of the FMLN were dismantled and its combatants reintegrated into civilian life.

By the evening of 29 December, only two issues remained to be agreed: the locations where the two sides' forces would be stationed at each stage; and the dismantling of the FMLN's military structure. The FMLN declined to discuss the second issue until they knew the outcome of the negotiations at the political table. As regards the first, my team plotted on a map all the places where one side or the other wanted its combatants to be stationed during the first stage. I summoned the two delegations and showed them the map: together, I said, they had asked for 478 locations; this was ridiculous; in Cambodia, a country nearly nine times the size of El Salvador and with over 200,000 people under arms, there would be only 95 locations in the first stage of the cease-fire; in El Salvador I could not agree to more than 100 for the government and 50 for the FMLN. There was much grumbling but both sides accepted the decision. There was a similar confrontation the next day, 31 December, about the stage two locations: the FMLN wanted 30; the government said they could agree to only three (but wanted over 60 for themselves). I decreed 15 for the FMLN, which was again reluctantly accepted by both sides.

I took this forceful line on the advice of David Escobar Galindo, a gentle poet and academic and one of the government's negotiators. He seemed out of place in that delegation of bureaucrats and soldiers but he was consistently helpful to the mediators. I had given him a preview of the map; he agreed that it was ridiculous; I should impose a decision; there was no time for haggling. His advice won me a success which received exaggerated praise; Escobar Galindo himself hailed a new diplomatic technique, *la cimitarra de Goulding* ('Goulding's scimitar').*

One of the most difficult decisions for a mediator is knowing when to turn forceful. Drawing on experience gained in negotiating the Law of the Sea Convention, de Soto had persuaded the parties to accept what is known as the single negotiating text procedure. The mediator discusses each issue separately with each of the parties and then drafts language which he hopes will bridge the gap between them. If, as is usually the case, it does not bridge the gap, the mediator shuttles through another round of discussions and produces a revised text. And so on, until a mutually acceptable text is arrived at. This is an iterative process and slow, and it does not give the mediator many opportunities to wield the scimitar. The whole idea is to find ways of accommodating the two sides' concerns, not to coerce or scold them into accepting the mediator's proposals. That New Year's Eve, it was Pérez de Cuéllar's imminent departure that acted as a spur and made it possible to use the scimitar. Both sides were aware how much personal effort Pérez de Cuéllar had put into this enterprise and both recognized how long it would take a new non-Latin Secretary-General to master the file.

But our successes at the cease-fire table were pale by comparison with those of Pérez de Cuéllar and de Soto at the political table. Agreement was reached there on the reduction and *depuración* of the armed forces, on the establishment of the new civilian police force and, in sketchy form that was going to cost us dear in the months to come, on a number of economic and social issues, especially a land transfer programme for the benefit of ex-combatants on both sides. Pérez de Cuéllar postponed his planned departure for the Bahamas and just before midnight the text of a brief 'New York Act' was agreed. This recorded that agreement had been reached on all substantive issues and on the technical and military aspects of the cease-fire. D-Day would be in one month's time, 1 February 1992. There would be a further meeting on 5 January to finalize the negotiation of two outstanding issues: the timetable for implementation of the agreements; and the procedures for demobilizing the FMLN. If these issues were not settled by 10 January, the parties committed themselves to accepting solutions proposed by the Secretary-General (who would by then, of course, be Boutros Boutros-Ghali). The final peace agreement would be signed in Mexico City on 16 January.

The New York Act was signed by the government negotiating team, by

---

* After the peace agreement was signed, he also named his new dog after me. This attracted some attention in the Salvadorian media, and when, sadly, the dog died young, I was sent newspaper cuttings with the alarming headline '*Goulding murió*' ('Goulding is dead').

the five *comandantes* of the FMLN and by de Soto, in the presence of Pérez de Cuéllar, the ambassadors of the four Friends, the members of de Soto's team and the support staff of the Salvadorian protagonists. Those who were not present were the UN cease-fire team, led by myself. We were in my conference room, waiting to be told that the political table had finished its work. Only when we heard excited voices in the corridor did we discover that the New York Act had been signed. We all felt deeply slighted and my staff demanded that I make a protest on their behalf.

I did so on 2 January, not to Pérez de Cuéllar who had left by then, but to de Soto. He said that the failure to check whether we were still in the building was an oversight due to the euphoria of the moment. But was it? De Soto had been an exemplary senior partner in this enterprise; he was scrupulous in keeping me informed about his part of the negotiations and complimentary when results were achieved in mine. My admiration for him will already be evident to readers of these pages. It would have been out of character for him to exclude the cease-fire team from the signing. When the cease-fire had been such a big issue, did no one think of calling us to witness the signature? Perhaps not.

But I have lingering doubts about Pérez de Cuéllar. Two months before, a senior colleague in the Secretariat, to whom I was not particularly close at that time, invited me to lunch to receive some unsolicited advice. When I had arrived in 1986, he said, I had been an outsider, but now I had become an insider. The other insiders wanted me to survive, because the standing of the UN depended so much on peacekeeping and I was 'virtually irreplaceable' as the head of it. As soon as Pérez de Cuéllar's successor took office, I should launch a 'blitzkrieg' to persuade him to institute a proper system for the planning and management of peacekeeping. Meanwhile, I should watch out: Pérez de Cuéllar did not like me and the 'palace guard' (Dayal, Picco, Diallo, but not Aimé) did not want me to survive. I asked why the SG did not like me. 'Because you come from a service which is highly efficient and in which it is normal to be direct with one's superiors. Jávier is an aristocrat who does not like that. He was especially upset by your complaint about his lunch with Peres.' Was it paranoid to think that the failure to summon me and my team to the signature might have been a parting shot in the closing minutes of Pérez de Cuéllar's Secretary-Generalship?

I accompanied Boutros-Ghali to Mexico City for the signing of the peace agreements on 16 January 1992. Eight days before, I had had an operation on my right hand to correct a condition known as Dupuytren's contracture (which I believe to be the only feature I share with Margaret Thatcher). As a result, my hand was bandaged and my arm in a sling. This led one Mexican newspaper to describe me as 'the wounded British general'. More seriously, I was unable to take notes or write a diary – and did not resume the diary for six months, though this was due more to pressure of work than to the aftermath of surgery.

The Chapultepec Accords, as they became known, made it necessary to add a military division and a police division to ONUSAL's existing human rights division. It was also time to close down ONUCA, now that two of the three Central American conflicts had been brought to an end. ONUSAL was up and running much more quickly than any of the other peacekeeping operations that were deployed in 1991 and 1992 (in Iraq/Kuwait, Angola, Western Sahara, Cambodia, Yugoslavia, Somalia and Mozambique). Thanks to the San José agreement on human rights, the mission was already established; and the termination of ONUCA created a source of human and material resources on which the enlarged ONUSAL could draw.

The informal cease-fire was respected, as was the formal one which came into force on 1 February 1992. The first phase of the separation of forces was achieved without serious incident. The FMLN leadership began to return to El Salvador. But we were soon being told by the Americans that the FMLN were not observing the rules. About a quarter of their combatants had not assembled in the 'designated locations' and arms and ammunition were being stored in clandestine caches. And the Friends were telling us that ONUSAL should be more proactive and not appear to be more responsive to the government than to the FMLN. A visit from New York was needed and I spent four days in El Salvador in mid-March 1992.

Both sides were failing to respect the accords and the timetable for implementation was slipping. Each side tended to blame the other, but since one wrong did not justify another, I urged them to return to the spirit of New York and Chapultepec. Unilateral action must be avoided. If they had grievances, they should discuss them with the other side or with the UN; ONUSAL's good offices were available to help them resolve disputes. This did not cut much ice. Friendly relations between individuals who have come to know each other through years of negotiation cannot easily be transferred to a wider stage. Mutual distrust remained strong. El Salvador was still a highly militarized society and the FMLN were genuinely disturbed by the government's failure to start training the new civilian police force and disbanding the existing militarized police. The government, assailed by its right wing and fed Washington's intelligence about the FMLN, was genuinely nervous about the suspected intention (rightly suspected, as it turned out) of some FMLN leaders to retain the capacity to resume war.

None of this was surprising. What did surprise was the tension created by the land issue. This had been negotiated only sketchily during the closing days of the December round in New York. Now its complexity was becoming clear to the UN officials involved. One of the issues that caused the war was access to land. The FMLN insisted that in future distributions of land the government should give priority to former FMLN combatants (and, they had to accept, to former combatants on the other side). They also wanted to regularize the situation of their many supporters who had taken over land abandoned by landowners in *zonas conflictivas* and other places where the FMLN were predominant; these people should now be given title to the land they were working. Outline provisions to this effect had been included in the accords but with little detail about how they were to be put into effect; and the accords themselves acknowledged that the existing agrarian legislation was 'haphazard, contradictory and incomplete'. Where there was detail in the accords, it placed unrealistic burdens on the government and the FMLN. The latter, for instance, were required to produce within thirty days an inventory of all land and buildings in the *zonas conflictivas*; but nowhere in the accords were the *zonas conflictivas* defined. Nor did the accords say how the land distribution programme was to be financed.

The resulting delays and uncertainties caused tension in the countryside; peasant groups occupied land; landowners sought the help of the hated police in evicting them; the FMLN combatants, cantoned in their designated locations, wondered whether there would be any land left for them when they were eventually demobilized. The land issue dominated the meetings which Riza and I had with the two sides. On the last day, there was a joint meeting at which it was agreed that they would try to prevent both new occupations of land and the eviction of existing occupants; the status quo would be maintained while COPAZ, which as required by the accords had set up a special commission on the land issue, investigated the cases submitted to it. The two sides also agreed to consult regularly on these issues. But I feared that this would not be the end of the story.

One month later Handal came to New York, bursting with indignation about the government's failure to demilitarize law and order and Riza's alleged inactivity. The FMLN had, he said, been misled by the UN in the negotiations; we had assured them that UN involvement constituted a guarantee that the other side would honour its commitments. That was not working; the FMLN now had to find its own guarantees. This was a bad sign; Handal seemed to be trying to establish a pretext for the FMLN not to demobilize the first 20 per cent of its combatants on 1 May. Sure enough there was no demobilization. Nor was there on 1 June when the accords required another 20 per cent to be demobilized. The El Salvador process was beset by the same problems as those in Angola and Cambodia. Had we lost the knack of implementing peace settlements? Was defiance of the UN a virus that was spreading world-wide?

In mid-June Riza reported that the two sides had agreed to adjust the timetable for implementation and the process was back on track. But by mid-August the process was again in trouble and I had to return to El Salvador. Eighty per cent of the FMLN combatants were still in the designated locations and the FMLN were ruthlessly playing the demobilization card to win more tricks against the government. It was crude diplomacy but effective. Cristiani recognized the weakness of his position and was ready to strike deals with the FMLN. But he was not well served by his mediocre team, who lacked both imagination and discipline. I decided to propose a second revision of the timetable, on the understanding that one month later the parties and the UN would review the progress made and decide whether conditions existed for the cease-fire process to be completed on 31 October. This was crude diplomacy too, designed to impress upon the government that if it did not carry out its commitments there would be a real risk of renewed conflict. As expected, the FMLN liked this approach; so did Cristiani, confirming that he at least understood the necessity to do a deal with the FMLN. But it took almost a week of hard negotiation to get agreement on the revised timetable.

This second revision won us the demobilization of the second 20 per cent of the FMLN fighters. But matters soon came to a halt again; the mid-September review gave the FMLN another opportunity to exploit its advantage. The accords, they said, required that the transfer of land be completed three months *before* demobilization was completed; it had not even begun. The first units of the new civilian police were supposed to be deployed a few days before the final demobilization; the training of the police had only just begun. Back I went to a tense San Salvador. The tension was aggravated by the fact that the ad hoc commission on the *depuración* of the armed forces had just presented its report to Boutros-Ghali and Cristiani. The commission was composed of three Salvadorians appointed by the Secretary-General. Its task was to evaluate the suitability of each officer for service in the reformed armed forces created by the accords and to make recommendations accordingly. The government was to take the necessary administrative decisions not more than thirty days after receiving the report and those decisions were to be put into effect not more than sixty days thereafter. To the fury of the FMLN, Boutros-Ghali had decided to keep the commission's recommendations confidential.

It was a grinding visit of long, over-sized, bad-tempered meetings – I was a squash ball smashed alternately against the wall by two angry players. On the land issue, my instructions were to put forward a proposal which, if accepted, would make it possible to begin the transfer of land to ex-combatants on both sides. I was accompanied by Graciana del

Castillo, a Uruguayan economist from the Secretary-General's office. The first two meetings, with the government and then with the FMLN, were preliminary sparring. We were looking for common ground on which we could build our proposal. It was not to be found. The government was concerned about the resource constraints: there was neither enough land nor enough money to meet the demands of the FMLN. The latter insisted that they had always made clear that 'reintegration' of their combatants had meant giving them land; promises had been made; if they were not kept, then the FMLN were relieved of their commitments. Del Castillo and I shared the government's concerns about resources; the FMLN's demands amounted to more than a quarter of the country's arable land and pasture. Riza and his team were more inclined to sympathize with the FMLN.

Overnight we refined our proposal and put it the next day to Cristiani and his numerous advisers. It provided for beneficiaries of the land transfer programme to receive on average 3.5 hectares each. Cristiani was outraged by it. It took no account of the realities, he said, and the amount of land demanded for the FMLN was politically unacceptable. He asked me 'vehemently' not to give the proposal to the FMLN until we had received his government's considered observations. I reluctantly agreed to this. There followed an even more difficult meeting with the FMLN. My inability to inform them of the proposal made them suspicious. Handal repeated at length all he had said the previous day. At the end of that meeting he had given us a meticulously detailed list of all the points, however minor, on which the government had failed to honour its commitments. In a telephone call that evening, de Soto and I had agreed that the FMLN were simply striking poses before the serious negotiations on land began. We were wrong. Handal now said that on the basis of this analysis of the government's performance the FMLN had decided to demand a complete revision of the implementation timetable, covering not only the items which were supposed to be completed by 31 October 1992 but also those beyond that date. It was necessary to revert to the logic of the original timetable: the FMLN would not complete its demobilization until the government had done all that it had been supposed to do by 31 October; nor would it demobilize the third 20 per cent who were supposed to return to civilian life that very day (30 September). I said that the FMLN were giving the government a pretext for suspending the reduction of the armed forces and going slow on *depuración*. Handal said that he and his colleagues had taken this into account before reaching their decision.

The next morning there was nothing important to do in San Salvador: Cristiani was studying our proposal and the FMLN were closeted with Bernie Aronson, the Assistant Secretary for Inter-American Affairs at the

State Department, who was our main American interlocutor on this subject and something of a hardliner. He too was on a visit to El Salvador to explore what could be done to put the peace process back on track. So del Castillo and I went to Perquín to see what a *tenedor* looked like, a '*tenedor*' being a person illegally working land that belongs to someone else. Perquín is a mountain village in a *zona conflictiva* which had been an FMLN stronghold during the war and the clandestine site of their Radio Venceremos. The *tenedor* we met was a woman living with a man, an aunt, a grandmother, seven children, two pigs and two chickens in a house which they had reconstructed from a bombed ruin, with just over two hectares of maize and beans. We also met a group of recently demobilized FMLN combatants who had occupied a couple of hectares of vacant land and were clearing it to plant maize. They did not know, and cared less, who the owner was.

Back in San Salvador there was another long meeting with Cristiani and his team. They had been working on our proposal all morning and set out to destroy it. Cristiani produced a stream of statistics to show that our figure of 3.5 hectares per beneficiary was unjustified and unworkable. I felt out of my depth. Del Castillo fought gallantly but she was the only economist in my team and I wished that I had brought more. The government was swamping us with selective information which we had no means of verifying. At the end I asked for a restricted meeting and told Cristiani of the FMLN's demand for a new timetable. His reaction was bitter and truculent; the reduction of the armed forces would be suspended and so would the legalization of the FMLN as a political party. Next I told the FMLN that I still had no proposal for them on land and that the government had been strongly opposed to their demand for revision of the timetable. I would have to return to New York and report to the Secretary-General. The last meeting in a heavy day was with Aronson who was calmer than I had expected. The FMLN decision, he said, was regrettable and should be resisted, but some revision of the timetable was inevitable; the important thing was that the FMLN should demobilize the third contingent soon and be more honest about the weapons they held.

Interwoven with these discussions about land and the timetable was the question of *depuración*. I first raised it tête-à-tête with Cristiani. He said that the ad hoc commission's report was drastic; it required him to remove a large part of the senior command structure, including three out of five generals and half the colonels. This was made more difficult by the fact that the commission had given no reasons for its recommendations. How could he cashier officers without telling them why? To do so would be dishonourable; *institucionalidad* again. As for Handal, he complained bitterly about Boutros-Ghali's decision not to share the report with

COPAZ, which would have given the FMLN access to it. I said that Cristiani had received a copy of the report; if the FMLN felt that they were entitled to see it they should raise this matter with the government in COPAZ.

After our return to New York, Graciana del Castillo worked quickly to produce a detailed proposal on land which Boutros-Ghali would send personally to the two sides. This he did on 13 October. Within a few days both had accepted it, to my surprise and relief. Most of the credit for this success was due to del Castillo who drafted a professional, coherent and well-balanced programme of action. One can now see that once it had been personally endorsed by the Secretary-General, it would have been difficult for either side to refuse it. It also had the full support of the four Friends, who had now been joined by the United States in a formation known as 'the Four plus One'.

Boutros-Ghali reported to the Security Council that he would shortly present to the two sides a proposal on the demobilization of the FMLN and a possible third revision of the timetable. It was sent to them on 23 October, proposing limited adjustments to the timetable and completion of demobilization on 15 December. The FMLN accepted; Cristiani set conditions related to submission by the FMLN of a satisfactory inventory of their weapons and of the action taken to destroy them. He also sent a schedule for the *depuración* of the armed forces, which Boutros-Ghali decided he could not accept because it did not satisfy the requirements set out in the peace accords. As a result I became the recipient of daily telephone calls from Aronson and from Cristiani himself pleading for understanding of the problems he faced. They were real problems and I had much sympathy for him. Riza reported that tension was rising again in San Salvador; it was becoming known that the ad hoc commission had recommended a major purge and there was fear that right-wing extremists would be provoked into restarting the death squads' 'dirty war' of the 1980s. But *depuración* had been a central feature of the peace settlement and the accords were precise about the action Cristiani now had to take. If the Secretary-General condoned his not taking it, the UN itself could become responsible for unravelling the whole process.

On 30 October I was back in San Salvador, accompanied this time by de Soto as well as del Castillo. The FMLN's third demobilization took place that day and ONUSAL reported that for the first time real fighters had been demobilized and real weapons handed over. The principal issue discussed was *depuración*. Cristiani was in agony over his obligation to remove 103 officers from the armed forces within a few weeks. He was particularly unwilling to cashier the Minister of Defence, General Ponce, and thirteen other officers whose presence in the list was in his view inexplicable; he wanted these fourteen to stay until his term of office ended eighteen months later. None of his ideas for doing this was remotely acceptable to Handal (from whom we had, of course, to conceal the identities of the officers concerned). De Soto and I tried to persuade Cristiani that he could not escape drastic action; perhaps he could dress it up as part of a much wider reform of the armed forces which he would announce at the planned ceremony to celebrate the end of the armed confrontation. But all the ideas that we floated ran aground on the rock of Ponce and the thirteen. By the end of the second day we had to advise Boutros-Ghali that we had got nowhere and that he should take a tough line with Cristiani, perhaps even threatening to publish the ad hoc commission's list.

At that point Boutros-Ghali ordered me back to New York and on to Luanda as a result of the resumption of civil war in Angola. De Soto stayed on for another five days and achieved an agreement of some complexity, which Boutros-Ghali reported to the Security Council in necessarily opaque terms, given the secrecy surrounding the identity of the *depurables*. Cristiani had agreed to implement the commission's recommendations 'within a specified time-frame' and would inform the Secretary-General on 29 November of the administrative decisions he had taken. If those decisions were found by Boutros-Ghali to match the commission's recommendations, the FMLN would provide ONUSAL with a final inventory of its weapons, conclude their concentration on 30 November and start destroying them on 1 December, whereupon the government would resume the reduction of the armed forces.

From this point on, de Soto took the lead in the endless negotiations that were needed to get the Chapultepec Accords implemented. Overwhelmed by other responsibilities, I was happy for him to do so, though I missed the frequent visits to El Salvador. I did, however, accompany Boutros-Ghali to a ceremony that was held in San Salvador on 15 December to mark the formal ending of the armed conflict, following the legalization of the FMLN as a political party the previous day. The ceremony was held in a long, low, hot building with seating for three thousand. National reconciliation was not much in evidence. When the national anthem was sung, the government supporters had their hands on their hearts *à l'américaine* and the FMLN supporters had their clenched fists in the air *à la soviétique*. Handal was in rabble-rousing mode; when his tribute to Cuba and the Sandinistas was met with boos and hisses, he repeated the sentence 'so that they can shout again'. Cristiani, apparently exhausted by the strain of the previous weeks, spoke in low key and the event ended peacefully. On the way back to New York we stopped in Managua to lunch with President Chamorro, who sought the UN's help in dealing with some residual post-Contra problems in her country. It seemed decades since I had made my first visit to Nicaragua when ONUCA was set up; but it was less than three years.

Implementation of the Chapultepec Accords continued for a further two years in the same erratic way. ONUSAL's good offices remained much in demand. It was not surprising that implementation took a long time, for some of the provisions relating to human rights and the economic and social issues were long-term and not of finite duration like the ending of the armed conflict. Neither side hesitated long before violating the accords if it felt that that would advance its interests. De Soto kept an eagle eye on the process from his perch in the Secretary-General's office and, later, the Department of Political Affairs and advised Boutros-Ghali to pounce whenever he detected a serious violation. The fact that the party to be censured was more often the government than the FMLN is not necessarily an accurate measure of the relative non-compliance of the two sides. Boutros-Ghali spotted this after a while and became less willing to harry Cristiani and his successor Calderón Sol. But if de Soto was sometimes a little harsh towards the government, that should not detract from his astonishing achievement in negotiating the peaceful revolution which brought to an end a grim period in El Salvador's history. I am proud to have been involved in the enterprise.

Two down, one to go. With the wars ended in Nicaragua and El Salvador, the UN turned its attention to Guatemala. Peacemaking there was to be a major issue during my four years as Under-Secretary-General for Political Affairs. Another long negotiation, skilfully conducted by Jean Arnault, a French member of the Secretariat, led in December 1996, two days before the end of Boutros-Ghali's term as Secretary-General, to the signature of an 'Agreement on a Firm and Lasting Peace'. The signatories were the Guatemalan Government and an insurgent movement known as the *Unidad Revolucionaria Nacional Guatemalteca* (URNG). Like the Chapultepec Accords the agreement brought to an end a long and cruel civil war and included a wide range of provisions to address the root causes of that war. Although there were differences between the two conflicts, the negotiators of the Guatemalan settlement were able to draw on lessons learnt from the earlier process in El Salvador. In no region of the world were the United Nations' post-Cold War efforts for peace more successful than in Central America.

14

Cambodia

The United Nations Transitional Authority in Cambodia (UNTAC) was deployed in Cambodia from April 1992 until November 1993. It was the UN's largest peacekeeping undertaking since the operation in the Congo in the early 1960s. In concept it was the child of UNTAG which had been sent to Namibia three years before; it was a multifunctional peacekeeping operation whose task was to help four Cambodian factions implement a peace agreement which settled an internal conflict fuelled by the Cold War. But UNTAC's circumstances were different from UNTAG's. In 1989–90, other peacekeeping operations were either small or long-established and for a whole year UNTAG was able to command the attention of the Secretary-General and his senior staff. In 1992–3, on the other hand, UNTAC had to compete with four new operations which had been established during the preceding twelve months (in Iraq/Kuwait, Western Sahara, Angola and El Salvador) and with two other large operations which were being set up in the former Yugoslavia and Mozambique. In addition, Boutros Boutros-Ghali had only just assumed office and lacked Pérez de Cuéllar's encyclopaedic knowledge of UN peace operations during the preceding decade.

Cambodia, one of the three countries of Indo-China, gained independence from France in 1953. Its ruler, Prince Norodom Sihanouk, tried to keep it out of the Vietnam War but the country was subjected to massive bombing by the United States and in 1970 Sihanouk himself was overthrown in a military coup by his army commander Lon Nol, who promptly received support from Washington. Civil war ensued and after five years victory was won by the Khmer Rouge, a fundamentalist Communist party officially known as the Party of Democratic Kampuchea and led by Pol Pot. There followed five years of so-called 'genocide' in which 20 per cent of the country's inhabitants are estimated to have died.* On Christmas

---

* Not strictly genocide, because Cambodians were killing Cambodians and the slaughter was due to ideological and class motives, not ethnic ones. For sound political and legal reasons Pérez de Cuéllar did not like this misuse of language and coined a

Day 1978 Vietnamese forces invaded Cambodia to overthrow the Khmer Rouge.

At this point the Cold War dimensions of the Cambodian tragedy became explicit. Vietnam's action received full support from the Soviet Union and its allies. The West, however, condemned Vietnam for 'aggression' against Cambodia and denied recognition to the government (the People's Republic of Kampuchea (PRK)), which Vietnam installed in Phnom Penh under a renegade member of the Khmer Rouge, Heng Samrin. Instead the West supported a rival government which was headed by Sihanouk and called itself the Coalition Government of Democratic Kampuchea (CGDK). This had three components: the Khmer Rouge; Sihanouk's United National Front for an Independent, Neutral, Peaceful and Cooperative Cambodia (FUNCINPEC); and the smaller Khmer People's National Liberation Front (KPNLF), led by Son Sann. The West ensured that the CGDK retained Cambodia's seat at the United Nations, where it was represented by an unrepentant member of the Khmer Rouge.

A quarter of a century later, in a post-Cold War age of humanitarian intervention and international tribunals for the punishment of *génocidaires*, these events have become difficult to believe. They show how much the West's worldwide struggle against Soviet-led Communism had distorted the values which the West itself claimed to be defending. As a member of the British Mission to the UN at that time I dutifully condemned the Vietnamese action and coupled it a year later with the Soviet invasion of Afghanistan as twin manifestations of the wickedness of what Ronald Reagan dubbed the 'Evil Empire'. But inwardly I knew that Afghanistan and Cambodia were quite different. The Soviet action in Afghanistan *was* wicked; Vietnam had been wicked too in using force to establish control over another country, but by today's humanitarian standards its action can be justified as something that had to be done, like Tanzania's military intervention in Uganda in 1979 to topple the monster Idi Amin.

At the United Nations, the West's position was shared by the Association of South-East Asian Nations (ASEAN).* ASEAN was able to muster enough Non-Aligned votes in the General Assembly for the adoption of a series of resolutions calling for the withdrawal of all foreign forces from Cambodia and self-determination for its people. The

---

(continued)

euphemistic alternative which was eventually incorporated in the Paris agreements on Cambodia – 'the policies and practices of the past'.

* At that time consisting of Indonesia, Malaysia, the Philippines, Singapore and Thailand.

Assembly also set up an International Conference on Cambodia, which was boycotted by Vietnam and its allies. Cambodia had been part of Pérez de Cuéllar's bailiwick when he was one of the Under-Secretaries-General for Special Political Affairs in the Secretariat and as soon as he became Secretary-General he put it high on his agenda. He was, however, obliged to proceed discreetly because his only formal mandate came from the one-sided resolutions of the General Assembly; if he was to succeed as a mediator, he would have to prove his impartiality.* His principal aide on Cambodia was Rafeeuddin Ahmed, a long-serving Pakistani member of the Secretariat, whom he appointed in 1983 as his Special Representative for Humanitarian Affairs in South-East Asia. This title gave Ahmed access where he needed it but disguised the political nature of his task. Pérez de Cuéllar had great confidence in Ahmed whose courtesy, shrewdness, determination and patience matched Pérez de Cuéllar's own qualities as a diplomat.

The two of them quickly identified the essential ingredients of a peace settlement in Cambodia – cease-fire, withdrawal of Vietnamese forces, dissolution or suspension of both the PRK and CGDK governments, free and fair elections, adoption of a new constitution, international supervision of all the foregoing. They quietly and persistently advocated to all parties a solution on these lines. The negotiation, which is well described in Pérez de Cuéllar's *Pilgrimage for Peace*, took almost ten years, with a host of international actors on an ever more crowded peacemaking stage. Ahmed played a central role and methodically planned the eventual deployment of a UN operation. He kept me informed as the negotiations proceeded and I made Timothy Dibuama available to advise him on the military aspects.

In mid-1989 the pace quickened. The end of the Cold War was marked not only by East–West détente. There was also a rapid rapprochement between China and the Soviet Union. In December 1988 the Chinese Foreign Minister visited Moscow, the first such visit in more than thirty years. Less than two months later, a return visit to Beijing by the Soviet Foreign Minister produced a joint statement on Cambodia in favour of a political settlement which would include the withdrawal of Vietnamese forces. These developments had obliged Vietnam to reconsider its position. China was Vietnam's historic enemy. Vietnam's overthrow of the Khmer Rouge, China's proxy in Cambodia, had enhanced Vietnam's value to Moscow, winning it political and financial support for its occupation of Cambodia. Now the sands were shifting, demonstrating that peace between major powers can be more threatening to their lesser

---

* The partiality of the General Assembly gave him a similar problem in the case of Palestine: see Chapter 6.

protégés than war. Vietnam had already committed itself to a progressive withdrawal of its forces from Cambodia. Two weeks before the Soviet Minister's visit to Beijing, it announced that it would have them all out by September 1989.

This created the possibility of a political breakthrough at a conference which was to take place in Paris in August. At this point, it emerged that many of the negotiators had unrealistic ideas of how long it would take to deploy a UN operation. Pérez de Cuéllar therefore stated very clearly at the Paris conference what the UN could do and what conditions would have to be fulfilled for it to succeed. He went on to propose the immediate dispatch to Cambodia of a fact-finding mission which would gather the technical data needed for planning purposes. This was agreed and the mission left a few days later under the leadership of Lieutenant-General Martin Vadset, Chief of Staff of UNTSO.

In Paris there was also talk of the early dispatch of a small UN military observer mission to verify the withdrawal of the Vietnamese troops. I was opposed to this, fearing that it would suffer the fate of UNGOMAP, the observer mission deployed in Afghanistan to verify the withdrawal of Soviet troops, which had done its limited task and then stood ineffectually by as the civil war raged on. But the Paris conference failed to reach agreement and no significant decisions were taken, though useful groundwork was done for the future, including acceptance of the need for an 'International Control Mechanism' to ensure implementation of an eventual settlement. The technical mission encountered political difficulties, thanks in part to some injudicious public statements by its leader, but returned with a report that made clear the logistical difficulties that would confront any UN peacekeeping operation in Cambodia.

The turning point came at the beginning of 1990 when, in response to an initiative by the Australian Foreign Minister, Gareth Evans, the five permanent members of the Security Council took charge of the negotiations. Although a little put out at Evans' failure to consult him, Pérez de Cuéllar welcomed this initiative. As already mentioned, he was quick to spot the opportunities that the end of the Cold War was creating for the Security Council to resolve some long-standing regional conflicts fuelled by the Cold War. He had successfully engaged the Permanent Five in his efforts to end the Iran–Iraq conflict. Their readiness to work together on Cambodia was even more important, and more surprising, for most of them had been directly involved in Cambodia – China as the patron of the Khmer Rouge and enemy of Vietnam, France as the former colonial power, the Soviet Union as the ally of Vietnam and the government it had installed in Phnom Penh and the United States as the enemy of the Soviet Union and Vietnam. Even Britain was reported to have been providing covert military support to the forces of the CGDK. Cambodia is thus the most telling example of how the end of the Cold War made it possible to extinguish the proxy wars which East–West rivalry had ignited in the Third World. The peace that was to be established there was, and remains, fragile. But in Cambodia, unlike Afghanistan and Angola, the stalemate was hurtful enough for the local protagonists to permit the international community to help them re-establish peace – not a perfect peace, but a state of affairs infinitely better than that endured by the people of Cambodia for the previous quarter-century.

By the time the P-5 took the lead, it was becoming accepted that the UN would provide the 'International Control Mechanism'. But, with the Khmer Rouge continuing to hold Cambodia's seat in the General Assembly, Vietnam and the Phnom Penh government remained doubtful whether the UN would be impartial. They nevertheless asked to be briefed on UN peacekeeping, with special reference to the supervision of elections. I was also quizzed on this by the representative of the CGDK at the Namibian independence dinner in Windhoek in March 1990, thinking how odd it was that he should be there when SWAPO was so close to the Soviet Union and its allies, including Vietnam.

The Five held six meetings in 1990. At the sixth, in Paris at the end of August, they reached agreement on a framework document, which outlined in some detail the ingredients of a comprehensive political settlement. The four Cambodian parties would establish a Supreme National Council (SNC), which would be 'the embodiment of the independence, sovereignty and unity of Cambodia' during a transitional period; the Five hoped that Sihanouk would chair it. The SNC would delegate to a 'United Nations Transitional Authority in Cambodia' (UNTAC) all powers needed for implementation of the settlement, including 'relevant aspects' of administration. UNTAC would monitor a cease-fire and supervise the cantonment of the parties' armed forces at agreed locations. UNTAC would also organize and conduct free and fair elections for a constituent assembly. Human rights would be respected and measures taken to 'ensure the non-return to the policies and practices of the past'. International guarantees would be provided to ensure that the settlement was implemented in its entirety. The framework document also endorsed two earlier papers, one on the repatriation of refugees and the other on reconstruction of the country.

This document had been laboriously negotiated by the Five, both amongst themselves and between them and the parties. The parties promptly confirmed their acceptance of it and the Security Council endorsed it on 20 September 1990. Pérez de Cuéllar, for whom this welcome outcome was a daunting new commitment, instructed the Cambodia Task Force, which he had set up earlier in the year, following the successful Namibian model, to ensure that the UN took charge of the planning for implementation of the settlement and not allow this task to be assumed by the Paris conference or the Australians. For the latter too the Council's endorsement of the framework document was a diplomatic triumph and they were ever ready to step into the breach if they felt that the Secretariat was lagging.

More than a year was to pass before the peace agreements for Cambodia were signed in Paris on 23 October 1991. They were an amplification of the previous year's framework document. Ostensibly the delay was due to differences between the government in Phnom Penh and the three factions opposed to it over the detail of arrangements which had been described only in outline in the earlier document. These included especially the UN's 'control' of the existing administrative structures and the proportion of each faction's troops that was to be demobilized before the elections. But the real reason for the delay was that both the Khmer Rouge and the Phnom Penh government, led by Hun Sen and now called the 'State of Cambodia' (SOC), were having second thoughts about the risks they saw in the plan. The leaders of the four factions nevertheless met from time to time in the Supreme National Council (of which Sihanouk was duly elected President in July 1991) and in May 1991 a voluntary cease-fire came into effect in response to an appeal by the Secretary-General and the Co-Chairmen of the Paris Conference (France and Indonesia). The process was beginning to look irreversible.

In July the factions began talking about the possibility of the UN sending an advance 'good offices mission' that would station some UNMOs at the headquarters of each faction and would monitor the voluntary cease-fire. Neither Ahmed nor I was keen on this idea; if the Cambodians wanted a UN peacekeeping operation, they must sign the peace agreements. Initially we were supported by the Five but the idea steadily gained ground and when the Five plus Indonesia* met with the SNC in New York in September, they endorsed the idea of an advance mission. The UN Advance Mission in Cambodia (UNAMIC) was established in mid-October and would be deployed immediately after the agreements were signed, in order to ensure a UN presence on the ground in the interval between signature and the deployment of UNTAC.

The birth of UNAMIC was troubled by an unseemly squabble. The fault was mine. The French wanted the new mission to be composed exclusively of francophone personnel. I told the Five that this would not be possible. But when asking member states to contribute military observers for it, I agreed that the working language would be French. A storm broke. The other four permanent members expressed strong

---

* This unusual grouping reflected the fact that Indonesia was, with France, a co-chairman of the Paris conference.

objections. The ASEAN countries, all of them anglophone, protested to the Secretary-General. The Australians, I was told, were accusing me of colluding with the French to block Australia's well-known ambition to provide the Force Commander of UNTAC. Ahmed denounced me in the Cambodia Task Force. The Secretary-General said wearily that we would just have to say that I had been misunderstood; the universal practice in the UN, including its peacekeeping operations, was that English and French had equal status as the Organization's two working languages. This was true in theory but far from true in practice, even in francophone stations like Paris and Geneva.

Meanwhile, my presence was required in Angola, where implementation of the Bicesse Accords was not going well, and I did not think about Cambodia again until I arrived in Paris ten days later for the signature of the peace agreements. By this time there was a new issue. The Five and the ASEAN states all wanted Rafee Ahmed to be the Secretary-General's Special Representative and Head of UNTAC. But Ahmed had told Pérez de Cuéllar that he did not wish to go to the field; he believed that the mission would need exceptional direction from New York, given its size and complexity and the number of member states involved, and he would prefer to head a department in New York that would be given this task. This was, of course, a challenge to my own department's claim to unique responsibility for peacekeeping, but at that time I was so overworked and short-staffed that I decided to expend no energy on trying to block Ahmed's plan. Pérez de Cuéllar shared the view that Ahmed should be the SRSG but, having failed to persuade him to go to Phnom Penh, started looking for other candidates. His choice fell on two North Africans, Mohamed Sahnoun, an experienced Algerian diplomat who had held high office in the secretariats of both the OAU and the Arab League, and Mahmoud Mestiri, a former Foreign Minister of Tunisia. The ASEAN countries, led by Tommy Koh from Singapore, continued to lobby strongly in favour of Ahmed, and Pérez de Cuéllar eventually decided to leave this decision to Boutros-Ghali, who would have assumed office by the time UNTAC was deployed.

The signature ceremony, in the Kléber Conference Centre, was long and oddly anti-climactic. Given the horrors that had been perpetrated in Cambodia, some sign of jubilation at the restoration of peace seemed called for. A wordy ceremony conducted by diplomats in dark suits did not fit the bill. The agreements signed there gave the UN a larger role than it had had in Namibia. Three provisions in particular broke new ground. They all derived from the reluctance of the Khmer Rouge and their supporters, especially China, to accept that the government in Phnom Penh (the SOC) should continue to function as a government during the transitional period. Equally, the SOC and Vietnam would not accept the appointment of an all-party provisional government. Nor would China accept that Pol Pot and his accomplices be removed from the scene before the transitional period began. Did this mean that the UN itself should assume responsibility for the administration of Cambodia during the transitional period? During the negotiations Pérez de Cuéllar had rejected this as being beyond the Organization's capacity. He was right to do so, as has been demonstrated by the difficulties which, at the time of writing, the UN is encountering in administering East Timor and Kosovo, both of them smaller and less devastated territories than Cambodia was in 1992. If the UN could not do the job, some other means had to be found of ensuring that the country was administered in a way that did not give the administrators electoral advantage.

The first of the three provisions concerned the relations between the Supreme National Council and the head of UNTAC. Under the agreements the SNC delegated to the United Nations all powers necessary to ensure that they were implemented. The SNC would offer advice to UNTAC and UNTAC would comply with such advice provided that there was consensus in the SNC and that the advice was consistent with the objectives of the agreements, a point which would be determined by the Secretary-General's Special Representative, not the SNC. If there was no consensus, Sihanouk could decide what advice to offer and UNTAC would comply, provided, again, that the SRSG found the advice to be consistent with the agreements. If Sihanouk was, for whatever reason, unable to offer advice, 'the power of decision will transfer to the Secretary-General's Special Representative'. This provision gave the SRSG considerable power, if he chose to use it, in the event of dissent within the SNC.

The second innovation related to the 'existing administrative structures', by which was meant the SOC government in Phnom Penh and the administrations which the CGDK unconvincingly claimed to have set up in the small areas of Cambodia controlled by it. Under the agreements all structures which could directly influence the outcome of elections, and especially those concerned with foreign affairs, national defence, finance, public security and information, were to be 'placed under direct United Nations supervision or control'. In theory this too gave the SRSG considerable powers. In practice it gave him an exceptionally difficult task, given the impenetrability of both the Khmer language and the party and state structures in the Communist SOC. The Khmer Rouge were to complain repeatedly about UNTAC's failure to place the SOC government under 'direct supervision or control' and this was to be one of their excuses for refusing to demobilize and take part in the elections. Their complaints were justified, but the task given to UNTAC was an impossible one. Pérez de Cuéllar knew this. He had pressed throughout that the mandate given to the UN should be clear and practicable; but when peace was so close he did not feel that he could put the agreement at risk by insisting on the impracticability of 'direct supervision or control' of the SOC. This is a dilemma that Secretaries-General and their staff often face. Disasters can happen if the Secretariat is lax on such points. But in this case events proved that Pérez de Cuéllar was right to take the risk.

The third innovative provision was that UNTAC would be responsible for the 'organization and conduct' of the elections. This was different from Namibia where the UN's task had been to exercise supervision and control over an electoral process conducted by the South African Administrator-General. In Cambodia UNTAC itself was the electoral authority: it had to draft the electoral law, register political parties and voters, supervise the electoral campaign, provide the parties with access to the media, establish static and mobile polling stations, count the votes and declare the results. These tasks were to be carried out with considerable success, notwithstanding the Khmer Rouge's refusal to participate in the elections and, at one point, their apparent intention to disrupt them by violence.

When Boutros-Ghali became Secretary-General in 1992, his first decision on Cambodia was to appoint Yasushi Akashi as his Special Representative. Akashi, formerly a member of the Japanese diplomatic service, had been an Under-Secretary-General in the Secretariat since 1986, with responsibility first for public information and then for disarmament. The appointment provoked the usual speculation attributing some hidden motive to the Secretary-General. My own inclination, perhaps a naive one in such cases, was to accept the obvious explanation. In this case it was that Boutros-Ghali had decided to abolish Akashi's existing post as Under-Secretary-General for disarmament, knew that Japan, as the second largest contributor to the budget, must have at least one USG and wanted Japan to play a larger part in peacekeeping; so sending Akashi to Cambodia was an obvious move.

The Secretary-General submitted his detailed implementation plan to the Security Council in mid-February. The speed with which it was prepared was largely due to careful preparatory work by Ahmed during the long years of negotiation. His view of Cambodia as his *chasse gardée* had troubled me, because I did not enjoy being excluded from the planning of an operation for which I would eventually be responsible. But it made sense for Ahmed, given his hopes of running the operation from New York. I also had to confess that Ahmed's way of preparing an implementation plan was better than the agony we had been enduring for years in the Western Sahara Task Force.

At the end of February 1992 the Council established UNTAC and two weeks later Akashi and the Force Commander, Lieutenant-General

Sanderson of the Australian Army, arrived in Phnom Penh to assume their duties. The Supreme National Council began to meet regularly, notwithstanding a violent assault by supporters of the SOC on Khieu Samphan, the Khmer Rouge member of the council, on the day he arrived in Phnom Penh. Boutros-Ghali visited the mission in April and came back impressed by what he had seen. He did not include me in his party nor any member of my department. As mentioned earlier, his reluctance to allow senior officials to travel was to be a perennial problem during his Secretary-Generalship.

By the end of May, however, the operation was in serious trouble. For the Khmer Rouge, one of the most important provisions in the Paris Agreements was verification by UNTAC that all Vietnamese troops had been withdrawn from Cambodia. Vietnam stated formally that the withdrawal of its troops had already been completed in September 1989. The Khmer Rouge insisted that this was not the case; if all Vietnamese military personnel were not withdrawn, they would not proceed to phase two of the cease-fire (cantonment of each faction's armed forces and demobilization of at least 70 per cent of them). UNTAC was sure that no formed units of the Vietnamese Army remained in Cambodia but suspected, and later confirmed, that some Vietnamese staff officers were still working for the SOC armed forces.

Akashi, however, directly challenged the Khmer Rouge in the SNC by calling on 'the four parties, and the Party of Democratic Kampuchea in particular', to take twelve measures to show that they were ready for phase two. He then travelled with the Force Commander to the town of Pailin, close to the Thai border, which was the Khmer Rouge's capital and the centre of their illegal mining and logging operations. Akashi and his retinue were denied access to the town; the world saw on television the Special Representative of the Secretary-General of the United Nations being turned back at a Khmer Rouge checkpoint. At Akashi's request, Boutros-Ghali then wrote to Khieu Samphan seeking assurances that the Khmer Rouge would enable UNTAC to start phase two on 13 June. He received no such assurances; nor did Akashi at the next two meetings of the SNC. Boutros-Ghali informed the Security Council that this non-cooperation by the Khmer Rouge raised the question of whether phase two should be delayed. He had come to the conclusion, he said, that it was necessary to press on regardless; any further delay would jeopardize UNTAC's ability to hold the elections in April or May 1993.

A week after phase two was supposed to begin I made my first visit to Cambodia. When I arrived, Akashi was in Tokyo at a conference of donor countries which the Japanese had organized to obtain pledges of aid for the rehabilitation and reconstruction of Cambodia. The five-day visit was the usual mixture of briefings and visits to the field. The briefings were not cheering. No cantonment had taken place because the other three factions were not prepared to proceed unless the Khmer Rouge did so. Akashi was talking about the need to impose economic sanctions on the latter. Another area of concern was UNTAC's excessively military image. As a multifunctional mission of the new breed it had large and important civilian components covering human rights, police, civilian administration, elections, information and education, repatriation and rehabilitation. But the recruitment of civilians was behind schedule and some of the components were not yet very visible. There were also the usual (and justified) complaints about the inadequacy of the support provided by UN headquarters and a civilian-military dispute about logistics: the civilians wanted an integrated logistical service for the whole mission, while the military, who had most of the assets at this early stage, wanted to reserve them for the military component and leave the civilians to fend for themselves.

Underlying all these issues was another problem, which was hinted at but not stated openly until I had individual meetings with each of the civilian directors later in the visit. This was their unhappiness at the way Akashi was running the mission. Some of their misgivings coincided with those felt in New York, especially about his feud with the Khmer Rouge. But what bothered them most, they said, was that they were not being taken into his confidence. Policy cables exchanged with New York were not shared with them and there was almost no collective discussion of strategic issues. Such matters were reserved for Akashi's private office, to which he had recruited some very bright young people. There were also murmurings about the amount of time he devoted to briefing the media, especially the Japanese media. I defended him on the last point: having a Japanese as head of the UN's largest peacekeeping operation was helping to spread understanding of peacekeeping in Japan, where it had hitherto been viewed with some reserve. But I was worried by the other points and wondered how to raise them with Akashi on his return from Tokyo.

It was an interesting time to be visiting the field. The rains were about to begin and the Mekong was already rising more than a metre a week, forcing water back up one of its tributaries into the Tonle Sap, the great lake in the centre of the country. When the flood reached its peak, most of the country's flatlands would be inundated. As one could see from the helicopter, all human habitations were of necessity on hillocks in the flood-plain or on bunds along the waterways. The first outing was to a town called Kampong Thom to the north of the capital, where one of UNTAC's two Indonesian battalions was stationed. It had been the scene of serious cease-fire violations, lying as it does on a strategic highway running north-west to the Thai border and areas dominated by the

Khmer Rouge. The latter's representative on the local 'mixed military working group' was an apparatchik who looked twenty years old and whose only contribution to the discussion was to parrot the party line; I began to feel more sympathy for Akashi's impatience. Back in Phnom Penh I met Chilean and Uruguayan marines manning an as yet unused naval cantonment site on the Mekong and a German field hospital whose doctors insisted on admitting local patients as well as UN ones. Hippocrates would have been proud of them but the UN budget office was motivated by less lofty principles.

Another expedition was to Siem Reap at the northern end of the great lake. The battalion there was from Bangladesh and sappers from the Netherlands and New Zealand were running a training centre for de-miners. There was also a UNHCR reception centre for refugees return-ing from camps in Thailand. It was run by an Irish birdwatcher (who confirmed my impression that birds were extraordinarily few for a tropical country with abundant water; had they all been eaten during the Khmer Rouge years?). The refugees were invited to choose between three options: two hectares of land; or materials to build a house; or fifty US dollars and food for a year. Most were choosing the last and moving on into areas controlled by the Khmer Rouge, who had been the dom-inant presence in the camps in Thailand. There was time for a fleeting visit to the temples at Angkor Wat, before we left for Sihanoukville, the country's main port. The battalion was French but UN civilian police from Ghana and Ireland had taken control of the almost empty streets to ensure a clear passage for the visiting VIPs. From there we flew on to UNTAC's southernmost checkpoint on the Cambodian-Vietnamese border, whose task was to verify that no Vietnamese troops returned to Cambodia. It was commanded by a Russian lieutenant-colonel. We flew back to Phnom Penh as dusk fell, amazed by the ubiquitous craters left by the B-52s' carpet bombing of the border areas twenty years before.

As usual, these visits to the field cleared some of the gloom created by the briefings at headquarters. John Sanderson seemed to be an effective Force Commander and the many nationalities were working well together. I was also impressed by how well the UNTAC personnel were coping with their rudimentary living conditions and wished that it were thus in Angola.

Akashi returned from Tokyo, ebullient at the success of the recon-struction conference, where $880 million had been pledged, almost 50 per cent more than the Secretary-General had asked for. We spent the next morning together, initially at his meeting with his directors and then tête-à-tête. This gave me plenty of time to tell him what I thought of the mission. The meeting with the directors had confirmed that he was some-what reluctant to discuss strategic issues with them but he subsequently accepted my various comments, bridling only when I urged him to remain strictly impartial between the factions. 'How can you ask me to be impartial when three of the factions are cooperating with UNTAC and the fourth is not?'

This was a question I often heard from Special Representatives and Force Commanders. The best answer I could manage was: never turn a blind eye to a party's failure to respect an agreement that it has signed, for peacekeeping can succeed only if it is founded on a solid agreement between the parties; so confront a party immediately if it breaks the agreement; but bear in mind that it may genuinely feel that its behaviour is justified by things done or not done by you or another party; you should therefore be firm in explaining that its failure to cooperate is not justified by any action or inaction of others and will have to be reported to the Security Council unless it is put right very soon; but do this privately and without raising issues of 'face' which will make it more difficult for the party to mend its ways; do not draw unfavourable comparisons between it and the others; do not discriminate against it socially or in any other respect; if you do so, you will undermine its confidence in you as an impartial mediator; above all, do all you can to ensure that further negotiation remains possible; close no doors. This was not easy advice to follow, especially for those inclined to indignation, but it had to be followed if the mediator was to avoid being drawn into the conflict.

In a further report to the Security Council in mid-July the Secretary-General was able to report little progress. Three of the factions were cooperating well with UNTAC but the Khmer Rouge were not. Indeed they were now saying that they would resume cooperation only if the Phnom Penh government was dismantled; this would violate the Paris Agreements which required UNTAC to work with the 'existing administrative structures', UN-speak for the SOC government and the 'government' the three anti-SOC factions claimed to have established in territory controlled by them. In the view of the Americans the Khmer Rouge's plan was to hold on to the territory where they were already dominant, keep their forces intact and hope that a post-UNTAC government would be so corrupt and weak that they would be able to seize power again; there were indications also that some elements in the Khmer Rouge were considering military action against UNTAC; it should be cautious about operating in Khmer Rouge areas.

Between September and November further efforts were made, initially by Thailand and Japan and then by the Paris conference co-chairmen, to persuade the Khmer Rouge to come back into the implementation process. None succeeded. Meanwhile registration of voters for the elections had begun and was proceeding smoothly. In mid-November Boutros-Ghali again recommended to the Security Council that the UN should continue to implement the Paris Agreements as best it could, not-withstanding the Khmer Rouge's non-cooperation. At that time fighting had begun again in Angola after Savimbi rejected the results of the election there. I feared that the same fate would befall Cambodia, where almost no troops were being cantoned or demobilized and the Khmer Rouge were becoming increasingly aggressive in killing Vietnamese residents,* violating the cease-fire and harassing UN personnel. But the Security Council readily accepted the Secretary-General's recommendation and, contrary to his advice, 'called on those concerned' to take action to prevent the delivery of petroleum products to areas occupied by any party that was not complying with the Paris Agreements (i.e. the Khmer Rouge). A consequence of the decision to abandon the cantonment and demobilization provisions of the Paris Agreements was that we could revise the deployment of UNTAC's military component, whose main task now would be to protect the electoral process from disruption by the Khmer Rouge. This redeployment was completed by the end of the year.

Meanwhile Boutros-Ghali, who had advocated 'quiet diplomacy' in his report to the Council, continued to seek ways of persuading the Khmer Rouge to cooperate. He felt that he had to get across to them the message that the UN was not hostile to them and wanted them to remain engaged in the peace process. Who could deliver that message? A number of names were considered but the choice eventually fell on Rafee Ahmed, whom Boutros-Ghali had dispatched to Bangkok as head of the UN Economic and Social Commission for Asia and the Pacific after he had declined to be the SRSG in Phnom Penh. Though ostensibly acting in a personal capacity, he would seek the ASEAN countries' support for what he was doing. He had some interesting ideas about how to respond to the Khmer Rouge's not unreasonable complaint that UNTAC's inability to exercise effective control over 'the existing administrative structures' meant that the SOC had an unfair political advantage in the areas under its control, areas in which 90 per cent of the population lived. One idea was that the SNC should appoint Sihanouk immediately as head of state with executive authority, the appointment to be ratified by referendum at the time of the eventual elections; another was that a government of national reconciliation should be appointed and its composition adjusted later in the light of the election results. These would be departures from the Paris Agreements but they could be justified if they brought the Khmer Rouge back into the process. But would the SOC accept them? And would the Khmer Rouge?

---

* Almost all Vietnamese military personnel had been withdrawn from Cambodia, but almost 5 per cent of the country's population were Vietnamese, most of whom had lived there for generations.

Ahmed's mission did not prosper and at the beginning of 1993 the process looked in poor shape. On 3 January Sihanouk informed Akashi that he was withdrawing his cooperation from UNTAC. Two days later Sihanouk's son, Prince Norodom Ranariddh, who was now President of the FUNCINPEC party, told the Secretary-General that he was following his father's example in protest at UNTAC's weakness in failing to protect members of his party from murderous attacks which (though the Prince did not say so) came more from Hun Sen's party than the Khmer Rouge. Hun Sen himself wrote to the Secretary-General on the same day asking him to seek the intervention of the co-chairmen of the Paris conference and, if necessary, Security Council authority for enforcement action against the Khmer Rouge.

In a progress report to the Council, Boutros-Ghali expressed satisfaction with the success of voter registration and the return from Thailand and resettlement of a quarter of a million refugees (two-thirds of the total) but acknowledged that it had not been possible to create the neutral political environment needed for free and fair elections. He went on to endorse one idea which had emerged from Ahmed's efforts and had found favour with Sihanouk. This was that, instead of waiting for the constituent assembly to be elected in May and the new constitution to be approved some months thereafter, a presidential election, in which Sihanouk would be a candidate, should be held at the same time as the election of the constituent assembly. Boutros-Ghali and Ahmed thought that popular endorsement of Sihanouk as head of state would contribute to national reconciliation and stability during the possibly turbulent interval in which the assembly was drafting the new constitution. The purists amongst us said that this was a departure from the Paris Agreements and raised questions about what the basis of Sihanouk's power would be before the new constitution was adopted. But in this crisis, Boutros-Ghali was right to look for innovative ways forward.

I was due to visit Cambodia during the last week in January, before going on to a meeting of the SNC in Beijing, where Sihanouk was 'convalescing'. Boutros-Ghali told me to meet first with Ahmed and Akashi in Bangkok for a frank talk about how to re-engage the Khmer Rouge. All things considered, the meeting went well. Ahmed stated the case for patient diplomacy and floated some of the ideas he had already discussed with me. Akashi was sceptical (rightly, as it turned out) about our chances of getting the Khmer Rouge back into the process but did not object to our trying, provided that nothing was said or done that would enable them to say that the Secretariat in New York condoned their violations of the agreements. The three of us agreed that Sihanouk's enthusiasm for an early presidential election was probably helpful but that very careful thought was needed about what this would imply for UNTAC. After

Sihanouk had been democratically elected as an executive head of state, could the SRSG retain the power of final decision given to him in the Paris Agreements? If he did, would that not smack of neo-colonialism? At the same time, UNTAC had a mandate from the Security Council to achieve certain objectives, for instance on questions of human rights and the rule of law, which it could not simply transfer to the elected President. We also had to bear in mind that many in Cambodia did not want Sihanouk to recover the absolute powers he had enjoyed in the sixties.

The subsequent visit to Phnom Penh revealed, not unexpectedly alas, that UNTAC remained riven by the usual jealousies and that the civilian directors still felt that they were denied their due role in policy-making. A particularly awful battalion of untrained and drunken Bulgarians had been deployed in Phnom Penh where they had done so much damage to UNTAC's standing that they were being repatriated. But it was not all bad news. In the electoral component's computer centre a hundred handsome young Cambodians were entering the names of registered voters, pioneering a new Khmer keyboard which had been developed by UNTAC for the purpose; and the human rights component had made much progress, driven by its director's conviction that the election could not be free and fair unless the human rights environment was radically improved by election day. Also fascinating was a meeting of the Phnom Penh mixed military working group which had been convened to discuss major cease-fire violations resulting from a push by Hun Sen's forces along two roads leading to Pailin. The SOC and Khmer Rouge representatives joined battle; the other two factions said not a word. The Khmer Rouge officer also stated his faction's uncompromising rejection of the UNTAC military's new mandate to protect electoral activities.

There followed a good day in the field, with visits to Cambodia's second city, Battambang, and to an UNTAC position at a settlement called Sok Sann, close to the Thai border in an enclave inhabited by supporters of the small Buddhist faction, the KPNLF. The Khmer Rouge surrounded the enclave and in order to avoid possible small arms fire, the helicopter had to fly in high before making a precipitous descent into Sok Sann. The UNTAC position was manned by highly motivated Dutch marines who were using national funds to build a bridge, a school, a clinic and other philanthropic works. But they admitted that their understanding of what was going on locally was very limited; there seemed to be all sorts of deals between the KPNLF, the Khmer Rouge, the Thai military and civilian traders but they had learnt that enquiries about them met a wall of silence. We visited the local voter registration post, run by a bubbling UN volunteer from New Zealand and a police officer from Bangladesh. The young New Zealander was cock-a-hoop at having just registered a one-legged Khmer Rouge general, who had turned up on the pillion of a motorbike driven by one of his soldiers, in spite of his faction's refusal to allow people to leave its areas in order to register. We had passed them on the road, not realizing what a political aberration we were witnessing. As the helicopter lifted out of Sok Sann, a few rounds were fired in our direction, presumably by the Khmer Rouge, enabling me to add an exotic name to the list of parties which had fired at or near me during my service with the UN (hitherto they had all been from the Levant or the Balkans). Our last port of call was a Japanese engineering battalion. It was well-organized and lavishly equipped, but it was Japan's first military contribution to a UN peace-keeping operation and its personnel seemed overwhelmed by their responsibility for ensuring that it was a success.

The next day I flew with Akashi and his senior colleagues to Beijing for a day-long meeting of the SNC. It took place in Sihanouk's residence which had once, he said, been the French Legation. I had never met him before and started the day with some prejudice against him: during the last three difficult months he had been a recluse in Beijing, making unfair and damaging accusations against UNTAC, when his leadership as Chairman of the SNC was needed if we were to keep the process on track. This seemed irresponsible. But throughout that long day I was exposed to the full blast of his personality and charm and, like so many before, I succumbed. He can be infuriatingly unpredictable and intoler-ant of criticism; but he is also intelligent, generous, witty and warm (when he wants to be) and a more serious person than his squeaky voice, nervous giggles and writhing body movements lead one to expect.

There were four moments of drama during the day. The first came when Sihanouk announced his decision that the presidential elections should come after the constituent assembly had adopted the new consti-tution. This was an abrupt reversal of the position he had been vigor-ously advocating for weeks and caused consternation to the French, who, for reasons I did not understand, had been strongly supporting his previ-ous position. It also upset the Cambodian parties, especially FUNCIN-PEC, led by his son Ranariddh. Sihanouk said that his change of mind was partly due to a message from the Australian Foreign Minister, Gareth Evans, who, like us, was worried about giving the president executive powers before there was a new constitution.

The second drama came when a UNESCO official asked the SNC to approve, there and then, ten pages of legislation 'to save Angkor Wat'. This triggered from Sihanouk fifteen minutes of passionate oratory about Cambodia's heritage. But the other members of the Council said that they needed time to study the bill, which they had not previously seen. The meeting adjourned. When it reconvened, three of the factions were ready to approve the legislation but Khieu Samphan of the Khmer Rouge declined to do so. Sihanouk raged and cajoled and pleaded but Khieu remained firm. As the SNC's decisions had to be unanimous, Sihanouk was obliged to accept defeat. The third drama followed immediately: a representative of his son's party reopened the question of the timing of the presidential elections and begged Sihanouk to reconsider and not betray his people. This provoked a blazing response from Sihanouk which lasted almost half an hour, mostly in English: 'I have a solid and bad reputation for being a changing and mercurial prince, but this time I will not change my mind . . . How dare you accuse me of betraying my people? My patriotism is stronger than yours.'

The fourth drama was one I provoked. At the end of the meeting I spoke frankly about the factions' failure to cooperate with UNTAC. It was not, I said, a foreign presence imposed on Cambodia but something which the Cambodians themselves had asked for and to which they had promised their cooperation. I was not speaking only of the Khmer Rouge; the SOC had also violated the rules. Sihanouk looked glum and when I had finished he apologized for his own recent criticism of UNTAC. The American Ambassador then spoke about the harassment of UNTAC personnel, whereupon Sihanouk proposed that the SNC issue a statement condemning all acts of violence against UNTAC. Everyone agreed except Khieu Samphan; for the second time Sihanouk was impotent and vented his rage with a most unparliamentary denunciation of Khieu personally. For me, this was an own goal; during the recess I had spent some time trying to reassure Khieu that the Secretary-General wanted to deal even-handedly with all the factions and recognized that the SOC was also a sinner; but now, as a result of my intervention, he was being humiliated by Sihanouk.

One other memory of this event: during Sihanouk's diatribe against the young man from FUNCINPEC who had reopened the issue of the presidential elections, flunkeys entered the room carrying trays of chicken sandwiches and apple pies from the McDonald's round the corner: 'my favourite food', said Sihanouk, 'even though Monique [his wife] does not approve'.

This was my last involvement with peacekeeping in Cambodia. In May 1993 the elections were held without serious disruption by the Khmer Rouge and with a turnout of almost 90 per cent of registered voters. This proved that Boutros-Ghali, and before him Pérez de Cuéllar, had been right to take the risks they did. FUNCINPEC won 45.5 per cent of the votes, with 38.2 per cent for Hun Sen's Cambodian People's Party. Sihanouk appointed an interim joint administration with Ranariddh and

Hun Sen as co-chairmen. The constitution was promulgated on 24 September 1993. Cambodia became a kingdom with Sihanouk as its king. His first act was to appoint Ranariddh and Hun Sen as respectively First and Second Prime Ministers. The constituent assembly became the legislative assembly. UNTAC's mandate was done.

In assessments of the UN's post-Cold War peace operations, Cambodia is not usually placed in the top division of acclaimed successes such as Namibia, Mozambique, El Salvador and Guatemala; nor is it in the bottom division of admitted failures like Angola, Somalia, Bosnia and Rwanda. The Khmer Rouge insurgency continued and there have been some violent and unconstitutional episodes in the country's political life, in which Hun Sen has consolidated his party's power at the expense of Ranariddh's FUNCINPEC. The injection into Cambodia's traumatized and impoverished society of almost twenty thousand foreign personnel, most of them unaccompanied males and extremely well-paid by local standards, had a variety of social consequences, especially in the cities, and these did not help to heal the wounds created by two decades of civil war. This is a worrying and under-studied aspect of UN peacekeeping.

But it would be neither correct, nor fair to those who worked so hard to bring about the Paris Agreements and put them into effect, to allow these less fortunate consequences to detract from what was in fact a success for the international community. Cambodia may still be a corrupt and violent society. But there is no longer a civil war there fuelled by major powers; there are no longer a third of a million refugees in Thailand; international and national institutions for the promotion of human rights function in Phnom Penh; procedures are being defined, admittedly with great difficulty, to bring to justice those responsible for the crimes of the Pol Pot years; elections take place. The success is not yet total, but it is a success.

One of the lessons to be learnt from the international community's intervention in Cambodia is that peacemaking and peacekeeping are not enough. There is also a need for peacebuilding – that is, international action to help a society torn by civil war to identify the root causes of the conflict that has just ended and to devise means of eradicating those root causes. This takes time, for the roots often turn out to be deep. It requires a more profound understanding of the society than peacemakers or peacekeepers usually have. It is very sensitive, because it touches on issues deep within the domestic jurisdiction of the state concerned. It will not succeed if it is seen as something which outsiders are trying to impose; it must be a process of which the locals feel that they have ownership. For all these reasons, it is not a task which foreign governments or inter-governmental organizations are well-qualified to perform. The lead has to be taken by advocates of peace within the society itself, with discreetly provided help from well-intentioned outsiders. The outsiders should normally be international non-governmental organizations rather than foreign governments, though the latter can be a source of funding for the former.

New Threats

15

Collapsing States

In the situations described in the preceding chapters, it was the end of the Cold War which made it possible for the Security Council to take action to resolve regional conflicts, in most cases because neither East nor West judged that continuation of the conflict would serve its interests. In one case, however, the Cold War connection was less direct: the Iran–Iraq war was not a proxy conflict of the Cold War; its resolution would be of positive benefit to both superpowers; their emerging harmony enabled the Security Council to take effective action to end the war.

These developments generated enormous optimism in the late eighties. But the successes also bred over-confidence, which caused the United Nations – member states and Secretariat alike – to make mistakes in a number of new peacemaking and peacekeeping initiatives. The level of risk and the prospects of success were not thoroughly analysed; mandates were not clearly defined; the necessary resources were not provided; and there was too much reliance on things being all right on the night. Moreover, the backlog of regional conflicts that had accumulated during the Cold War commanded so much attention that we were slow to spot the emergence of two new categories of conflict.

The first of these was internal conflicts in collapsing states, that is countries where, for one reason or another, the institutions of state became incapable of governing and were challenged by warlords or other illegitimate institutions. The second category was conflicts arising from the unplanned break-up of two Communist-ruled federations – the Socialist Federal Republic of Yugoslavia and the Union of Soviet Socialist Republics. And in 1990 the United Nations was caught unawares by the reappearance of an ancient category of conflict – the forceful annexation of one state by another.

Few of the conflicts in collapsing states emerged clearly during my seven years as Under-Secretary-General for peacekeeping but they became a major preoccupation during the subsequent four years when I headed the political department. There were, however, two in which I was briefly involved during the peacekeeping period – Haiti and Somalia.

HAITI

The internal conflict in Haiti had no international dimensions other than US anxiety that conflict there could generate an uncontrollable flow of refugees. The problem it presented, and still presents, to the international community is humanitarian rather than political or strategic. Concern at the plight of its people and a wish for democracy to thrive in the Western Hemisphere are the factors that have motivated international intervention in Haiti, not advancement of the political or economic interests of the intervening powers. During the 1990s Haiti was a laboratory in which the international community experimented with a number of techniques for dealing with collapsing states in the post-Cold War world. The experiments included joint action by the UN and a regional organization, the observation of elections in an independent state, the deployment of a field mission to monitor respect for human rights, the use of force to restore an elected ruler to power, the recruitment and training of a new police force and the use of economic sanctions to coerce a small political élite into changing its policies. Several of these experiments failed, especially the sanctions, which had little political effect but increased human suffering.

Haiti was not always poor. In the eighteenth century it had been a jewel in the French imperial crown. The indigenous population was exterminated, slaves were imported from Africa (constituting 90 per cent of the population in 1750) and the French colonists lived like kings – so much so that the slaves rebelled and in 1804 made Haiti the first country in Latin America, and the second in the Western Hemisphere, to declare itself an independent state. During the twentieth century it experienced nineteen years of military occupation by the United States (1915–34) and twenty-nine years of autocratic rule by François 'Papa Doc' Duvalier and his son Jean-Claude 'Baby Doc' (1957–86). As described in Graham Greene's *The Comedians*, their regime was maintained by the *tontons macoute*, a violent paramilitary force, and at the local level by military prefects, known as *chefs seksyon*. After Baby Doc was forced into exile in 1986, the country endured a series of military coups. During the Duvalier years the economy and the environment had deteriorated radically; by the late eighties almost 80 per cent of the population were illiterate and lived in abject poverty.

In 1989, Canada, France, the United States and Venezuela decided to cooperate in an attempt to establish democracy in Haiti. Prompted by them, Pérez de Cuéllar sent Jean-Claude Aimé, who was by now his Executive Assistant and is himself a Haitian, on an exploratory visit to Port-au-Prince. In June 1990, the president of a precarious interim government asked the United Nations, and the Organization of

American States, to support the holding of a democratic election. The support was to take three forms: the provision of technical assistance to the electoral authorities; observation of the election and the campaign that would precede it; and the deployment of 'specialized observers' who would help the *Forces Armées d'Haiti* (FADH) to carry out their responsibility for ensuring the security of polling stations and voters. Pérez de Cuéllar appointed a Brazilian diplomat, João de Medicis, to be his Personal Representative for Haiti and to head an electoral mission which, if approved by the member states, would be known as the United Nations Observer Group for the Verification of the Elections in Haiti (ONUVEH).

But how was ONUVEH to be established? The Interim President had stated explicitly that Haiti did not want a peacekeeping operation, but she had also asked that the mission include 'specialized . . . observers . . . with solid experience in the public order field'. Normally this would mean uniformed personnel whose deployment would have to be approved by the Security Council. But the Latin Americans, sensitive about sovereignty, did not want the Council to be involved. Nor did the five permanent members of the Council because they pay a lower share of the costs if a mission is established by the General Assembly. On the other hand, deployment could begin sooner if the Security Council was the authorizing body. This argument rumbled on for some weeks, costing us valuable time. In the end, it was agreed that the General Assembly would establish the operation but the Security Council would be kept informed, as uniformed personnel were going to be deployed. It was also agreed, to my satisfaction, that in New York responsibility for ONUVEH would be entrusted to my department – a modest release from the peacekeeping cage in which I had been imprisoned for the previous two years. The General Assembly acted on 10 October; the first round of elections was to be held on 16 December. There was not much time.

João de Medicis turned out to be a calm, wise and effective head of mission. He had served in the Brazilian Embassy in Port-au-Prince, spoke some Creole and enjoyed the confidence of the Haitian political class. I made a brief visit to the mission in early December 1990. Poverty, dilapidation and lurking violence were everywhere. From the air it was evident that most of Haiti's trees had been cut down for firewood; great swathes of soil were being washed from the denuded hills into the Caribbean. As usual, ONUVEH's headquarters were plagued by logistical shortages and civilian-military jealousies. The military personnel, or 'security observers' as they were called, complained that the civilians, who had been deployed first, had grabbed the few vehicles and other equipment that were available. The Chief Security Officer, a Canadian brigadier called Gaby Zuliani, put it bluntly: '*l'ennemi est l'administration de l'ONU'*. For their part, some civilians characterized the military as drunken cowboys who did not know what they were there for (partly, it has to be said, because of the government's lack of precision about what it wanted the 'security observers' to do). Another issue was the army. The security observers had a frosty reception on arrival but in most places succeeded in establishing a good working relationship with their Haitian counterparts. The civilians, on the other hand, preferred to keep their distance, seeing the army as a potential threat to a democratic election. This was not unreasonable, given the frequency with which the FADH had disrupted elections in the past, but it did not contribute to civilian-military harmony in ONUVEH.

There were two principal contenders in the presidential election. One was Jean-Bertrand Aristide, a populist priest in his late thirties whose political activities had led to his dismissal from the Salesian Order two years before. The other was Marc Bazin, a politician who had been in exile for much of the Duvalier period, working for the World Bank and the World Health Organization. After Baby Doc was forced into exile, Bazin returned and founded a political party. His campaign was the better organized of the two but he lacked Aristide's oratorical skills and his appeal to the impoverished young. The election was not only for the president; voters were also to elect the members of both chambers of the legislature and various local councils. This required a complicated ballot paper for a largely illiterate electorate. Another worry was the appalling condition of the roads and the scarcity of telecommunications in the rural areas. There were to be 14,000 polling stations; how could the ballot papers be distributed and recovered promptly and securely?

A trip was made to the town of Hinche in the interior. As the crow flies, Hinche is only 75 kilometres from the capital but to go there by road would have involved a journey of 180 kilometres and the fording of three rivers; it would have taken seven hours. So de Medicis and I were to go by light aircraft. At the airport there was a Cessna but no pilot. A stand-in was sought. Waits at airports usually provide opportunities for bird-watching, but at Port-au-Prince there was nothing. A pilot was eventually found; he had evidently had a good time the previous evening. The flight revealed why so many polling stations were required. The rural population lived in hundreds of tiny roadless settlements and it was difficult to see how an efficient election could be carried out, let alone 'verified' by a handful of international observers. When we arrived over Hinche, no airfield could be seen. The pilot asked for my binoculars, found what he was looking for, made a low pass over a field of cows, turned and made a landing amongst the scattered beasts. We spent the day with the ONUVEH team and the Haitian authorities with whom they were working. As so often, this visit to the field corrected the gloomy impressions created by the briefings at HQ. Harmony prevailed in the ONUVEH team under the tactful leadership of a Ugandan civilian, Francis Okelo, and they seemed to have good relations with the OAS observers too. The Haitians also appeared to be working well together; if there was a threat to the election, it would not be from the army but from former *tontons macoute* and possibly from excessive enthusiasm among the young supporters of Father Aristide.

In a report to Pérez de Cuéllar on the eve of the elections, de Medicis did not disguise the difficulties of organizing a free and fair election in a country which had never before experienced such an event and where 'violence has always been the means of settling conflicts and choosing leaders'; he acknowledged that irregularities had taken place during the campaign and that the death of seven people nine days before in a grenade attack on a crowd dispersing from an election rally had 'darkened the prevailing mood'; but he concluded that ONUVEH's presence had helped to create a climate of confidence and that 'the future, like the present, is in the hands of the Haitian people'.

The first round of elections went extraordinarily well. About two-thirds of the electorate voted and there were no serious incidents. ONUVEH personnel were present, for at least part of the day, at about 10 per cent of the polling stations. As expected, there was a good deal of logistical confusion but no major irregularities were observed. Jointly with the OAS observer mission, ONUVEH did a 'quick count', a technique which had been pioneered in Nicaragua ten months before. At an early point in the vote-counting process, a small but representative sample of results is used to make a projection of what the overall results will be. This provides a check against fraud in the later stages of the counting. It also enables international monitors to give the protagonists advance notice of the results. In Nicaragua, for instance, the UN and the OAS had been able to warn the Sandinista government that they were almost certainly going to lose the election. The incumbents were thus put discreetly on notice that the international community knew how the electorate had voted and would detect any subsequent tampering with the results.

The accuracy of the quick count depends on how representative the sample is. In Haiti the counting of votes was to be done in the 14,000 polling stations. One hundred and fifty of these were chosen at random; in a few cases substitution was necessary because the station chosen was so inaccessible that its results would not be available in time for the quick count. The sample turned out to be remarkably representative. Less than six hours after polling ended, the model indicated that Aristide would win 66.4 per cent of the votes for president and Bazin would be the runner-up with 13.2 per cent. The actual results, announced twenty-six days later, were 67.5 per cent for Aristide and 14.2 per cent for Bazin. No second round would therefore be necessary for the presidential election but the voters would have to go to the polls again on 20 January 1991 to complete the parliamentary and local elections. The success of the first round in a country which had never before enjoyed a truly democratic election was a triumph for the United Nations. But, as I asked my diary on the evening of 16 December, 'can Aristide govern?'

'Will he be allowed to govern?' would have been a more appropriate question. Early on 6 January 1991, two weeks before the second round, when I was at Heathrow en route to Cyprus and Lebanon, I learnt that there had been a *coup d'état* in Haiti by Roger Lafontant, an unrepentant Duvalierist who had been chief of the *tontons macoute* under Baby Doc, but by the time I reached Nicosia the news was that the coup had been foiled. Nine months later an army officer called Michel François succeeded where Lafontant had failed. Aristide was forced into exile and General Raoul Cédras, the Commander of the FADH, assumed the functions of head of state. The coup was condemned by the OAS, which called upon its members to impose economic sanctions, and by the UN. Bazin became Prime Minister but his government received no international recognition. Both Pérez de Cuéllar and, later, Boutros-Ghali expressed support for the efforts of the OAS to restore legitimate government and the UN was represented in an OAS mission which went to Haiti in August 1992. Later that year international attention turned to the violations of human rights that were taking place under the military regime. In December Boutros-Ghali appointed Dante Caputo, former Foreign Minister of Argentina, as his Special Envoy for Haiti and a month later the Secretary-General of the OAS did the same. This was the first time that the Secretary-General of the United Nations and the Secretary-General of a regional organization had made a joint appointment. It reflected Boutros-Ghali's interest in regional organizations, which had been the topic of his doctoral thesis at the Sorbonne.

In January 1993, Aristide requested the UN and the OAS to deploy a joint civilian mission to monitor respect for human rights and promote dialogue between the parties as a step towards solving the political crisis created by the coup. Surprisingly, the military and Bazin agreed to both proposals. Caputo quickly obtained the regime's agreement to the terms of reference of the 'International Civilian Mission in Haiti' (MICIVIH) and an advance party was sent to Haiti. The mission would contain no military personnel and, formally speaking, was outside the remit of the peacekeeping department in the Secretariat. It was not until I moved to the Department of Political Affairs in March 1993 that I again became directly involved in international efforts to restore democracy and good governance to Haiti. They have not succeeded yet.

SOMALIA

Unlike Haiti, Somalia is a large country, strategically located in a politically important part of the world. It had been much affected by the Cold
War, first as a Soviet asset used against the Westward-leaning regime of
Emperor Haile Selassie in Ethiopia and then as a Western asset against
the Marxist government which overthrew the Emperor in 1975. In both
modes it had been ruled by a military dictator, General Siyad Barre. He
was overthrown in early 1991 by a coalition led by another general,
Mohammed Farah Aidid, who had been Siyad Barre's chief of staff when
he seized power, was subsequently imprisoned by him and was then
appointed Somalia's ambassador to India. After Siyad Barre's overthrow,
Ali Mahdi Mohammed was appointed interim president by Aidid's party,
the United Somali Congress (USC). A businessman, he was, like Aidid, a
member of the powerful Hawiye clan which controlled the USC and the
capital city, Mogadishu.

By mid-1991, Aidid and Ali Mahdi had fallen out and in November of
that year heavy fighting broke out in Mogadishu, leading to effective partition of the capital. In addition to the militias of the two protagonists,
there were a number of other armed groups controlled by lesser clan
leaders and entrepreneurs. A similar situation prevailed in the country's
second city, the port of Kismayo. Troops loyal to Siyad Barre were establishing an enclave in the south-west. In the north, a secessionist movement was asserting itself in the part of the country which had been the
British protectorate of Somaliland. The country was thus without an
effective government and undisciplined armed groups proliferated.
Because of superpower rivalry during the Cold War this part of Africa
was awash with arms. The battles were not fought with small arms; even
quite small gangs had 'technicals', civilian vehicles mounted with heavy
machine guns and anti-tank guns.*

This political crisis and breakdown of law and order coincided with a
prolonged drought. The country faced starvation. By 1992, 300,000 were
estimated to have died and a quarter of the population had been displaced from their homes. International agencies and NGOs endeavoured
to distribute relief supplies but these had become assets which the armed
groups seized for their own use. Anarchy reigned and the perils faced by
humanitarian workers became ever more severe. In the closing days of

---

* The term 'technical' was invented by non-governmental organizations engaged in
relief work. When heavy fighting began in Mogadishu, some of them hired the services
of armed groups to protect their convoys of humanitarian supplies. The question arose
of how to describe this expenditure in their accounts. The answer: 'technical expenses'.

his Secretary-Generalship, Pérez de Cuéllar informed the President of the Security Council that, with the concurrence of his successor, he had decided to launch an initiative for the restoration of peace. Boutros-Ghali had been much involved with Somalia when he was in charge of Egypt's policy in Africa. He had no illusions about the magnitude of the task the UN would be taking on, but he was determined to correct what he saw as neglect of Africa in the UN's peacemaking and peacekeeping priorities. This was not an entirely accurate perception, given the efforts already made in Namibia, currently under way in Angola and Western Sahara and soon to be launched in Mozambique, but it was a perception that would govern his thinking throughout his mandate. And right at the beginning it caused him to score an own goal by criticizing the Western members of the Security Council for their preoccupation with 'the rich man's war' in the former Yugoslavia and their indifference to far greater suffering in Somalia.

So James Jonah, who had recently succeeded Abby Farah (himself a Somali from Somaliland) as Under-Secretary-General for Special Political Questions, was sent to Somalia to explore what could be done by the United Nations to restore peace and to support humanitarian operations. He found that while everyone wanted the UN to assist national reconciliation, the protagonists were divided on the military issues. Ali Mahdi wanted a cease-fire; Aidid did not. The Security Council imposed an arms embargo and asked the Secretary-General to continue his efforts to negotiate a cease-fire. Delegations of the two main parties came to New York in February 1992. Both agreed on a cease-fire, which was signed in Mogadishu on 3 March, but Ali Mahdi wanted a full-scale peacekeeping force to disarm civilians and protect humanitarian operations, whereas Aidid would accept only unarmed personnel, without uniforms, to monitor the cease-fire.

A month later, Boutros-Ghali decided that Aidid had moved far enough for him to recommend the establishment of a peacekeeping operation (UNOSOM). It would consist of fifty military observers to monitor the cease-fire in Mogadishu and an infantry battalion to provide security for UN relief convoys. I was not at all happy with this: Aidid's consent had not been expressly stated and it was proposed that the battalion should be accommodated in a ship. This seemed likely to serve the interests of any faction which wanted to prevent the troops coming ashore to carry out their duties. But I was not able to prevail over the three Africans – Boutros-Ghali, Jonah and Annan – who were determined that this operation should go ahead. The Council, however, also doubted the viability of the infantry battalion and authorized only the deployment of the UN military observers and the appointment of a Special Representative. Boutros-Ghali chose Mohamed Sahnoun, the

Algerian diplomat whom Pérez de Cuéllar had considered the previous year for the post of Special Representative in Cambodia. Two months later, Aidid's consent to the military observers was finally obtained.

As soon as they began to arrive, however, Aidid demanded that their deployment be suspended because an aircraft chartered by the UN World Food Programme had brought from Nairobi a consignment of Somali currency for delivery to Ali Mahdi. Sahnoun persuaded Aidid to change his mind. It was not until August that the Secretary-General was able to inform the Council that consent had been obtained for the deployment of the infantry battalion. Meanwhile he had proposed that a UN presence should be established throughout Somalia based in four operational zones in each of which there would be a consolidated programme of humanitarian relief, cease-fire monitoring, disarmament and demobilization, and national reconciliation. There would be a UN infantry battalion in each zone. All these things needed to be done and consolidated programmes made good sense. But the Secretary-General's thinking was running way ahead of what the factions would agree to and the resources he proposed were insufficient to do the job. But again I found myself confronting a steamroller that would not be stopped.

Sahnoun too was now out of step with Boutros-Ghali and Jonah. He saw his role as being to engage the faction leaders in discussions that would lead to the negotiation of a political settlement – under UN auspices, it was hoped. While I wanted to delay military deployment out of fear that Aidid had not given his full consent, Sahnoun was concerned that all the talk of a military role for the UN was complicating his efforts to win Aidid's confidence and was exacerbating tensions between Aidid and Ali Mahdi. As a result, Sahnoun tended to distance himself from the UN operation, opposed the deployment of the infantry battalion and sided with the humanitarian agencies. The latter had by now worked out their own security arrangements by engaging the services of various of the armed groups and thought that any involvement with the UN military would aggravate their already difficult relations with Aidid. The crunch came in late October when Brigadier-General Imtiaz Shaheen, the commander of UNOSOM, let slip in a meeting with Boutros-Ghali that Sahnoun was in the Seychelles discussing with a group of Somali intellectuals how a peace process could be started. Boutros-Ghali sent Sahnoun a reprimand for absenting himself from his duty station without approval and criticized him for seeking close relations with warlords who were no better than criminals. Sahnoun resigned. He was replaced by Ismat Kittani, a wise and cautious Iraqi of Kurdish origin who had alternated between the Iraqi diplomatic service and the UN Secretariat for forty years.

Boutros-Ghali's anger at the wickedness of the warlords was justified.

But the wickedness was the symptom of a sickness for which there were only two cures: either we would have to overthrow them by force (which was not a viable option) or we would have to mediate a political settlement which would either remove them from office or oblige them to mend their ways. Perhaps Boutros-Ghali's long experience of Somalia convinced him that a political settlement was not possible. But he had recommended to the Security Council that the UN should try to bring one about and that required his Special Representative to establish good working relations with the faction leaders, however wicked they were. As we were being reminded in Yugoslavia at the time, peacemakers must eat with long spoons, for they are obliged to sup with many devils.

Meanwhile Boutros-Ghali reported to the Security Council in late November that the situation in Mogadishu had become intolerable. Aidid had banned the UNOSOM battalion from the streets of the city, and though it had managed to retain control of the airport, it regularly came under fire from Aidid's forces. Ali Mahdi's forces shot at ships approaching the port in the hope that this would cause UNOSOM to seize the port from the sub-clans that controlled it. Only a trickle of humanitarian supplies was reaching the needy. It was necessary to review the UN operation; perhaps a move to enforcement action was necessary. The Council agreed and asked Boutros-Ghali for specific recommendations. The same day, Lawrence Eagleburger, the acting Secretary of State in Washington, told him that if the Council decided to authorize the use of force to ensure the delivery of humanitarian supplies, the United States would be ready to take the lead in organizing and commanding a multinational force like the 'Desert Storm' coalition which had liberated Kuwait the year before.

The Secretary-General presented the Council with five options: withdrawal of military protection; continuing the existing operation; a show of force in Mogadishu to deter the factions from refusing to cooperate with UNOSOM; a country-wide enforcement operation undertaken by a group of member states authorized by the Council to do so; or a country-wide enforcement operation under UN command and control. He recommended the fourth option; the force's tasks would be to protect humanitarian operations, disarm the irregular armed groups and bring under international control the heavy weapons of the organized factions. Once those objectives had been achieved, the enforcement operation would be replaced by a reinforced UN peacekeeping operation, which would be known as UNOSOM II. The Council agreed to the fourth option and the Americans immediately began to assemble the force, which they called the Unified Task Force (UNITAF). The Security Council resolution defined its mandate as being to 'help create a secure environment for the delivery of humanitarian aid'. The resolution made no mention of the disarming of irregulars or international control of the factions' heavy weapons. Nor did it state specifically that the multi-national force would be deployed throughout Somalia.

These matters immediately became a bone of contention between Boutros-Ghali and the Americans. He wrote to President Bush, who was in the last weeks of his presidency, to say that the transition from UNITAF to UNOSOM II would have to be dependent on, first, disarmament of the gangs and control of the factions' heavy weapons and, secondly, extension of UNITAF's authority over the whole country. But the American military steadfastly refused, in public and in private, to accept these tasks; the incoming Clinton Administration made no attempt to persuade them to do so.

UNITAF arrived in Mogadishu on 9 December 1992 and encountered no opposition. Within the limited mandate permitted by the Americans, it was a great success: it had overwhelming military superiority (with a maximum deployment of 37,000 troops, though in only 40 per cent of the country); it displayed the political will to use that superiority, if necessary; and it was impartial, using force against any person who threatened humanitarian operations, irrespective of the faction or gang to which that person belonged. The fact that UNITAF had no mandate other than the protection of humanitarian operations reinforced the perception that it was truly impartial and thus enhanced its ability to carry out its limited task. In that respect it set a standard for future operations deployed for such purposes. But its refusal to disarm the gangs or take control of the factions' heavy weapons meant that the weaker UNOSOM II, which would replace it five months later, was doomed to fail.

16

Iraq vs. Kuwait

Invasion and annexation of one state by another was an international practice that had gone out of fashion since the end of the Second World War. During the Cold War, each of the two superpowers occasionally invaded an independent state but never with the purpose of annexing it. Invasion for the purpose of reunification was attempted unsuccessfully in Korea but succeeded in Vietnam; and Israel annexed some Jordanian and Syrian territory after the 1967 war in the Middle East. But Iraq's invasion of Kuwait on 2 August 1990 was the first time since the Second World War that one country had invaded another with the purpose of annexing it and extinguishing its sovereignty and independence.

I was on holiday with my family in Suffolk at the time. The news did not interrupt the holiday; the action required from the United Nations would be peacemaking, not peacekeeping, and at that time I no longer had any part in peacemaking. But I worried about the security of UNIIMOG, the UN military observer group on the front line between Iran and Iraq, when, in the usual knee-jerk way, the Security Council imposed sanctions on Iraq.

The news did, however, revive memories of an earlier Kuwait crisis. I had been a novice diplomat in Kuwait in June 1961 when a previous Iraqi dictator, Abdul Karim Qasim, threatened hostile action against the newly independent State of Kuwait. Whether the threats were real is still unclear. But Britain's reaction was rapid – some would later say rashly so, given the strength of the forces that Qasim could, in theory, unleash against British troops newly arrived from temperate climates at the height of the Kuwaiti summer. Four days after the first threat, the Political Agent (as the British representative in Kuwait was still called) received instructions to persuade the Amir of Kuwait to ask for British military intervention. The instructions were successfully carried out the next day and by the evening of the following day Britain had deployed 600 marines, a squadron of tanks, three squadrons of fighter aircraft and two frigates in Kuwait and its territorial waters. The next day brought a battalion of the Parachute Regiment and advance units from an infantry brigade which would be flown in from Kenya. At that time Britain was still the superpower in the Persian Gulf and had forces in Bahrain and Aden. But even allowing for that, the deployment in Kuwait was an astonishingly rapid reaction by the standards of today.

Three decades later the response to an actual invasion was very much slower. On 29 November 1990, the Security Council adopted SCR 678 which authorized the use of 'all necessary means' (UN-speak for 'force') by 'Member States cooperating with the Government of Kuwait' (UN-speak for the multinational coalition led by the United States) to compel Iraq to comply with SCR 660 (UN-speak for withdraw its forces from Kuwait) if it had not done so by 15 January 1991. As that date approached, there was growing concern, both in New York and in the field, about the security of UN civilian and military staff not only in Iraq but elsewhere in the Middle East, especially Israel and the Arab territories occupied by Israel. But dining with six UN colleagues in West Beirut on 8 January 1991, I asked who thought there would be a war before the end of the month; only Lars-Eric Wahlgren, commander of UNIFIL, the UN force in southern Lebanon, and I thought there would be. Pérez de Cuéllar, sharing our view, decreed the mandatory 'relocation' (UN-speak again) of all UN dependants and non-essential staff from Israel and the Occupied Palestinian Territories. Later, in Damascus, I heard the BBC report the Red Army's seizure of the radio and TV station in the capital of Lithuania and had a horrid vision of a repetition of 1956 – a Western military adventure in the Middle East coinciding with the assertion of Moscow's military might in Europe. On 16 January, I arrived home in New York just as the first air raids hit Baghdad, covered live by CNN. My wife wept; I shared her distress, but felt excitement too.

At that time, my responsibilities were still confined to peacekeeping and I had accepted, without enthusiasm, that I would have no part to play in Pérez de Cuéllar's courageous efforts to forestall the war. But I was angered to learn from Aimé that since August he had, on Pérez de Cuéllar's instructions, been discussing a possible peacekeeping operation with the US Ambassador to the UN, Tom Pickering, and, it later turned out, with the Nordic countries. Once the war started Pérez de Cuéllar began speaking publicly about a peacekeeping role for the UN after the hostilities were over. This generated much interest in the media who sought clarification from me; it was difficult to deal with their inquiries without seeming to be out of the loop or disloyal to my boss or both.

Meanwhile, the start of Iraqi missile attacks on Israel caused panic amongst the civilian staff who remained in UNTSO, the military observer group based in Jerusalem, and in UNIFIL, almost all of whom lived in Nahariya, a town in northern Israel. I had to speak sternly to a couple of the senior civilians (whose behaviour the Chief of Staff of UNTSO, Hans Christensen, described as 'disgusting') and remind them of their duty to set an example to the others. Behrooz Sadry, the Director of Field Operations Division, also favoured the early return of the Field Service Officers in UNTSO and UNIFIL who had been 'relocated' to Cyprus and arranged for them to receive danger money. Dayal, Pérez de Cuéllar's Chef de Cabinet, who had hitherto taken the side of the panicking civilians, in both Iraq and the Levant, finally accepted that peacekeeping operations are a special case; they are by definition deployed in areas of potential conflict and their staff have to stay as long as possible at their duty stations if the conflict becomes actual.

In mid-February 1991, before the land war had begun, the Norwegian Defence Minister, Johan Jörgen Holst, visited New York to discuss a possible peacekeeping operation between Iraq and Kuwait. Pérez de Cuéllar painted on a broad canvas: peacekeeping, return of refugees, reconstruction (including Iran), regional security arrangements, arms control and, especially, elimination of any weapons of mass destruction developed by Iraq.* Some of this agenda echoed the request to the Secretary-General in SCR 598 that he 'examine, in consultation with Iran and Iraq and with other states in the region, measures to enhance the security and stability of the region'. Picco had never disguised his hope that he would be put in charge of this project when peace had been restored between Iran and Iraq. It was for this reason that political offices were to be retained in Baghdad and Tehran when UNIIMOG was closed down after the liberation of Kuwait.

In a separate meeting with Holst, I highlighted some of the complications which Pérez de Cuéllar had glossed over – the need for complete Iraqi withdrawal, the relationship between a UN operation and the coalition forces who would presumably remain in Kuwait for a while, and doubts about Iraqi consent. Pérez de Cuéllar, Dayal and Picco, however, still hoped that a land war could be avoided and were desperate to get the UN back into the act. Caution and realism were not welcome. I was instructed to concentrate on finding troop contributors for an early peacekeeping operation.

On the evening of 23 February President Bush announced that the land war had begun. Within four days the coalition forces won an astonishing victory. Bush announced a suspension of hostilities to give Saddam time to consider various ultimata conveyed to him by the coalition. Having consistently predicted that the Iraqi Army would be a tough nut to crack, I was both relieved and embarrassed by the shortness of the land war. But I was also distressed by the victors' ferocity against the

---

* By weapons of mass destruction is meant biological, chemical and nuclear weapons.

retreating Iraqis. Pérez de Cuéllar sent Ahtisaari to Iraq and Kuwait to assess war damage and humanitarian needs.*

The time had arrived for serious discussion of a peacekeeping operation. It gave rise to a doctrinal problem. Peacekeeping requires the consent of the hostile parties; but it was already clear that the post-war sanctions and other constraints which the coalition intended to impose on Iraq would require the Security Council to act under Chapter VII, the enforcement chapter of the UN Charter, in which context the question of Iraqi consent would be irrelevant. Would the military operation in that case be a peacekeeping operation? More worrying was the scale of the operation initially envisaged by the coalition: a huge armed force to monitor a demilitarized zone and associated areas of arms limitation stretching from Basra to the Iraq–Jordan border, a distance of more than 1,000 kilometres. But this was soon scaled down to an observer force astride the Iraq–Kuwait border, which is barely 200 kilometres long.

Away in Nepal, in search of a new Force Commander for UNIFIL, I played no part in the negotiation of SCR 687, the 'mother of all resolutions', which set out the arrangements that Iraq had to accept before a formal cease-fire could come into effect. These included the establishment of the demilitarized zone and deployment of a UN observer mission to monitor it. The briefing on the DMZ which the Pentagon provided to the Secretariat in New York was discouraging. Iraqi forces, we were told, remained in both the Iraqi and the Kuwaiti sectors of the zone. Some 37,000 refugees from southern Iraq, survivors of the failed Shi'ite uprising against Saddam, were also at Safwan in the Iraqi sector, protected and supported by the Americans. Little work had yet been done on the rules which the UN would apply in the zone. Mines and unexploded ordnance were everywhere. SCR 687 was adopted on 3 April 1991 and Iraq accepted its terms on 6 April. By then, the Secretary-General had already submitted his recommendations for UNIKOM, as the new mission was to be called, and these were accepted by the Security Council on 9 April.

The political necessity of early deployment was evident and constantly reaffirmed by the Americans and their allies. My department's ability to bring it about, however, was limited. When the Council took its decision, I was already in Mexico City for a new round of negotiations on the peace settlement for El Salvador. During the next five weeks I was to spend only three weekdays in New York. This placed on my staff a burden which was beyond their capacity to bear and it was at this time that unfair complaints about their performance reached crisis point.

---

* Ahtisaari had been the Special Representative in Namibia and was now back in New York as Under-Secretary-General for Administration and Management.

Managing the deployment of UNIKOM from a hotel in Mexico City was a frustrating business and tempers on all sides were soon fraying.

Our first draft of the Secretary-General's recommendations for UNIKOM had proposed that monitoring of the DMZ should initially be done by three battalions of infantry who would gradually be replaced by unarmed military observers as the situation stabilized; we also proposed a field engineering squadron to deal with unexploded ordnance; the initial military strength would be about three thousand personnel. This was very badly received by the P-5. The British and Soviets wanted no infantry or engineers at all, just military observers. Peacekeeping doctrine was also a problem: Fleischhauer on legal grounds, and I on practical grounds, argued that Iraqi 'consent' had to be obtained; the P-5 were not prepared to accept anything stronger than 'readiness to cooperate'.

I decided to compromise on troop strength and proposed that all the monitoring would be done by UNMOs but for the first month or two their security would be assured by infantry temporarily borrowed from UN operations elsewhere in the Middle East; if after four weeks the commander thought that there was a continuing need for infantry he would so recommend to the Secretary-General. This was accepted by the P-5. On doctrine, the resolution was adopted under Chapter VII and provided that UNIKOM could be terminated only if there was a Security Council vote to that effect. The mission could not therefore be terminated simply because its current mandate had come to an end nor because Iraq withdrew its consent. This was a historic departure from (some would say 'betrayal of') the principle of consent so laboriously established by Hammarskjöld with Nasser when the first UN Emergency Force in Sinai was set up in 1956. But it was justified by the fact that UNIKOM was the first peacekeeping operation to be deployed in the aftermath of UN-authorized enforcement action.

Pérez de Cuéllar offered Timothy Dibuama, the Military Adviser, the command of UNIKOM but he was reluctant to leave his post in New York. The choice then fell on Günther Greindl from Austria who had served long and well as Force Commander of the UN forces on the Golan Heights (UNDOF) and in Cyprus (UNFICYP).

A major issue was the extent of the UN's responsibility for the 37,000 Iraqi Shi'ites in the Iraqi sector of the demilitarized zone. UNIKOM had neither the mandate nor the resources to take on this responsibility; the most we could offer was that it should establish a visible presence at each of the camps in the hope of deterring atrocities by the Iraqi secret police after the Americans had left. This looked feeble and UNIKOM's apparent heartlessness became an issue in the US media.

Peacekeeping is rightly presented as a noble and selfless activity in which soldiers from distant lands risk their lives in trying to control and end other peoples' wars. But peacekeepers are often obliged to appear heartless and to face the opprobrium this generates. Every peacekeeping operation has (or should have) clearly defined tasks and the resources needed to carry out those tasks. But it is inevitable that the peacekeepers' presence arouses other expectations. They have transport, communications, shelter, food, medicaments, doctors and the weapons to ensure the security of those they befriend. They are impartial in the conflict and they are, usually, decent people. It is only natural that they should want to respond to the expectations created by their presence. But their commanders, or the bureaucrats in New York if the commanders shirk this responsibility, sometimes have to tell them that they may not do what their humanity impels them to do. There are various reasons for this constraint: resources are already strained by the peacekeepers' mandated tasks; the proposed action has not been authorized by the Security Council; civilian relief agencies will resent military intrusion on their turf; the operation's impartiality will be impaired if it seems to be providing relief to civilians of one side rather than the other. Though valid, these reasons are nonetheless very difficult to explain, be it to the media or to young soldiers agonized by the suffering they see around them.

In the end the Americans persuaded the Saudis to take in most of the displaced Iraqis whose lives were judged to be at risk. But a much greater humanitarian problem now surfaced in the north of Iraq. During the air campaign, President Bush had publicly encouraged 'the Iraqi people to take matters into their own hands and force Saddam Hussein, the dictator, to step aside'. The Shi'ites in the south rose up against the regime and the Kurds in the north soon followed their example. After the land war ended, it became known that nearly two million Kurds were fleeing towards Iran and Turkey to escape reprisals by Saddam's army and pro-Baghdad Kurdish irregulars. Whether or not they had revolted in response to Bush's exhortations, the coalition powers felt an obligation towards them.

On 5 April 1991 the Security Council adopted SCR 688 which demanded that Iraq end the repression of its civilian population, including the Kurds, and allow immediate access by international humanitarian organizations. On 18 April, Sadruddin Aga Khan, a former UN High Commissioner for Refugees who had been given the task of overseeing the UN's response to the humanitarian needs created by the war, signed with the Iraqis an agreement on the UN's expanded humanitarian operations in Iraq, which would include the establishment of a number of UN Humanitarian Centres (UNHUCs).* Two days before, Bush had told

---

* Sadruddin's title, a long one even by the wordy standards of the UN, was 'Executive Delegate of the Secretary-General for the United Nations Inter-Agency Humanitarian Programme for Iraq, Kuwait and the Iraq/Iran and Iraq/Turkey Border Areas'.

Pérez de Cuéllar that the Americans, the British and the French had decided to introduce troops into northern Iraq to build and protect refugee camps for the Kurds. A few weeks later they declared, and began to monitor, a no-fly zone to exclude Iraqi aircraft from northern Iraq; a similar zone was later established in the south after it came to light that large numbers of the Shi'ite rebels had taken refuge in the marshes there. The legality of these military measures, which were taken after the formal cease-fire had come into effect, is disputed; but they are still justified by Britain and the United States on the grounds that the cease-fire agreement authorized them to impose controls over Iraqi military flights.

At the end of April the British proposed that a UN civilian police force be deployed in northern Iraq so that the coalition's troops could be withdrawn. They wanted it to be deployed by the Secretary-General 'at his initiative', lest it be blocked in the Security Council by a Chinese veto inspired by that permanent member's sensitivities over Tibet. This seemed to me a mad idea: once the coalition forces had withdrawn, the Iraqis could commit as many atrocities as they wanted and the UN would have no effective way of stopping them; and how would the operation be funded if it had not been established by decision of the Council or the General Assembly? A more practicable proposal would be a normal peacekeeping operation to take over from the coalition forces the 'humanitarian protection zone' that they had cleared of Iraqi forces and their Kurdish allies. At a coordination meeting in Geneva on 30 April neither Sadruddin Aga Khan nor Sadako Ogata, the UN High Commissioner for Refugees, who had taken up her appointment only a few months before, supported the British proposal. But the Iraqi representative in New York expressed interest in it and Pérez de Cuéllar told me to raise it with the Iraqis in Baghdad, where I was about to go on my first (and only) visit to UNIKOM.

There were still no airlines flying into Kuwait and, accompanied by Dermot Earley from the Military Adviser's office in New York, I had to go first to Bahrain. The next morning we flew to Kuwait in an old, ill-maintained and smelly BAC-111 chartered from the Romanian airline TAROM. Eastern European aircraft were to become a disagreeable feature of UN peacekeeping in the 1990s. After the fall of Communism, they flooded the charter market at rates so low that the UN's strict procurement regulations permitted no escape from using them. Their dilapidated condition and the nonchalance of their chain-smoking crews raised the fear that every flight was going to be one's last. But very few of them crashed.

As we approached Kuwait, I was invited into the cockpit to see the oil wells which the Iraqis had set alight as they withdrew and which were still burning fiercely. Even worse than the fires were the lakes and rivers of crude oil which turned the desert black. At the airport American and British troops were everywhere, the Americans so heavily armed that they suggested an army of occupation rather than one of liberation. We flew on to the demilitarized zone in one of UNIKOM's light planes. It was a sobering flight; just north of Kuwait we passed over the wreckage created by the 'turkey shoot' when allied aircraft mercilessly destroyed every vehicle in sight as the Iraqis fled the city on the last day of the land war; and at the western end of the zone there was the debris of the armoured battle fought and lost by units of Saddam's Republican Guard. We landed at Safwan, where US aircraft were flying out the Iraqi displaced persons to their new camps in Saudi Arabia, and in Umm Qasr we inspected the excellent buildings that had been found for UNIKOM's headquarters.

Back in Kuwait, I went to look at the house where my wife and I had lived in the early sixties. It was still standing but had evidently been used as a billet for the occupying troops. For fear of booby traps I did not go in, but peering through what had been our drawing-room window I saw that the wall bore the following slogan, beautifully executed in classical Arabic script: 'Long Live the Great Leader Saddam Hussein. Down with Husni and Fahd and 'Ali and Hafiz and, behind them all, the filthy Bush'. Husni was the President of Egypt, Fahd the King of Saudi Arabia and Hafiz the President of Syria. But who was 'Ali?

Greindl seemed to have done a good job in getting the mission on its feet but it was already evident that it had more military observers than it needed. I recalled the recent review of UNFICYP in Cyprus where we had concluded that it made no sense for officers to do jobs which private soldiers could do as well, if not better. Was not this as true of UNIKOM's DMZ as of UNFICYP's Buffer Zone? I wished we had resisted more firmly the P-5's rejection of infantry.

The calls on Kuwaiti ministers were not cheering. Even after making allowances for the terrible trauma their country had endured, it was difficult to accept the spoilt-child tone of the demands they were making on the international community. In my case the demands were for immediate demarcation of the border and the immediate expulsion to Iraq of the stateless people, known as *bidūns*, who had gathered on Kuwaiti territory just south of the border.* The *bidūns* are residents of Kuwait who do not have Kuwaiti nationality for one reason or another, usually because they did not apply for it when they had the opportunity to do so. Most of them have a tribal background and many serve in the armed forces and police. Those of concern to Kuwaiti ministers in 1991 were people whom the government suspected of having collaborated with the Iraqis

---

* *Bidūn* means 'without' in Arabic. These unfortunate people were without nationality.

during the occupation; in the government's view, they were Iraqis who should be returned to Iraq.

We flew on in the stinking BAC-111 to Habbaniyah in Iraq and drove into Baghdad, finding very little visible damage in either the country or the city. My instructions were to prepare the way for a visit which Sadruddin was to make a week later. I was to say that Pérez de Cuéllar was interested in the British proposal for a UN police force as a means of reassuring the Kurds and accelerating the withdrawal of coalition forces from Iraq. But he was open-minded about the modalities; perhaps a peacekeeping operation might be more effective and more acceptable to Iraq. Either way, these would be transitional arrangements; the Secretary-General hoped that the government's current negotiations with Kurdish leaders would open the way to reconciliation and a political settlement. The UN was increasingly involved in helping to resolve conflicts within states and Pérez de Cuéllar had ideas to contribute, if Iraq so wished.

I started with the Deputy Foreign Minister, Muhammad Sa'id Sahhaf, and the Ministry's Legal Adviser, Riad al-Qaisi. They firmly rejected any idea of a UN police operation, even the attachment of a few police to Sadruddin's UN humanitarian centres; nor would Iraq accept a UN peacekeeping operation; and as for the Kurds this was a domestic matter in which the UN had no right to involve itself; the UN should get on with implementing Sadruddin's programme and thus remove any pretext for the coalition forces to remain in the north. The next day I put to the Foreign Minister, Ahmed Hussein, a more modest proposal: let Iraq invite the Secretary-General to attach UN civilian observers, with police experience, to the Iraqi security forces in the Kurdish area so that they could verify that the Kurds' human rights were being respected. The Minister said that he would put this to 'the leadership'.

I spent the next day at UNIIMOG's former headquarters, the Canal Hotel, drafting a report on the enlargement of the UN operation in Angola to enable it to monitor the imminent cease-fire there. The Canal Hotel now housed not only UNIKOM but also a new acronym UNOSGI, the UN Office of the Secretary-General in Iraq. When UNIIMOG was disbanded, Pérez de Cuéllar had obtained the Council's agreement to the retention of small UN offices in Baghdad and Tehran to help the parties implement the political provisions of SCR 598, but they turned out to have little to do and were phased out by the end of 1992. The military member of UNOSGI showed Earley and me gruesome pictures of about a hundred stripped, bound, blindfolded and disfigured corpses which the Iraqis claimed were Iraqi soldiers killed by Iranian-controlled infiltrators. I wondered whether they might not in fact be some of the missing Kuwaitis (or had the Kuwaitis been killed in the allied 'turkey-shoot' as they were taken from Kuwait by the retreating Iraqis?). In the evening I received a rebuke from Pérez de Cuéllar for having put forward such a minimalist proposal for a UN police presence in the north; I was to remain in Baghdad until instructed to leave.

After two days, I received the Iraqi reply: total rejection of all our ideas for a police presence. I asked Sahhaf what he thought would now happen in the north. He replied that the talks with the Kurds were going well. As for the coalition forces, they would leave sooner or later; the wiser they were, the sooner it would be. This bravado was typical of Iraqi attitudes at that time, and since. From the moment we arrived at Habbaniyah I had been struck by the resilience and cheerfulness of the ordinary people. What I was seeing was very different from the apocalyptic report presented by Ahtisaari when he visited Iraq immediately after Desert Storm. The city had been cleared up; the bridges were being repaired; two-thirds of the power and water supplies had been restored; Saddam, I felt, looked secure and Western perceptions of a defeated and humiliated Iraq were wishful thinking.

Pérez de Cuéllar let me leave Baghdad the next day. Back in New York, there was talk of a new Security Council resolution to impose a UN police force on Iraq. This seemed to me fanciful. What was eventually agreed was the deployment of a contingent of 'UN Guards', carrying side arms provided by the Iraqis, whose task would be to protect UN personnel and property, including those of NGOs working within the UN programme. I played no part in the negotiation of this arrangement and the visit to Baghdad ended my involvement in the major issues relating to Iraq. For the remainder of my time as the Under-Secretary-General for peacekeeping, my only task was to manage UNIKOM and Kofi Annan relieved me of this task when he joined the peacekeeping department in March 1992. For most of that year there were no serious problems. UNIKOM, like UNDOF in Syria, was of use to both the parties and therefore enjoyed their strategic consent, though this did not stop them causing mini-crises from time to time by breaking the rules in some minor way or by harassing UN personnel. Early in 1993, however, at a time of tension resulting from Iraqi violations of the no-fly zones enforced by the United States and Britain, there were a number of incursions by Iraqi troops into the Kuwaiti sector of the demilitarized zone. These were observed by UNIKOM which protested to the Iraqi authorities, but the incursions continued. The Western powers decided that UNIKOM should be converted into an armed 'trip-wire' force.

The Secretariat had favoured an infantry-based force in 1991, primarily to provide security for the UN observers and other international bodies operating in the DMZ, especially the Border Demarcation Commission. But for financial reasons the P-5 had insisted that

UNIKOM consist only of military observers. Now the roles were reversed but again the major Western powers had their way.

The Secretariat did not like the trip-wire concept. At one time it was thought that UN troops could deter aggression not by their military strength but by raising the political price that the aggressor would pay for attacking them. But when Israel invaded Lebanon in 1982 the UN force did not have the military capacity to resist the Israel Defence Forces, which pushed through it with hardly a shot being fired; political deterrence had failed and the UN had been humiliated. This taught the Secretariat that in peacekeeping, as in real soldiering, deterrence works only if you deploy all the resources you would need if the aggressor were to attack. This was why Boutros-Ghali, on the advice of his military staff, told the Security Council in 1993 that 34,000 additional troops would be needed if the UN force in the former Yugoslavia was to have the capacity to deter attacks against the 'safe areas' in Bosnia. His reluctant submission to Western pressure to do the job with only 7,600 extra troops was, in my view, a mistake which had disastrous consequences for both the people of Srebrenica and the UN itself.

If by 'trip-wire' is meant international eyes and ears to observe and report the act of aggression, then unarmed military observers are sufficient for the task. For them to be brushed aside by the invading army is less of a humiliation than if armed UN troops are involved, as was the case in Lebanon in 1982. This, though, gives rise to what might be called the Thermopylae question. Suppose the United Nations troops in Lebanon or Srebrenica had joined battle with the aggressors. They would have lost the fight and many would have died. That *would* have made the aggressor pay a political price. We remember Thermopylae today not because it was an overwhelming Persian victory but because three hundred Spartans fought and died, all with their wounds in front. So perhaps there is a case in theory for an armed trip-wire; but in practice Thermopylae would never happen, for it is difficult to think of circumstances in which troop-contributing nations would be ready to sacrifice their soldiers' lives in this way. If the UN had its own army, the concept might be less fanciful, but there are many political and financial reasons why the UN will never have an army of its own.

17

Yugoslavia

The year 1991 was busier and more disagreeable than any of my preceding five years in the Secretariat. In the first place, the volume of peacekeeping had more than doubled. In 1986 there had been five peacekeeping operations in the field and no new ones were being planned. By mid-1991 there were ten operations in the field and three more were in the active planning phase. By now also Pérez de Cuéllar's edict in late 1988 that I should be responsible only for peacekeeping had been somewhat eroded: in El Salvador and, to a lesser extent, Western Sahara, I was fully involved in the negotiation of peace agreements and happy to be so. To add to my busyness, the gaps created in my office in late 1988 had not been adequately filled and a reliable deputy had still to be found. In the first ten months of 1991, I spent 134 days away from New York, coming back from each trip to a mountain of unprocessed paperwork.

At the same time, continuing tensions in my relations with Pérez de Cuéllar were making life difficult, and these difficulties were compounded by uncertainty as to who his successor would be. No African had yet been Secretary-General and it was widely felt that it was now Africa's turn. But there was no obvious African candidate and in May the French were openly advocating a third term for Pérez de Cuéllar. Later the rumour was that the permanent members of the Security Council would ask him to stay on for a couple more years. But by the autumn Africa had fielded two credible candidates in Boutros Boutros-Ghali (Egypt) and Bernard Chidzero (Zimbabwe), who were running neck and neck. On 21 November 1991 Boutros-Ghali won the vote in the Security Council and twelve days later he was formally appointed by the General Assembly. I was pleased by this outcome. I had occasionally called on him in Cairo and admired him for his intellect, his diplomatic experience, his charm and his wit. Although most African states might well have preferred Africa's first Secretary-General to be a sub-Saharan, Boutros-Ghali would cover many bases as a Christian citizen of a Muslim country with a Jewish wife.

Given my workload, the weakness of my office and the uncertain

291

relations with Pérez de Cuéllar, the last thing I wanted that autumn was another major peacekeeping project. But it came with horrid suddenness in mid-November as a result of the fragmentation of what we would soon be calling 'the former Yugoslavia'.

Tito's Socialist Federal Republic of Yugoslavia (SFRY) was composed of six republics: listed by size of population, they were Serbia, Croatia, Bosnia and Herzegovina (hereinafter abbreviated to 'Bosnia'), Slovenia, Macedonia and Montenegro. Serbia included two autonomous provinces: Kosovo (with an Albanian majority) and Vojvodina (with a large Hungarian minority). Most of their inhabitants belonged to a number of Slav ethnic groups, distinguished by language and/or religion, of which the most important were Serbs, Croats, Muslims (sometimes called 'Bosniacs'), Slovenes, Montenegrins and Macedonians, but there were also a number of non-Slav groups, of which the most important were Albanians and Hungarians. By the early 1990s, however, a significant number of people defined themselves simply as Yugoslavs, either for political reasons (loyalty to the SFRY) or social ones (mixed marriages). Only Slovenia was ethnically homogeneous. The population of Serbia was only 66 per cent Serb and that of Croatia only 78 per cent Croat; in Bosnia the population was 44 per cent Muslims, 31 per cent Serbs, 17 per cent Croats and 7 per cent 'Yugoslavs' and others.* The SFRY had a collective presidency of eight persons, each of them representing one of the six republics or two autonomous provinces; the chairmanship rotated annually.

During the late eighties this constitutional structure began to buckle under the pressure of economic and political crisis and the collapse of Communism in Eastern Europe. The Serb Communists who had dominated the SFRY, and especially the Yugoslav People's Army (JNA), lost credibility; nationalist and separatist tendencies came out into the open. By early 1991 it was clear that the federation was doomed. The republics of Slovenia and Croatia held referendums in which the majority voted for independence. Both republics seceded from the SFRY in June 1991. The Serbian President, Slobodan Milošević, did not attempt to block Slovenia's departure. But the secession of Croatia was strongly opposed by the Croatian Serbs who were concentrated in three areas – the Krajina, Western Slavonia and Eastern Slavonia.† They refused to accept rule by an independent Croatia, rose up in arms against the embryonic Croatian

---

* All this makes the nomenclature of the Yugoslav wars confusing. The practice in this book is to use the shorter form of the noun or adjective as the indicator of ethnicity and the longer form as the indicator of the republic of domicile: a 'Croatian Serb' is an ethnic Serb domiciled in Croatia; a Serbian Croat is an ethnic Croat domiciled in Serbia.

† See map, page xxi.

army and declared their own sovereign 'Republic of the Serbian Krajina'. They were openly supported by the JNA and by Milošević who wanted to exploit the break-up of the SFRY to create a Greater Serbia, incorporating the Serb minorities in Bosnia and Croatia. A savage war resulted.

I had followed these developments during the summer but had not foreseen that the UN would become involved. The European Community (EC), as it then was, took the lead in international efforts to control and resolve the conflict and in September 1991 established a Conference on Yugoslavia, with Lord Carrington as Chairman. Carrington succeeded in getting the three leaders primarily involved, President Franjo Tudjman of Croatia, President Milošević of Serbia and General Veljko Kadijević, Federal Minister of Defence, to accept three principles for a political settlement: federal Yugoslavia would be replaced by a loose alliance of independent republics; the human rights of minorities would be protected, with certain areas possibly being given a special status; and there would be no unilateral modification of borders.

The EC was less successful on the military front. It sent to Croatia a European Community Monitoring Mission (ECMM), whose members wore a much-mocked civilian uniform (though many of them were in fact serving officers in their country's armed forces). Half a dozen ceasefires were negotiated but none was respected for any length of time. As the fighting intensified, the EC decided to involve the United Nations. On 25 September the Security Council adopted a resolution which endorsed the Community's efforts, invited the Secretary-General to assist all those who were working to restore peace and imposed a general embargo on the delivery of weapons and military equipment to any party in Yugoslavia. As its efforts stumbled, the Community urged Pérez de Cuéllar to take a more active role and he appointed Cyrus Vance, a former US Secretary of State, as his Personal Envoy for Yugoslavia. By mid-November Vance had made two visits there. Officially they were fact-finding visits; but Carrington and Vance had long been friends and Vance soon became a major player in the peace process.

Macedonia declared its independence in September. In October the Bosnian Muslims and Croats staged a vote for independence in the Bosnian legislative assembly, whereupon the Bosnian Serbs walked out and declared their intention to secede from Bosnia. Milošević, with the help of the President of Montenegro and the JNA, replaced the remnants of the collective presidency with a new federal government in Belgrade, a move that was difficult to reconcile with his acceptance of Carrington's three principles for a settlement. All the other republics denounced this move as illegal and refused to have anything to do with the 'rump government'. The UN and other international organizations did likewise.

The members of the EC were divided about how to respond to these developments. From the beginning, the Germans said they wanted to recognize Croatia and Slovenia as quickly as possible. More prudent members argued that recognition and the economic benefits the EC could bring to the successor states should be used as levers to persuade them to negotiate a peaceful dismantling of the SFRY. Initially this view prevailed; in a declaration in Rome on 8 November, the EC linked recognition to an overall settlement which would include human rights guarantees. But there was already a tendency in the EC to treat the Serbs as the guilty party in Croatia. Pérez de Cuéllar and Vance were rightly troubled by this; if the UN was involved, it had to be impartial between the parties, at least until the Security Council formally determined who was the aggressor.

The collapse of the SFRY's political structures meant that there was no recognized civilian authority over the JNA, which was already fighting on the side of the Croatian Serbs and arming the Serbs in Bosnia. Was its purpose to preserve the SFRY or to help create a Greater Serbia? Ostensibly it was under the political control of the minister of defence in the unrecognized rump federal government. But he was a soldier and a Serb, General Veljko Kadijević. His deputy, Admiral Stane Brovet, was a Slovene but had remained loyal to the JNA. It was assumed that the real political authority was Milošević. As the fighting intensified in Croatia, JNA garrisons were blockaded in their barracks by Croatian forces and told that they could not withdraw unless they left their equipment behind. The military scene was further confused by a proliferation of territorial defence forces, reserve units, paramilitaries and volunteers, who were armed by, and fought in the interest of, the emerging political authorities but whose often atrocious doings the latter could, if necessary, disown.

On 12 November I was asked out of the blue to give Pérez de Cuéllar a note on the conditions that would have to be met before a UN peacekeeping operation could be deployed in Yugoslavia. The next day I was summoned to a meeting at which Vance was to brief the members of the Security Council. Thus was I sucked into a vortex from which I would not emerge for fifteen months. Many member states were by now pressing for a UN military operation but Pérez de Cuéllar was admirably robust in saying that this would require a cease-fire and a genuine readiness to negotiate a political settlement. Vance gave a gloomy assessment of the prospects and showed little interest in peacekeeping.

But when Carrington announced the next day that all the parties in Yugoslavia were now in favour of a UN operation, Pérez de Cuéllar decided to send Vance back to Yugoslavia, accompanied by me and a small peacekeeping team. For the latter I chose Heikki Purola, a Finnish colonel, and Shashi Tharoor, an Indian official whom I had recently brought into my department from UNHCR as my Special Assistant. It was already clear that his talents were such that he ought to have a major substantive task as well; Yugoslavia it was to be. When the Secretary-General reported his decision to the Security Council, the Western members expressed their satisfaction but none of the Non-Aligned spoke; their loyalty was still to the SFRY, which had been a leader of the NAM since the Bandung Conference of 1955 and the first Non-Aligned Summit in Belgrade in 1961.

We flew first to Amsterdam for an airport meeting with Hans van den Broek, the Netherlands Foreign Minister and current President of the Council of Ministers of the European Community. He jealously protected the EC's activities; a UN operation might be the only way to get the JNA to withdraw from Croatia; but the EC Monitoring Mission must remain in place alongside the UN operation. Vance expressed doubts about whether this would work. We flew on to Belgrade in a luxurious executive jet (provided by the Swiss Government as its contribution to the search for peace) and arrived on 17 November, the day that the town of Vukovar in Croatia fell to the JNA after a siege of eighty-five days.

Slavko Jović, the former commander of the UN military observer group in Iran and Iraq, was waiting for me at the hotel. He seemed fully recovered from the heart attack he had suffered in Baghdad a year before. But in other respects he was a changed man, vehement in his hatred of the Croats: the *ustashi** had been reborn, he said; Germany was trying to create a Fourth Reich, based on a Catholic federation; the JNA should be using flame-throwers to get 'the rats' out of the cellars of Vukovar; were it not for his heart condition, he would be fighting there as a volunteer; if the Croats would not accept a sensible settlement, the Serbs would have to kill them all, every one of them. This tirade from a man whom I had previously respected for his judgement and clear-headedness was chilling evidence of how deep the hatred was between two peoples separated only by history and religion; but then I remembered that similar things could be heard in a province of my own country.

Already that evening there were rumours of atrocities in Vukovar. Vance decided to go there the next morning. 'Impossible; it is still too dangerous,' said our Serbian minders. A cheerless day was rounded off by an unproductive session with the local ECMM team; their distaste for a UN operation was evident and they had told the EC Presidency that at least twenty-six battalions would be required (a force of this size was

---

* The name given to the Croatian fascists who fought on the German side in Yugoslavia during the Second World War and carried out a campaign of genocide against the Serbs in Croatia.

inconceivable; our largest current operation, in southern Lebanon, had only seven battalions). They confirmed what Van den Broek had led us to suspect; the EC institutions were already prejudiced against the Serbs; the only impartial briefing we were to receive from the ECMM on this trip was from its team in Sarajevo.

The next day we saw Milošević. I had not met him before and knew little about him. The first impression was positive – calm, expansive, supremely self-confident, a good listener but long-winded in his own remarks. At Vance's request, I gave the lecturette that he had dubbed 'Goulding's Peacekeeping 101'. Milošević said that peacekeeping seemed to be just what Yugoslavia needed. He went on to define, at great length, the political basis of the conflict. Serbs had been settled in the Krajina and the Slavonias as privileged front-line defenders of the Austro-Hungarian Empire against the Turks; they had always been responsible to Vienna, never to Zagreb. The republics formed after the Second World War were only administrative divisions, not states; when Croatia decided to secede, the Serbs residing there had 'the sovereign right' to assert their wish to remain in Yugoslavia; the JNA had no choice but to intervene and protect them when they were attacked by the Croatian authorities. We then saw Kadijević and Brovet who were also in favour of a peacekeeping operation; once it was deployed, they said, the JNA would withdraw from Croatia.

Vance and I initially had in mind a force that would be deployed in what he called 'ink-spot' mode; in order to limit its size it would be stationed only in 'crisis areas' where intercommunal tension was high and fighting had taken place. But I became increasingly uneasy about this concept. Would the ink-spots be the only places where a UN military presence was needed? Intercommunal tension can spread very fast, as UNFICYP had found during its first ten years in Cyprus (1964–74) when it too had been deployed in ink-spot mode. It did not have much success in preventing intercommunal violence until there was a clear front line between the opposing forces; and that came about only after an extensive and cruel exchange of populations.

The next day we were allowed to visit Vukovar. The tales of atrocities had multiplied; particularly awful things were alleged to have been done at the hospital. From the outset Vance insisted that a visit to the hospital was our top priority. We stopped first at Šid, an ugly agro-industrial town just on the Serbian side of the border with Croatia. The Croatians had shelled it lightly a few days before and time was wasted as we were briefed about, and then visited, 'the crimes of the fascist *ustashi* regime' – further evidence that the Serbs were reviving the abusive vocabulary of the Second World War. For the next leg of the journey we were required to travel in armoured personnel carriers 'because of the snipers'. I asked the commander of ours, a disarmingly charming Bosnian Serb, what it felt like to be fighting his countrymen: 'I was worried at first but now I have got used to killing Croats.' It was a slow journey up the line to Vukovar. The road was congested with military traffic, much of it convoys carrying bridging material, presumably for the next push across the fields and ditches to Osijek, the capital of Eastern Slavonia. A few kilometres short of Vukovar we stopped at a brigade headquarters for another briefing. Lunch was then offered. 'No, thank you,' we replied; 'we want to see the town and the hospital.'

So we were taken to the town. More time was wasted as we were shown the JNA barracks which the Croat inhabitants had (not surprisingly) blockaded during the siege. Then we drove through the town; many houses had been hit by shellfire and there were a couple of knocked-out tanks. But we did not see anything like the devastation described by the media. It soon became clear why; we were being shown the outskirts of the town, not the most damaged central area. Next we were taken to a JNA reception centre for displaced civilians. This was a painful introduction to the human realities of this conflict: the civilians dazed and hopeless; the army triumphant; the Serb irregulars bizarre and threatening in their rag-tag attire. At first, Vance was allowed to speak to whom he chose, but the minders soon began producing people 'who want to talk to you, Mr Vance'; all of them, of course, said what a wonderful humanitarian job the JNA was doing. There were even some staged reunions: a sudden cry of excitement from an individual who would rush through the crowd to embrace an allegedly re-found family member.

We had been told that after the reception centre we would be taken to the hospital. But as we drove away, I noticed that we were going south, whereas the hospital was to the north-west. Vance and I, by now quite angry, insisted that the convoy halt. It did. There followed an altercation with a bristling, two-metre tall JNA major. He produced the usual excuses: the road to the hospital was mined; there were snipers; the other brigade would have to be consulted; he had no direct communications with it; and so on. When I said that I could not understand why all these problems, if they really existed, had not been resolved during the course of the day, he flew into a rage, complaining that I had impugned his and the JNA's honour by accusing him of lying. In the end we had to concede and drive unhappily back to Belgrade; but we had made our point and the incident had been filmed by several crews. The bristling major was one Veselin Slivancanin who has since been indicted by the International Criminal Tribunal in The Hague for his alleged role in the massacre of some three hundred Croats, many of them wounded, who were taken from the Vukovar hospital the previous day.

The authorities in Belgrade had placed an embargo on all flights to

Croatia. To get to Zagreb, therefore, we had to fly in Swiss luxury to Graz in Austria and then drive for two hours through Slovenia to the Croatian capital. Franjo Tudjman, President of Croatia, intelligent but gauche, wore a perpetually pained expression and was very different from the self-confident and extrovert Milošević. He had with him Antun Tus, a renegade JNA colonel who now commanded the Croatian National Guard, and Hrvoje Kacić, a Dubrovnik shipowner and politician and the only moderate we met in Zagreb. Tudjman opened with a long diatribe against Serbian 'imperialism' and the JNA, 'the largest Communist army in Europe after the Soviet Union'. I responded with 'Peacekeeping 101'. Tudjman was initially hostile but he was worn down by Vance (and helpful interventions from Kacić) and eventually accepted that demilitarization of the 'crisis areas' was the only way to get the JNA out of Croatia.

The next morning I sent Purola and Tharoor to take a look at Western Slavonia. In Zagreb, Vance and I called on the Foreign Minister, aptly named Separović, and other dignitaries, before visiting the JNA's Marshal Tito barracks which had by now been under blockade for over two months. We were received by the Commander of the Fifth Military District, Colonel-General Andrija Rašeta, and a dozen of his senior officers in an unlit and unheated room (electricity cut off) with the rain pouring down outside. They spoke about the humiliation to which they were being subjected: confinement to the barracks, cutting off of all utilities, seizure of their apartments, harassment of their families, no release unless they left behind their arms, equipment and personal property. This they refused to do. It was a matter of honour; they would rather die where they were. All this was said calmly, with emotion controlled. I admired the qualities of leadership which had enabled Rašeta to keep his men together and disciplined for so long. There was evidently no chance of a cease-fire in Croatia until this issue was resolved.

Later that day Vance saw Tudjman alone. Tudjman confirmed his acceptance of our concept, which was beginning to be called 'the Vance Plan', and agreed to a secret meeting with Milošević and Kadijević three days later. Vance wanted the meeting to be in Sarajevo. But Tudjman rejected Sarajevo and insisted on Geneva.

The next morning we undertook the long journey via Graz to Sarajevo for meetings with the Bosnian President, Alija Izetbegović, and his Foreign Minister, Haris Silajdžić, both of them Muslims. They spoke anxiously about the likelihood of fighting between the Serb and Croat communities in Bosnia and wanted a UN peacekeeping operation to be deployed there too. Although I did not realize it then, this was not honest. The greater danger in Bosnia at that time was fighting between Serbs and Muslims if, as soon happened, the Serbs tried to turn the eastern part of the republic into an ethnically cleansed Serb domain which could be annexed by Serbia; and the two districts in which he asked for UN military observers to be stationed as soon as possible, Mostar and Bihać, were places of Serb-Muslim, not Serb-Croat, tension. With hindsight, Izetbegović's aim was probably to create for the Muslims a privileged role as the UN's ally in its efforts to control Serb-Croat enmity throughout Yugoslavia; as we left, he suggested that the head-quarters of a UN force in Croatia should be located in Sarajevo, as a place that would be neutral between Belgrade and Zagreb.

My poor understanding of the deeper currents of Yugoslavia's ethnic politics at this time was symptomatic of a persistent weakness in the UN's efforts to prevent and resolve conflict. Unlike the hardy annuals in Cyprus, the Middle East and Namibia, most of the conflicts which the Security Council wanted the Secretariat to tackle in the nineties were new to the United Nations. Pérez de Cuéllar had established a unit called the Office for Research and the Collection of Information, which was headed by James Jonah until he succeeded Abby Farah as Under-Secretary-General for Africa. But its research capacity was limited and, in any case, my department was so stretched that we did not have time for the extended briefing by experts which we should ideally have received before plunging into these turbulent waters.

From Sarajevo Vance and his party flew back to Belgrade. We had earned good marks with Kadijević for the visit to the JNA barracks in Zagreb, but he now made lifting of the blockades on all JNA barracks a condition for JNA acceptance of our peacekeeping proposal. Both he and Milošević agreed to come to the meeting with Tudjman and both, like the latter, rejected Sarajevo, so it was agreed that we would meet two days later in Geneva; the meeting would be kept secret. Milošević expressed strong opposition to the possible deployment of military observers in Bosnia. Again it was only later that I understood the reason for his vehemence: he did not want any international presence to stand in the way of his plans for the Bosnian Serbs.

Meanwhile our problem was with the Croatian Serbs. We saw first their leader in Eastern Slavonia, Goran Hadžić, and then his colleague in the Krajina, Milan Babić. Contrary to what Milošević had led us to expect, these were difficult and unproductive meetings. Both men went on at length about Croatian atrocities and both vigorously rejected the ink-spot concept; they could not accept any demilitarization of the Serb-held parts of the 'crisis areas' (though Babić wanted all of Croat-held Croatia to be demilitarized!) and they insisted that the peacekeeping operation be deployed along the cease-fire line, with no restrictions on movement between Serb-held areas in Croatia and either Serbia proper or Serb-held areas in Bosnia. The Greater Serbia project was now emerging clearly.

We flew to Geneva on the morning of the meeting, 23 November. On arrival we learnt that the Dutch Ambassador in Belgrade had described the meeting to the BBC as an emergency meeting arranged by Carrington to which the Yugoslav leaders had been 'summoned'; an explanation of the continuing assault on Osijek would be 'demanded' from Kadijević. Vance was livid at this further evidence of meddling by the European Community and its taking of sides against the Serbs. Vance had briefed Carrington over dinner in Belgrade the previous evening and had invited him to come to the meeting. Were it not for the long friendship between them, the Dutch indiscretion could have caused a major rift between the European Community and the United Nations.

After this inauspicious prelude, the meeting went well. Vance planned that it should begin with just the three Yugoslavs, Vance and Carrington. Vance would read a statement describing the conclusions he drew from his conversations in Yugoslavia. They would then discuss, and, it was hoped, reach a new agreement on, deblocking the JNA barracks and a cease-fire. I would then be called in to present a paper I had drafted in Belgrade about a peacekeeping operation that would monitor the cease-fire and subsequent separation of forces. I was not happy about being excluded from the first part of the discussion but assumed that Vance's purpose was to avoid giving the impression that the United Nations had usurped the EC's political role; I was the technician who would be brought in when the political agreements had been reached.

This was how it worked out. The atmosphere was tense at times. Milošević and Kadijević were on the whole reasonable and supportive of our proposals. Tudjman, by contrast, was strained and emotional, very much the underdog. Carrington was also ill at ease, constantly leaving the room to telephone Van den Broek, who seemed to be running him on a tight rein and was insisting that any agreement should include condemnation of the JNA assault on Osijek. Carrington's patience finally broke and he left. On the peacekeeping operation, the main issues were the geographical delineation of the 'crisis areas', the arrangements for policing within them (Tudjman insisted that these should be 'in accordance with the constitution of the Republic of Croatia') and our ideas about UN deployment in Bosnia. It was agreed that more work should be done on these issues and that we would meet again within ten days.

The next day we flew to Rome to brief Pérez de Cuéllar. Pleased with the election of his successor, he did not have a great deal to say about Yugoslavia. We accompanied him to the Italian Foreign Minister, the ebullient Venetian Gianni di Michelis who, a few weeks earlier, had vigorously opposed a UN operation; now he was vigorously in favour and castigated me as 'just another bureaucrat' when I said that we first had to confirm the principals' ability to control their extremists, that there were procedures to be followed in New York and that we were likely to have trouble with the P-5 about the costs of the operation.

Back in New York, Yugoslavia was top of the agenda. France tried to get the Security Council to adopt an instant resolution in favour of a peacekeeping operation but was blocked by the Non-Aligned, who were uneasy about this United Nations intervention in the Socialist Federation of Yugoslavia to which they remained loyal, and by the Americans, who were concerned about the costs and had to consult Congress before agreeing to such an operation. The Secretariat itself thought that a resolution would be premature at that stage and was more concerned about continuing violations of the cease-fire and the lack of progress on deblocking the JNA barracks. Vance wanted to go back immediately but, since there are violations at the start of every cease-fire, I urged that we should keep him in reserve for larger crises. Instead Vance's senior adviser, Herb Okun, was sent to Zagreb to try to persuade Tudjman to do what he had said he would do; but Vance insisted that he and I should follow a few days later. Meanwhile the JNA put their own pressure on Tudjman by resuming the shelling of Dubrovnik. As a result I spent a weekend under remorseless telephonic pressure from Bernard Kouchner, the Minister for Humanitarian Action in the French Government, who wanted us to deploy UN guards like those in Iraq to deter further shelling. Having seen the mood on both sides, I knew that such a deployment would only demonstrate how impotent the UN was.

Vance and I returned to Belgrade on 1 December. This time the UN team included Behrooz Sadry, Director of Field Operations Division. He was in belligerent mood: our concept, he said, was not workable and the Secretariat did not have the capacity to take on another major operation when Cambodia and Angola were already on the agenda. I had much sympathy for the second point and some for the first. Vance and I were mainly concerned with violations of the cease-fire agreed in Geneva and the question of whether the two sides were either able or willing to control their irregulars. Kadijević admitted that some of the Serb irregulars were beyond his control. Milošević was less honest and became evasive when Vance said that if he wanted a peacekeeping operation he would have to get the Serb leaders in Slavonia and the Krajina, Hadžić and Babić, to accept it. Milošević was more concerned about what was happening in the European Community: the Germans were insisting on the recognition of Slovenia and Croatia by 10 December and the Community's Political Committee was meeting that day to discuss tightening sanctions against Serbia. Milošević justifiably asked whether the Community was still capable of playing a mediatory role. Vance shared his doubts but could not say so.

It is not yet known why Germany was so impatient about recognition of Slovenia and Croatia and so eager to abandon the wise policy which had been adopted at Rome only one month before, linking recognition of the new republics to an overall settlement. Nor is it clear why the British and the French, and indeed the Americans, allowed Germany to get its way, when the damage that was likely to result from recognition was so evident. Various motives have been attributed to the Germans: a desire to assert leadership in Europe following reunification of the country; pressure from Catholic Bavaria to strengthen relations with new Catholic republics to the south; historic hostility to Serbia and friendship with Croatia, which was Germany's ally during the Second World War; access to the Mediterranean. None of these alleged motives is very convincing in the Europe of the 1990s. As for Germany's allies, it is said that recognition became an element in the negotiations which led to the adoption of the Maastricht Treaty on European Union in December 1991 and, in particular, that British acceptance of recognition was traded for German acceptance of British insistence that social policy should not be included in the treaty but covered in a separate agreement to which Britain would not be a party. But this has never been admitted by Britain and if it was true there would still be the question of why France allowed Germany to get its way. This puzzle may not be resolved until details of the Maastricht negotiations are released for public scrutiny.

That afternoon we saw Radovan Karadžić, the psychiatrist-poet leader of the Bosnian Serbs. Intense, dishevelled and with wild eyes, he looked more like someone who needed psychiatric care than someone who could provide it. He gave us a lecture on the constitution of Bosnia, a republic with three nationalities or peoples where no important decision could be taken without the consent of all three. This would apply to the deployment of UN troops in Bosnia. He would strongly oppose any such deployment; Izetbegović wanted a UN presence only because he thought it would help him promote Bosnian separatism; we must remember, he said, that Izetbegović was more fundamentalist than Khomeini himself and intended to make Bosnia a strictly Muslim country when in ten years' time the Muslims' high birth-rate would have made them the majority.

The next day we visited Osijek, the capital of Eastern Slavonia which was still besieged by the JNA. In a town called Dalj, we received a bloodthirsty and mendacious briefing from the JNA corps commander, whose field headquarters were in the commandeered premises of a huge Catholic church. Until the Geneva agreement, he said, his task had been to 'break the *ustashi* forces on the right bank of the Danube'; this had been accomplished; since Geneva not a shot had been fired by his troops or the irregulars, who were all fully under his control; there had never been any indiscriminate shelling of Osijek; but some buildings there had been destroyed by the Croatians themselves in order to provide fuel for their propaganda. This last point was to become familiar as a standard ingredient in all sides' responses to the charge that they had broken the rules: 'the other side did it themselves, so they could turn you against us'.

To get to Osijek we had to pass through the front lines, escorted by the EC monitors. Egged on by his adviser Herb Okun, Vance wanted to take our retinue of journalists across with us. I advised against this: crossing an active front line is a hazardous business at the best of times and cameras are particularly unwelcome; we should take just one journalist with us, on a pool basis, and there was to be no filming or photography in no man's land. To my relief, Vance accepted this advice. Since our first trip together I had been worried by his openness to the media and had tried in vain to persuade him to give one statement in the morning and another in the evening, instead of a stream of off-the-cuff, and sometimes inconsistent, comments during the course of the day.

The JNA's front was a line of muddy trenches, backed by an impressive array of armour and artillery. No man's land was about a kilometre of unharvested maize. The road had evidently been shelled – wrecked vehicles and broken trees lined our route. At one point we came across some fine wires stretched across it. The Danish 'civilian' monitor who was in command of our little convoy responded professionally to this potential hazard, burning the wires with a lighter and declaring them to be the relics of a wire-guided anti-tank missile. As we approached the Croatian front line, anti-tank mines were casually removed from the road to let us pass. We were received by more EC monitors. For them the only villain was the JNA and their moral indignation against it exceeded even that of the BBC's Kate Adie who was amongst the waiting journalists. The town seemed to be little damaged, but a visit to the hospital provided evidence of recent heavy shelling.

On the way back to Belgrade, we stopped in Dalj to upbraid the corps commander for his untruthful briefing. He admitted (as did Kadijević the next day) that the Serbs' 'territorial defence units' had shelled Osijek from the north since the Geneva cease-fire agreement but denied that the JNA itself was responsible for any violations. This too was typical of the mendacity of all sides in the Yugoslav wars. One day they would tell you, with earnest sincerity, that they had not broken the rules; the next day when you confronted them with evidence that they *had* broken a rule, they would admit with a charming smile that this was the case and would then go into a sulk when you lectured them about the need for trust and honesty if peace was to be restored. We left Dalj at sunset, a memorable moment with the sun just visible through the fog, the great church, the camouflaged command vehicles and the tough corps commander crushing one's hand as he said goodbye.

In Zagreb the mood was sour. Tudjman and his ministers held the UN responsible for the shelling of Dubrovnik and resented the pressure which Okun was putting on them to deblock the JNA barracks and an aircraft maintenance facility owned by the JNA, a new issue which had arisen since our last visit. But the Croatians did not raise any serious objections to the latest version of the Vance Plan. We returned to Belgrade to try once more to persuade Milošević to get the Croatian Serb leaders, Hadžić and Babić, to accept the plan. He filibustered: this was a matter for the Federal Presidency; he was only the President of Serbia; as it happened, the two leaders were in Belgrade; perhaps Goulding should speak to them again. Goulding did so, but the two budged not an inch. The demilitarization of the 'crisis areas' (which we were now beginning to call the 'UN Protected Areas' (UNPAs)) was unacceptable; their people would never disarm; the 'Republic of the Serbian Krajina' must be treated as the equal of the Republic of Croatia. Babić did most of the talking; he was a dentist by profession and evidently pulled teeth slowly.

The next day, in Sarajevo, Izetbegović and Silajdžić were even more worried than before: European recognition of the republics as independent states would precipitate a war in Bosnia because the JNA would again intervene to support the Serbs. They asked us to discuss with representatives of the three communities (Muslims, Serbs, Croats) the possible deployment of elements of the peacekeeping operation in Bosnia. We did so in a painful and deeply disturbing meeting. There were six of us seated in a semicircle in a huge room in the Presidency building: Rusmir Mahmutčehajić for the Muslims, Karadžić for the Serbs, Stjepan Kljuić for the Croats, a gentle middle-aged woman as interpreter, Vance and myself. The Muslim and the Croat were strongly in favour of UN deployment in Bosnia 'in order to forestall Serb hegemony'. Karadžić, the Serb, was strongly opposed to it, the other two having made it clear that a UN presence would be misused to promote their secessionist aims; the Serbs in Bosnia could not live without the protection of 'a federal state', by which he apparently meant some successor to the SFRY in which all republics with a significant Serb population would be included. This debate was interspersed with virulent attacks by each of the three on one or both of the others for what their people had done to his. So violent was the discussion that more than once the interpreter broke down in tears; and when the Muslim reached down to take something from the briefcase by his feet I felt for a moment that it was going to be a gun; in fact, it was a luridly illustrated picture book about the butchery visited on his community during the Second World War. One felt that war might be only days away and that there was little the UN could do about it, other than persuading the Germans not to recognize Slovenia and Croatia. As we lunched with Izetbegović, news came in of synchronized JNA bombardments of Dubrovnik and Osijek, the south-western and north-eastern extremities of Croatia – a clear message. Vance sent a fierce protest to Kadijević.

We returned to Belgrade and protested to Milošević too. Typically, he said he was as shocked as we were. He also feigned innocence when we reported the unsatisfactory meeting with the dentist and his colleague. The Krajina and Eastern Slavonia, he said, were genuinely autonomous and would take no orders from Serbia, but he would institute political action, appealing to the people over the heads of their leaders and trying to get them to see where their interests really lay. The next day Kadijević too was apologetic about the bombardments; the commanders concerned would be disciplined (how easy it is for such meaningless assurances to be given in closed societies). But his worry was about recognition; if German policy continued unchecked, we would see the real war in Yugoslavia. This was one of the few issues which united the Serbs and the Muslims.

Boutros Boutros-Ghali, the newly-elected Secretary-General, was in New York and had asked to see me there. I was reluctant to leave Vance at such a formative moment in the design of a new peacekeeping operation and it was agreed that I would instead see Boutros-Ghali in Cairo on 9 December. He plunged straight into Yugoslavia. His misgivings were strong. Failure there could be disastrous for the Organization's standing. We were probably on a loser already: if he recommended against the peacekeeping operation, the Secretariat would be accused of spinelessness by France and others, and terrible things would happen in Yugoslavia; if he said yes, the operation would almost certainly fail, possibly after being enlarged to include other parts of Yugoslavia, and the UN would have to withdraw in ignominy. He asked what I would recommend (tough first question from a new SG!). If the cease-fire held for the next week and if Milošević could deliver the Croatian Serbs, I said, I would recommend in favour; to say no at that stage would do more damage to the UN's standing than if we had to withdraw after having made an honest effort; and success, if achieved, would be a great prize. He looked doubtful – and his remarks turned out to be remarkably prescient.

On his plans for the Secretariat, he said only that he intended to complete his reorganization within the first sixty days. Aimé had told me a few days before that he thought I would be asked to stay. The present conversation left me with the impression that Aimé was right, but Boutros-Ghali had taken care to say nothing specific. It had nevertheless been a good conversation, confirming my impression of him as a man of high intellect who liked to analyse a subject at length and would not be easily distracted from the path of analysis. That would make for long meetings but he had said that he believed in decentralization and he wanted the heads of departments, not his own staff, to have substantive responsibility for the major issues.

In New York the French, with some support from the British, were pressing for the instant deployment of a military observer group in advance of the main operation, as we were doing for Cambodia at precisely that time. But all of us who had been to Yugoslavia, except Okun, thought that this would be premature unless Milošević had delivered Babić and Hadžić. On 15 December the Security Council approved the Secretary-General's plans for a peacekeeping operation but endorsed his view that conditions did not yet exist for it to be established. The Council decided only that a preparatory mission should be sent.

Meanwhile Pérez de Cuéllar, like Carrington, had written to Genscher and others urging that recognition of Slovenia and Croatia be delayed. His efforts were in vain. At a meeting of EC Foreign Ministers on 15–16 December Genscher browbeat his eleven colleagues into inviting all Yugoslav republics which sought EC recognition to apply for it within seven days; their applications would be reviewed by a special commission to ensure that they met the EC's criteria (which related mainly to the rights of minorities); the commission would report by 15 January. Germany, however, confirmed that it would recognize Slovenia and Croatia anyway, even though the republics concerned might not meet the criteria (which Croatia, in the event, did not). On 20 December Izetbegović gave in to German pressure and applied for recognition; the drums of war beat ever more loudly in Bosnia. I have never understood why the other EC countries (and the United States) allowed this disaster to happen.

Boutros-Ghali arrived in New York just before Christmas. At a meeting with Pérez de Cuéllar and Vance on Christmas Eve, he said that he wanted to disengage from Yugoslavia as soon as possible; there was no law that obliged the UN to assume responsibility for every problem in the world; Yugoslavia was a European problem; let the Europeans deal with it. Initially, both Pérez de Cuéllar and Vance went along with this, as did I; Dayal was the only dissenter. But three days later, following Okun's return from the field and his eager advocacy of a UN operation, Vance decided to make one last try to create the necessary conditions. I could not go with him because of the El Salvador negotiations which were to reach their climax between Christmas and the New Year, but I sent Tharoor, my desk officer for Yugoslavia, to advise him on the peacekeeping issues. On 1 January Tharoor reported from Belgrade that Vance was again in favour of early deployment. The prospect of coping with a new operation on top of Cambodia, Angola and the now urgent enlargement of the operation in El Salvador was daunting. But Vance returned with a convincing assurance from Milošević that Hadžić and Babić would be brought to heel, and with a new and more detailed cease-fire agreement which enabled him to persuade a reluctant Boutros-Ghali to send fifty 'military liaison officers' to help the parties maintain the cease-fire. Boutros-Ghali would not, however, recommend the main deployment until the cease-fire had held for at least four weeks.

But it did not hold. So back I went to Yugoslavia at the end of January 1992, after a brief visit to Western Sahara, to look for a way forward. The main problem was not in fact the cease-fire; it was refusal on both sides to accept our basic concept. From the outset Vance's and my position had been that this would be a traditional peacekeeping operation; its objective would be to prevent a resumption of fighting while the EC's Conference on Yugoslavia helped the parties to negotiate a political settlement. To that end there would be a cease-fire, demilitarization of the areas controlled by the Serbs which would be protected by the UN, and withdrawal of both sides' heavy weapons to agreed locations. These arrangements would not prejudge the political settlement; as was standard practice in peacekeeping they would be interim arrangements only. The real problem we now faced was that both the government of Croatia and the Krajina Serbs were trying to manipulate the peacekeeping arrangements to create facts which according to the UN's concept could be created only through the political negotiations.

The Croatians, for instance, continued to insist that their police and other structures of local government, which had been swept away by the Serb uprising in 1991, should be reinstated during the interim period; the constitution of Croatia must be respected. To this we had to say no; the concept was to freeze things as they were (other than demilitarization and the separation of forces) until political negotiation had produced agreement on the future status of the Serb-majority districts in Croatia. But that did not go far enough to satisfy the Krajina Serbs. They rejected the very idea that they were 'in Croatia'; they had exercised their right of self-determination and had seceded from Croatia; the UN had to respect that. They also doubted, rightly as was to be shown three years later, whether the UN force would have the capacity to protect them. Would it really fight if Zagreb decided to recover by force the territory it claimed? What guarantee was there that Tudjman's 'friends in the Security Council' (that is, the United States) would not one day veto renewal of its mandate?

I started in Belgrade with General Blagoje Adžić, the JNA Chief of Staff. Belgrade, he said, continued to give its full support to the Vance Plan; discipline prevailed in the JNA; it had opened fire only thirty-one times since the cease-fire was signed, always in response to Croatian fire, which had killed twenty-four of its men. But Serbs in the crisis areas were genuinely afraid; the United Nations must allay their fears.

A meeting with Hadžić, the Serb leader in Eastern Slavonia, confirmed that Milošević had been making an effort to bring the Croatian Serbs into line. He expressed his concerns about the description of his region as being 'in Croatia'. But he listened carefully to my assurances that nothing was being prejudged and that this would be stated firmly in the Secretary-General's report to the Security Council. On this basis he agreed to accept the plan. I obtained a similar assurance from the leader of the Serbs in Western Slavonia.

However, two meetings with Babić in Knin, the capital of the Krajina, showed that he remained impervious to Milošević's powers of persuasion. The Vance Plan, he said, had been overtaken by the EC's recognition of Croatia on 15 January; we should remember the doctrine of 'changed circumstances' in international law. How could we demand that the Krajina Serbs be demilitarized and denied the protection of the JNA when they were the potential victims of Croatian aggression? If there must be demilitarization, let it be fair and balanced between the two potential enemies. Milošević might have accepted the Vance Plan; the Krajina Serbs had not. Babić was a major thorn in our flesh but I liked him and admired the power of his intellect and his fearless defence of what he saw as his people's interests. Just as I now feel it was wrong to have pressed the Angolan Government to believe that the independence of Namibia would end Savimbi's capacity to wage war against them, it was wrong to try to persuade the Krajina Serbs that the UN could protect them against ethnic cleansing by Tudjman. It could not, and hardly tried to, when Tudjman launched his assault on the Krajina in August 1995.

General Ratko Mladić was also in Knin. He was one of the JNA officers who in 1990 had developed a clandestine plan to organize and arm the Serbs outside Serbia in preparation for the creation of a Greater Serbia when the SFRY eventually fell apart. I saw him separately from Babić. He expressed the same views but in a bluff and direct way that was very different from Babić's reasoned statement of the Krajina's case. He too was scornful of the UN's ability to protect the Serbs from the Croatian Army; his corps was responsible for only part of the Krajina but it was much larger than the proposed UN force, which would have to cover Eastern and Western Slavonia too. I tried to explain that the deterrent power of a UN force is political, not military, but found no common ground. Before dawn the next morning he came round for breakfast with Tharoor and me in the freezing JNA facility where we had been billeted. Persuaded to talk about his past he described, in a matter of fact way, how his parents had been killed by Croatian *ustashi* during the Second World War.

In Zagreb, Tudjman restated the known Croatian position: Croatia's sovereignty must be respected and Croatian displaced persons must return to their homes. The operation, he added, should last for six months or, at the most, one year. I explained why this would never be accepted by the other side. Tudjman then proposed a compromise: the UN operation would have a civilian head who, after due consultation, would appoint a provisional council; that council would assume responsibility for local government, including the police, until the UN held elections for a new council; these would take place at a time to be determined by the UN official, taking into account the extent to which displaced persons had returned to their homes. I undertook to put this to the other side but doubted that it would be accepted. It was not. I was told in Belgrade that the only obstacle on their side was Babić; they would work on him. There might be a slight delay but the UN should continue with its preparations.

The Secretary-General's report to the Security Council stated bluntly that Tudjman had retracted the unconditional acceptance of the peacekeeping plan which he had previously communicated to Vance and that Babić's position suggested that a UN force would not receive cooperation from the Krajina Serbs. He could not yet recommend deployment of the force. Vance went to work on Tudjman and got from him, in writing, an unequivocal acceptance of the concept and the plan. Milošević summoned Babić to Belgrade and tried to bully him into accepting the plan. Babić refused. With the assistance of Milan Martić, the chief of police in Knin, Milošević then arranged for a meeting of the Krajina assembly to be held away from Babić's stronghold in Knin. Babić challenged its legality and did not attend. It voted overwhelmingly to dismiss Babić and to accept the plan.

The way was now clear for Boutros-Ghali to recommend that the Security Council establish the new force. The complexity of Yugoslavia's political geography at that time meant that no place name could be included in the force's title. We therefore called it 'the UN Protection Force' (UNPROFOR);* those to be protected were of course the Serbs in Croatia. The headquarters would be in Sarajevo. This idea had prospered since Izetbegović first mentioned it in November. Vance favoured it because he believed that it would have a stabilizing effect in Bosnia; I favoured it on grounds of impartiality. With hindsight we should have paid more attention to the likelihood of war in Bosnia and the operational consequences for UNPROFOR of having its headquarters there.

The force would be deployed in four sectors, two of them in the Krajina, one in Western Slavonia and one in Eastern Slavonia. Although

---

* For similar reasons the UN force deployed on the Golan Heights in Syria in 1974 was called only 'the UN Disengagement Observer Force'.

the operation would have extensive political, legal, police and information functions, with a civil affairs office in each sector, it would be headed by a military officer who would be supported by a Director of Civil Affairs. The more normal arrangement of entrusting overall responsibility for such an operation to a civilian Special Representative was avoided in order to retain a clear distinction between the peacekeeping, which was the UN's responsibility, and the political negotiations, which belonged to the European Community. The core of the force would be twelve enlarged infantry battalions and its military strength would exceed 13,000 all ranks, almost as large as the force that was to be deployed simultaneously in Cambodia. There would also be more than 500 civilian police officers. The Force Commander would be an Indian officer, Lieutenant-General Satish Nambiar, and his Director of Civil Affairs would be Cedric Thornberry who had performed a similar function in Namibia. The Security Council approved the Secretary-General's recommendations on 21 February 1992 and established UNPROFOR for one year.

Thus was born the UN's largest ever peacekeeping operation. During its first year the Council adopted twelve resolutions adding new tasks to its mandate. It was to remain in the field for four years, peaking at over 57,000 all ranks in 1995; one tiny remnant of it is still deployed on the Prevlaka peninsula in Croatia.

Nambiar and his senior staff arrived in Sarajevo in mid-March. The situation in the UN Protected Areas was disturbing. Alleged cease-fire violations averaged about one hundred per day and people were being driven from their homes for ethnic reasons as each side tried to 'create facts' before UNPROFOR's deployment. Tensions were high in Sarajevo itself and in New York we became increasingly uneasy about the decision to locate UNPROFOR's headquarters there. Nambiar pressed for the earliest possible deployment of his force and this was quickly authorized by the Security Council.

But already the Council, led by Austria and Hungary, was devoting more attention to the deteriorating situation in Bosnia than to UNPROFOR's tasks in Croatia. It was an unfortunate coincidence that both Austria and Hungary were members of the Council at this time, for together they had been the imperial power in Bosnia and Croatia and both were historically hostile to the Serbs; their representatives brought to the Council a passionate bias which did not help the Council to find a way through the very difficult problems it was to encounter in Bosnia.

It had been evident for at least a year that if Yugoslavia broke up piecemeal without an overall political settlement there would be war in Bosnia. Milošević's ambitions for a Greater Serbia were known; they could be realized only if northern Bosnia was under Serb control; otherwise the

Croatian Serbs in the Krajina would be cut off from Serbia itself. Equally well known was Tudjman's desire to annex western Herzegovina, where Croats were the majority ('you must remember, Mr Goulding,' he once said, 'that western Herzegovina is the nicest part of Croatia'). And it was an open secret that, even during the Serb-Croatian hostilities in the Krajina and the Slavonias, Serbian and Croatian leaders had been discussing the partition of Bosnia. But if Bosnia was to be carved up between Croatia and Serbia, what was going to happen to the Muslims? It seemed better to preserve Bosnia as a tri-ethnic state. The alternative would be to partition Bosnia, with the Muslim plurality (43.7 per cent of the population) retaining only a small rump state. For many good reasons, the international community ruled out partition and its peace-making efforts were concentrated on the first alternative. It was on that basis that the war was eventually brought to an end by the Dayton Agreement of December 1995. It is too soon to judge whether that settlement will endure.

The EC's offer in December 1991 to recognize Bosnia's independence required that a referendum be held. It took place on 29 February and 1 March 1992, by which time the Bosnian Serbs had already declared their 'Republika Srpska'. The vote, in which few Serbs took part, was strongly in favour of independence. Within days fighting began in northern Bosnia, as the Serbs asserted their control over the vital corridor between Serbia and the Krajina and started clearing it of other nationalities. By early April this fighting had become the dominant Yugoslav issue in the Security Council. It was embarrassingly evident that Vance and I had made a mistake in recommending that UNPROFOR's headquarters should be in Sarajevo.

Boutros-Ghali sent Vance to Bosnia in mid-April. A cease-fire agreement had just been negotiated but was not being respected – the usual story. Vance returned with a grim report: fighting was widespread and escalating; much of it involved undisciplined irregular forces; already a quarter of a million people had been displaced; none of the parties was without blame; conditions did not exist for deployment of the peace-keeping operation which Izetbegović wanted; but there was still life in the political negotiations conducted by José Cutileiro, a Portuguese diplomat who was Carrington's envoy for Bosnia. He had been exploring the possibilities of a cantonal structure for Bosnia; that might yet be the solution, though it was not at that time acceptable to the Muslims.

Boutros-Ghali was in Paris at the end of April and came under pressure from President Mitterrand to recommend a peacekeeping operation in Bosnia. He doubted the feasibility of this and was concerned about the Secretariat's capacity to manage another large peacekeeping undertaking at that time. But two days later he sent me to Bosnia to evaluate the possibilities. I spent six days in Yugoslavia. The circuit was Belgrade–Sarajevo–Zagreb, with an excursion from Belgrade to Eastern Slavonia to see UNPROFOR at work.

The plan was to take a UN plane from Belgrade to Sarajevo. But the airport was closed because of shelling, so the JNA provided a helicopter to fly me and my party to Pale, Karadžić's base in the hills above the city. It deposited us on the town's football field. Nambiar, who was supposed to meet us, was not there. Nor was anyone else except a couple of policemen. After an hour or so a man who described himself as the director of the 'Republika Srpska's' news agency invited us to his office. He offered a meeting with Karadžić. I declined, thinking it politic to see President Izetbegović first; we would wait in his office till Nambiar showed up. Nambiar eventually turned up, having been delayed for hours at a Serb checkpoint down the hill. Whether the Serbs' purpose was to force me to see Karadžić first or simply to demonstrate who was in control, I do not know.

Sarajevo was already in deep distress. It was besieged by the Serbs and shelled daily. Food was in short supply. The airport was usually closed and no public transport was functioning. Economic activity was at a standstill. The JNA installations within the city, including a cadet school, were blockaded, as they had been in Croatia. Two days before my arrival, UNPROFOR had helped negotiate an agreement under which the Muslims guaranteed safe passage for JNA personnel to vacate the JNA headquarters in the city centre. But as they left along a narrow street, accompanied by UNPROFOR personnel, they were shot down in cold blood by Muslim militiamen. The UNPROFOR officers were powerless to stop the slaughter and were subsequently abused, detained and disarmed by Serb militiamen who accused them of complicity in the plot.

When I called on Izetbegović, he offered to take me on a tour of the city and show me the havoc wrought by the Serb shelling. Mindful of Vance's and my experience at Vukovar, I accepted the offer on condition that I could decide the itinerary. This was agreed. So that afternoon we set off in his vast armoured Mercedes. True to his promise, he let me go first to the street where the JNA personnel had been killed and to the JNA barracks and other blockaded installations. I then invited him to take over. He said that what he most wanted me to see was the destruction by Serb artillery of the mosques in the old city, which was a UNESCO world heritage site.

The media were there in force but destruction was far from evident; just a heap of broken tiles on one of the cobbled streets, without any obvious damage to the adjacent buildings. Suddenly there was a short burst of fire from what I judged to be a heavy machine gun some hundreds of metres away. Staged panic ensued. The armoured Mercedes was reversed up the street at high speed, presenting a much greater threat to all of us than the putative Serb machine-gunner. I was so angered by this performance that I declined to be bundled into the car until I had finished telling Izetbegović about the real damage done to Beirut's city centre during the Lebanese civil war. This apparent courage under fire won me a number of admiring letters from people in Britain who saw the episode on their television screens.

Outside Sarajevo, there were many other places at war in Bosnia but no consistent pattern. In the north-west, Serbs were fighting Muslims; in the north-east, they were fighting Croats; in the east, Serbs were driving Muslims from their homes; in the south-west, Croats, including members of the Croatian Army, were fighting the JNA – but as soon as the JNA withdrew, Croats and Muslims would fight for control of Mostar and the Neretva valley, Bosnia's outlet to the Adriatic. In the month since Vance's visit the number of displaced persons had doubled to more than half a million.

Boutros-Ghali presented his report to the Security Council on 12 May. It stated that all international observers agreed that what was happening was a concerted effort by the Serbs to create 'ethnically pure' regions. Though an accurate description of the views of most international observers at the time, this was not an accurate description of what was actually happening. The disagreeable reality was that the Serbs had indeed begun the ethnic cleansing; but once cantonization was on the agenda, each of the three parties wanted populations to be redistributed in a way that would suit that party best either in a cantonized republic or in the event of partition. For the Serbs that meant consolidating their people in the regions they would need to control if the dream of a contiguous Greater Serbia was to be realized; for the Croats it meant consolidating their control of the largest possible swathe of territory adjacent to Croatia; for the Muslims it meant maintaining a foothold in as many places as possible to demonstrate that the partition of Bosnia could not be achieved without grievous damage to the interests of the Muslim people. But for hundreds of thousands of Bosnians those politicians' priorities were subordinate to their desire to preserve the homes in which they had invested their savings. Ethnic cleansing involved appalling human suffering; and, as one could see so clearly from the air, it also involved the destruction of tens of thousands of family homes.

In this complicated conflict, reported Boutros-Ghali, the three parties had one thing in common. None of them respected the United Nations. Promises made to it were broken. Its personnel (myself included) were denied free passage and fired upon. Its property was stolen and its emblems and uniforms misappropriated by all three parties. But they differed about a peacekeeping operation. The Muslims and the Croats wanted one that would 'restore order' or at least 'reopen communications' in Bosnia, by which they meant take their side against the Serbs. The Serbs wanted no UN peacekeeping in Bosnia. This being so, Boutros-Ghali concluded that the conditions did not exist for peacekeeping there, other than UNPROFOR's existing activities in Sarajevo and Mostar (where a few military observers had been stationed, at some peril to their lives); the European Community must continue its peacemaking efforts; only when it had succeeded would peacekeeping become a possibility. Meanwhile, UNPROFOR's headquarters could no longer operate in Sarajevo and would be temporarily moved elsewhere.

Boutros-Ghali's report stated that UNPROFOR's operations in Croatia were also suffering from the parties' failure to respect or cooperate with the United Nations. A significant error in the Vance Plan had come to light. The plan's purpose had been to demilitarize areas controlled by the Croatian Serbs, pending the negotiation of a political settlement. But the four UN Protected Areas did not include certain areas (which came to be known as 'pink zones') in which Serbs were the majority and the JNA was still in control. Belgrade wanted these areas to be incorporated into the UNPAs; Zagreb demanded that the JNA and Serb irregulars be withdrawn immediately. I felt some responsibility for this problem; more thorough research into the demographics of the zones and the location of forces at the end of 1991 would have led to their inclusion in the UNPAs (which was the obviously sensible solution). But now it was too late; Tudjman could not concede more territory. In his report Boutros-Ghali supported the Croatian position, while asking the JNA and the Serbian authorities to use their influence to calm the fears of the Serb communities who were outside the UNPAs and not therefore under the protection of UNPROFOR.

The report disappointed most members of the Council. There was much wringing of hands; they had wanted to be told what the UN could do in Bosnia; instead the Secretary-General had told them what it could not do; his arguments were irrefutable but there was still a frustrated feeling that 'the UN must do something'. The Hapsburgs (as we now called Austria and Hungary collectively) had resort to invective, equating Serbia with Iraq and Libya and, by implication, inviting the United States to bomb that pariah too. It would be more than three years before this happened. Meanwhile the Council adopted a wordy resolution in which the only instructions to the Secretary-General were to keep under review, first, the feasibility of protecting international humanitarian programmes and ensuring secure access to Sarajevo airport and, secondly, the deployment of a peacekeeping operation in Bosnia.

Boutros-Ghali reported on these matters two weeks later, on 26 May. By then the situation in Sarajevo had deteriorated further. The UNPROFOR headquarters had departed and the only international presence remaining in the city, apart from the media, was a small UNPROFOR group commanded by the Chief Military Observer, the excellent Colonel John Wilson of Australia. The displacement of civilians throughout Bosnia was 'proceeding on a scale not seen in Europe since the Second World War'. Boutros-Ghali still held to the view that the best way of protecting humanitarian activities was through respect for agreements; the problem was that the Bosnian parties' performance in respecting agreements was lamentable. Ethnic cleansing was carried out by deliberately inflicting hardship on civilians. As a result, humanitarian agencies which delivered relief to those civilians were frustrating the war aims of the party concerned and ran the risk of becoming targets themselves. The provision of armed protection for humanitarian convoys would not, on past form, deter the Bosnian parties from blocking or even attacking the convoys; if protection was to be guaranteed, troops would have to be deployed in some force to clear the route in advance and protect the convoy as it passed. A less ambitious objective would be to seek an agreement for the reopening of Sarajevo airport and UNPROFOR protection of convoys distributing supplies in the besieged city.

The Secretary-General's next report, on 30 May, described the confused situation that had resulted from the proclamation in Belgrade in late April of a new Federal Republic of Yugoslavia (FRY), consisting only of Serbia and Montenegro. One of the first decisions of the new federal government was to withdraw from the other four republics all JNA personnel who were citizens of the FRY, leaving the others to return to civilian life or join the armed forces in the new republics. As more than 80 per cent of the JNA personnel in Bosnia were Bosnians and most of them were Bosnian Serbs, this decision placed up to 50,000 former JNA troops and their equipment at the disposal of the 'Republika Srpska'. They would be under the command of General Mladić who had resigned from the JNA – and had immediately ordered a night-time bombardment of Sarajevo in apparent defiance of orders from the JNA leadership in Belgrade, another example of Yugoslav theatre-to-deceive. As requested by the Council in its last resolution but one, Boutros-Ghali analysed the options for international assistance in disbanding Mladić's forces. None of the options bore any relationship to reality. The report led to more agony in the Council. But it also sparked an overdue reaction to Hapsburg hyperbole; several speakers, including France, reminded the Council that it must maintain its impartiality.

At the beginning of June, there was at last some good news. Thornberry, assisted by John Wilson, succeeded in negotiating with the three parties in Sarajevo an agreement under which Sarajevo airport would be vacated by the Bosnian Serb forces and reopened for the delivery of humanitarian supplies. UNPROFOR would operate the airport and ensure its security; all anti-aircraft systems on the approaches and all artillery and missile systems within range of the airport would be concentrated in areas agreed and supervised by UNPROFOR. This was a remarkable achievement but would the agreement be respected? Would the Serbs really give up such an important asset in their siege of the city? The Council was sceptical. It therefore decided to enlarge UNPROFOR's mandate as proposed but to delay deployment of additional troops until the Secretary-General confirmed that they would be able to carry out the tasks entrusted to them. The prospects did not seem promising but on 28 June, in a brave *coup de théâtre*, President Mitterrand of France flew into Sarajevo for a few hours. The next day the Secretary-General was able to inform the Council that the Serbs were at last withdrawing their troops and that the way was clear for the UN to take over; the deployment of additional UN troops was immediately authorized.

In early July I accompanied Boutros-Ghali on a brief visit to London, following Britain's assumption of the Presidency of the European Community for the second half of 1992. At lunch at Lancaster House, the Foreign Secretary, Douglas Hurd, let it be known that if the Serbs continued to use force against international humanitarian operations the Security Council might be asked to authorize air-strikes by NATO powers. Boutros-Ghali and I responded that such action could not be reconciled with UNPROFOR's peacekeeping mandate; the force's personnel would be vulnerable to reprisals if the Serbs (or either of the other parties) concluded that the UN was hostile to them; for its own safety UNPROFOR would have to be withdrawn before the bombers went in; the Security Council had to decide whether it was engaged in peacekeeping, which requires the consent of the parties, or peace enforcement, which does not; the two could not be mixed. This issue was to be an irritant in the Secretariat's relations with the major Western powers for the next three years.

Since becoming Secretary-General, Boutros-Ghali had consistently taken the position that there was a division of labour in Yugoslavia: the European Community was responsible for peacemaking and the UN for peacekeeping. That evening at 10 Downing Street he abandoned this position. Now that Britain held the EC Presidency, he proposed that the EC's Conference on Yugoslavia should be chaired jointly by Carrington (for the EC) and Vance (as the UN Secretary-General's Special Envoy). The UN was so deeply involved in Yugoslavia that the previous division of labour no longer made sense. Prime Minister Major was attracted by this idea but wondered how the French would react. It was agreed that Hurd would consult Carrington and that Major would then pursue the idea at a G-7 meeting the following week.

Back in New York two weeks later I caused, through inadvertence, a major rumpus between Boutros-Ghali and the Security Council. Late on 16 July I received word from José Cutileiro in London that the three Bosnian parties would sign a cease-fire agreement the following day under which the UN would 'supervise' their heavy weapons throughout Bosnia. The next morning David Hannay, the British Ambassador to the UN, confirmed this information, adding that London wanted the Council to authorize the proposed UN role that very day. I replied that we would need details about quantities and locations, so that we could determine the resources required. I asked Annan and Tharoor to monitor the proceedings in the Council but omitted to tell them to brief the Secretary-General (who was engaged in negotiation with Vassiliou and Denktash, the two Cypriot leaders). Under pressure from Hannay, the Council announced its decision in principle to accept the Bosnian parties' request. When I eventually saw Boutros-Ghali late that evening, he exploded with rage at not having been informed. Both Carrington and Vance, he said, had told him during the morning that the cease-fire agreement would not work and he had intended to urge the Council not to approve UN involvement. How could I have allowed the Council to take such a decision without the Secretary-General's knowledge?

On his instructions I drafted a firm letter from him to the President of the Council, followed by a report in which he declined to recommend that the United Nations accept the three parties' request. As a matter of principle, he said, the UN should not be subordinate to regional organizations (like the European Community). Under the Charter the UN could 'utilize' them; there was no provision for them to utilize it. Nor had the UN played any part in the negotiation of the cease-fire agreement. The cease-fire had not come into effect; none of the parties had declared its weapons to UNPROFOR as they were supposed to do. No spare resources, human or logistical, were available and it would take at least three months to deploy the 1,100 military observers that Nambiar believed would be required. And to put yet more effort into Yugoslavia would reduce even further the Organization's capacity to deal with equally cruel and dangerous conflicts elsewhere, such as the one in Somalia.

These themes were to reverberate in Boutros-Ghali's relations with the major Western powers throughout his term of office. Their effect was aggravated by the fact that Boutros-Ghali, unlike his predecessor, rarely put in an appearance at the Council's 'informal consultations'. These were (and still are) private meetings, in a stuffy and uncomfortable little room, which are not open to non-members of the Council nor to the media. The fact that the Council members do so much of their business in private has long been a cause of resentment. Given the power that has accrued to the Council since the end of the Cold War many delegations feel that its proceedings should be more transparent; non-members should be able to observe the political bargaining which precedes its decisions and not be presented with faits accomplis accompanied by bland and uninformative statements in the Council's open meetings. Pérez de Cuéllar's willingness to sit, expressionless and doodling, through hours of these informal consultations won him respect in the Council; Boutros-Ghali, a less patient man, soon concluded that he had more valuable ways of using his time and rarely appeared. This was seen as a slight by some members of the Council and his appointment of Chinmaya Gharekhan, a popular and able Indian diplomat, as his representative on the Council did little to assuage the discontent.

Douglas Hurd came to New York on a conciliatory mission. He told Boutros-Ghali that the British Government, as the Presidency of the European Community, had decided to convene an 'International Conference on the Former Yugoslavia' in London at the end of August. The purpose would be to relaunch the negotiating process in a new format; Carrington's recent efforts in the EC's Conference on Yugoslavia had failed to break the deadlock, he was inclined to pass the chairman's baton to someone new and every day brought worse news from Bosnia. Bearing in mind what Boutros-Ghali had said on his visit to London about revising the division of labour between the European Community and the United Nations, the British Government now proposed that he and Prime Minister Major should jointly chair the new conference.

The Secretary-General was glad that his idea of a new partnership between the EC and the UN had been accepted. But it now sat ill with his announced desire to reduce the UN's involvement in Yugoslavia and I was unhappy with it. I had hoped that he would succeed in getting the Europeans (and the United States) to assume responsibility for both peacemaking and peacekeeping in Yugoslavia – and for the peace enforcement that daily seemed more likely. Even with the appointment of Kofi Annan to reinforce my department, we were hopelessly over-stretched and Yugoslavia was distracting me from other conflicts (Cambodia, Central America, Angola) where there seemed a better chance that the UN could produce results. But I found little support from my UN colleagues; most of them took the view that UN involvement in Yugoslavia was inescapable and that it would anyway not be in the Organization's interest to withdraw from efforts to resolve the most flagrant conflict then troubling the world.

A new issue was the Serbs' siege of a number of Muslim-majority towns in eastern Bosnia, notably Goražde. The Serbs, wanting to drive out their Muslim populations, prevented the delivery of humanitarian supplies. The Hapsburgs pressed for air-drops or for UNPROFOR to provide the humanitarian convoys with armed escorts. The Secretariat made it clear that we had no mandate to do this; the Secretary-General had already warned the Council of the operational complexities of such a task. A related issue was the discovery by the media that detention camps existed in Serb-controlled parts of Bosnia. Some of these were close to the border with Croatia and international personnel on the Croatian side had received reports of atrocities. Quite properly, they had shared this information with the International Committee of the Red Cross (ICRC), which had delegations in Bosnia and Croatia and is responsible under the Geneva Conventions for investigating such matters. But the media, prompted by the Bosnian Ambassador to the UN, Muhamed Sacirbey, demanded an explanation as to why the atrocities had not been reported to the Security Council rather than to the discreet ICRC. The US presidential election campaign was under way and Clinton exploited the furore, prompting President Bush to propose that the Security Council authorize member states to use force to bring relief to the besieged and abused in Bosnia. The British and the French, with the shameful reluctance to face reality that was to characterize their Bosnian policy for the next two and a half years, thought the task should be given to UNPROFOR.

Boutros-Ghali remained admirably firm in maintaining the position that it is impossible to mix peacekeeping and peace enforcement and that in any case the tasks proposed by the Western powers would be very difficult operationally. The upshot was the adoption of two Security Council resolutions on 13 August 1992. The first, adopted under Chapter VII (the enforcement chapter in the UN Charter), called upon states to take 'all measures necessary to facilitate in coordination with the UN' the delivery of humanitarian assistance to Sarajevo and other places in Bosnia. Hannay correctly pointed out that this was a more limited authority than that given to the coalition which used force to liberate Kuwait. But Gharekan, still at that time the Indian Ambassador to the UN, said that this distinction would be lost on the Serbs; if the Council's decision led to their being bombed, they would wreak vengeance on UNPROFOR. Gharekhan was correct too. The second resolution condemned violations of international humanitarian law, including 'ethnic cleansing', and demanded that all such behaviour cease. It recognized the role of the ICRC under the Geneva Conventions but at the end it had recourse to Chapter VII, threatening to 'take further measures' against any party in the former Yugoslavia and any military force in Bosnia which failed to heed the Council's demands. This baring of the Council's teeth may have satisfied the Hapsburgs and met the requirements of the American presidential campaign, but it did nothing to restore peace in Bosnia.

Boutros-Ghali formally warned the Council that enforcement action in Bosnia would have very serious implications for the security of

UNPROFOR personnel stationed there. Unexpected support came from the Pentagon which stated publicly that 100,000 troops would be required to open and hold a corridor from Split (on the Adriatic coast) to Sarajevo and Goražde. A week later delegations came from London, Paris and Washington to discuss implementation of the first resolution. Their proposal was that UNPROFOR should assume responsibility for protecting humanitarian convoys, when so requested by UNHCR, using normal UN rules of engagement (that is, firing only in self-defence) and that it should be reinforced for the purpose by troops from Britain, France and other countries (but not the US) at the expense of the contributing governments. Boutros-Ghali reluctantly accepted this; he did not want to be drawn further into the Bosnian morass but politically he could not turn down such a proposal when the populations of Sarajevo and other besieged cities were suffering such hardships.

I accompanied Boutros-Ghali and Vance to the International Conference on the Former Yugoslavia (ICFY) in London. Boutros had sent Petrovsky ahead to represent the UN in the preparatory commission. He was not amused to learn that, without consulting New York, Petrovsky had accepted the British wish to set up 'contact groups' on sanctions, humanitarian issues and confidence-building measures. Boutros-Ghali feared that it would be difficult for the small UN delegation to ensure that he, as Co-Chairman, was kept abreast of all that was happening. But the pass had already been sold. At a meeting with Major and Hurd we were told that the British were having difficulty in persuading their EC partners that David Owen should succeed Carrington as the EC negotiator.* It also emerged that the British intended the Conference to set up a Steering Committee, chaired jointly by Vance and Owen, which would oversee six working groups on Bosnia: humanitarian issues, succession issues, economic relations, minority and ethnic issues and confidence-building measures. All this was news to us. Our news for them was that the Secretary-General wanted to appoint Martti Ahtisaari to succeed José Cutileiro as the negotiator on Bosnia and to chair the working group concerned.

The Conference lasted for two exhausting days, 26 and 27 August, during which it was almost impossible to keep up with everything that was going on. The first day was all speeches and no negotiation. We sat in a square: the EC and UN had most of one side and the various Yugoslav leaders, all identified by name, not country, had most of the side opposite; the rest of the space was occupied by about thirty foreign

---

* Owen had been Foreign and Commonwealth Secretary from 1967 to 1970. He and I were exact contemporaries at a small prep school in Devon in the 1940s but we found that neither could remember anything of the other.

ministers. The meeting began with points of order by various of the Yugoslavs: Why were there no name-plates for the republics? Why was there no interpretation into Slovenian or Bosnian? Why was Macedonia not recognized by the EC?* Carrington gave a sometimes moving account of his efforts during the past year. The foreign ministers took up most of the rest of the day. The mood was strongly anti-Serb, with several calls for an international war crimes tribunal. The Yugoslavs spoke last; the hatred between them was evident; so was the hatred between Milošević and the Prime Minister of the new Federal Republic proclaimed four months before, Milan Panić, a pharmaceuticals tycoon from California and a newcomer to politics. I spent much of the day in bilateral meetings with foreign ministers of countries which either wanted to participate in convoy protection in Bosnia or were wanted by us to participate in convoy protection in Somalia.

The second day began with a UN–EC consultation. Major recognized that the key issue was whether or not the Muslims would agree to negotiate. If they would not, the Conference would have failed. His second objective was to get the Conference to endorse a number of documents which the British had prepared overnight. Some were familiar to us from consultations the previous day; others were emerging from the contact groups about whose deliberations we knew little. I realized then that the UN delegation should have been larger, with delegation meetings at least once a day. But who should have arranged this – the Secretary-General's office before we left New York, Petrovsky as the Under-Secretary-General for Political Affairs or myself as head of peacekeeping? As so often happened in the UN, no one had made clear who was responsible for what. The most controversial document was a strong criticism of Serbia-Montenegro's involvement in the wars in Bosnia and Croatia. By late afternoon the Conference was in deadlock: the Serbs said that if that document was tabled they would walk out; the Bosnians said that if it was not tabled they would withdraw their agreement to attend negotiations in Geneva. Major resolved the problem by tabling the document and immediately gavelling the Conference to a close before anyone could object. The Muslims were deeply upset: they had obtained no real condemnation of the Serbs, no promise of Western military intervention and no exemption from the arms embargo; and they had had to commit themselves to negotiations.

---

* Unlike the other successor states of the SFRY, Macedonia had not been recognized by the European Community because of Greek insistence that Greek Macedonia alone was entitled to use the name Macedonia. In 1993 Vance mediated a compromise: the country would call itself 'the Former Yugoslav Republic of Macedonia'. As such it was recognized by the EC and admitted to membership of the UN.

But the conference had succeeded in achieving the main purpose the British had in mind. It established a negotiating structure which was more robust and better resourced than the EC's previous Conference on Yugoslavia. On the whole, the new Steering Committee and its six working groups functioned well. So did the two Co-Chairmen, David Owen for the EC and Cyrus Vance and, later, Thorvald Stoltenberg for the UN. Its weakness, perhaps, was that after Vance retired the United States was not directly engaged and this somewhat reduced the Steering Committee's effectiveness and credibility. Towards the end of the conflicts in Bosnia and Croatia, it was largely superseded by a 'Contact Group' consisting of Britain, France, Germany, Russia and the United States.

Meanwhile, there was another surprise to come. In the evening Major and Boutros-Ghali gave a press conference. To my astonishment Major announced that an agreement had been signed with Karadžić: within four days the Bosnian Serbs would declare to the UN all their heavy weapons around Sarajevo and three other besieged cities (Bihać, Goražde, Jajce) and within seven days they would place the weapons under permanent UN supervision. This agreement had been negotiated with Karadžić by Douglas Hogg, a junior minister at the Foreign Office. Evidently it was the price that had had to be paid to get Izetbegović to agree to negotiations. But none of us in the UN delegation had any inkling that the British were negotiating an agreement committing the UN to do something which Boutros-Ghali had said only a month before the UN could not do.

I spent the next seven days in Yugoslavia. UNPROFOR was now installed in its new headquarters in Zagreb and no one envisaged its returning to Sarajevo. Nambiar, whom I admired more and more, had formed a harmonious and cohesive command group. The force was responding calmly and effectively to the almost monthly enlargements of its mandate in Bosnia.

In Croatia I visited all four of the sectors and found the same problem in each: the Serbs were not respecting their commitment to demilitarize the Protected Areas. The JNA had indeed been withdrawn and the 'Territorial Defence Forces' disbanded. But the latter's personnel and equipment, plus personnel from the previous paramilitary groups, had been reorganized into a variety of new formations – 'border militia', 'special police', 'multi-purpose police brigades'. Undisciplined and often drunk, these groups were continuing the work of ethnic cleansing. In the Baranja district in Eastern Slavonia, for instance, there had been 150 police before the war; now there were 800 'regular police', most of them with no previous police experience, and 1,500 'militia'. Almost no displaced persons had returned to their homes and of those that tried a significant proportion had been murdered. The Croatian Government, increasingly impatient at UNPROFOR's failure to create conditions in which refugees could return, was threatening military action.

I was firm to the point of rudeness at a meeting with the 'Government of the Republic of the Serbian Krajina', now headed by Hadžić and Martić, the police chief from Knin who had succeeded Babić: their militias, I said, were a gross violation of the Vance Plan; it was beyond belief that they could allow their so-called government to be controlled by militia thugs (one of them, of course, being Martić himself); they were responsible for paralyzing the work of a joint commission which had been set up to resolve the problem of the pink zones; the Croatian Government's threats to use force were entirely their fault; and, as far as I was concerned, they deserved what might be coming to them. This diatribe received the usual Yugoslav response of smiling admission that there might be something in what I was saying but let's have lunch.

I saw Tudjman at the beginning and the end of the trip. At both meetings he was angry and impatient, not without justification, at the UN's inability to get the Serbs to conform with the Vance Plan. He was especially indignant about the economic consequences. The UN Protected Areas, he said, were effectively cutting Croatia into three. He wanted UNPROFOR to open the motorway between Zagreb and the Serbian border and to protect non-Serb traffic as it passed through Western Slavonia. The Peruca Dam in one of the pink zones was the source of electricity for all of southern Dalmatia; if it was not back in operation within a week, Croatia would have to act (this was a somewhat empty threat because the Serbs were likely to blow up the dam if the Croatians attacked). But he did undertake to stop the press-ganging of Muslim refugees in Croatia for the war in Bosnia and he gave me a helpful proposal on the Prevlaka peninsula. This is a strategic feature at the extreme southern tip of Croatia, which controls the entrance to the Gulf of Kotor, the FRY's only access to the sea following the independence of Croatia. The JNA had not yet withdrawn from it. Tudjman's proposal was that it should be demilitarized and heavy weapons removed from the neighbouring parts of both Croatia and the FRY (Montenegro). This was eventually accepted by the FRY authorities and a small group of UN military observers was deployed to monitor the arrangement. At the time of writing they are still there, the only remnant of UNPROFOR. However the two meetings with Tudjman and the visits to the Protected Areas made me increasingly doubtful about the viability of the Vance Plan; renewed hostilities seemed likely within months. They occurred, but on a limited scale. It was not until the summer of 1995 that Tudjman finally lost patience and used massive force to drive the Serbs out of Western Slavonia and then out of the Krajina.

The second meeting with Tudjman began with a tête-à-tête. He wanted to seek my advice on 'a most delicate matter'. The previous evening an Iranair 747 had landed at Zagreb airport to unload humanitarian supplies for onward delivery to the Bosnian Muslims. The Croatian customs boarded the aircraft and found armed *mujāhidīn*, with 4,000 rifles, 1.2 million rounds of ammunition and over 1,000 cases of two unidentified liquid chemicals. What should he do? The correct course, I said, was to arrest the plane, confiscate the cargo, protest to Iran and report to the UN committee responsible for oversight of the arms embargo. An easier, but less correct, course was to send the plane back to Iran with its cargo. He favoured the first course but said he would first have to consult the Americans. I was intrigued as to why he thought that necessary but subsequently learnt that it was the Americans who had told him that the plane was worth inspecting. When I reached Geneva that evening, there was a message from Nambiar that Tudjman had lost his nerve and was letting the plane go. I telephoned the US chargé d'affaires in Zagreb. He confirmed Nambiar's report but said that the cargo had been unloaded; Tudjman wanted UNPROFOR to take charge of it but was not willing to make a report to the sanctions committee; let his conversation with me suffice.

In Belgrade, there were huge queues for petrol and for the first time I felt that sanctions were having an impact. Milošević was at his most suave. No one had told him, he said, about the violations of the Vance Plan; he would try to get Hadžić and Martić to mend their ways. The meeting with Federal Prime Minister Panić was surreal. It took place in the parliament building where a motion of no confidence in him was being debated, as a result of his erratic performance at the London Conference where he had fought openly with Milošević. The debate was adjourned so that he could meet us. He expressed strong disapproval of the Krajina leaders' failure to implement the Vance Plan; he would try to help. But what really interested him was the Prevlaka peninsula. He rejected Tudjman's proposal (withdrawal of the JNA, demilitarization, monitoring by UNPROFOR) and made a counter-proposal (a permanent JNA presence, with demilitarization of the hinterland) which I told him Tudjman was certain to reject. 'Tell Tudjman to give me that rock with only the sun on it and I will give him the Peruca Dam and four other things in the pink zones. We gotta make a deal.'

In Sarajevo the airport had been open for over two months. It was in no man's land; there was an agreement, much resented by the Muslims, by which Serb ambulances carrying soldiers wounded in the fighting on one side of the airport were allowed to cross to the Serb field hospital on the other side; but they had to run the gauntlet of Muslim snipers and some did not make it. At lunch news came in that contact had suddenly been lost with an Italian aircraft on its way to the airport with humanitarian supplies. Everyone assumed that it had been shot down and there was a general air of helplessness. It was eight hours before an UNPROFOR convoy got to the site and found that there were no survivors.

I began my meeting with Izetbegović by telling him about the plane. He instructed his staff to establish the facts immediately; there was much rushing to and fro; within fifteen minutes a report was made: Zagreb air traffic control (ATC) confirmed that the plane had been hit by a missile fired from somewhere near Kupres (Serb-held territory, of course); for ten minutes the pilot had wrestled to save the plane, all the time in contact with Zagreb ATC, but alas he had failed; the plane had come down near Dubina, in Croat-held territory. Knowing, as I did, that Zagreb ATC had suddenly lost contact, without any explanation, I received these lies with what I hoped was a contemptuous glare and staged a loss of temper when Izetbegović pressed for his officials to accompany the UNPROFOR search party (which would have meant delays at every Serb checkpoint en route).* Izetbegović further annoyed me by insisting that the agreement negotiated by Douglas Hogg in London covered *all* Serb heavy weapons in Bosnia and not just those around Sarajevo, Bihać, Goražde and Jajce. He spurned our plans for the protection of humanitarian convoys and revived his unrealistic demands for UNPROFOR to open, and keep open, secure corridors between all the main cities.

The final meeting in Sarajevo was with Karadžić in the late afternoon at the Serbs' base on the outskirts of the city. This was the hour of the Sarajevo sunset chorus and sure enough our conversation was punctuated with some loud bangs. But Nambiar's expert ear led him to think that these were probably orchestrated by the Serbs to substantiate Karadžić's complaints about the 'continuous offensives' launched by the Muslims since the London Conference. Predictably he held the Muslims responsible for the loss of the Italian aircraft and for attacks on Serbs around Goražde after the 'withdrawal' ('defeat' would have been more accurate) of Serb forces which had been besieging the town. If this went on, he said, his people would not let him honour his commitments under the Hogg agreement.

Back in New York, the Security Council leapt into action again. Boutros-Ghali reported that in discussion with a number of Western powers and UNHCR a plan had been worked out for UNPROFOR to protect humanitarian convoys when so requested by UNHCR. The force would be strengthened with four or five battalion groups for this purpose but at no expense to the United Nations. This arrangement was approved by the

---

* The UN was never able to establish who had shot down the plane.

Council on 14 September, with the added proviso that UNPROFOR was authorized to protect convoys of released detainees as they left Bosnia. On 6 October the Council adopted a resolution asking the Secretary-General to appoint a committee of experts to investigate violations of international humanitarian law in Bosnia. Three days later there was a resolution banning military flights in Bosnian airspace; UNPROFOR was to monitor compliance with the ban by stationing observers at airfields in the neighbouring republics. A month later, after receiving Vance's and Owen's first report as Co-Chairmen of the Steering Committee of the London Conference, the Council adopted an omnibus resolution which, in addition to reaffirming many previous decisions, tightened the sanctions on Belgrade and asked Boutros-Ghali to study two new ideas. These were the stationing of UN observers on Bosnia's international borders and the establishment of safe areas for humanitarian purposes.

Nor did the Council neglect UNPROFOR's activities in Croatia. The Secretary-General submitted a gloomy report on these at the end of September. It contained only two positive elements. Croatia and the FRY had reached agreement on the demilitarization of the Prevlaka peninsula and its monitoring by UNPROFOR; and the force's Kenyan battalion had taken control of the Peruca Dam after consultants had produced an alarming report about the condition of its structure; it had not yet, however, been possible to remove the explosive charges allegedly placed in it by Serb forces. A further report by Boutros-Ghali two months later had even less good news to impart. The Krajina Serbs were less and less cooperative and the Secretary-General stated bluntly that they bore responsibility for the non-implementation of the peacekeeping plan. None of the outstanding issues had been resolved; even the JNA's withdrawal from Prevlaka had been bungled and had led to extensive fighting in the hinterland.

In December Tudjman proposed that UNPROFOR be authorized to use force to implement the Vance Plan. In January, his patience broke and the Croatian Army launched an offensive into one of the pink zones to retake a damaged bridge which needed repair in order to restore road communications along the Dalmatian coast. The Serbs broke into the depots where their heavy weapons had been stored under UNPROFOR's control and battle was joined; the Croatians won; two French soldiers of UNPROFOR were killed. The Security Council wrung its hands and adopted another resolution. The Serbs seized the Peruca Dam; the Croatians took it from them. The Serbs blamed UNPROFOR for their losses, threatened UNPROFOR personnel and refused to return their heavy weapons to the storage areas.

In November Boutros-Ghali had warned the Council that peacekeeping in Croatia seemed likely to create for the Council the same dilemma as

UNIFIL in southern Lebanon: non-cooperation by one or more of the parties would prevent the force from fulfilling its original short-term mandate but it would nevertheless reduce the level of hostilities and alleviate the suffering of the civilian population. The Council would then face a difficult choice between withdrawing it, in the knowledge that this could lead to a resumption of fighting, or keeping it in place, in the knowledge that this could mean a large and expensive commitment of indefinite duration. After the Croatian offensive, he told the Council that he did not believe that UNPROFOR's mandate in Croatia should be renewed unless two issues were successfully addressed. The first was implementation of the original peacekeeping plan; the second was progress in negotiating a political settlement between the Croatian Government and the Krajina Serbs. This task should be entrusted to the Co-Chairmen of the International Conference's Steering Committee, Vance and Owen. This recommendation was accepted; negotiations proceeded intermittently and with limited success; in 1995 Tudjman's patience broke again and he used force to drive the Serbs from Western Slavonia and then from the Krajina. Only then was a political settlement negotiated for Eastern Slavonia of the kind that we had envisaged in 1991.

As for Bosnia, the Co-Chairmen were picking up speed and submitting regular reports on their progress in defining constitutional principles for a reconstituted multi-ethnic state. This work would lead in May 1993 to the Vance–Owen plan for a Bosnia consisting of ten provinces which, had it been accepted, would probably have been a better settlement than the Dayton Agreement adopted in November 1995 after thirty more months of murderous warfare. In the Secretariat we continued to wrestle with simplistic and impracticable ideas for adding new tasks to UNPROFOR's mandate. A good example was the issue of stationing United Nations observers on Bosnia's borders.

The Bosnian Prime Minister proposed in August 1992 that such observers should be stationed 'along' the republic's borders in order to stop the illegal entry of military personnel and supplies and the illegal transfer of Bosnian assets to neighbouring countries. In November the Security Council endorsed the idea and asked the Secretary-General to make recommendations. Analysis identified three possible operational concepts: observe and report; observe, search and report; or observe, search, deny passage and report. Given that in Bosnia what is now called 'naming and shaming' did not persuade any of the parties to honour its commitments, we concluded that only denial of passage would have any real effect. Most of the 123 border crossings were in places where, on the Bosnian side, control was exercised by enemies, or potential enemies, of the Sarajevo government. This meant that the denial of passage would have to take place on the territory of the neighbouring state whose consent would have to be obtained. But the neighbouring states themselves were, or could become, hostile to Sarajevo, so the UN observers would have to be numerous, armed and well-endowed logistically. This would indicate at least 10,000 additional troops. The cost for the first year would be about $1.3 billion. The Council did not proceed with the idea.

Just before I left the peacekeeping department, UNPROFOR was given an additional task in Macedonia (or, rather, 'the Former Yugoslav Republic of Macedonia' as we had to call it). Kiro Gligorov, the Macedonian President, asked for UN military and police personnel to be deployed for preventive purposes along his country's borders with Serbia and Albania. Ostensibly the request was due to concern that the small Serb minority in Macedonia might create problems similar to those in Croatia; but a greater, and undeclared, concern related to secessionist sentiment in the much larger Albanian minority. Gligorov felt that a UN presence would have a stabilizing effect. His request was readily accepted by Vance, Boutros-Ghali and the Council and the troops were deployed.

This was an interesting innovation. In all previous cases, UN peacekeeping operations had been deployed after a conflict had broken out and on the basis of an agreement between the hostile parties. In Macedonia there was not yet a conflict and the UN deployment was undertaken at the request of one party only, without specific identification of who the potential adversary might be – the Macedonian Serbs, the Federal Republic of Yugoslavia, the Macedonian Albanians, Albania? The UN force was to remain in Macedonia for over six years, until in 1999 the government's ill-judged recognition of Taiwan caused China to veto extension of the force's mandate. The UN (the author included) has tended to hail this experiment in preventive peacekeeping as a success. Certainly Macedonia was spared civil war until some months after the UN force was obliged to leave. But can we be sure that this was because of the UN presence? We cannot. One of the problems with preventive action is that if the conflict to be prevented does not occur one can never be certain whether the happy outcome is due to one's own preventive efforts or to other unrelated factors.

Boutros-Ghali's decision in early 1993 to transfer me to the Department of Political Affairs released me from the Yugoslav vortex into which I had been plunged fifteen months before. I regretted the move but was not sorry to pass to Kofi Annan the burden of UNPROFOR. After the London Conference in August 1992, I began to feel that this enormous operation was spinning out of my department's control. Nambiar had a similar feeling in the field. One problem was the size and complexity of the operation and the constant expansion of its tasks. Another was the appalling cruelty of the conflicts and the passion this generated in the West and in the Islamic world. A third was the deceitful and uncooperative nature of all the protagonists; in no other conflict with which I was concerned were so many lies uttered or the parties' promises so rarely fulfilled. A fourth problem was the inclusion in UNPROFOR of Western contingents which were funded exclusively by their governments and not by the UN membership as a whole. The result was that those contingents tended to give more heed to the instructions which (improperly) their governments sent them than to the orders of the Force Commander. This distortion of the chain of command was so severe that Boutros-Ghali soon recommended that these contingents should be subject to the same financial arrangements as all others. A fifth factor was the presence in Geneva of two powerful and senior personalities, Cyrus Vance and David Owen. I liked and admired them both but it was not easy to fit them into the usual management structures of UN peacekeeping and peacemaking.

Finally, in the last quarter of 1992 my department was facing major crises not only in Yugoslavia but also in Angola, Cambodia, El Salvador and Somalia, as well as trying to establish a new operation in Mozambique. We were little larger than we had been when there were only five peacekeeping operations and barely ten thousand uniformed personnel in the field. We simply did not have the capacity to unravel the complexities of the largest conflict in Europe since the Second World War, digest the huge flow of information it generated, maintain good relations with the interested delegations in New York and devise more effective ways of carrying out the tasks laid upon the Secretary-General by the Security Council, in the former Yugoslavia and elsewhere. With hindsight, I should have confronted the Secretary-General and the member states with this reality and pressed more insistently for extra staff. Perhaps, too, Boutros-Ghali was right; I should have spent more time in New York running the department and less time in the field. But the trips to Yugoslavia were not 'promenades', as he alleged (though they were enjoyable and a blessed relief from the pressures in New York). They were needed both for the management of the operation and for the inevitable negotiations with the parties. Again with hindsight, it was a mistake not to appoint, from the outset, a senior civilian to head UNPROFOR. A Special Representative of the Secretary-General could have handled more of the negotiations and lightened the load on the head of the department in New York. This was not put right until Boutros-Ghali appointed Thorvald Stoltenberg as SRSG in March 1993. But Stoltenberg soon found that it was impossible to combine the leadership of UNPROFOR with his duties as Co-Chairman of the ICFY Steering Committee and it was not until January 1994 that UNPROFOR received, in the person of Yasushi Akashi, a civilian who was exclusively devoted to the direction of that huge operation.

Endings

18

Lessons Learnt

The move in March 1993 from the Department of Peacekeeping Operations to the Department of Political Affairs altered my job. I was still working in the field of peace and security. But a well-defined and operational task – directing thirteen peacekeeping operations, with 55,000 uniformed personnel in the field – was exchanged for the ill-defined one of running a large and amorphous department in New York. It had been hastily composed the previous year by sweeping together more than 300 officials from six 'political' offices which Boutros-Ghali had decided to abolish or transform in his restructuring of the Secretariat. There had been no time to assess how well those officials' skills would match the tasks of preventive diplomacy and peacemaking which he intended to be the new department's primary responsibility. Initially it was headed by two Under-Secretaries-General, Vladimir Petrovsky and James Jonah. When I replaced Petrovsky, Jonah was already in charge of Africa and the Middle East, the regions in which I had most expertise. My own portfolio covered Europe and the Americas, plus a variety of more menial bureaucratic tasks. After a year, Jonah left to join the government in Sierra Leone and Boutros-Ghali decided that the department needed only one USG. This enabled me to remodel it in ten divisions – six geographical ones, one for disarmament, one for electoral assistance and one each for servicing the General Assembly and the Security Council.

There was some satisfaction to be gained from my new post but there was not much travel and I enjoyed less autonomy; the vineyards in which I laboured were no longer missions in the field but committees in New York. Although pleased at first to be relieved of a burden that had become almost intolerable, I watched with envy as Kofi Annan took charge of peacekeeping and launched six new operations in his first eight months in the job. The relationship between his department and mine was complicated by Boutros-Ghali's insistence that the political department should deal with the 'political aspects' of peacekeeping. I continued to believe in the integrity of peacekeeping and the impossibility of dividing it into 'political' and 'operational' aspects. But Boutros-Ghali and

Jean-Claude Aimé, who was now his Chief of Staff, would not accept this. Annan's department, for instance, drafted the reports on peacekeeping operations which the Secretary-General presented to the Security Council. But Boutros-Ghali insisted that the drafts should all be vetted by me before being forwarded to him for approval. This caused understandable resentment in DPKO, as did the behaviour of some firebrands in my own department who tried to assert its supposed responsibility for the political side of peacekeeping. Annan and I controlled the damage by agreeing early on that neither of us would entertain complaints from our staff about the alleged iniquities of the other's staff; complainants would be told to resolve the problem at their own level.

Meanwhile United Nations peacekeeping ran into increasing difficulties. By late 1994 there would be 78,000 uniformed personnel in the field in fifteen operations. Already during my own time as head of peacekeeping, overload was evident and, though I did not notice it at the time, we were becoming careless. This was partly due to the burden of work but perhaps also to the fact that our judgement had been blunted by the intoxicating effect of peacekeeping's successes in the years following the end of the Cold War. Many of the later mistakes were my mistakes, for I was as intoxicated as everyone else. One example was our failure to recognize the fragility of the agreements on which we based what was to become a vast operation in Yugoslavia. Another was the imprudent insertion of United Nations military personnel into a conflict in Somalia whose dynamics were poorly understood in New York.

Kofi Annan wisely set up a 'lessons learnt unit' in DPKO, but by the time the importance of its work was recognized by the Secretariat and the member states, the United Nations had suffered major setbacks in Rwanda, Somalia and Bosnia. As a result, the worth of United Nations peacekeeping came under question, especially in Washington, and in two years the number of personnel in the field fell to barely 20,000. Analysis of the failures has produced a high level of agreement on their causes and on the measures needed to ensure that they do not recur. There is rather less readiness on the part of governments to take those measures.

The first set of 'lessons learnt' relates to the nature of conflict. A conflict usually starts because one side decides that violence is the best means it has of achieving an objective; the conflict continues because the other side decides that violence is the best, or only, way of defending itself against its adversary. Each of the two sides is thus fighting because it sees fighting as the best, or least bad, option available to it. The task of peacemakers is to persuade each side that continuation of the conflict will not produce the outcome which that side desires and that a better option is to negotiate a settlement which will enable each side to achieve some part of its objectives; it is better to have a fraction of a loaf than no loaf at all. Professor Zartman of Johns Hopkins University is right when he says that such persuasion will not succeed until a conflict has been made 'ripe' for settlement by the pain that both sides are experiencing. This means, however, that at any one time few of the actual or potential conflicts in the world will be ready for third-party involvement; years, even decades, can pass before the necessary level of pain is reached. Of course, the Secretary-General must regularly take the temperature of each conflict in order to assess whether it is becoming ripe for third-party treatment. But he should discourage governments and public opinion from assuming that because fighting is taking place, 'the United Nations must do something'. All too often there is nothing that it can do, other than to provide humanitarian relief to suffering civilians. As President Clinton said in a speech to the General Assembly, 'the United Nations must learn to say no', a precept which applies as much to governments as it does to the Secretariat. The scarce resources that are available for peacemaking and peacekeeping must be reserved for conflicts where it is clear that expenditure will produce results.

A second set of lessons relates to the agreements on which peacekeeping is based. Whenever a new operation is established or an existing one is given new tasks, there has to be a written agreement or agreements between the parties to the conflict and between each of them and the United Nations. These agreements must, at the very least, record the parties' agreement to stop fighting, register their consent to the United Nations operation, commit them to cooperate with it, define the tasks it is to undertake and establish the status which its personnel will enjoy in territory controlled by each of the parties. Such agreements can take time to negotiate. It can be tempting to deploy immediately and tie up the loose ends afterwards, and governments and the media often urge the Secretary-General to do this. But the temptation must be resisted, both for operational reasons and because the readiness of parties to negotiate expeditiously on such matters is itself a measure of the seriousness of their intent. Strong though the pressure may be for the UN to do something, it is a mistake for it to beg the parties to accept its peacekeeping services; let them do the begging; they should be indebted to the United Nations, not vice versa.

Success in peacekeeping is also dependent on how the peacekeepers react to breaches of the agreements on which the operation is based. These can call for tough decisions and universal precepts are hard to define. Compare, for instance, the operations in Angola and Cambodia. In both cases, one or more of the parties failed to respect the military provisions of the peace settlement. This raised the question of whether the scheduled elections could or should be held when one of the key conditions for holding them was not going to be fulfilled. In both cases, it was agreed between the mission in the field, the Secretary-General in New York and the members of the Security Council that the risk should be taken. In Cambodia that turned out to be the right decision; in Angola it was the wrong one. But I have not been able to derive from these two cases any universal guidelines, other than the thought that there may be less risk of the election failing when several major parties are contesting it, as in Cambodia, than when it is a head-to-head battle between only two parties, as in Angola.

It is, however, possible to define tactical precepts for peacekeepers to observe when agreements are violated. The first is never to turn a blind eye; the parties must be persuaded that the United Nations is a tireless and fearless monitor of their respect for agreements they have signed. Sometimes a force commander would urge that the violating party be given time to get to know the peacekeepers; only then could the whistle be successfully blown if rules were broken. My reply should always have been that this was mistaken; every condoned violation creates a precedent; ground lost at the beginning cannot be recovered; start tough and continue tough. But I have to confess that there were occasions when I too paled at the prospect of an early confrontation with one of the parties and agreed that a violation should not be challenged until later.

A second precept is never to humiliate the violating party; criticism of its actions should be communicated to it in private, not in the presence of its opponents; nor should it be pilloried in the Secretary-General's published reports to the Security Council. 'Face' is important in these situations and not only in eastern countries. A third precept is to enlist the help of others when an agreement is violated. In almost all cases, governments or other international organizations will have played a part in negotiating the cease-fire agreement or peace settlement; and in every case the members of the Security Council will have taken the decision to field the peacekeeping operation. A number of governments will therefore have a stake in its success. Discreet intervention by governments which have already played a part in the peace process and are friendly to the violating party can be a valuable addition to the diplomatic resources at the Secretary-General's disposal, as was particularly well demonstrated by the 'Friends of the Secretary-General' in El Salvador.

A third set of lessons relates to the military and police personnel required for United Nations peacekeeping operations. Member states are under no formal obligation to make them available. The UN Charter provides for member states to enter into 'special agreements' with the Security Council by which they would undertake to provide military resources on call if the Council needs them for the purpose of maintaining international peace and security. For political reasons related to the Cold War, no such agreement has ever been concluded. Nor has the

Security Council ever assumed direct command of an enforcement operation. When such action has been required, as in Korea in 1950 or Kuwait in 1990, the Council has authorized a group of member states (now referred to as a 'coalition of the willing') to use force to achieve a purpose approved by it. When the UN is required to provide peacekeeping, by which is meant the use of international military personnel with the consent of the hostile parties, the Council has always entrusted the command of the operation to the Secretary-General. In both cases, governments' contribution of troops and police is purely voluntary. This can mean, as it did in Rwanda in 1994, that the Secretary-General is unable to recommend action to the Security Council because governments are unwilling to make the necessary troops available.

This factor has, since the early days of the United Nations, caused a number of experts, notably Brian Urquhart, to argue that the UN itself should recruit a rapid reaction force some 5,000 strong which would be immediately available when needed. It would be deployed only if the Security Council so decided, and its role would be to get a new operation started and to hold the ground until troops contributed by member states were available to take its place. At that point it would return to base and be on stand-by for the next crisis. This idea has attracted much support from individuals and non-governmental organizations who desire a more effective United Nations and who recognize that total reliance on troops volunteered by governments is an impediment to rapid deployment. But the idea has attracted few governments, for two reasons. First, the cost of recruiting, accommodating, training, arming and managing such a force would be a heavier charge on the UN budget than member states are prepared to accept. Secondly, member states would not like the Secretary-General to have an 'army' at his beck and call. Even though the force would be deployed only by decision of the Security Council, its very existence could seem to give the Secretary-General a degree of political authority not envisaged in the Charter. An army, it is argued, is the prerogative of a sovereign state; if entrusted to an international official, it could inspire dangerous illusions of grandeur.

Instead of pursuing the option of a standing army, the Secretariat has worked hard to conclude 'stand-by agreements' in which governments undertake to have troops and equipment on stand-by for rapid deployment when the United Nations needs them. In their full form such agreements define the categories of troops that will be contributed, the vehicles and other equipment they will bring with them, the training they will have received and the minimum notice required for their deployment. These agreements have gone some way to ease the problem but not far enough to resolve it. Their main weakness is that governments invariably reserve to themselves the right to wait until the details of the

new peacekeeping operation are known before deciding whether to contribute personnel to it. In many cases this is a constitutional obligation
(and may require lengthy proceedings in national parliaments) but it also
reflects an understandable reluctance of governments to write a blank
cheque for the deployment of their troops into the middle of someone
else's war.

Another suggestion aimed at strengthening the Secretary-General's
military capacity and ability to deploy rapidly is that he should have a
'general staff'. This would be composed of officers who would leave their
national forces in mid-career and join the United Nations with the intention of spending the rest of their time there (in the same way that I
moved from the British Diplomatic Service to the UN Secretariat, not on
secondment but on a permanent basis). The role of the UN general staff
would be threefold: they would be the main source of military advice to
the Secretary-General; they would do the military planning in New York;
and they would provide the core staff officers at the field headquarters of
all UN military operations. Not only would this improve planning and
ease the establishment of new operations. The general staff would also
ensure that the established principles, procedures and practices of peacekeeping were uniformly applied world-wide. A number of episodes
described in this book have illustrated the problems that can arise when
a group of officers from heterogeneous backgrounds find themselves
charged with setting up in a foreign land a new military operation of a
type not previously known to many of them.

This idea likewise finds little favour with governments. It would be
expensive and difficult to manage; like the standing army, it would put
too much apparent power in the hands of the Secretary-General; and it
would deny governments the ability to influence the Secretariat's military
policy by lending their own officers to the United Nations on short-term
secondments. As the growing volume of peacekeeping in the early 1990s
overwhelmed the exiguous military staff in New York, governments
became increasingly ready to provide officers to the peacekeeping
department at no expense to the United Nations. The governments were
primarily Western governments, which found it easier than others to
meet the not inconsiderable costs of posting officers to New York. The
arrival of these 'gratis officers', as they were called, added to the concern
of many member states that, following the end of the Cold War, the
Western powers were taking over the United Nations and other international institutions and using them to advance their own interests. The
gratis officers also made it even easier than before for Western governments to monitor the Secretariat's work and intervene with the Secretary-
General if they did not like what was going on.

Because peacekeeping is wholly dependent on the willingness of governments to contribute troops, the Secretariat, in its relations with the troop contributors, has tended to wear kid gloves. Criticism of the quality of their personnel or of their interference in the UN chain of command has been avoided except in the most egregious cases. Freed now from the shackles of official responsibility, I offer some frank precepts to troop-contributing governments. First, send your best; their performance will enhance your standing amongst the nations. Secondly, prepare them for peacekeeping; it differs from the combat duties for which they have been trained but it too can be difficult and dangerous. Thirdly, pay particular attention to the quality of the contingent commander. Make sure that he or she is an officer who will ensure that discipline is enforced. Some societies are tolerant of the excesses of young men in uniform, but others are not; violation of the host country's social norms can turn its people against the peacekeepers. So can corruption. Special care is needed in poor countries where the comparative opulence of the peacekeepers can have destructive social effects. Fourthly, choose carefully the staff officers who will be assigned to the operation's headquarters. They must be suited to work with officers from other countries. Even more than the formed units, they will be the measure of your army's quality. Fifthly, respect the United Nations chain of command. Do not attempt to countermand orders which your contingent receives from the UN commander; if you do not like the orders, take the matter up with UN headquarters in New York. Sixthly, tell your contingent commander not to establish a local identity separate from that of the rest of the force. The winning of hearts and minds in your battalion's area of operation is welcomed but your contingent must not aspire to a wider political role in the host country. It was for the latter reason that in the early days there was an informal convention that permanent members of the Security Council would not participate in peacekeeping and that former colonial powers would not contribute troops to operations in their ex-colonies. Both rules were broken by the British contingent in Cyprus and the French contingent in southern Lebanon. In recent years the convention has been largely ignored, with particularly unhappy consequences in some former colonies.

The fourth set of lessons relates to the United Nations Secretariat and its perceived inefficiency. In some respects inefficiency did (and does) exist, as in most international bureaucracies. Few memories of my UN days disturb me more than the recollection of how little I knew when we plunged into new conflicts in places like Yugoslavia and Somalia. The Secretariat is not a Foreign Ministry. Its research capacity is limited; its knowledge about member states and their disputes is selective, depending primarily on whether the United Nations has previously been involved. What we lacked was a systematic procedure for enlisting the help of governments, academics, journalists and NGOs in briefing Secretariat officials when a new crisis broke and the United Nations seemed likely to be asked to provide its peacemaking and peacekeeping services.

In other respects the Secretariat is unfairly held responsible for inefficiencies which are not its fault. This is especially true of its failure to deploy rapidly when a new peacekeeping operation is required at short notice in a distant theatre. The damaging consequences of slow deployment in such circumstances have recurred throughout this book; the damage is suffered not only by the unfortunate people in the war zone; the standing of the United Nations also suffers. All of us who had responsibility for peacekeeping were agonized by our inability to meet the political need for rapid deployment. But it was not our fault. The problem lay in governments' insistence that the peacekeeping activities of the United Nations be subject to the same regulations and procedures as are applied to the activities of its bureaucracies in New York, Geneva, Vienna and other UN centres.

The member states' unwillingness to approve special arrangements for new peacekeeping operations had dire consequences. Take, for instance, the posting of a press officer to the field. This should be almost the first thing that happens, for there needs to be an authoritative United Nations voice to explain to the local media why the operation is being deployed and what it is going to do. Otherwise the parties to the conflict will propagate unchallenged their own one-sided interpretations of events. But if the rules are strictly followed, it is almost impossible to deploy the press officer at the outset. For the rules say that he or she cannot go to the field unless a post for a press officer has already been established. But a post cannot be established until the new operation's budget has been adopted by the General Assembly. However, the General Assembly cannot adopt the budget until it has been approved by its Fifth Committee, and the Fifth Committee cannot approve it until it has been examined in detail by an expert body called the Advisory Committee on Administrative and Budgetary Questions (ACABQ). But the ACABQ cannot start examining it until the Security Council has taken the political decision to establish the new operation.

In the early 1990s, the average passage of time between the Security Council's decision and the General Assembly's adoption of the budget was twenty-six weeks. So if we were to meet the needs of the new operation, we had to break the rules and rely on our ability to justify this to the auditors *ex post facto*. We usually succeeded. But rules are made to be obeyed and it is unhealthy for an organization, and unfair to its employees, if they are obliged to break the rules to get their jobs done.

This unsatisfactory state of affairs has been evident to successive Secretaries-General. They have seen that it is unwise and impractical to subject UN peacekeeping operations to administrative rules devised for a static Secretariat whose functions and budget change little from year to year. The rapid deployment of a military force to a distant theatre requires a financial and logistical agility unknown to most bureaucracies. So Secretaries-General have asked the member states to approve special rules for the initial phase of new peacekeeping operations. They have had some success. The Secretary-General can, for instance, apply to the ACABQ for a limited authority to commit money as soon as the Security Council has taken the political decision to establish a new operation. Some progress has also been made in setting up a reserve stock of peace-keeping equipment at Brindisi in Italy. But much remains to be done if the United Nations is to be able to respond adequately to the political need for rapid deployment.

Another besetting problem of the Secretariat is the internal strife within its ranks. This too is said to be endemic in international bureau-cracies, though it is not clear to me why that should be so. Some of the difficulties which arose between my colleagues and me have been described in this book with a frankness that is not customary in the United Nations. I have done this deliberately, not to settle old scores or denigrate the individuals concerned but to give the reader a fuller under-standing of what it was like to work in the United Nations and the extent to which internal strife undermined its efficiency. Endemic strife is not a condition that can easily be cured in any organization or society. Successes ought to help but in practice they seem not to; the award of the Nobel Peace Prize to the UN peacekeeping forces in 1988 did nothing to improve my department's relations with others. Good leadership is obvi-ously important and so are the attitudes of governments. Members of the Secretariat want to be appreciated by the member states; they want to be recognized for the good job that most of them do. Lack of respect and support for them from member states does not unite the UN staff in defence of their organization and their own reputations; on the contrary, it tends to undermine morale and have a divisive effect.

The fifth and final set of lessons relates to the member states of the United Nations, for it is they who have the power of decision, in matters great and small.* It is they who, in the Security Council, decide that a peacekeeping operation should be deployed and what its tasks should be. It is they who, in the General Assembly, decide what resources should be made available to the operation. The Secretary-General's role is to provide them with recommendations on these points and to prepare an operational plan. Most of the disasters which brought UN peacekeeping into disrepute in the mid-nineties occurred when governments and the

---

* A secretary could not be added to my department without a decision of the General Assembly.

Secretary-General were at odds. In Western Sahara Pérez de Cuéllar pressed ahead with his doomed plan, notwithstanding governments' unease about whether the two sides had given their consent to it. In Somalia Boutros-Ghali's insistence on early deployment of the Pakistani battalion in Mogadishu was accepted by governments with great reluctance. In Bosnia governments rejected the Secretary-General's advice that the 'safe areas' concept was unlikely to be viable and then denied him the military resources he judged necessary to make the concept work. In a few cases, notably Namibia, an operation succeeded despite strong differences between governments and the Secretary-General. But the general lesson to be learnt would seem to be that if there is a serious level of disagreement between governments and the Secretary-General, the viability of the action proposed should be very carefully reviewed.

Likewise the international standing and therefore the effectiveness of the United Nations depends on how its member states treat it. All member states are duty-bound to fulfil the obligations assumed by them under the Charter and to assist the United Nations in any action it takes in accordance with the Charter. But this is not just a duty. If the member states value the United Nations, as almost all say they do, their own national interests require that they avoid any action which would undermine or discredit it. During my years in the Secretariat it was far from evident that member states saw the United Nations in this way. Too often they seemed to see it as a receptacle for problems which they themselves had no interest in resolving or which were insoluble. Bosnia was a good example. The atrocities committed there from 1992 onwards aroused indignation both in the Western democracies and in the Islamic world. Governments came under pressure from public opinion to do something to stop the atrocities. Their reaction was to pass the burden to the United Nations, imposing on the Secretary-General impossible tasks and denying him the resources he needed to attempt them. As Boutros-Ghali remarked at this time, the primary function of the Secretary-General of the United Nations seemed to be to serve as the scapegoat on which member states could heap the blame for their own shortcomings.

Also needing reinforcement is what might be called the 'ethical dimension' of the United Nations. When Tony Blair's first government assumed power in 1997, the Foreign Secretary, Robin Cook, famously said that '[Britain's] foreign policy must have an ethical dimension', a remark for which he has sometimes since been mocked. The mockery was unfair. Any decent state has often to debate how far policy dictated by narrow national interest should be modified to take account of moral imperatives. It is the role of governments to decide where the balance should be struck between these two factors. But the United Nations is different. The message of its Charter is that, notwithstanding the sovereignty of the UN's member states, their individual national interests should not prevail over the ethical purposes for which the Organization was established in 1945. This vision can still be found amongst the elderly idealists who grace meetings of United Nations Associations around the world. Some members of the Secretariat are still inspired by it. But it is now rare amongst governments.

The value they attach to the United Nations is related more to the advancement of their national interests than to advancement of the collective interest of all its members in creating a more peaceful, just and prosperous world. This has contributed to a widespread perception amongst the countries of the Third World that the end of the Cold War has enabled the countries of the West to take over the United Nations and to use it, and other international organizations, to promote the West's interests to the detriment of the interests of the developing countries. This perception is exaggerated but it is not without foundation. There has, for instance, been a significant shift of resources and political energy in the United Nations from economic and social development to peace and security. The developing countries' dissatisfaction with this trend is aggravated by two other factors. First, some of the West's ideas for promoting peace and security, such as preventive action, humanitarian intervention and democratization, seem to threaten the sovereignty of the countries of the Third World, where most contemporary conflicts are being fought. Secondly, there have been some blatant cases of double standards by the West: it spent hundreds of millions of dollars on stopping comparatively minor violations of human rights in Kosovo but would do nothing to stop the murder of 800,000 people in the Rwandan genocide; and it has imposed punitive sanctions for a decade on one Middle Eastern country which occupied its neighbours' territory and sought to develop weapons of mass destruction but it has placed no pressure on another Middle Eastern country which remains in occupation of territory belonging to two of its neighbours and actually has weapons of mass destruction. How, it is asked, can these facts be reconciled with the first Principle stated in the Charter: 'The Organization is based on the principle of the sovereign equality of all its Members'?

Pious and naive though it may sound, I believe that the shortcomings which have been described in this book will be corrected only if the United Nations can find a way back to the ethical role defined in its Charter. Let it cease to be a forum in which governments compete to advance their national interests; let it become a forum in which governments work together 'to achieve international cooperation in solving international problems'. The Secretary-General can help to make this happen, as Kofi Annan is currently doing. But the main responsibility lies on governments and especially the governments of the OECD countries.

They finance most of the activities of the United Nations and the wider UN system. Fortunately they include several countries which remain faithful to the ideals enshrined in the Charter.

My seven years in charge of the peacekeeping operations of the United Nations have been the most satisfying period of my working life. The day-to-day direction of expeditionary forces in distant lands, which at their peak numbered 55,000 people in eleven operations, gave me a level of responsibility that I would never have attained if I had remained in the British Diplomatic Service. The size of the job did sometimes give rise to illusions of grandeur. But just before I left it the illusions were neatly dispelled by the United Nations itself. A future daughter-in-law, Claire Holt, and a friend were staying with us in Manhattan and went on a guided tour of the United Nations building. I primed them with a question for the tour guide: 'Who is in charge of peacekeeping in New York?' The answer, they told me, came without a second's hesitation: 'It's a committee of generals. The chairmanship rotates every four months. An Indian general is the current chairman.' Pure fabrication. But it brought me down to earth.

Epilogue

The British edition of this book went to press in mid-December 2001, just three months after the terrorist attacks on New York and Washington on 11 September. The unprecedented nature, scale and success of those attacks raised the question of whether *Peacemonger* should end with a chapter analysing their repercussions on peace and security world-wide and, in particular, on the United Nations. I decided against writing that chapter for three reasons: the book's narrative was about a past period, not the present; it was already more than 50 per cent longer than the publishers had stipulated; and, most important, the consequences of 9/11 seemed likely to be so far-reaching that it would be premature and imprudent to attempt to analyse them at that stage.

This American edition of the book is now going to press in the aftermath of another cataclysmic event. The war of March 2003 against Iraq has unsettled, to put it mildly, several institutions of great importance in the contemporary architecture of international relations. They include the European Union and NATO, both of which were already stressed by imminent and ambitious increases in their membership. Transatlantic relations have not been subjected to such strain since the United States used its economic power to block the attack by Britain and France, in collusion with Israel, against Egypt in 1956.

As the future of the United Nations, the primary subject of this book, is now being questioned, I have been persuaded by the Johns Hopkins University Press (who have been as friendly to, and supportive of, this novice writer as John Murray Publishers were in London) that this American edition should include some tentative thoughts about the impact that 9/11, the consequent hostilities in Afghanistan and now the war against Iraq will have on the United Nations.

The United Nations lies at the heart of the international system established at the end of the Second World War. The maintenance of international peace and security was (and remains) the first of the purposes assigned to it. Its Charter defined norms which, if respected, would make it a more effective instrument for preventing and resolving conflict than the inter-war League of Nations had ever been. Initially the Cold War prevented the new United Nations from fulfilling many of its creators' hopes and expectations, but its moment seemed at last to have come when the Cold War ended in 1989. During the next few years it achieved important successes in promoting peace and security. But success led to over-confidence and over-stretch, and some grievous errors were made both by the member states in the tasks they gave the UN and by the UN Secretariat in executing those tasks. As a result, the major powers had, by the mid-1990s, lost confidence in the United Nations' ability to fulfil this role and had become less ready to finance its efforts to do so.

As mentioned in the preceding chapter, the United Nations – both its member states and its Secretariat – analysed their errors and drew lessons from them. Various reforms were implemented. Peacekeeping doctrine, for instance, was amended, enabling peacekeepers to use force for specific purposes authorized by the Security Council, without compromising the impartiality and neutrality that are necessary conditions for successful peacekeeping. In Eastern Slavonia, Kosovo and East Timor the United Nations established and directed transitional administrations in the aftermath of conflict (though in the case of Kosovo the conflict has only been suspended, not resolved, and could break out again at any time). Peacebuilding was also recognized as an essential sequel to successful peacemaking and peacekeeping; the fruits of peace would wither on the vine unless action was taken to ensure that the root causes of the war were eradicated. By the beginning of the twenty-first century the United Nations had digested the mistakes of the past and was able to offer its member states a better defined, more realistic, more cautious and more professional peacemaking and peacekeeping service than had been available before.

Meanwhile, a shift in the worldwide balance of power suggested that the demand for that service might fall. Indeed, the very concept of 'balance' no longer seemed to apply; the United States was now the only remaining superpower. The collapse of the Soviet Union had led to a rapid decline in Russia's war-making capacity. China, while spending heavily on strengthening its armed forces, still fell far short of superpower status. The countries of the European Union, for all their talk of a common foreign and security policy, continued to spend less of their GDP on defence than the Americans and were making very slow progress in developing joint military structures. In 2001 the United States' defence expenditure amounted to $322.4 billion, a figure that exceeded the aggregate of defence spending by the next ten countries in the defence budget league.*

---

* International Institute for Strategic Studies, *The Military Balance 2002–2003*, London, 2002, Table 26. The next ten were: Russia, China, Japan, United Kingdom, France, Germany, Saudi Arabia, Italy, India and South Korea.

An increase of 6.6 per cent in the US defence budget for fiscal year 2002 further widened the gap.

The Clinton administration came to power in 1993 proclaiming its commitment to 'assertive multilateralism', but by the mid-1990s the United States was the first major power to lose confidence in the United Nations after seeing the organization fail to meet US expectations. By the end of the decade, however, Secretary-General Annan made some progress in improving perceptions of the UN in Washington, especially on Capitol Hill. This revived hopes that the lone superpower would see the United Nations as a useful adjunct to its military supremacy, a universal organization that could assist it in building international coalitions and give legitimacy to Washington's own efforts to maintain peace and security and promote the other purposes set out in the UN Charter.

This may yet happen. But at the time of this writing (early May 2003, with the hostilities in Iraq just ending) it seems unlikely to happen while the neo-conservative administration headed by President George W. Bush remains in power in Washington. Senior members of that administration have not hidden their low regard for the UN and their lack of confidence in its ability to achieve goals important to Washington. This has disturbed many of America's friends and allies, as has President Bush's predilection for the use of military force, the prominence of pre-emptive action in his new security strategy and his distaste for the tedious process of consensus-building in international organizations.

At the core of the current turbulence in long-standing alliances and friendships are the rules about use of military force set out in the UN Charter. When states join the United Nations they enter into an obligation to settle their disputes by peaceful means. The only exception to that rule is the Charter's recognition of 'the inherent right of individual or collective self-defence if an armed attack occurs against a Member of the United Nations'. But even that right lasts only 'until the Security Council has taken measures necessary to maintain international peace and security'. The Charter envisaged the Security Council itself taking military action against states that committed acts of aggression or otherwise broke the peace; member states were to provide military resources to the Council for that purpose. But the Cold War rendered those provisions unworkable, and when North Korea invaded South Korea in 1950 the Council authorized a coalition led by the United States to use force to repel the invasion.

This procedure was not used again during the rest of the Cold War because most armed disputes were proxy wars in which the East supported one side and the West the other. In these cases, Council authorization of the use of force was usually blocked by the veto, actual or threatened, of one or more of its permanent members (as it would have been in 1950 if the Soviet Union had not been boycotting the Council at that time). As a result both the United States and the Soviet Union (and Britain and France in 1956) used military force against other states without authorization from the Council. After 1989, however, the nature of conflict changed. Most of the proxy conflicts of the Cold War were resolved and almost all the remaining conflicts in the 1990s were either conflicts within a state, especially in Africa, or wars of succession resulting from the dismemberment of the Soviet Union and Yugoslavia.

Nevertheless, very few acts of aggression by one state against another occurred during this period – the notable exception being Iraq's occupation of Kuwait in 1990. But the prompt liberation of Kuwait by a US-led coalition authorized by the Security Council was seen as a triumph for the United Nations and as the birth of a new world order in which the Security Council would assume its role as the source of collective action in response to acts of aggression and other breaches of the peace. The Council began to authorize the use of force by 'coalitions of the willing' for these purposes and sometimes to bring internal conflicts under control. It also began to authorize the use of force by UN peacekeeping operations for specific purposes. This controversial development initially had some unfortunate consequences, especially in Bosnia, which were mainly due to the failure of the Security Council and the UN Secretariat to reconcile the use of force with the prevailing doctrine that required peacekeepers to be impartial in all circumstances.*

But respect for the Charter's constraints on the use of force was not universal. Following the 1998 bombing of the American embassies in Kenya and Tanzania, the United States launched missile attacks against targets in Afghanistan and Sudan, which it claimed were linked to Osama bin Laden's terrorist network, al-Qaʿida. These attacks attracted much international criticism, not least because one of the Sudanese targets turned out to be a pharmaceuticals factory. A further setback occurred in 1999 when NATO launched a bombing campaign against Serbian forces in Kosovo without authorization from the Security Council, further exposing the fragility of the new order that had seemed to be emerging. Major powers were still ready to use military force without UN authorization if they felt that their interests so demanded.

The terrorist attacks on New York and Washington on 11 September 2001 created both an opportunity and a danger for the United Nations. The opportunity was to demonstrate the UN's continuing relevance in the face of a new kind of threat to international peace and security. The

---

* As already mentioned, the necessary revision of peacekeeping doctrine has since taken place.

danger lay in the possibility that the blow to US security and morale would be so severe that the UN would be bypassed by the Bush administration, whose unilateralist tendencies had already become evident during its first eight months in office.

The Security Council acted immediately. A resolution adopted the day after the attacks recognized the 'inherent right of individual or collective self-defence in accordance with the Charter', unequivocally condemned the attacks and called on nations everywhere to redouble their efforts to prevent and suppress terrorism. Eight days later, President Bush, in an address to Congress and the American people, declared a 'war on terror' and told the nations and regions of the world that 'either you are with us, or you are with the terrorists'. This hyperbole, which the President was to repeat more than once in the following weeks, seemed to raise doubts about the extent of Washington's commitment to multilateral action. But Washington continued to seek support from the United Nations. Before the end of September, the Security Council adopted a long and unprecedented mandatory resolution that required all member states of the UN to take effective action against terrorism and defined at length the form that action should take. It also established a committee to which states were to report, within ninety days, the action they had taken and which would thereafter monitor each state's implementation of the resolution.

A few weeks later Washington raised no objection to Secretary-General Annan's appointment of the distinguished Algerian diplomat Lakhdar Brahimi as his Special Representative for Afghanistan. Brahimi, who had served the UN in Afghanistan from 1997 to 1999, now had the task of planning post-conflict nation-building in Afghanistan while the United States carried out its military campaign of self-defence against al-Qaʿida and the Taliban government that supported it. Some of America's actions in that campaign, especially its treatment of prisoners of war and its tolerance of atrocities by its Afghan allies, aroused international concern. But it continued to play a positive role in the Security Council, supporting Brahimi's successful efforts to set up a transitional administration in Kabul and encouraging the Council to authorize the deployment of an 'International Security Assistance Force', whose personnel would be provided by a coalition of the willing led by Britain. In the case of Afghanistan, therefore, the United States cannot be accused of having side-lined the United Nations; on the contrary, it used the Security Council to win international support and legitimacy for its policies and established a viable division of labour between itself and the UN.

Meanwhile, President Bush made no secret of his determination to use force to remove Saddam Hussein's regime in Iraq. In the autumn of 2002, he reluctantly accepted advice that it was in the United States' interest to have the operation authorized by the Security Council. This raised hopes that the need for UN approval would be respected. If the Council authorized the impending operation, NATO's unauthorized use of force in Kosovo in 1999 could be dismissed as an aberration; and if the operation succeeded in finding and destroying weapons of mass destruction, the UN might even win again the accolades it had received after the liberation of Kuwait. But, as in the case of the 'war on terror', President Bush's decision to seek Security Council authorization also created a danger for the UN. If authorization could not be obtained from the Security Council and the United States went ahead unilaterally, the credibility and relevance of the United Nations in the age of the lone superpower would be undermined, and it might even go the way of the League of Nations – an outcome that, it seemed, would not be unwelcome to some of the President's closest advisers.

The likelihood of unilateral action by the United States was heightened by what many governments, including some of Washington's closest allies, saw as arrogant neo-imperialist tendencies in Washington. Would not this impression make it even more difficult for the United States and its British ally to obtain authorization of a war for which they could provide little convincing justification? Their allegations that Iraq still held biological and chemical weapons and was still seeking to create or acquire nuclear weapons could not be proven. Nor could claims that Saddam's regime had links with al-Qaʿida. Members of the UN, who are after all the governments of sovereign states, offered little support for the idea that a government should be removed by force simply because it was a brutal tyranny and violated its people's human rights. US and British efforts to justify the war also gave rise to charges of double standards: Why was Iraq being threatened with war because it might have nuclear weapons when North Korea, which had just admitted to possessing them, was merely being engaged in negotiations? And when nothing at all was being done about Israel's nuclear arsenal, not to mention those of India and Pakistan?

To its credit, the Bush administration persevered in the negotiations and in November 2002 the Security Council adopted unanimously SCR 1441, which required Iraq to re-admit UN weapons inspectors and which set out clearly the conditions Saddam had to fulfill if he was to avoid 'serious consequences', a typical UN euphemism for the use of force. This was something of a diplomatic triumph and gave Saddam the option of avoiding a war and his own overthrow. But he continued to prevaricate. The weapons inspectors found and destroyed some banned weapons but none of them was in the mass destruction category. As the heat of the Mesopotamian summer approached, impatience grew in Washington. Opposition to war, however, remained strong, even in some of America's closest and strongest allies, and by late February 2003 deadlock pre-vailed in the Council. A second resolution explicitly authorizing the use of force could not be obtained, and the United States, with Britain's sup-port, decided to go to war on the basis of SCR 1441.

The legality of that decision is much debated. In an attempt to justify it, the British government published not entirely unconvincing legal ar-guments, but they traced authority for the war back to the resolution of November 1990 in which the Security Council authorized the US-led coalition to use force to liberate Kuwait. A long and slender thread must be woven to establish that that resolution, and others derived from it, constitute, twelve years later, authorization of the use of force for the quite different purpose of changing the regime in Baghdad. It must also be remembered that when SCR 1441 was adopted in November 2002, the Permanent Representative of the United States to the UN said that it contained 'no hidden trigger', a statement difficult to reconcile with Washington's subsequent insistence that the use of force did not require a second resolution.

At the time of this writing, Saddam's government has been over-thrown and victory has been declared by the United States and its allies. But most of the concerns expressed by opponents of the war have turned out to be well-founded. Material destruction was massive, not only because of bombing and combat but also because of the looting that followed the fall of the regime and that the United States and Britain apparently failed to foresee. Civilian casualties seem to have been signif-icant (though the Pentagon has so far declined to estimate their number). No weapons of mass destruction have been found. The use of Amer-ica's overwhelming might against another Muslim country has further fu-elled hatred of the United States (now joined by Britain) in the Arab and Muslim worlds. The Iraqis are not the joyous, liberated, united and dem-ocratic people whom Secretary Rumsfeld promised us; they remain the divided and fractious people they have been ever since the victors of the First World War enclosed them in artificial borders. A credible post-war plan has yet to be developed for the promised reconstruction and de-mocratization of Iraq; there seem to be several plans, prepared by differ-ent agencies in Washington but not coordinated.

That is the pessimist's perception of the situation in Iraq in May 2003. Here is the optimist's: The United States has committed itself to a major effort to bring about post-war reconstruction and nation-building in Iraq. This differs from its policy in Afghanistan where its energies are primar-ily devoted to the continuing military campaign against remnants of the Taliban and al-Qaʻida and where post-war reconstruction has not been a priority. For the United States the stakes are higher in Iraq than in Afghanistan, and the resources available from Iraq's oil exports will make reconstruction easier to achieve. Iraq is also one of the best educated of the Arab countries. Saddam's tyranny caused many Iraqi professionals to emigrate, pursuing their careers and raising their families elsewhere. It is hoped that many of these émigrés will now come home. With their education, their professional skills and their experience of other countries, they could help bridge the political gaps between the Shi'ite, Kurdish and Sunni communities and create in Iraq a modern, democratic and secular system of government.

To establish a stable government in Iraq could be the first step to political reform in the Middle East more widely. The Arab Human Development Report, written by Arab scholars and officials and published by the United Nations Development Programme (UNDP) in 2002, has provided a painfully frank analysis of under-development in the Arab countries. Their growth in per capita income is the lowest in the world except for sub-Saharan Africa. The root-causes for this, according to the report, are three 'deficits': in freedom and the good governance to which freedom and democratic practices can lead; in the empowerment of women; and in knowledge. In education and in social development more generally, Iraq has been one of the more successful of the Arab countries. The new Iraq could, therefore, lead the way for other Arab countries that wish to modernize their societies and address the deficits identified in the UNDP report.

Whatever the outcome of the war in Iraq, it is difficult to predict how the United Nations will be affected. Most important will be the roles the UN is permitted to play now that actual combat has ended and how well it performs in those roles. The establishment of a stable, just and democratic Iraq would bring glory to all the institutions involved in its development. If the United Nations has been allowed to play an important role, it will share in the glory. If it has not, its future usefulness in similar circumstances will be called into question: 'we did not need the UN in Iraq; why should we use it now?' On the other hand, if the victors' plans do not succeed and Iraq becomes another 'failed state', it will be better for the UN not to have been given a major role and, therefore, a share of the blame. If excluded, it could perversely draw some benefit: 'if the Americans had followed the UN rules and made more use of its services, this mess would never have occurred'.

The United Nations *could* shoulder many responsibilities in the rebuilding of Iraq, if governments agreed. Expressions of neo-conservative contempt for the UN in Washington may suggest that such agreement is unlikely, but the Bush administration did have recourse to the UN in the aftermath of the war in Afghanistan; the same could happen for Iraq.

Efforts to build a democratic state in Iraq will need legitimacy and security. As Secretary-General Annan has said, legitimacy is probably the most valuable contribution that the United Nations can offer. But patient diplomacy would be needed to obtain a Security Council resolution giving UN approval to the efforts of the United States and its allies. The Arab and Muslim worlds are strongly opposed to the American occupation of Iraq, and some states would argue that Security Council endorsement of America's post-war efforts there would be perceived as condoning an illegal and illegitimate war. But awareness seems to be growing, especially in Europe, of the need to start repairing the damage done to existing international institutions by last winter's crisis; international consensus on how to handle the aftermath of the war would be an admirable way of mending fences.

Security is a necessary condition for the political and economic reconstruction of Iraq. If security is neglected by the international community, Iraq will either revert to tyranny or, like Afghanistan or Somalia or Lebanon during their long civil wars, become a 'failed state' composed of mutually hostile fiefdoms, like those established in 1991 under Western protection in the Kurd-controlled regions of northern Iraq. The armed forces of the United States are ill-suited to peacekeeping in an Arab and Muslim country since the intimacy of the US relationship with Israel makes them suspect and since their *combativité* and the violence inherent in their doctrine of force protection generate hatred, complicating their attempts to master the quasi-civilian police aspects of peacekeeping.

The early withdrawal of United States troops from Iraq is, therefore, viewed favourably by both the international community and the Pentagon. Still the Americans must be replaced by an international force with the mandate and capacity to use its weapons, if necessary, to prevent the emergence of illegal forces and to assist in the maintenance of civil order. Given the size of Iraq and the complexity of the post-war situation, this task is probably too large and difficult for a UN peacekeeping operation. A multinational force, provided by a coalition of the willing, including significant contingents from Arab and other Muslim countries, would be a better option. It would need robust command and control structures, a high level of mobility and strong logistic support; and because it might have to use force, it would need Security Council authorization, as have other multinational forces.

Some have advocated for Iraq a UN transitional administration similar to those established in Eastern Slavonia, East Timor and Kosovo. I do not believe this is a realistic solution. Iraq is vastly larger than those three very small territories and it is essential that the government of Iraq be returned to its own people. This delicate process is currently controlled by the Americans, who must advance quickly and not allow provisional ad hoc arrangements to become permanent. To put the present process on hold while the UN assembled a transitional administration would be folly. Again, the legitimacy of the process would be enhanced if the Security Council was kept informed and was able to give, if merited, its approval to the progress in the restoration of Iraqi governance.

Nevertheless, the United Nations is not just about war and peace. The many programmes, funds, offices and specialized agencies that together constitute the 'United Nations System' have the capacity to make a major contribution to Iraq's reconstruction and a return to normalcy in the economic, social and humanitarian fields. But political issues must also be addressed. At the time of this writing, Washington's plan seems to be to entrust many of these functions to American agencies, with the US private sector playing a major role, and to place Iraq's oil sector under US control. This is imprudent. For various and deep-rooted reasons Iraqis do not want their country to become a US protectorate or trust territory. Nor do other Western countries want to see the United States assume such a role; they know that the Iraqi people will oppose it and they want a share of the cake themselves. These concerns strengthen the arguments for giving an extensive, but not exclusive, role to UN agencies, which have accumulated much experience in working in other war-torn countries.

One caveat has to be made, however: A persistent weakness in the wider UN system is its ineffective coordination. Each of its many agencies has its own inter-governmental policy-making body, its own chain of command and its own sources of finance. As a result, each agency feels autonomous and tends to resist coordination by others. Given the scale of what needs to be done in Iraq, a person of great ability will be needed to coordinate the UN system's contribution to the reconstruction of Iraq and its conversion into a stable, just and democratic state.

Two historical factors also need to be taken into account when assessing the Iraq war's likely implications for the United Nations. First, how will governments and peoples judge the United Nations' efforts to neutralize Iraq after its expulsion from Kuwait in 1991? Will its failure to hold Saddam to the promises he made then cause it to be blamed for the 2003 war?

The United Nations was given a wide range of responsibilities in Iraq during those twelve years. Most of them were set out in SCR 687, the 'mother of all resolutions',* and SCR 688, both of which were adopted in April 1991. They included the management of punitive sanctions against Iraq; the provision of humanitarian relief; the monitoring of Iraq's compliance with the disarmament provisions of SCR 687; the payment of compensation for losses incurred by individuals, corporations

---

* See page 283.

and governments during the Iraqi invasion and occupation of Kuwait; the recovery of Kuwaiti property seized by Iraq; the return of displaced persons; the demarcation of the Iraq-Kuwait border; and peacekeeping on that border. Four years later the UN also assumed responsibility for the 'oil-for-food' programme that permitted Iraq to export oil, with the proceeds from the exported oil being used by the UN to purchase food and other humanitarian supplies for distribution to the Iraqi population.

The UN's handling of two of these tasks was controversial. The economic sanctions inflicted great hardship on the Iraqi people. They created opportunities for the ruling elite to profit from sanctions-busting; they enabled Saddam to pose, in the Middle East and beyond, as the victim of vindictive Western powers; and they failed to persuade him to change any of his policies – on the contrary, the sanctions regime was of great political and economic benefit to him. Successive UN humanitarian coordinators in Iraq resigned from their positions in protest at the sanctions' inhumane consequences for the Iraqi people. In his January 1995 *Supplement to an Agenda for Peace,* Secretary-General Boutros-Ghali described sanctions as 'a blunt instrument' that, he said, 'raise the ethical question of whether suffering inflicted on vulnerable groups in the target country is a legitimate means of exerting pressure on political leaders whose behaviour is unlikely to be affected by the plight of their subjects'. But the United States and its British ally insisted on maintaining the sanctions regime until Saddam Hussein was overthrown.

The handling of weapons-related tasks was also controversial. A Special Commission was established to work with the International Atomic Energy Agency in documenting and dismantling Iraq's programmes for the development and acquisition of nuclear, biological and chemical weapons and long-range delivery systems. The Commission's ability to carry out these tasks depended critically on Iraqi cooperation, which was never consistent enough for the Commission to account satisfactorily for all of Iraq's banned weapons programmes. On the contrary the Commission was repeatedly obliged to ask the Secretary-General and the Security Council to exert pressure on Saddam to comply with the commitments he had entered into in 1991. In December 1998 his persistent non-compliance led the United States and Britain to launch air attacks on strategic targets in Iraq. In retaliation Iraq expelled the Special Commission and no further inspections took place until UN weapons inspectors returned in late 2002 in accordance with SCR 1441.

The other tasks entrusted to the United Nations after the liberation of Kuwait proved less difficult to perform and gave rise to little dissent within the Security Council. In the aftermath of the 2003 war, however, the media seem to have been fed allegations of impropriety by the UN Secretariat in its management of the oil-for-food programme. Whether irregularities did occur or whether these allegations reflect anti-UN 'spin' by neo-conservatives in the United States is not yet clear. With the possible exception of this last point, there is nothing in the UN's performance in Iraq between the 1991 and 2003 wars that could be held to disqualify it from continuing to play a central role in that country's reconstruction.

The second historical factor that must be considered when assessing the implications of the Iraq war for the United Nations relates to the crisis in the Security Council during the winter of 2002–2003. Where does responsibility lie for that crisis and the damage it has inflicted on the international political architecture? Has it disqualified the Security Council from arbitrating the use of force in the future? Or will the Council's failure to agree on action be attributed not to the Council as an institution but to unreasonable positions adopted by certain of its members?

A decision by the lone superpower to ignore the Charter's restrictions on the use of force is obviously a major setback for the United Nations, especially when the superpower has just declared its intention to take preemptive action against potential enemies. The unauthorized and doubtfully legal war of 2003 may therefore have reversed the progress made by the Security Council in the 1990s in having states obtain authorization before using force, other than in self-defence.

But whose fault is that? The United States and Britain cannot be blamed for seeking authorization for the use of force against Iraq; they did what the Charter required of them. Nor can other powers be blamed for questioning whether the war was justified and for pressing its proponents for more convincing evidence. The founders of the United Nations intended the Security Council to debate precisely this kind of question. The United States and Britain can, however, be blamed for pressing on regardless when it became clear that authorization could not be obtained. But other powers share that blame.

The Council had after all voted unanimously in favour of SCR 1441, which included the reminder to Iraq that it would face 'serious consequences' if it continued to violate the obligations it accepted at the end of the Kuwait war in 1991. The uncompromising position adopted by France, supported by other opponents of the war, closed the door to further negotiation about what the 'serious consequences' would be and when and how they would be imposed on Iraq. France's stance also created the impression that it had a hidden agenda and that more was at stake than whether or not to authorize the use of force against Iraq. That agenda was, perhaps, related to distaste for the policies and style of the Bush administration or to the future distribution of power within the European Union or to France's national interests in Iraq or to any combination of those factors.

Still, the Council's inability to reach a decision was an unwelcome reminder of the paralysis that so often afflicted the Council during the Cold War. Over time it is possible that the principal recipients of blame will not be the United States and Britain for their unauthorized use of force but the countries that irresponsibly prevented the Council from defining a course of action that complied with the Charter and that could be endorsed by the Council. In that case the Iraq débâcle will add to the Third World's demands for reform and 'democratization' of the Council.

Meanwhile the damaged Western alliance is in urgent need of repair. The industrialized democracies share so many common values and so many common objectives that our own interests oblige us to restore harmony. Europeans may be tempted to criticize and mock the United States for what we see as a tendency towards arrogant unilateralism and a predilection for the use of force, especially since the present administration assumed office in Washington, and Americans may find it tempting to criticize Europe's lack of cohesion, the feebleness of our efforts to develop a common security policy and the low level of our spending on defence. Both temptations need to be resisted. Mutual respect must be restored, and both sides of the Atlantic need to develop a more understanding perception of each other's viewpoints.

Grotesque though it may sound to some, I believe the United Nations can play a helpful role in this endeavour. True, success in the war against Iraq, if success it turns out to be, will strengthen the hand of those in Washington who favour the use of military force and are not averse to proceeding unilaterally if authorization by the Security Council is not available. This would constitute a major setback for the United Nations. But in today's world many of the threats to the security, prosperity and health of developed countries cannot be neutralized by military means. Foremost among them is international terrorism. Terrorist networks are too small and dispersed a target for military might to prevail against them, notwithstanding the precision of modern weaponry, and they are too deeply embedded in civilian society for the attacker to avoid causing collateral casualties that will generate further hatred and further terrorism. The weapons needed to defeat terrorism are good intelligence; good police work; just and efficient courts; political action to address the perceived injustices that have led otherwise peaceful communities to support terrorists and give them shelter; and, above all, effective international cooperation. The resolution adopted by the Security Council soon after 9/11 was a step in the right direction.

International cooperation can address many other threats, as well: International crime, including trafficking in drugs, arms and human beings; infectious disease; environmental pollution; persecution and underdevelopment; and the uncontrolled migration to which they often give rise, are a few examples. As I already mentioned, the United Nations is not just about war and peace; the various institutions that together constitute the United Nations System have expertise in every field of human activity and provide fora in which countries can work out collective policies and programmes of action.

In US opinion polls, about two thirds of those polled normally give the UN a favourable rating. Research has consistently shown that this high level of approval for the UN is not based on its role in maintaining peace and security; Americans have confidence in the US armed forces' ability to defend them. Their approval of the UN is based on their belief that it provides a means of getting governments to agree on collective policies to deal with the many external threats to Americans' prosperity and health that cannot be dealt with by military means.

Perhaps the countries of Europe should initially concentrate their efforts to restore a harmonious and productive relationship with the United States in these non-military fields of common interest. But opening a dialogue on less contentious issues than those raised by the Iraq war would only be a first step. Prolonged failure to use the UN's peacemaking and peacekeeping services would return it to the Cold War refrigerator and undo fifteen years of progress in giving it a real and credible role in the maintenance of world-wide peace and security.

Appendix I
*Abbreviations and Acronyms**

ACABQ	Advisory Committee on Administrative and Budgetary Questions
ACMO	Assistant Chief Military Observer (UNIIMOG)
AO	Area of Operation
ARENA	*Alianza Republicana Nacionalista* (National Republican Alliance) (El Salvador)
ASEAN	Association of South-East Asian Nations
ASG	Assistant-Secretary-General
ATC	Air Traffic Control
BBC	British Broadcasting Corporation
CAO	Chief Administrative Officer
CGDK	Coalition Government of Democratic Kampuchea
CIAV	*Comisión Internacional de Apoyo y Verificación* (International Support and Verification Commission) (Central America)
CMO	Chief Military Observer
COPAZ	*Comisión Nacional para la Consolidación de la Paz* (National Commission for the Consolidation of Peace) (El Salvador)
DFC	Deputy Force Commander
DFF	*De Facto* Forces (UN euphemism for the South Lebanon Army)
DMZ	Demilitarized Zone
DPA	Department of Political Affairs, created by Boutros-Ghali in 1992, in which the author served from March 1993 until February 1997
DPKO	Department of Peacekeeping Operations, created by Boutros-Ghali in 1992, in which the author served from March 1992 until February 1993
DSRSG	Deputy Special Representative of the Secretary-General
EC	European Community
ECMM	European Community Monitoring Mission
ECOMOG	ECOWAS Monitoring Group
ECOWAS	Economic Organization of West African States
EOSG	Executive Office of the Secretary-General
EPS	*Ejército Popular Sandinista* (Sandinista People's Army) (Nicaragua)
ERP	*Ejército Revolucionario Popular* (People's Revolutionary Army) (El Salvador)
FAA	*Forças Armadas de Angola* (the new national army envisaged in the Bicesse Accords)

---

*A full list of United Nations peacekeeping operations created from 1948 to 1996 can be found in Appendix II.

359

FADH	*Forces Armées d'Haiti*
FAES	*Fuerzas Armadas de El Salvador*
FALA	*Forças Armadas da Libertação de Angola* (UNITA's army)
FAPLA	*Forças Armadas Populares da Libertação de Angola* (the Government's army)
FC	Force Commander
FLS	Front Line States
FMLN	*Frente Farabundo Martí para la Liberación Nacional* (Farabundo Martí Front for National Liberation) (El Salvador)
FOD	Field Operations Division
FRY	Federal Republic of Yugoslavia (Serbia and Montenegro)
FUNCINPEC	*Front Uni National pour un Cambodge Indépendent, Neutre, Pacifique et Coöpératif* (United National Front for an Independent, Neutral, Peaceful and Cooperative Cambodia)
FYROM	Former Yugoslav Republic of Macedonia
GDP	Gross Domestic Product
GOES	Government of El Salvador
ICFY	International Conference on the former Yugoslavia
ICRC	International Committee of the Red Cross
ICTY	International Criminal Tribunal for Yugoslavia
IDF	Israel Defence Forces
JNA	Jugoslovensko Narodna Armija (Yugoslav People's Army)
KPNLF	Khmer People's National Liberation Front
MECAS	Middle East Centre for Arab Studies
MICIVIH	*Mission Civile Internationale en Haïti* (International Civilian Mission in Haiti)
MINURSO	*Mission des Nations Unies pour l'organisation d'un référendum au Sahara Occidental* (UN Mission for the Referendum in Western Sahara)
MPLA	*Movimento Popular da Libertação de Angola* (People's Movement for the Liberation of Angola)
NAM	Non-Aligned Movement
NATO	North Atlantic Treaty Organization
NCO	Non-Commissioned Officer
NGO	Non-Governmental Organization
OAS	Organization of American States
OAU	Organization of African Unity
OC	Officer Commanding
OECD	Organization for Economic Cooperation and Development
OFOESA	Office of Field Operational and External Support Activities
OGL	Observer Group Lebanon
ONUCA	*Grupo de Observadores de las Naciones Unidas en Centroamérica* (United Nations Observer Group in Central America)
ONUSAL	*Misión de Observadores de las Naciones Unidas en El Salvador* (United Nations Observer Mission in El Salvador)
ONUVEH	*Groupe d'Observateurs des Nations Unies pour la vérification des élections en Haïti* (United Nations Mission for the Verification of Elections in Haiti)
ONUVEN	*Misión de las Naciones Unidas encargada de verificar el proceso electoral en Nicaragua* (United Nations Mission for the Verification of Elections in Nicaragua)

OP	Observation Post
OSPA	Office of Special Political Affairs, one of the 'Offices of the Secretary-General', in which the author served from 1986 until Boutros-Ghali's reorganization of the Secretariat in March 1992
P-5	The Permanent Members of the Security Council (China, France, Soviet Union/Russian Federation, United Kingdom, United States)
PESG	Personal Envoy of the Secretary-General
PLO	Palestine Liberation Organization
POLISARIO	*Frente Popular para la Liberación de Saguia el-Hamra y de Río de Oro* (Popular Front for the Liberation of Saguia el-Hamra and Río de Oro)
POW	Prisoner of War
PRSG	Personal Representative of the Secretary-General
RENAMO	*Resistência Nacional Moçambicana* (Mozambican National Resistance)
SADF	South African Defence Forces
SADR	Saharan Arab Democratic Republic
SCR	Security Council Resolution
SESG	Special Envoy of the Secretary-General
SFRY	Socialist Federal Republic of Yugoslavia
SG	Secretary-General
SLA	South Lebanon Army
SNC	Supreme National Council (Cambodia)
SOC	State of Cambodia
SOFA	Status of Forces Agreement
SRSG	Special Representative of the Secretary-General
SWAPO	South West Africa People's Organization
SWAPOL	South West Africa Police
SWATF	South West Africa Territorial Force
UK	United Kingdom
UN	United Nations
UNAMIC	United Nations Advance Mission in Cambodia
UNAVEM	United Nations Angola Verification Mission
UNDOF	United Nations Disengagement Observer Force
UNDP	United Nations Development Programme
UNEF	United Nations Emergency Force
UNFICYP	United Nations Peacekeeping Force in Cyprus
UNGOMAP	United Nations Good Offices Mission in Afghanistan and Pakistan
UNHCR	United Nations High Commissioner for Refugees
UNHUC	United Nations Humanitarian Centre
UNIFIL	United Nations Interim Force in Lebanon
UNIIMOG	United Nations Iran–Iraq Military Observer Group
UNIKOM	United Nations Iraq–Kuwait Observation Mission
UNITA	*União Nacional para a Independência Total de Angola* (National Union for the Complete Independence of Angola)
UNITAF	Unified Task Force
UNMO	United Nations Military Observer
UNMOGIP	United Nations Military Observer Group in India and Pakistan
UNOSGI	United Nations Office of the Secretary-General in Iran (or Iraq)
UNOSOM	United Nations Operation in Somalia

UNPA	United Nations Protected Area
UNPROFOR	United Nations Protection Force
UNRWA	United Nations Relief and Works Agency for Palestine Refugees in the Near East
UNTAC	United Nations Transitional Authority in Cambodia
UNTAG	United Nations Transition Assistance Group
UNTSO	United Nations Truce Supervision Organization
US(A)	United States (of America)
USC	United Somali Congress
USG	Under-Secretary-General
USS	United States Ship
VC	Verification Centre

Appendix II

United Nations Peacekeeping Operations, 1948–1996

Acronym	Full Name	Dates	Type*	Location
UNTSO	UN Truce Supervision Organization	1948–	T	Levant and Egypt
UNMOGIP	UN Military Observer Group in India and Pakistan	1949–	T	Kashmir
UNEF I	First UN Emergency Force	1956–67	T	Egypt, Gaza Strip
UNOGIL	UN Observer Group in Lebanon	1958	T	Lebanon
ONUC	UN Operation in the Congo	1960–4	CE	Congo
UNTEA/UNSF	UN Temporary Executive Authority and UN Security Force in West New Guinea (West Irian)	1962–3	MF	West Irian
UNYOM	UN Yemen Observation Mission	1963–4	T	Yemen, Saudi Arabia
UNFICYP	UN Peacekeeping Force in Cyprus	1964–	T	Cyprus
DOMREP	Representative of the Secretary-General in the Dominican Republic	1965–6	T	Dominican Republic
UNIPOM	UN India–Pakistan Observation Mission	1965–6	T	India, Pakistan
UNEF II	Second UN Emergency Force	1973–9	T	Egypt
UNDOF	UN Disengagement Observer Force	1974–	T	Syria (Golan Heights)
UNIFIL	UN Interim Force in Lebanon	1978–	T	Lebanon
UNGOMAP	UN Good Offices Mission in Afghanistan and Pakistan	1988–90	T	Afghanistan and Pakistan
UNIIMOG	UN Iran–Iraq Military Observer Group	1988–91	T	Iran, Iraq
UNAVEM I	UN Angola Verification Mission I	1989–91	T	Angola
UNTAG	UN Transition Assistance Group	1989–90	MF	Namibia
ONUCA	UN Observer Group in Central America	1989–92	T	Central America
UNIKOM	UN Iraq–Kuwait Observation Mission	1991–	T	Iraq, Kuwait
UNAVEM II	UN Angola Verification Mission II	1991–5	MF	Angola
ONUSAL	UN Observer Mission in El Salvador	1991–5	T, MF	El Salvador
MINURSO	UN Mission for the Referendum in Western Sahara	1991–	MF	Western Sahara

---

*The types, described more fully on pages 15–18, are abbreviated thus: CE = Complex Emergency; MF = Multifunctional; P = Preventive; T = Traditional.

Acronym	Full Name	Dates	Type	Location
UNAMIC	UN Advance Mission in Cambodia	1991–2	T	Cambodia
UNPROFOR	UN Protection Force	1992–5	T, CE	Former Yugoslavia

In 1995 UNPROFOR was subdivided into:

UNCRO	*UN Confidence Restoration Operation in Croatia*	*1995–6*	*T*	*Croatia*
UNPREDEP	*UN Preventive Deployment Force*	*1995–9*	*P*	*Macedonia*
UNPROFOR	*UN Protection Force*	*1995*	*CE*	*Bosnia and Herzegovina*
UNTAC	UN Transitional Authority in Cambodia	1992–3	MF	Cambodia
UNOSOM I	UN Operation in Somalia I	1992–3	T	Somalia
ONUMOZ	UN Operation in Mozambique	1992–4	MF	Mozambique
UNOSOM II	UN Operation in Somalia II	1993–5	CE	Somalia
UNOMUR	UN Observer Mission Uganda–Rwanda	1993–4	T	Rwanda, Uganda
UNOMIG	UN Observer Mission in Georgia	1993–7	T	Georgia
UNOMIL	UN Observer Mission in Liberia	1993–	CE	Liberia
UNMIH	UN Mission in Haiti	1993–6	MF	Haiti
UNAMIR	UN Assistance Mission for Rwanda	1993–6	MF	Rwanda
UNASOG	UN Aouzou Strip Observer Group	1994	T	Chad, Libya
UNMOT	UN Mission of Observers in Tajikistan	1994–2000	T	Tajikistan
MONUA	UN Angola Verification Mission III	1995–7	MF	Angola
UNMIBH	UN Mission in Bosnia and Herzegovina	1995–	MF	Bosnia and Herzegovina
UNTAES	UN Transitional Administration for Eastern Slavonia, Baranja and Western Sirmium	1996–7	MF	Croatia
UNMOP	UN Mission of Observers in Prevlaka	1996–	T	Croatia
MINUGUA	UN Mission for the Verification of Human Rights and of Compliance with the Comprehensive Agreement on Human Rights in Guatemala (*later* UN Verification Mission in Guatemala)	1996–	MF	Guatemala

Appendix III

Dramatis Personae Maiores

Abd al-Meguid, Esmat: Egyptian (1923–): Diplomat, politician. Foreign Minister 1984–91, Secretary-General of the Arab League 1991–2001.

Abdelaziz, Mohamed: Sahrawi (1948–): Politician. Co-Founder of POLISARIO in Western Sahara 1973. President of SADR since 1976.

Abdul Nasser, Gamal: Egyptian (1918–70): Soldier, politician. President of Egypt 1954–70.

Abu Nidal, pseudonym of Sabri al-Banna: Palestinian (1937–): Head of Palestinian terrorist organization, variously known as 'Fatah – the Revolutionary Council', 'Revolutionary Organization of Socialist Muslims' etc.

Adamishin, Anatoliy: Soviet/Russian (1934–): Diplomat. Deputy Foreign Minister 1986–90, Ambassador to Italy 1990–2, First Deputy Foreign Minister 1992–4.

Adžić, Blagoje: Yugoslav (Serbian) (1932–): Soldier. Chief of Staff of JNA 1991, Federal Defence Minister 1992.

Aga Khan, Sadruddin: Iranian (1933–): UN High Commissioner for Refugees 1965–77, Coordinator UN programmes in Afghanistan 1988–90, Head of UN humanitarian programmes resulting from Kuwait crisis 1990–1.

Ahmed, Rafeeuddin: Pakistani (1932–): Diplomat, UN official. Joined Secretariat 1970. Secretary-General's Chef de Cabinet 1978–83, USG for Political Affairs, Trusteeship and Decolonization 1983–6 and for International Economic and Social Affairs 1987–92. Also SRSG for Humanitarian Affairs in SE Asia 1983–91. Executive Secretary of the Economic and Social Commission for Asia and the Pacific 1992–4.

Ahtisaari, Martti: Finnish (1937–): Diplomat, UN official, politician, peacemaker. SRSG for Namibia 1978–90; USG for Administration 1987–91; Chairman of Bosnia Working Group of ICFY 1992–3; President of Finland 1994–2000.

Aidid, Mohammed Farah: Somali (1934–96): Soldier, politician. Chief of Staff to Siyad Barre when latter seized power in 1969. Led coalition which overthrew Barre in 1991. In resulting civil war fought for control of Mogadishu with Ali Mahdi Mohammed and international forces. Died in combat.

Aimé, Jean-Claude: Haitian (1935–): UN official. UNDP 1962–77; Senior Adviser UN peacekeeping operations in Middle East 1978–82; Director Office of Special Political Affairs 1982–8; Executive Assistant to SG Pérez de Cuéllar 1989–91; Chief of Staff to SG Boutros-Ghali 1992–6; Executive Secretary UN Compensation Commission 1997–2000.

Ajello, Aldo: Italian (1936–): Politician, UN official. UNDP 1984–92, SRSG Mozambique 1992–4.

Akashi, Yasushi: Japanese (1931–): Diplomat, UN official. USG for Public Information 1979–87 and for Disarmament 1987–91, SRSG for Cambodia 1992–3 and for former Yugoslavia 1994–5, USG for Humanitarian Affairs 1996–7.

Alarcón de Quesada, Ricardo: Cuban (1937–): Diplomat, politician. Cuban Ambassador to UN 1966–78, 1990; Deputy Foreign Minister 1978–90; Foreign Minister 1992–4.

Annan, Kofi: Ghanaian (1938–): UN official. Director of Budget 1984–7; ASG for Human Resources Management 1987–90; Controller of Budget etc. 1990–2; ASG (1992–3) and USG (1993–6) for Peacekeeping Operations; Secretary-General of the United Nations since 1997.

Aoun, Michel: Lebanese (Maronite) (1935–): Soldier, politician. Commander of Army 1984; nominated by outgoing President Amin Gemayel as Prime Minister of interim government 1988; evicted by Syrian forces from presidential palace 1990; in exile in France since 1991.

Arad, Ron: Israeli (1958–): Air Force officer, captured by radical wing of Amal when his plane came down over Lebanon in 1986. Fate unknown.

Arafat, Yasir (Abu Ammar): Palestinian (1929–): Resistance leader and politician. Chairman of Palestine Liberation Organization since 1968, President of Palestine National Authority since 1994.

Arens, Moshe: Israeli (1925–): Academic, diplomat, politician. Defence Minister 1983–4, 1990–2; Foreign Minister 1988–90.

Arias Sánchez, Oscar: Costa Rican (1940–): Academic, politician, peacemaker. President of Costa Rica 1986–90.

Aristide, Jean-Bertrand: Haitian (*c.* 1950–): Priest, politician. Expelled from Salesian Order 1988. Leader, National Front for Change and Democracy; President of Haiti 1991, 1993–6 and since 2000.

Aronson, Bernard: American. Public official, businessman. Assistant Secretary for Inter-American Affairs, State Department 1989–93.

al-Assad, Hafiz: Syrian (1928–2000): Soldier, politician. President of Syria 1971–2000.

Aziz, Tariq: Iraqi (1936–): Journalist, politician. Deputy Prime Minister 1981; Foreign Minister 1983–91; Deputy Prime Minister since 1991.

Babić, Milan: Yugoslav (Croatian Serb) (1956–): Dentist, politician. President of the 'Republika Srpska Krajina' 1990–2.

Baena Soares, João: Brazilian. Diplomat. Secretary-General of the OAS 1984–94.

Bailey, Clinton: Israeli (1936–): Academic, government official. Various advisory posts with IDF. Liaison Officer with Amal in southern Lebanon 1982–5.

Baker, James III: American (1930–): Lawyer, politician. Secretary of the Treasury 1985–8, Secretary of State 1989–92; UN Special Envoy for Western Sahara 1997–.

Bazin, Marc: Haitian (1932–): Lawyer, international civil servant (World Bank), politician. Formed political party 1986. Runner-up to Aristide in presidential election 1991. Prime Minister 1992–3 after military overthrew Aristide.

Béchir, Mustapha Sayid: Sahrawi (1950–): Politician. Deputy SG of POLISARIO 1976–82, member of Executive Committee responsible for foreign affairs since 1988.

Ben-Ben (*nom de guerre*; real name not known): Angolan, nephew of Savimbi. Soldier (UNITA). Chief of General Staff of FALA 1992–3.

Bernadotte, Count Folke: Swedish (1895–1948 (assassinated)): Peacemaker. UN Mediator for Palestine 1948.

Berri, Nabih: Lebanese (Shi'ite Muslim) (1938– (Sierra Leone)): Lawyer, politician. President of Amal movement 1980–. Speaker of National Assembly 1992–.

Bock (*nom de guerre*; real name not known): Angolan. Soldier (UNITA). Military adviser to Savimbi 1992.

Botha, Pieter Willem (PW): South African (1916–): Politician. State President of South Africa 1984–9.

Botha, Roelof Frederik (Pik): South African (1932–): Lawyer, diplomat, politician.

Boutros-Ghali, Boutros: Egyptian (1922–): Jurist, journalist, civil servant, politician. Minister of State (1977–91) and Deputy Prime Minister (1991–2) for Foreign Affairs; Secretary-General of the United Nations 1992–6.

Brahimi, Lakhdar: Algerian (1934–): Diplomat, politician, UN official. USG of Arab League 1984–91 and architect of Taif Agreement on Lebanon 1989; Foreign Minister 1991–3; SESG for Zaire 1993, Yemen 1994 and Liberia 1994; SRSG for South Africa (elections) 1993–4; SRSG for Haiti 1994–6.

Brovet, Stane: Yugoslav (Slovene). Naval officer. Federal Deputy Defence Minister 1991–2.

Bunche, Ralph: American (1904–71): Political scientist, government official, UN official 1946–71. Nobel Peace Prize 1950 for mediating armistice agreements between Israel and its Arab neighbours.

Bush, George: American (1924–): Politician. Ambassador to UN 1971–2 and to China 1974–5; director of CIA 1976–7; Vice-President 1981–9 and President 1989–93.

Buttenheim, Lisa: American. UN official. Political officer, UNTSO 1985–6, OSPA 1986–8, SG's Executive Office 1989–.

Calderón Sol, Armando: Salvadorian. Politician, leader of ARENA party, President of El Salvador 1994–9.

Callaghan, William: Irish (1921–). Soldier. Served in ONUC, UNFICYP, UNTSO. Force Commander UNIFIL 1981–6; Chief of Staff UNTSO 1986–7.

Camilión, Oscar: Argentine (1930–): Lawyer, diplomat, newspaper editor, politician. Foreign Minister 1981, SRSG for Cyprus 1988–93, Defence Minister 1993–6.

Caputo, Dante: Argentine (1943–): Academic, politician, UN official. Foreign Minister 1983–8, SRSG for Haiti 1993–4.

Carrington, Lord (Peter): British (1919–): Soldier, politician, peacemaker. Chairman EC Conference on Yugoslavia 1991–2.

Chamorro, Violeta Barrios de: Nicaraguan (1939–). Journalist, politician. President of Nicaragua 1990–6.

Chidzero, Bernard: Zimbabwean (1927–): Economist, UN official, politician. Minister of Finance, Economic Planning and Development 1980–95. Boutros-Ghali's principal rival for the Secretary-Generalship of the UN 1991.

Chirac, Jacques: French (1932–): Politician. Prime Minister of France 1974–6 and 1986–8. President of France 1995–.

Chissano, Joaquim: Mozambican (1939–): Freedom fighter, politician. Foreign Minister 1975–86, President of Mozambique 1986–.

Christensen, Hans: Finnish. Soldier. Chief of Staff of UNTSO 1990–2.

Cicippio, Joseph: American. Academic administrator. Comptroller at American University of Beirut, kidnapped 1986, released 1991.

Clerides, Glafcos: Cypriot (Greek) (1919–): Lawyer, politician. President of House of Representatives 1960–76, President of Cyprus 1993–.

Collett, Alec: British. Journalist employed by UNRWA, kidnapped 1985, presumed killed 1986.

Cordovez, Diego: Ecuadorian (1935–): Lawyer, diplomat, UN official, politician. USG for Special Political Affairs 1981–8, working principally on the Iran–Iraq war and Afghanistan. Foreign Minister of Ecuador 1988–92.

Cristiani Burkard, Alfredo: Salvadorian (1948–): Businessman, politician. President of El Salvador 1989–94.

Crocker, Chester: American (1941–): Academic, government official. Assistant Secretary for African Affairs, State Department 1981–9.

Cutileiro, José: Portuguese. Diplomat. EC negotiator on Bosnia 1991–2.

da Moura, Venâncio: Angolan. Politician. Vice-Minister for External Relations from early 1980s. Promoted to Minister December 1992.

Daoud, Daoud Sulaiman: Lebanese (Shi'ite Muslim). Moderate leader of Amal in southern Lebanon. Assassinated 1988, probably by Hizbullah.

Dayal, Virendra (Viru): Indian (1935–): Civil servant, UN official. Director, OSPA 1979–82, Chef de Cabinet of Secretary-General 1982–92.

de Klerk, Frederik Willem: South African (1936–): Politician. Chairman Council of Ministers 1985–9, State President 1989–94, Deputy State President 1994–6.

del Castillo, Graciana: Uruguayan (1951–): Economist, academic, UN official. Executive Office of Secretary-General 1992–4.

de Medicis, João: Brazilian. Diplomat. Head of of ONUVEH, Haiti 1990.

de Michelis, Gianni: Italian (1940–): Academic, politician. Foreign Minister 1989–92.

Denktash, Rauf: Cypriot (Turkish) (1924–): Lawyer, politician. President of 'Turkish Federated State of Cyprus' 1975–83 and of 'Turkish Republic of Northern Cyprus' 1983–.

de Soto, Álvaro: Peruvian (1943–): Diplomat, UN official. Special (1982–6) and Executive (1987–91) Assistant to SG Pérez de Cuéllar 1982–91 and his Personal Representative for the Central American Peace Process 1988–91; architect of the El Salvador peace settlement; Senior Political Adviser to SG Boutros-Ghali 1992–4; ASG for Political Affairs 1995–8.

Dhlakama, Afonso: Mozambican (1953–). Politician. Joined RENAMO 1977; President since 1980.

Diallo, Issa: Guinean (1939–): Diplomat, UN official. Special Adviser on Africa to SG Pérez de Cuéllar 1982–90 and architect of UN plan for Western Sahara; acting Executive Secretary, UN Economic Commission for Africa 1990–1.

Dibuama, Timothy: Ghanaian (1937–): Soldier, UN official. Joined Secretariat as Military Liaison Officer in OSPA on secondment from Ghanaian Army 1974; Military Adviser to USGs for Special Political Affairs 1981 and to SG 1987; CMO of UNIKOM 1992–3.

Dirani, Mustafa: Lebanese (Shi'ite Muslim) (1950–): Militiaman, politician. Joined Amal movement 1975 and became its head of security. Formed Believers' Resistance mid-1980s. Dismissed by Berri from his Amal position following kidnapping of Higgins 1988. Kidnapped by Israel 1994, still in prison there 2001.

do Nascimento, Lopo: Angolan (1940–): Politician. Prime Minister 1975–8, Minister of Planning 1980–6, Governor Huila Province 1986–90, Minister for Administration of the Territory 1991–.

dos Santos, José Eduardo: Angolan (1942–): Politician. President of Angola 1979–.

Dunne, Tommy: Irish (1932–). Soldier. Head of UNAVEM liaison team, Jamba 1991–2.

du Plessis, Barend: South African (1940–): Politician. Minister of Finance 1984–8. Runner-up to de Klerk in contest for leadership of the National Party 1989.

Eagleburger, Lawrence: American (1930–): Diplomat, politician. US Foreign Service 1957–84. Deputy Secretary of State 1989–92; Secretary of State August 1992–January 1993.

Earley, Dermot: Irish (1948–). Soldier. Member of OSPA military staff 1987–91.

Eliasson, Jan: Swedish (1940–): Diplomat, UN official. Swedish Ambassador to UN (and PRSG on Iran–Iraq) 1988–92, USG for Humanitarian Affairs 1992–4.

Erskine, Emmanuel (Alex): Ghanaian (1937–): Soldier. Chief of Staff UNEF II 1974–5, Chief of Staff of UNTSO 1976–8, Force Commander UNIFIL 1978–81, Chief of Staff UNTSO 1981–6.

Escobar Galindo, David: Salvadorian. Poet, scholar. Member of government negotiating team El Salvador 1990–2.

Evans, Gareth: Australian (1944–): Lawyer, politician. Foreign Minister 1988–96.

Fadlallah, Shaikh Sayyid Muhammad Husain: Lebanese (Shi'ite Muslim) (1935–): Born and educated in Iraq. Moved to Lebanon 1966. Spiritual leader (though he denies it) of Hizbullah since its foundation in 1978.

Farah, Abdelrahim 'Abby': Somali (1919–): Diplomat, UN official. Ambassador to UN 1965–9, USG for Special Political Questions 1973–91.

Feissel, Gustave: American (1937–): UN official. Various economic appointments 1963–84, Director OSPA 1984–8, SG's Executive Office 1988–90, Alternate/Deputy SRSG for Cyprus 1990–7.

Filali, Abdellatif: Moroccan (1928–): Diplomat, politician. Foreign Minister 1985–98, Prime Minister 1994–8.

Fleischhauer, Carl-August: German (1930–): International lawyer, diplomat, UN official. UN Legal Counsel 1983–94; Judge, International Court of Justice 1994–.

Fortier, Yves: Canadian (1935–): Lawyer, diplomat. Canadian Ambassador to the UN New York 1988–92.

França, António dos Santos ('Ndalu'): Angolan. Soldier. Chief of Staff of FAPLA from early 1980s. Had central role in the negotiation and implementation of the peace settlements for Namibia and Angola. Lost his positions in December 1992 after the failure of that year's elections.

Frasure, Robert: American. Diplomat. London Embassy member of Crocker's Angola–Namibia team; died in accident in Bosnia in 1995 when working with Holbrooke on the Dayton Accords.

Galeano, Israel ('Comandante Franklyn'): Nicaraguan. Contra commander.

Geagea, Samir: Lebanese (Maronite) (1952–): Militiaman, politician. A leader of the Kataeb and Lebanese Forces (Maronite militia).

Gemayel, Amin: Lebanese (Maronite) (1942–): brother of Bashir. Politician. President of Lebanon 1982–8.

Gemayel, Bashir: Lebanese (Maronite) (1947–82 (assassinated)): Politician. Elected President of Lebanon 1982; assassinated before he could assume office. Brother of Amin.

Genscher, Hans-Dietrich: German (1927–): Politician. Foreign Minister 1974–92.

Gharekhan, Chinmaya: Indian (1934–): Diplomat. Indian Ambassador to UN 1986–92, Senior Adviser to SG Boutros-Ghali 1992–6.

Gligorov, Kiro: Yugoslav (Macedonian) (1917–): Politician. President of Macedonia 1991–9.

Goksel, Timur: Turkish (1944–): UN official. Spokesman (1978–2002) and Senior Adviser (1994–2002), UNIFIL.

Gomes, Péricles Ferreira: Brazilian (1931–): CMO, UNAVEM I and II 1988–91.

Gómez, Luis María: Argentine (1924–): UN official. Acting USG for Administration during Ahtisaari's absence in Namibia 1989–90; Associate Administrator of UNDP 1990–6.

Gorbachev, Mikhail: Soviet, Russian (1931–): Politician. General Secretary, Central Committee of the CPSU 1985–91, President of Soviet Union 1990–1.

Greindl, Günther: Austrian. Soldier. Force Commander UNDOF 1979–81, UNFICYP 1981–9, UNIKOM 1991–2.

Gros Espiell, Hector: Uruguayan. Diplomat, politician. SRSG for Western Sahara 1988–90.

Hadžić, Goran: Yugoslav (Croatian Serb) (1958–): Politician. Leader of the Serbs in Eastern Slavonia (Croatia).

Hägglund, Gustav: Finnish (1938–): Soldier, Force Commander UNDOF 1985–6, UNIFIL 1986–8.

Hamadeh, Abdul Hadi: Lebanese (Shi'ite Muslim). Leading figure in Hizbullah's security apparatus.

Hammarskjöld, Dag: Swedish (1905–61 (air crash)). Diplomat, public servant. Secretary-General of the United Nations 1953–61.

Hamutenya, Hidipo: Namibian (1939–): Politician. Joined SWAPO 1960, Information Secretary 1981, Minister of Information and Broadcasting 1990–4.

Handal, Schafik: Salvadorian. Politician. President of the Salvadorian Communist Party; one of the five *comandantes* of the FMLN.

Hannay, David: British (1935–): Diplomat. British Ambassador to the UN 1990–5. UK and EU Special Representative for Cyprus 1996–.

Hassan Ben Mohammed: Moroccan (1929–99): King Hassan II of Morocco 1961–99.

Hassan bin Talal: Jordanian (1947–): Crown Prince of Jordan 1965–99.

Higgins, Robin: American. US Marine Corps. Wife of Colonel W. Higgins.

Higgins, William ('Rich'): American (1943–murdered 1988 or 1989). US Marine Corps. Commander, Observer Group Lebanon, UNTSO 1987–8. Kidnapped February 1988.

Hogg, Douglas: British (1945–): Politician. Minister of State, Foreign and Commonwealth Office 1990–5.

Holst, Johan Jørgen: Norwegian (1937–94): Politician. Minister of Defence 1986–9 and 1990–3 and of Foreign Affairs 1993–4.

al-Hoss, Salim: Lebanese (Sunni Muslim) (1929–): Academic, financier, politician. Prime Minister 1976–80, 1987–90.

Hrawi, Elias: Lebanese (Maronite) (1930–): Politician. President of Lebanon 1989–98.

Hun Sen: Cambodian (1952–): Politician. Khmer Rouge 1970–7, joined pro-Vietnamese Cambodians 1977, Foreign Minister 1979–85, Prime Minister 1985–93, Second Prime Minister Royal Government 1993–8, Prime Minister 1998–.

Hurd, Douglas: British (1930–): Diplomat, politician. Foreign and Commonwealth Secretary 1989–95.

Hussein, Ahmed: Iraqi. Politician. Foreign Minister 1991.

Hussein bin Talal: Jordanian (1935–99): King of Jordan 1952–99.

Hussein, Saddam: Iraqi (1937–): Politician. President of Iraq 1979–.

Husseini, Hussein: Lebanese (Shi'ite Muslim) (1937–): First SG of Amal movement mid-1970s. Speaker of National Assembly 1984–92.

Hütter, Joachim: German. UN official. Senior Adviser UNIFIL, UNFICYP, OSPA 1990–2, DPKO 1992–.

Iacovou, Georgios: Cypriot (Greek) (1938–): Diplomat, politician. Foreign Minister 1983–93.

Izetbegović, Alija: Yugoslav (Bosniac) (1925–): Politician. President of Bosnia and Herzegovina since 1990.

Janvier, Bernard: French (1939–): Soldier. Force Commander UNPROFOR, later UN Peace Forces in former Yugoslavia 1995–6.

Jobarteh, Ebrima: Gambian (1940–): UN official. UNTAG 1989–90, Executive Director UNAVEM II 1992–3.

Jonah, James: Sierra Leonean (1934–): UN official, diplomat, politician. Joined Secretariat 1963. Director in OSPA 1971–9. ASG for Personnel 1979–81, for OFOESA 1982–7 and Office for Research and Collection of Information 1987–90; USG for Africa 1991–2 and for Political Affairs 1992–4.

Jovel, Francisco: Salvadorian. Leader of the Revolutionary Party of Central American Workers; one of the five *comandantes* of the FMLN.

Jović, Slavko: Yugoslav (Bosnian Serb) (1926–): Soldier. CMO UNIIMOG 1988–90.

Jumblatt, Kamal: Lebanese (Druze) (1917–77 (assassinated)): Politician. Founder of Progressive Socialist Party (PSP). Father of Walid.

Jumblatt, Walid: Lebanese (Druze) (1949–): son of Kamal. Politician. Leader of PSP and Druze militia.

Kabalan, Abdul Amir: Lebanese (Shi'ite Muslim). Cleric, politician. Member of Political Bureau of Amal.

Kacić, Hrvoje: Yugoslav (Croatian). Shipowner, politician. Chairman, Foreign Affairs Committee, Croatian Parliament 1991.

Kadijević, Veljko: Yugoslav (Serbian) (1925–): Soldier. Federal Defence Minister 1989–92.

Källström, Per: Swedish (1942–): Soldier. ACMO UNIIMOG (Tehran) 1989–90.

Karamé, Omar: Lebanese (Sunni Muslim), younger brother of Rashid Karamé. Politician. Prime Minister 1990–2.

Karamé, Rashid: Lebanese (Sunni Muslim (1921–87 (assassinated)): Politician. Prime Minister 1958–69, 1975–87.

Kaunda, Kenneth: Zambian (1924–): Politician. President of Zambia 1964–91.

Keyes, Alan: American. Government official, politician. Assistant Secretary for International Organizations, State Department 1986.

Khaddam, Abdul Halim: Syrian (1932–): Politician. Foreign Minister 1970–84; Vice-President 1984–.

Khazraji, Nizar: Iraqi. Soldier. Army Chief of Staff 1988–91. Commanded Iraqi Seventh Division in Kuwait war. Survived wounds and capture by Shi'ite insurgents in southern Iraq after liberation of Kuwait. Reported to have defected to Iraqi opposition group 1996.

Khieu Samphan: Cambodian (1932–): Politician. Joined Khmer Rouge 1967, C-in-C Khmer Rouge High Command 1973–9, Head of State 1976–9, Vice-President (Foreign Affairs) PDK government in exile 1982–91, member of Supreme National Council 1991–3.

Khomeini, Ruhollah: Iranian (1900–89): Cleric (Ayatollah), politician. Leader of the Islamic Revolution in Iran in 1979.

Kissinger, Henry: American (1923–): Scholar, government official, politician, consultant. President's Assistant for National Security Affairs 1969–75, Secretary of State 1973–7, Chairman Kissinger Associates Inc. since 1982.

Kittani, Ismat: Iraqi (Kurd) (1929–2001): Diplomat, international official. Ambassador to UN 1961–4; UN Secretariat 1964–75; Deputy Foreign Minister 1975–82; Ambassador to UN 1985–90; SRSG for Somalia 1992–3; SESG for Tajikistan 1993; Special Adviser to SG 1994–6.

Kljuić, Stjepan: Yugoslav (Bosnian Croat). Politician. Croat member of Bosnian Presidency at various times following Bosnia's declaration of independence.

Knutsson, Rolf: Swedish (1942–): UN official. UNDP 1969–83. Peacekeeping assignments as Senior Political Adviser to UNIFIL 1985, UNTSO 1987, ONUCA 1990, MINURSO 1992. New York appointments in OSPA, DPKO and SG's Executive Office.

Koh, Tommy Thong Bee: Singaporean (1937–): Lawyer, academic, diplomat. Singaporean Ambassador to the UN 1974–84, Ambassador to the US 1984–90, Ambassador at Large 1990–.

Kouchner, Bernard: French (1939–): Physician, politician. Founder of *Médecins sans Frontières* and *Médecins du Monde*; Secretary of State for Humanitarian Action 1988–92; Minister of Health and Humanitarian Action 1992–3, 1997–9.

Kyprianou, Spyros: Cypriot (Greek) (1932–): Lawyer, politician. President of Cyprus 1977–88.

Lacayo, António: Nicaraguan. Son-in-law of Violeta Chamorro and leader of her transition team, 1990; later Minister for the Presidency.

Lafontant, Roger: Haitian. Led unsuccessful coup against Aristide January 1991.

Lahoud, Emile: Lebanese (Maronite) (1936–): Naval officer, politician. Armed Forces Commander 1989–98, President of Lebanon 1998–.

Larijani, Javad: Iranian (1951–): Politician. Deputy Foreign Minister late 1980s.

Legwaila, Legwaila Joseph: Botswanan (1937–): Diplomat. Botswanan Ambassador to the UN New York 1980–. Deputy SRSG for Namibia 1989–90.

Liu, Fou-tchin (FT): Chinese (1919–2001): UN official. Joined Secretariat 1949. Trusteeship Council 1949–60. OSPA, initially as Special Assistant to Ralph Bunche, 1960–86 (ASG from 1981).

Lumumba, Patrice: Congolese (1925–61): Politician. Prime Minister 1960. Murdered while in custody of Mobutu's troops 1961.

Mackenzie, Lewis: Canadian. Soldier. Acting CMO of ONUCA 1991, Commander Sarajevo Sector UNPROFOR 1992.

Major, John: British (1943–): Politician. Foreign and Commonwealth Secretary 1989, Prime Minister 1990–7.

Mahmutćehajić, Rusmir: Yugoslav (Bosniac). Politician.

Manuvakola, Eugénio: Angolan. Soldier, politician (UNITA). Deputy Secretary-General UNITA 1992.

Manz, Johannes: Swiss. Diplomat. SRSG for Western Sahara 1990–1. Subsequently Permanent Observer of Switzerland at the UN.

Martić, Milan: Yugoslav (Croatian Serb) (1945–): Police officer, politician. Police chief in Knin 1990–2, President of 'Republika Srpska Krajina' 1992–5.

Martinez Varela, Juan: Salvadorian. Minister of the Interior in Cristiani's government.

Masire, Quett: Botswanan (1925–): Politician. President of Botswana 1980–98.

Mestiri, Mahmoud: Tunisian (1929–): Diplomat, politician. Tunisian Ambassador to UN 1986–7, Foreign Minister 1987, Ambassador to Egypt 1988–90, SRSG for Afghanistan 1991–4.

Mills, Bernard: British. UN official (UNRWA). Director of UNRWA's operations in the West Bank 1987–8.

Milner, Clive: Canadian (1936–): Soldier. UNMO in UNTSO/UNDOF 1975–6, Force Commander UNFICYP 1989–92.

Milošević, Slobodan: Yugoslav (Serbian) (1941–): Politician. President of Serbia 1990–7, President of Federal Republic of Yugoslavia 1997–2000. Indicted by ICTY.

Misharin, Vladislav: Soviet (Russian). Director, OSPA 1985–90.

Mitterrand, François: French (1916–96). Politician. President of France 1981–95.

Mladić, Ratko: Yugoslav (Bosnian Serb) (1943–): Soldier. Commander Knin Corps JNA 1991–2, Commander of Bosnian Serb Army 1992–6. Indicted by ICTY.

Mohammed, Ali Mahdi: Somali. Politician. Participated with Aidid in overthrow of Siad Barre in January 1991 but subsequently fought with Aidid for control of Mogadishu.

Moriarty, Michael: Irish (1931–). OC UNTAG detachment in Angola 1989–90.

Mortlock, Roger: New Zealander. Soldier. UNAVEM Regional Commander, Huambo 1992.

Mubarak, Muhammad Hosni: Egyptian (1928–): Air force officer, politician. President of Egypt since 1981.

Mudenge, Stanislaus: Zimbabwean (1941–): Academic, diplomat, politician. Ambassador to the UN late 1980s; Foreign Minister since 1995.

Mugabe, Robert: Zimbabwean (1924–): Freedom fighter, politician. Prime Minister of Zimbabwe 1980–7, President 1988–.

Murphy, Richard: American. Diplomat. Ambassador to Syria 1978–81, Saudi Arabia 1981–3, Assistant Secretary for Near Eastern and South Asian Affairs, State Department 1983–9.

Mwinyi, Ali Hassan: Tanzanian (1925–): Teacher, diplomat, politician. President of Tanzania 1985–95.

Nambiar, Satish: Indian. Soldier. Force Commander UNPROFOR 1992–3.

Netanyahu, Benjamin (Bibi): Israeli (1949–): Diplomat, politician. Ambassador to UN 1984–8, Deputy Foreign Minister 1988–91, Prime Minister of Israel 1996–9.

Norodom Ranariddh: Cambodian (1944–): Politician. President of FUNCINPEC party, First Prime Minister 1993–7.

Norodom Sihanouk: Cambodian (1922–): King of Cambodia at various times since 1941. In exile 1978–91, founded FUNCINPEC party 1981, President of Supreme National Council 1991–3, crowned King of Cambodia 1993.

Nujoma, Sam: Namibian (1929–): Freedom fighter, politician. President SWAPO 1960–, President of Namibia since 1990.

Obando y Bravo, Cardinal Miguel: Nicaraguan (1926–): Churchman. Chairman, Nicaragua National Reconciliation Commission 1987.

Obasanjo, Olusegun: Nigerian (1937–): Soldier, politician. Head of Federal Military Government 1976–9, President of Nigeria since 1999.

Obeid, Abdul Karim: Lebanese (Shi'ite Muslim). Cleric. Kidnapped by Israel 1989, still in prison there 2001.

Ogata, Sadako: Japanese (1927–): Scholar, diplomat, UN official. UN High Commissioner for Refugees 1991–2000.

Okelo, Francis: Ugandan. UN official. ONUVEH 1990–1.

Okun, Herbert: American. Diplomat. Deputy Ambassador to the UN 1985–9. Special Adviser to Cyrus Vance on Yugoslavia 1991–3 and Macedonia 1993–7.

Omayad, Hisham: Ghanaian. UN official. Worked mainly on African issues. Director of UNTAG's electoral division, Namibia 1989–90.

O'Neill, Tadgh: Irish (1926–). Soldier. Chief of Staff, Irish Defence Forces 1986–9.

Opande, Daniel: Kenyan. Soldier. Deputy Force Commander UNTAG 1989–90.

Ortega Saavedra, Daniel: Nicaraguan (1945–): Member Frente Sandinista, resistance leader, politician. President of Nicaragua 1985–90.

Ortega Saavedra, Umberto: Nicaraguan. Younger brother of Daniel. Soldier, Minister of Defence in Sandinista government.

Panić, Milan: Yugoslav (Serbian) and American (1929–): Businessman (pharmaceuticals), politician. Emigrated to USA 1956, returned 1991. Prime Minister of FRY 1992, unsuccessful candidate for Presidency of Serbia 1992.

Parsons, Anthony: British (1922–96): Soldier, diplomat. UK Ambassador to the UN, 1979–82.

Patil, Venky: Indian. Soldier. ACMO (Baghdad) UNIIMOG 1988–90.

Pelletier, Michel: French. UN official in OSPA and later DPKO.

Peres, Shimon: Israeli (1923–): Government official, politician. Prime Minister 1984–6, Vice-Prime Minister 1986–90, Foreign Minister 1986–8 and 1992–5.

Pérez, Carlos Andrés: Venezuelan. Politician. President of Venezuela 1974–9 and 1989–93.

Pérez de Cuéllar, Jávier: Peruvian (1920–): Jurist, diplomat, politician. SRSG Cyprus 1975–7, USG for Special Political Affairs 1979–81, Secretary-General of the United Nations 1982–91.

Petrovsky, Vladimir: Soviet (Russian) (1933–): Diplomat, UN official. Deputy Foreign Minister 1986–91, USG for Political Affairs 1992, Director-General UN Office Geneva 1993–2002.

Picco, Giandomenico: Italian. UN official, international consultant. Joined Secretariat 1973. Worked with Pérez de Cuéllar in Cyprus, OSPA and SG's Executive Office; negotiated release of Western hostages held in Beirut 1990–1.

Pickering, Thomas: American (1931–): Diplomat. Ambassador to Jordan 1974–8, Nigeria 1981–3, El Salvador 1983–5, Israel 1985–8, UN 1989–92, India 1992–3, Russia 1993–6, Under-Secretary for Political Affairs 1997–2000.

Pienaar, Louis: South African (1926–): Lawyer, diplomat, politician. Ambassador to France 1975, Administrator-General of Namibia 1985–90, Minister of Home and Environmental Affairs 1990–3.

Pol Pot (pseudonym for Saloth Sar): Cambodian (*c.* 1925–98): Politician. Leader of Khmer Rouge, Prime Minister of Cambodia 1976–9, retired from leadership 1985.

Ponce, Emilio: Salvadorian. Soldier, Minister of Defence at time of Salvadorian peace settlement.

Prem Chand, Dewan: Indian (1916–): Soldier. Joined Indian Army in 1937. Served UN in ONUC, Congo 1962–3, Force Commander UNFICYP 1969–76, Force Commander UNTAG 1989–90.

Puna, Miguel N'zau: Angolan (from Cabinda). Soldier (UNITA) and politician. SG of UNITA 1968–91. Defected in February 1992 in protest at Savimbi's alleged killing of a number of UNITA officials.

Purola, Heikki: Finnish. Soldier. OSPA military staff in early 1990s.

al-Qaddumi, Farouq (Abu Lutf): Palestinian (1930–): Founder member of Fatah (Arafat's wing of the PLO). Head of PLO Political Department since 1974.

Qadhafi, Mu'ammar: Libyan (1942–): Soldier, politician. Led revolution which overthrew monarchy 1969, Chairman of Revolutionary Command Council (Head of State) 1969–.

al-Qaysi, Riad: Iraqi. Lawyer, diplomat. Legal Adviser at the Foreign Ministry late 1980s and early 1990s.

Qasim, Abdul Karim: Iraqi (1914–63): Soldier, politician. Overthrew Hashemite monarchy in Iraq 1958; overthrown by *coup d'état* and executed 1963.

Quesada Gómez, Agustín: Spanish. Soldier, CMO ONUCA 1989–90.

Rabin, Yitzhak: Israeli (1922–95 (assassinated)): Soldier, politician. Chief of Staff of IDF 1964–8, Prime Minister 1974–7, Defence Minister 1984–92, Prime Minister 1992–5.

Rafsanjani, Ali Akbar Hashemi: Iranian (1934–): Cleric, politician. President of Iran 1989–97.

Rana, Jai Pratap: Nepalese. Diplomat. Nepalese Ambassador to the UN in late 1980s.

Rašeta, Andrija: Yugoslav. Soldier. JNA Commander, Fifth Military District, 1991.

Richardson, Elliott: American (1920–99): Lawyer, politician. Many senior government posts during 1970s. PRSG for verification of the Nicaraguan elections 1989–90.

al-Rifa'i, Zaid: Jordanian (1936–): Diplomat, politician. Prime Minister 1973–6, 1985–9.

Riza, Iqbal: Pakistani (1934–): Diplomat, UN official. Director OSPA (Iran–Iraq) 1982–8, Chief of ONUVEN Nicaragua 1989–90, SRSG El Salvador 1990–3, ASG DPKO 1993–7, Chief of Staff to SG Kofi Annan 1997–.

Rizvi, Zia: Pakistani. UN official. DSRSG for Western Sahara 1991–2.

Rodrigues, Manuel Alexandre ('Kito'): Angolan. Politician. Minister of the Interior 1980–9. Headed Angolan team in US-led negotiations on the withdrawal of Cuban troops from Angola.

Roy, Armand: Canadian. Soldier, Force Commander of MINURSO 1991–2.

Sacirbey, Muhamed: Yugoslav (Bosniac) (1956–): Lawyer, banker, diplomat, politician. Ambassador to UN 1992–5, Foreign Minister 1995–6.

al-Sadr, Imam Musa: Iranian (1928–): Shi'ite cleric. Founder of the Amal movement in Lebanon. Disappeared 1978 in Libya.

Sadry, Behrooz: Iranian (1936–): UN official. Joined Secretariat 1957. Director FOD 1987–92, Deputy SRSG Cambodia 1992–3 and Mozambique 1994.

Sahhaf, Muhammad Sa'id: Iraqi. Politician. Minister of State for Foreign Affairs early 1990s, later Foreign Minister.

Sahnoun, Mohammed: Algerian (1913–): Politician, diplomat, UN official. Deputy SG of OAU 1963–74 and of Arab League 1973–4. Algerian Ambassador to UN 1982–4, USA 1984–8, Morocco 1989–90; SRSG for Somalia 1992; Special Envoy of SGs of UN and OAU for Great Lakes region of Africa 1993.

Samayoa, Salvador: Salvadorian. Senior member of the People's Liberation Forces (FPL); member of the FMLN negotiating team.

Sánchez Cerén, Salvador (alias Leonel Gonzales): Salvadorian. Leader of the People's Liberation Forces (FPL); one of the five *comandantes* of the FMLN.

Sancho, Eduardo (alias Ferman Cienfuegos): Salvadorian. Leader of the National Resistance (RN); one of the five *comandantes* of the FMLN.

Sanderson, John: Australian. Soldier. Force Commander UNTAC 1992–3.

Santamaria, Oscar: Salvadorian. Minister of the Presidency and Head of the government negotiating team 1989–92.

Savimbi, Jonas: Angolan (1934–2002): President of the UNITA movement in Angola from 1966.

Schiff, Ze'ev: Israeli (1932–): Analyst, writer, journalist. For many years Defence Editor of *Ha'aretz*.

Separović, Zvonimir: Yugoslav (Croatian) (1928–): Politician. Foreign Minister 1991–2, Ambassador to UN 1992.

Shaheen, Imtiaz: Pakistani. Soldier. Force Commander UNOSOM I 1992–3.

Shamir, Yitzhak: Israeli (1915–): Politician. Foreign Minister 1980–3, Prime Minister 1983–4, Foreign Minister 1984–6, Prime Minister 1986–92.

Shamkhani, Ali: Iranian. Politician. Minister for the Pasdaran in late 1990s. Subsequently Minister of Defence.

Shamsuddin, Shaikh Muhammad Mahdi: Lebanese (Shi'ite Muslim) (1935–2001): Cleric. Vice-President Supreme Shi'ite Council 1978, President 1994.

al-Shara', Farouq: Syrian (1938–): Airline manager, diplomat, politician. Foreign Minister since 1984.

Shearar, Jeremy: South African (1931–): Diplomat. Ambassador to the UN 1988–94.

Shimura, Hisako: Japanese (1934–): UN official. Was in Cordovez's part of OSPA when the author joined the UN in 1986. Became author's deputy from 1989 until Annan joined DPKO in early 1992.

Shultz, George: American (1920–): Academic, economist, industrialist, politician. Secretary of State 1982–9.

Silajdžić, Haris: Yugoslav (Bosniac) (1945–): Politician. Foreign Minister of Bosnia and Herzegovina 1991–3, Prime Minister 1993–6.

Siyad Barre, Mohamed: Somali (1919–): Soldier, politician. Seized power in 1969. Overthrown in January 1991 by coalition led by Aidid.

Skalli, Ali: Moroccan (1927–): Lawyer, diplomat. Ambassador to the UN 1990–1.

Smith, Rupert: British (1943–): Soldier. Military Commander UNPROFOR Bosnia 1995.

Sommereyns, Raymond: Belgian. UN official. Worked with Cordovez in OSPA. Senior Adviser UNIIMOG 1988–91. Assigned to DPA 1992.

Son Sann: Cambodian (1911–): Politician. Governor of National Bank of Cambodia 1954–68, Prime Minister of CGDK 1982–91, member of Supreme National Council 1991–3, Speaker of Constituent Assembly 1993.

Suanzes Pardo, Victor: Spanish. CMO of ONUCA 1991–2.

Tamir, Avraham: Israeli (1924–): Soldier, government official, politician. Close associate of Sharon until they fell out in 1982 over Israel's invasion of Lebanon. SG of Foreign Ministry 1986–8.

Tharoor, Shashi: Indian (1956–): Writer, UN official. Joined UNHCR 1978, moved to New York 1991 as the author's Special Assistant, remained in DPKO under Kofi Annan, was appointed the latter's Executive Assistant when he became Secretary-General in 1997.

Thornberry, Cedric: Irish (1936–): Lawyer, academic, UN official. Senior Adviser UNFICYP 1981–2, UNTSO 1982–4, Director SRSG's office UNTAG 1989–90, Director USG's office Department of Administration and Management 1990–2, Director Civil Affairs UNPROFOR 1992–5.

Tito, Josip Broz: Yugoslav (Croat/Slovene) (1892–1980): Politician. Prime Minister of Yugoslavia 1945–53, President 1953–80.

Titov, Dmitry: Soviet (Russian). Joined OSPA 1990. Desk officer for Angola.

Tudjman, Franjo: Yugoslav (Croatian) (1922–99): Soldier, academic, politician. Led campaign for Croatian independence 1990–1. President of Croatia from 1991 until his death.

Tus, Antun: Yugoslav (Croatian). Soldier, JNA officer. Commander JNA Air Force till 1991; Commander, Croatian National Guard 1991–2.

Unimna, Edward: Nigerian. Soldier. CMO UNAVEM II 1991–2.

Urquhart, Brian: British (1919–): UN official 1945–86; USG for Special Political Affairs 1974–86.

Vadset, Martin: Norwegian (1930–): Soldier. Chief of Staff UNTSO 1987–90.

Valentim, Jorge: Angolan (1937–): Politician (UNITA). Information Secretary 1991–2.

Vance, Cyrus: American (1917–): Lawyer, public servant, politician. Secretary of State 1977–80, SESG for Yugoslavia 1991–2, Co-Chair Steering Committee of ICFY 1992–3.

Van den Broek, Hans: Netherlands (1936–): Politician. Foreign Minister 1982–93, External Relations Commissioner, European Commission 1993–9.

Van Dúnem, Pedro de Castro ('Loy'): Angolan. Politician. Many ministerial posts since 1976. Foreign Minister 1989–92.

Vargas, Mauricio: Salvadorian. Soldier. Military member of GOES negotiating team.

Vassiliou, George: Cypriot (Greek) (1931–): Business consultant, politician. President of Cyprus 1988–93.

Velayati, Ali Akbar: Iranian (1945–): Physician, politician. Foreign Minister 1981–97.

Vendrell, Francesc: Spanish (1940–): Jurist, UN official. Joined Secretariat 1968. Worked closely with de Soto, especially on Central America and in DPA.

Villalobos Huezo, Joaquín: Salvadorian (1951–): Politician. Leader of the People's Revolutionary Army (ERP). One of the five *comandantes* of the FMLN.

Vorontsov, Yuliy: Soviet (Russian) (1929–): Diplomat. First Deputy Foreign Minister 1986–9, Ambassador to Afghanistan 1988–90, Ambassador to the UN 1990–2, Adviser to President Yeltsin 1992–4, Ambassador to United States 1994–8.

Wahlgren, Lars-Eric: Swedish (1929–): Soldier. Force Commander UNIFIL 1988–93, Force Commander UNPROFOR March–June 1993.

Waite, Terry: British (1939–): Church of England official. Kidnapped Beirut 1987, released 1991.

Waldheim, Kurt: Austrian (1918–): Diplomat, politician. Secretary-General of the United Nations 1972–81. President of Austria 1986–92.

Welin, Gustaf: Swedish. Force Commander UNDOF 1986–8.

White, Tom: Canadian (1938–): Soldier, UN official. FOD New York 1985–9, CAO UNAVEM I and II 1989–92.

Williams, Angela: British. UN official (UNRWA). Acting Director of UNRWA's operations in the Gaza Strip 1987–8.

Wilson, John: Australian. Soldier. Commander UN Military Liaison Officers Yugoslavia 1992, CMO UNPROFOR 1992–3.

Wisner, Frank: American (1938–): Diplomat. Ambassador to Zambia 1979–82, Deputy Assistant Secretary for African Affairs, State Department 1982–6, Ambassador to Egypt 1986–91, Under-Secretary of Defense 1993–4, Ambassador to India 1994–7.

Zartman, I. William: American. Scholar, Johns Hopkins University. Proponent of the concept of the 'ripeness' of conflicts for negotiated settlement.

Zuliani, Gaby: Canadian. Soldier. Chief Security Observer of ONUVEH 1990–1.

Appendix IV

The Peacekeeping Workload, 1986–1992

	1986	1987	1988	1989	1990	1991	1992
Cyprus							
Lebanon							
Palestine							
Iraq vs. Iran							
Namibia							
Angola							
Mozambique							
Western Sahara							
Central America							
Haiti							
Cambodia							
Iraq vs. Kuwait							
Yugoslavia							
Somalia							

Legend: Heavy Medium Light

Appendix V

A Week in the Levant, 1987

The following is the text of a letter which I wrote to my daughter Rachel two days after returning from a week-long trip to the Levant in January 1987, when I was still pursuing the dream of negotiating the withdrawal of Israeli forces from southern Lebanon, as described in Chapter 5. It conveys my mood at the time and gives an idea of how intense, and enjoyable, these trips were.

Another week in the life of a travelling peacekeeper. I left New York on Friday evening (the 2nd), with my Haitian colleague Jean-Claude Aimé, on a direct flight to Tel Aviv. Arrived there lunch time Saturday, with the first signs of flu already making themselves felt. Drove to Jerusalem, where our favoured hotel, pictur-esquely Ottoman in the summer, turned out to be quite incapable of protecting us against the bitter cold. Went for a walk in the Old City to get over the flight; had to accept the company of a Jerusalem-based American journalist who, after a multi-brandy lunch, could not manage the brisk pace I wanted. But he guided me to the spot where the yeshiva student was murdered a few weeks ago, sparking riots in the West Bank and Gaza. An ugly little street, full of mud and garbage; the victim's colleagues have already built a shrine inscribed with a menacing OT text about the justice of revenge. Many kestrels hunting in the dusk. Quiet dinner with Aimé; much gloom about our prospects of achieving anything on this trip.

Sunday: wake after bad night with flu developing nicely. Spend morning and lunch in shivering conference with Hägglund, Commander of UNIFIL. After lunch drive down to Tel Aviv for meeting with Defence Minister Rabin. Atmosphere very affable (even though I had recently sent him a rude letter after his Lebanese allies, the SLA, had wantonly killed one of our Irishmen – so rude that the Israeli mission complained to the SG about its tone!) but no give at all on the substance; Israel insists on maintaining its occupation of southern Lebanon but Rabin shows some signs of worry about the knocks the SLA have recently been taking from the Lebanese 'Resistance'. Back to Tel Aviv. Lines to NY per-manently engaged. Interesting dinner with an Israeli friend who knows a lot about Lebanon and, *mirabile dictu*, supports what we are trying to do.

Monday: survive the night, just. Up early to fly to Beirut in the UN Fokker. As always, I approach Beirut with some apprehension but it's all right once one is there. Land without mishap at the airport; only light shelling in the nearby 'Camps War'. Fly in UNIFIL helicopter over the sea to the point of Ras Beirut and thence by car through West Beirut to Prime Minister Karamé's office. The weather is superb – bright sun, and Mount Lebanon covered with fresh snow. But Beirut itself is as frightful as ever; heaps of garbage, queues for bread and petrol, armed

380

men everywhere. Karamé is even less realistic than usual – 'the UN must force Israel to withdraw; automatic renewal of the UNIFIL mandate is a humiliation for Lebanon; with so much chaos already, what difference would a little more chaos in the South make?' Back by car to Ras Beirut, out over the sea in the chopper and round to East Beirut, where we see President Gemayel. He is full of confidence about the prospects for national reconciliation and denies that he has played any part in the return of PLO fighters to the camps (not true). Then a heavy and not very palatable lunch with the Foreign Ministry, a couple of press statements, cables at the office and so up the hill to Brumana, where the hotel is full of rich émigrés enjoying, like UN officials, life on the cheap as a result of the collapse of the Lebanese pound. Excellent dinner with Aimé at the usual restaurant, who provide a bottle of Armagnac, compliments of the house.

Tuesday: a feverish night, with much thunder. Wake up to torrential rain and doubts whether the UNIFIL heli will be able to fly; passes to Syria blocked by snow; are we stranded in Brumana? No; our gallant Italian pilots say they will give it a whirl. We find an ever-narrowing corridor between a thunderstorm to the north and the guns of West Beirut to the south and reach the airport safely. Two-hour flight to Damascus; the Syrians make you go a long way round. Damascus even colder and wetter than Beirut. Working sandwiches with Welin (Swedish Commander of UNDOF) and his staff. Return to hotel to await confirmation of constantly changing appointments with Syrian ministers. Not a penance because it gives time to work on the SG's report on UNIFIL which has to be ready by Sunday evening; and, astonishingly, the hotel sports a charming chamber trio who play familiar things by Mozart, Schubert etc. each afternoon to uncomprehending Syrian security men and harassed businessmen (and UN officials). Eventually see Foreign Minister at about 7 p.m. He could not be more friendly (gainsaying some of my enemies here who had been putting it about that the Hindawi trial and all that would have destroyed my credentials in Syria) and speaks with great passion about the iniquities of Yasir Arafat. We then rendezvous with bodyguards of Nabih Berri, leader of the Amal movement in Lebanon, who drive us off into the night for what turns out to be a two-hour meeting with him. Very relaxed and useful meeting; he is confident that the Resistance will force the Israelis to vacate Lebanon but worried about whether he is going to win his war with Arafat. Finally reach the dinner table of charming and patient Mrs Welin at 11.30. Get to bed at 0130.

Wednesday: up at 0630. Drive from Damascus across Golan Heights in thick fog. Cross cease-fire line and are given breakfast by the COs of the Canadian and Finnish contingents of UNDOF. Just what a breakfast should be: HM the Queen on the mess wall, fried eggs, bacon and baked beans. The Canadian cooks had a remarkable ability to crack an egg with one hand and decant it, with yoke unbroken, into the frying pan. Then on over the Golan and down into Israel. Aimé maddeningly vague about which engagement was fought where; must do my homework before I ride this road again. Across northern Galilee (I hadn't realized there were still so many Arab villages there) and reach the sea at Acre. North on the coast road to the Israel–Lebanon frontier and so to UNIFIL HQ, which we reach at 11. Still cold and wet. Long but not inconclusive conference (plus inevitable sandwiches) with Hägglund and his staff about how we can improve UNIFIL's ability to control hostilities without getting its own people killed. See the Swedish medics who give me killer pills which they swear will not impair my mental functions. Off by helicopter, dodging the showers, into the operational area. First stop, the HQ of the Finnish Battalion, where I have a meeting with Daoud Daoud, the Amal chieftain in the south. He disconcerts me by kissing me three times (it was only our first meeting); hope I didn't give him the flu. Speak to him severely about the fuss he is making about Hägglund's plan to replace Irish troops with Nepalese in three crucial villages; assure him Nepalese even better than Irish; say how much Argies feared Gurkhas in the Malvinas (he knows about that war). Second stop, the HQ of the unloved Nepalese battalion. Inspect them inadequately clad (me, not them) in freezing drizzle; they are dear people (and give me a pretty Buddha scroll) but not, contrary to what I told Daoud, very competent. Third stop, HQ of newly arrived Swedish troops who stepped into the breach after the French decided to pull out most of their people. Another inspection; I tell them, honestly and with real feeling, that they saved the ship in its moment of crisis. And so back to HQ UNIFIL for another two-hour conference followed by dinner with the Hägglunds. During dinner a message comes in that the Israelis have indicated that they intend to ask us to take over three of their positions which have given us the most trouble. If true, this would mean that we, with of course the help of the Resistance, had succeeded in getting the Israelis to resume their withdrawal from Lebanon. I want to believe it but do not allow myself to do so. Leave UNIFIL at 9 p.m. for the three-hour drive back to Jerusalem. Aimé, maddening again, sleeps all the way; I can't, being too keyed up. Reach Jerusalem at midnight; in bed by 0100.

Thursday: Meeting with Foreign Minister Peres at 10, then more work on the SG's report, then meeting with DG of Foreign Ministry (refreshingly dovish, but who does he speak for?), then lunch with Callaghan (Commander of UNTSO), then interviews with Israeli journalists, then conference with Callaghan, then drive down to Tel Aviv again for key meeting with Defence Minister Rabin. Was last night's gen pukka gen? Of course it wasn't. Rabin takes a harder line than ever before; it is clear that recent successes of the Resistance have led the Israelis to conclude, predictably enough, that they must respond with harsher, not gentler, policies. We have a bad-tempered exchange about harassing fire against UNIFIL troops and the meeting ends on very depressing note. Have drink with an Israeli friend who confirms that Israel has decided to use the iron fist. Dinner with American Ambassador in Tel Aviv and Dick Murphy, who is in charge of ME affairs in the State Department. Manage to behave well in spite of general gloom, flu and fatigue. In bed in hotel in Tel Aviv by 0100.

Friday: HOME. Reach NY at 1030 p.m. and go to bed, where I sleep for 13 hours continuously. Wake up at lunchtime on Saturday to learn that there has been a shoot-out between the unloved Nepalese and the locals who don't want them to take over from the Irish. The Nepalese have acted with determination and restraint and make me feel guilty about the doubting thoughts I had on Wednesday. Two hours later I learn that an Irish corporal has been killed by fire from an Israeli tank. I don't think UNIFIL can, or should, survive much more of this.

Index

383

Index to the Epilogue